Stoicism

by Tom Morris, PhD and
Gregory Bassham, PhD

Stoicism For Dummies®

Published by: **John Wiley & Sons, Inc.,** 111 River Street, Hoboken, NJ 07030-5774, www.wiley.com

Copyright © 2024 by John Wiley & Sons, Inc., Hoboken, New Jersey

Published simultaneously in Canada

For general information on our other products and services, please contact our Customer Care Department within the U.S. at 877-762-2974, outside the U.S. at 317-572-3993, or fax 317-572-4002. For technical support, please visit https://hub.wiley.com/community/support/dummies.

Wiley publishes in a variety of print and electronic formats and by print-on-demand. Some material included with standard print versions of this book may not be included in e-books or in print-on-demand. If this book refers to media such as a CD or DVD that is not included in the version you purchased, you may download this material at http://booksupport.wiley.com. For more information about Wiley products, visit www.wiley.com.

Library of Congress Control Number is available from the publisher.

ISBN 978-1-394-20627-8 (pbk); ISBN 978-1-394-20628-5 (ebk); ISBN 978-1-394-20629-2 (ebk)

SKY10061262_112823

Table of Contents

INTRODUCTION 1

About This Book. 1

Foolish Assumptions. 2

Icons Used in This Book 3

Beyond the Book 3

Where to Go from Here 4

PART 1: ANCIENT STOICISM 5

CHAPTER 1: **Stoicism: A Philosophy for Our Time** 7

A Way of Thought for Our Time 8

Hot philosophy in America. 9

The Stoic formula 9

What Does "Philosophy" Even Mean?. 10

What Wisdom Is and Is Not 11

Two sides of philosophy. 12

Philosophy and life 14

Using Wisdom with the Stoics 17

Happiness and freedom. 18

When to go to philosophy 20

CHAPTER 2: **Socrates and the Beginnings of Western Philosophy** 21

Heraclitus the (Cranky and) Obscure 22

Socrates: The Barefoot Gadfly and General
Pain-in-the-Patootie of Ancient Athens 24

Care for the soul 25

Virtue is sufficient for happiness. 26

No harm can come to a good person. 26

Virtue is knowledge. 27

No one does wrong willingly 27

Diogenes of Sinope: Socrates on Steroids. 27

Virtue is the only true good 28

Virtue is sufficient for happiness. 28

"Follow nature". 29

Be a citizen of the world. 29

CHAPTER 3: **The First Stoics** 31

The Basic Teachings of Zeno and His Stoic Followers 32

Materialists through and through. 32

Belief in Logos 33

Strict determinists 35
Belief in an afterlife 35
Live rationally 36
The good, the evil, and the indifferent 36
Only virtue leads to happiness 37
Why Stoicism Had Its Moment in Ancient Greece and Rome 39

CHAPTER 4: **Stoicism Comes to Rome** 41
Seneca and Epictetus 42
Seneca: Wealthy but Frugal 42
Philosophy as a therapy for the emotions 43
Coping with life's hard knocks 44
Controlling anger 45
Epictetus: Slave Turned Philosopher 47
True freedom 48
The dichotomy of control 49
Radical acceptance 50

CHAPTER 5: **Marcus Aurelius: Philosopher-Emperor** 53
A Stoic Philosopher Comes to the Throne .53
Early influences 54
Conversion to Stoicism 55
Reign as emperor 55
Personal tragedies and death 56
Two Themes in Marcus's Philosophy 58
Impermanence: Reality is flux 58
Pessimism 59
The Demise of Ancient Stoicism 63
The demise of "the old gods" of paganism 63
The rise of competing philosophies 63
Failure to appeal to the masses 63
Attacks by rival philosophical schools 64
Down but not out 64

PART 2: THE STOIC WORLDVIEW 65

CHAPTER 6: **The Stoic View of Reality** 67
Everything Is Made of Matter 68
God and Nature 69
Stoic pantheism 69
The Earth's place in the universe 70
Stoic arguments for God 70
Stoic belief in periodic conflagrations .72

The Place of Humanity in the Cosmos 73
    An anthropocentric view 73
    Belief in a (temporary) afterlife 74
    Finding truth in outdated notions. 76

CHAPTER 7: Providence, Fate, and Free Will 77
    "Everything Is Fated" 78
        Fatalism gone rogue 79
        Free will and responsibility. 81
    Is God to Blame for Evil?. 85
        Seneca's response. 85
        Natural evils and animal pain 86
        Are sin and evil caused by God? 87
    Stoic Fate and Passivity. 88
        Divine Providence 89

PART 3: STOIC ETHICS 93

CHAPTER 8: Virtue as the Goal of Life 95
    Virtus and Arete. 96
        Virtus. 96
        Arete 97
    Virtue at the Center. 98
        May the Force be with you. 98
        Vice: The opposite of virtue 99
        Can you progress toward virtue? 99
    Happiness and Virtue 101
        The surface complexity of happiness. .103
        The Stoic simplification of it all 105
        Virtue and happiness coincide 105
        Only virtue is good, and only vice is bad 106
    The Good, Bad, and Indifferent. 107
        What's different about the Stoic indifferent 109
        Inner and outer things 113
        A good person can't be harmed 114
        Use and value. 115

CHAPTER 9: Things We Can Control. 119
    The Dichotomy of Control 120
    Your wants and your power. 121
    Exploring the Concept of Control 124
        Value judgments, desires, and goals 125
        More options about control. 126
        The inner citadel or fortress 128
        Another spectrum 130

The Problem of External Goals 131
    Relationships, reason, and common good 131
    A modern Stoic's strategy. 133
Trying Our Best 137
An Alternate Strategy 138
    Our emotional relationship to goals. 139
    The proper path of action 140

CHAPTER 10: **Desire and the Happy Life**. 143
Getting Clear about Desire. 144
    Commitments 144
    Thought, desire, and action 145
    Managing desires 147
    Whatever should be will be 147
    Desiring only what is true. 148
    The problem of evil 149
Desire and Happiness. 150
    The Desire Satisfaction View of Happiness 151
    Finding the real flaws here. 154
An Opportunity for Hope 156
    The gap is good 157
    Can you rid yourself of desires? 158
    The many facets of happiness. 160
    Desire for that which is. 160
    Happiness comes from within. 162

CHAPTER 11: **Pleasure and Pain** 163
The Epicurean Pull of Pleasure 163
    Epicurus on pleasure 164
    Stoic objections to Epicureanism 166
Pleasure and Pain with the Stoics. 167
    Epictetus has his say. 168
    Marcus Aurelius weighs in 170
    Seneca joins the fray. 175
Using Sensations and Situations. 178

CHAPTER 12: **Natural Law** 183
What Is Natural Law? 184
    Cicero on natural law 185
    Basic elements of natural law 186
Natural Law in Roman Law 189
Modern Stoicism and Natural Law 190
    Natural law: Pros and cons 191

CHAPTER 13: **Building Strong Communities** 197

    Philosophers as Social Advisors 197

    The Two Roots of Community. 199

        Reason and relationality. 199

        The self and society. 200

    Plato and Aristotle Behind It All. 202

        Our need to belong. 203

        Aristotle on the power of partnership 203

        Platonic perspectives 205

        Community and political virtues 206

    Circles of Community and Care. 207

        The rings of our lives. 207

        Making the most of our circles 209

        The Four Foundations. 210

        The demands of love. 211

        Citizens of the world 213

PART 4: PASSIONS AND EMOTIONS 217

CHAPTER 14: **Stoic Apathy: Why You Should Care** 219

    Two Ideas of Apathy 220

        Two big problems 220

        An ancient idea and a modern translation 220

    Definitions and Images in Film 221

    Digging Deeper into Stoic Apathy. 222

    The Discipline We Need 224

    The Nature of Emotions 225

    Apathy and Ataraxia 227

        Stoic serenity 228

        The extremes of Epictetus 229

    Finding Sensible Peace 232

    Concluding Thoughts on Apathy. 234

CHAPTER 15: **Love and Friendship**. 235

    Two Big Ideas for Friendship and Love 235

        The Stoic idea of agreement 236

        The idea of appropriation 237

    True Friendship 238

        Aristotle on friendship 238

        Stoic friends 240

The Interpenetrating Unity of Souls 245
    Is the self a walled fortress? 245
    Distributed cognition 246
    A unique virtue 247
    Virtue or vulnerability? 248
Stoics in Love and on It 249
Sex and Love with the Stoics 251

CHAPTER 16: **The Fear of Death** 257
Matters of Life and Death 257
Philosophy as Preparation for Death 258
    The Socratic acceptance of mortality 259
    The Stoics' concerns 259
Two Epicurean Efforts to Calm Us Down 261
    The Symmetry Argument 261
    The Impossibility of Harm Argument 262
Epictetus Against Fearing Death 264
    The Judgment Argument 266
    The Avoidance Argument 268
    The Ignorance Argument 271
    The Acceptance Argument 271
Marcus Aurelius Weighs in on Death 274
    The Sameness Argument 275
    The Natural and Liberating Argument 276
    The Normal Change Argument 279
Seneca's Quantity or Quality Argument 281

PART 5: STOIC VIRTUES 285

CHAPTER 17: **The Master Virtues** 287
The Nature of Virtue 287
    Arete, or excellence 288
    Good habits 288
The Stoic View of Virtue 289
    From the Cynics 289
    From Socrates 290
    Stoic paradoxes relating to virtue 290
The Four Cardinal Virtues 291
    Courage 292
    Self-control 294
    Justice 296
    Wisdom 297
    Evaluating the four cardinal virtues 298

CHAPTER 18: Finding Resilience and Inner Peace 299

Resilience: The Art of Bouncing Back 300
    Live in the present moment. 300
    Adopt the view from above 301
    Look at the situation objectively 302
    Cut people some slack 303
    Take a walk on the wild side 304
    Keep Stoic basics ready to hand 304
The Stoic Quest for Inner Peace 306
    Anticipate possible adversities 306
    Practice morning and evening meditations. 307
    Start journaling 308
    Act with a reserve clause 308
    Practice voluntary discomfort 309
    Contemplate impermanence. 310
    Adopt good role models. 312
    Focus on what you can control 312
    Curb your desires for externals. 313
    Practice *Amor Fati* 314

PART 6: STOICISM TODAY 317

CHAPTER 19: The Stoic Next Door: The Popular Revival of Stoicism Today 319

The Rise of Modern Stoicism 320
    The therapists 321
    The sixties. 322
    Existentialism. 323
    Virtue ethics 323
    A renewal of scholarly work. 324
    Cultural attention 324
Leading Figures in Modern Stoicism. 327
    William B. Irvine 327
    Donald Robertson 331
    Massimo Pigliucci 333
    Ryan Holiday. 335

CHAPTER 20: Modern Stoicism 339

What Is Modern Stoicism? 339
Key Differences: Ancient and Modern 341
    Theoretical ambitions. 342
    Intellectual foundations 342
    Attitude toward religion 343
    Plausibility. 343

Central focus 345
Intended audience 346
Argumentative and rhetorical styles. 346
Modern Stoicism: Down and Upsides 349
Modern Stoicism: The cons 349
Modern Stoicism: The pros 353

PART 7: THE PART OF TENS 357

CHAPTER 21: **Ten Books Every (Budding) Stoic Should Read** 359
The Inner Citadel: The Meditations of Marcus Aurelius. 360
A Guide to the Good Life: The Ancient Art of Stoic Joy. 360
The Stoic Art of Living: Inner Resilience and Outer Results. 361
How To Be a Stoic 361
How to Think Like a Roman Emperor: The Stoic Philosophy
of Marcus Aurelius 362
The Stoics (2nd edition) 362
The Obstacle Is the Way 363
The Daily Stoic 363
Epictetus: A Stoic and Socratic Guide 363
Breakfast with Seneca: A Stoic Guide to the Art of Living 364

CHAPTER 22: **Ten Great Stoic Blogs and Podcasts** 365
Daily Stoic Blog. 365
Stoicism Today Blog 366
Figs in Winter Blog. 366
Stoicism: Philosophy as a Way of Life. 366
Traditional Stoicism Blog 367
Daily Stoic Podcast 367
The Walled Garden Podcast. 367
Stoic Meditations Podcast 368
Stoicism: Philosophy As a Way of Life Podcast 368
Stoic Coffee Break Podcast 368

INDEX 369

Introduction

Half the secret to living a good and happy life may be in knowing what to embrace and what to release. Most of us seem to get this wrong much of the time, embracing what we should release and releasing what we should embrace. There is some great ancient wisdom right now sweeping across the world and changing lives for the better that can show us how to get this right, and what it means to do so properly, in ways that really matter.

A group of philosophers in ancient Greece and Rome known as Stoics powerfully addressed the question of how best to live in a world of challenge and change. They had distinctive views about happiness and the good life, which they thought of as arising from personal excellence and moral virtue lived well in healthy communities. Their best insights have survived through the centuries to burst forth anew in our time. They offer deep and practical perspectives on finding a sense of real meaning, on joyful resilience, personal power amid turbulence, and a sense of inner calm in confronting uncertainty that may be just what's needed in our day.

About This Book

This is the right book for you if you've heard about Stoicism from a podcast or through friends and want to learn more, or if you've read one of the bestselling books that are reintroducing this distinctive philosophy into our time and would like an opportunity to work more fully through the powerful and fascinating array of ideas to be found in this way of thinking and living. It's also the right book for you even if you hardly know much about the Stoics at all but are ready for some fresh perspectives on your life, for some new ways of handling what's challenging and difficult, and perhaps even for liberating yourself from so many of the forces that seem to hold people back from being their best, feeling their best, and doing their best in the world.

The most helpful philosophers seek to understand life better and live it more meaningfully. They want to attain the deepest perspectives possible about this world to enhance and improve their own experiences of living. They take nothing for granted but question and probe in search of illumination and perspective. And then they seek to bring their discoveries to the rest of us.

We all want to understand the best wisdom there is for how we can live and move and grow. And you're in luck, because getting at least a good start on that task is the purpose of this book. We'll give you the key background history and the greatest thoughts of some of the most interesting practical thinkers in history, in many ways just normal, smart people who used their curiosity and their talents well, and in that way reached extraordinary heights in their thoughts and daily practices for living well. And now they can help us to do the same in our own lives.

You don't need to be an academic or a world-class visionary to benefit from looking more closely at the fundamental issues of your life, as framed by some of the wisest guides who have tackled these questions before us. This book is really about the challenges you face in your everyday life. And any new measure of understanding you can gain from smart people who have grappled with these issues before you will be a step in the right direction of practical and perhaps even life-changing results. You may find that you agree with the Stoic philosophers in all ways, or you may choose rather to cherry-pick their ideas for approaches you can use with the things that mean the most to you. In the end, despite how it may seem, a book like this is less about the information it holds than the possibilities for transformation it suggests.

In our look at the ancient and practical philosophy of Stoicism, we will ask basic and probing questions about what it is to exist as a human being in this world, what life is all about, and how we can live in the most satisfying ways every day. We'll ponder some of the most important things for our own personal self-understanding. We'll even tackle head-on some of the most fundamental life issues that we too often merely dance around, and rarely ever address directly. This will be a book about some of the most fundamental human questions and insights.

Foolish Assumptions

In the way we present the ideas in this book, we're basically going to assume that you're new to philosophy as a way of thinking and living, but not that you're new to all the questions and issues that philosophers ponder. We're also going to assume you're not a historian of the ancient world, or a classicist trained in Greek and Latin. And we're not expecting that you're already an expert on Stoicism and just want to read every new book written on this fascinating philosophy, as some big-time Stoic fans now seem to do.

If you are, however, a proud and credentialed representative of any such group, you're also most welcome here. We have a lot for you. We cover the basics but break new ground, too. We pledge to work hard to keep you engaged and even entertained and to give you the chance to dig deep and think in new ways about matters that are vital to your life. And finally, we won't assume but fervently will hope that you'll have as much fun and as inspirational an experience probing this important and interesting philosophy as we have had and continue to experience as we ponder all these things in new ways.

Icons Used in This Book

Throughout this book, icons in the margins highlight certain types of valuable information that call out for your attention. Here are the icons you'll find, and a brief description of each.

TIP

The Tip icon marks suggestions and perspectives that can help you think through an issue.

REMEMBER

The Remember icon indicates information that's especially important to know and keep in mind.

TECHNICAL STUFF

The Technical Stuff icon alerts you to information of a more difficult nature that you can skip over initially if you prefer.

ANECDOTE

We'll occasionally use an interesting story to aid in making a point.

WARNING

The Warning icon tells you to watch out! It flags important cautionary notes that can save you intellectual confusion, needless effort, or the fallacious *faux pas* to be avoided.

Beyond the Book

In addition to the abundance of information and guidance related to the philosophical questions to be found in this book here in these pages, you can get access to even more help and information online at dummies.com. Check out this book's Cheat Sheet there. (But don't worry, it's not the sort of cheating the very ethical Stoics would frown upon and steer you away from.) Just to go www. dummies.com and type "Stoicism For Dummies Cheat Sheet" in the search box.

Where to Go from Here

In the order of our chapters, we start by commenting on the incredible revival of Stoicism in our day, and especially among people who don't ordinarily pursue ancient ideas for modern living or dive into philosophy with an eager zest to use it well. Then we begin from the beginning of ancient thought to give you a full context, in brief, for understanding the rise and nature of Stoicism, to help you get your bearings as we go on to explore their biggest ideas in later chapters.

We hope you'll launch into your reading of the book in the normal manner, sequentially, cover to cover, as we've laid things out here, but you don't have to — you can read it any way you like! Each chapter has been written in such a way as to basically stand on its own. Big ideas are introduced in early chapters that are revisited and developed more fully in later chapters. This means that there are certain recurring ideas, cropping up in more than one place, but in their various appearances, they're developed in a variety of ways and tested from different angles in different contexts.

You can scan the table of contents and jump in anywhere you'd prefer to satisfy your appetite for whatever topic is on your mind right now, or to scratch any existential itch you may have. And yet, as in all things philosophical, the ideas here are all related to each other, and the perspective of any given chapter will be understood most fully and deeply in the context of what's come before and what's to be developed afterward. But you're never locked in. Explore as you wish. And enjoy. We want you to have an adventure here and a great experience. Stoicism is in many ways a philosophy of liberation, and so we want you to feel free to read this book as you like. And then tell us what you think. We mean it! Philosophy is a very big conversation, across space and time. We'd love to hear your thoughts. But to start, now let us give you ours.

1

Ancient Stoicism

IN THIS PART . . .

Discover why Stoicism is so popular in our time.

Dip into the history of ancient Stoicism.

Meet some Greek and Roman philosophers, and one amazing emperor.

Chapter **1**

Stoicism: A Philosophy for Our Time

As we write these words and then you read them, AI may be taking the world by storm. Yes, Artificial Intelligence, but also at the same time, Ancient Ideas. And to be more specific, some powerful perspectives from Stoic philosophers of long ago are suddenly spreading across contemporary culture in many countries at once and making a big difference in people's lives and work. Ancient Stoicism, born in Greece and then refreshed and in a sense rebranded in imperial Rome, can help you think in new and powerful ways about the challenges and opportunities you face every day. Its aim is to free you from whatever troubles you and may be holding you back. Its purpose is to give you a new form of strength and courage that's crucial in such a turbulent and uncertain world that we all face right now. And it's rooted in the greatest source of power for good that you have: your character.

In this chapter, we look at what's behind the current appeal of this very old and yet revolutionary way of thinking, feeling, and acting. And in the process, we can rediscover what's perhaps the most profoundly useful view of philosophy ever developed.

A Way of Thought for Our Time

In just the last few years, Stoic philosophy has suddenly become wildly popular around the world, gaining massive attention across such diverse cultural domains as business, sports, entertainment, and the military. Books about the Stoics and their ideas are selling in the millions and hitting national bestseller lists over and over. Podcasts, websites, online discussion groups, and even sales of Stoic-themed T-shirts, medallions, and coffee mugs are surging. Tattoo artists are turning out renderings of Greek and Latin words, variously placed on the bodies of adherents to this ancient philosophy. Public speakers are picking up on the trend. There are business meetings, professional sports team gatherings, and military mindset training sessions that now focus on Stoic ideas. Top executives at banks, hospitals, tech companies and manufacturing firms are waking up and coming alive to the possibilities that Stoic ideas awaken. And at college campuses across the country, overflowing classes are now being offered on Stoicism, while even much younger students are beginning to show an interest.

It may be that this surprising trend is in part a rebound effect from a widespread sense of cultural distress, and even an entertainment industry in dynamic interplay with it, that in many ways have together become increasingly coarse, loud, and superficial over the years. It could also be a reaction against the toxic aspects of social media, the ever-growing stressors of modern work and family life, the decline of organized religion, and the increasing political ugliness on display around the world. In addition, this development might in part be a reasonable response to all the fear and uncertainty highlighted by the many new dangers of sudden lethal violence in everyday life, an ongoing global war on terrorism and gang threats that has no clear end in sight, and increasingly obvious and catastrophic climate change. Then, add in all the fast-paced economic and technological disruption that threatens to increase more, along with emerging threats to democracy and world peace, the lingering effects of the last Great Recession and, of course, the frightening and massively destabilizing Covid-19 pandemic.

While artificial general intelligence looms over us as both a great promise and big peril, and we're often told a large asteroid careening through space just might have us in the crosshairs, it's understandable that people want to get their bearings, calm down, and find ways of dealing with all the dangers and challenges that surround us. Whatever the sources are of this new hunger for a sense of purpose, personal meaning, inner strength, mental balance, and resilience in life, Stoicism as a result is going viral. There is a huge new desire expanding through many parts of the world for more information on the ideas deriving from this school of ancient Greek and Roman thought that has influenced major thinkers from distant times to the present day.

Hot philosophy in America

It's rare for any form of philosophy to become highly popular in the United States, where we the co-authors live, and where a great deal of this new interest in the Stoics has been centered. To be blunt, our nation is a country that's often considered a nonintellectual or even anti-intellectual place of practical-minded "doers." But philosophy in fact has made major incursions into American life before.

During our founding period, the political ideas of thinkers like Aristotle, John Locke, David Hume, and Charles de Montesquieu were widely discussed. For a couple of decades in the late 19th century, the thoughts of Ralph Waldo Emerson, Henry David Thoreau, and many other philosophers in New England, within and around a form of thought known as transcendentalism, became common table talk among educated people and strongly influenced many aspects of life at the time. Then at the dawn of the 20th century, philosophers like William James and John Dewey sparked a brief boom across several decades in what came to be known as pragmatist philosophy, with ideas that filtered into many domains of American life.

Existentialism had a cultural run in the postwar 1940s and '50s, but mostly among the Beat poets, authors, artists, and musicians. Zen Buddhism and other Eastern philosophies then experienced a broad popularity in the 1960s and '70s, at first in what was broadly called the peace and love hippie counterculture, and then with widely spreading effects, spurred in part by the Beatles and other prominent celebrities and culture influencers, along with the increasing popularity of such healthful practices as yoga and meditation. And of course, the reverberation of that movement continues today.

But the current wave of fascination with Stoicism may be the biggest and broadest spread of interest in an ancient philosophy that America has ever seen. It certainly seems to be the fastest growing, at least if current trends continue.

The Stoic formula

At its core, the philosophy of Stoicism is about personal freedom, individual excellence, inner power, human equality, healthy communities, vibrant societies, and a radical recipe for inner tranquility and the possibilities of outer peace in the face of challenge, threat, adversity, massive uncertainty, and wildly unprecedented opportunity. We obviously live in a time of high anxiety, widespread throughout the population. While the dangers around us seem to be increasing at a rate never experienced before, our trusted institutions for helping us deal with the challenges of life appear to be stumbling and crumbling around us, throwing us more on our own in recent times. Where can we turn for help and resources?

Stoic philosophy seems to answer the life guidance needs that we now have in abundance. And a broad generalization may be safe to make about the motives most people have for their interest in it at present. Some people are attracted to Stoicism as a way to cope, while others see it as a way to conquer. But both these paths are based on developing inner character.

REMEMBER

In fact, if Stoicism had a general motto, it just might be:

To Cope and Conquer with Character.

Many people combine within themselves these two desires, to cope and conquer, to shun all feelings of victimization and emerge victorious from our crazy cauldron of modern challenges. Individuals who want both these things perceive in this ancient philosophy a collection of surprisingly novel resources they never suspected they could find in ancient thought and use for practical results. On the surface of Stoicism, there are many tips and techniques for thinking and acting in new ways that can be amazingly helpful for dealing with the stresses we all face, affording us a new sense of calm and confidence as we navigate our daily difficulties and race into the future.

What Does "Philosophy" Even Mean?

The word "philosophy" comes from two Greek root words: *philo*, meaning love, and *sophia*, meaning wisdom. In its origins, philosophy was thought to be, simply, "the love of wisdom." And of course, an object of love is always a distinctive thing: When you lack it, you pursue it, and when you have it, you embrace it. So, philosophy is etymologically the pursuit and embracing of wisdom, which is itself just embodied insight for living well.

The Roman lawyer, political advisor, and prominent Stoic author Seneca (4 BCE–65 CE) once put the insight like this:

> In the first place then, if you approve, I'll draw a distinction between wisdom and philosophy. Wisdom is the perfect good of the human mind. Philosophy is the love of wisdom and the endeavor to attain it. (*Letters* 89.4)

WARNING

In another place, Seneca says what he thinks philosophy isn't, as well as what it really is. And his words are as relevant now as they were in his day:

> Philosophy is no trick to catch the public — it's not devised for show. It's a matter not of words but of facts. It's not pursued so that the day may yield some

amusement before it ends, or that our free time might be relieved of a tedium that irks us. It shapes and builds the soul. It orders our lives, guides our conduct, shows what we should do and what we should avoid. It sits at the helm and directs our course as we hesitate among uncertainties. Without it, no one can live fearlessly or with peace of mind. Countless things that happen every hour call for guidance, and such advice is to be sought in philosophy. (*Letters* 16.3)

Reflecting later on why he or anyone needs philosophy as a help in this world, the same Stoic thinker writes these words, as if addressing philosophy itself with his urgently felt needs:

What should I do? Death is on my trail and life is slipping by. Teach me something I can use to face these troubles. Give me courage to meet hardships, make me calm in the face of the unavoidable. Relax the confines of the time allowed me. Show me that the good in life doesn't depend on life's length but on the use we make of it. (*Letters* 49.9–10)

We can see here the depth and urgent practicality of what Seneca seeks. He values philosophy and the wisdom it brings for its needed usefulness in helping us to use all other things well. To pursue and practice wisdom is the key to everything else. But then, what is wisdom, exactly? How should we think about it? Many people in our time seem to get it wrong.

What Wisdom Is and Is Not

Wisdom is never just a collection of short, clever, and insightful sayings about life. It's not mainly about slogans that could fit on a bumper sticker, ball cap, or T-shirt. In fact, it's never at all at its essence a matter of simple statements or propositions about the world, or even about living in it, but rather it's meant to be an inner reality within the soul, a progressively realized capacity of deep discernment for living well. When we attain a measure of genuine, authentic wisdom, we begin to grow stronger in it, or it begins to grow stronger in us. It's a lifetime adventure of deepening that will help any other adventure go better.

REMEMBER

Some aspects of this life-discernment can be captured in proverbs, aphorisms, or epigrams, but such statements at their best simply spark reminders, or new insight, a better orientation, a little needed tranquility, or a proper form of action in the world, and are never themselves the heart and soul of what wisdom really is. It's a state of heart and mind. And in saying that, we're using the ancient metaphor of the heart as referring to the center or core of our souls or selves in our fullness and complexity.

In a real sense, wisdom is a form of being in the world that doesn't live in sentences but in you, if you're wise. Wisdom is a state of mind and heart that affects your thoughts, feelings, attitudes, choices, and actions — forming and molding them all to better suit who you are and what the world is.

The prominent Stoic philosopher Epictetus ("ep-ic-TEE-tus," c. 55–c. 135 CE) once said this about philosophy and the wisdom it brings:

> What is it to do philosophy? Isn't it to prepare yourself for whatever happens? (*Discourses* 3.10.6)

The Roman emperor Marcus Aurelius (121–180), another prominent Stoic thinker in his own right, and a man who had studied the thoughts of Epictetus, puts it this succinctly:

> What then can guide us through life? Only philosophy. (*Meditations* 2.17)

TIP

Essentially, wisdom is about two things — guidance and guardrails. It's then manifested in two ways. Imagine first a bright light shining forth in the darkness at the top of a steep hill far away, signaling where the key to your best life may be found. Wisdom is your ability to see and follow that light. Or envision wisdom alternatively as the capacity to use a GPS with directions giving you guidance on how to get to that illuminated hilltop. The road to it will be steep and twisty and there will be many dangers along the way.

The other aspect of wisdom, in augmentation of the guidance it gives, is the system of guardrails it provides. Like those low metal barriers found alongside modern roads through mountainous terrain, the guardrails of wisdom will protect you as you proceed and keep you from falling off the side of the road into an abyss, and crashing down in the valley below. Wisdom points you in the right direction and protects you as you go. Philosophy at its best is simply about pursuing and embracing the powerful inner and outer transformation that real wisdom can provide in your life.

Two sides of philosophy

These statements about philosophy and wisdom in the previous sections may surprise you if you've had an introductory philosophy course in almost any college or university in the past 50 years. About a hundred years ago, academic philosophy — the study of philosophy in the context of higher education — took a more formal or theoretical turn, perhaps in emulation of the natural sciences whose success and progress have been extraordinary.

And yet those sciences themselves were once part of philosophy. Throughout much of early modern history, the discipline of philosophy was divided into

"Natural Philosophy" and "Moral Philosophy." Natural philosophy was thought of simply as a study of the natural world in which we live. But as specific investigative techniques for learning more about various subject matters in the world began to be developed, natural philosophy gradually gave rise to the various disciplines of science that we know today, like biology, astronomy, physics, chemistry, psychology, and so on. In ancient times, it was the philosophers who studied all those things, trying to get their bearings in the world and seeking a deeper knowledge of the context in which we all live.

When the various empirical sciences defined themselves as distinct disciplines and spun off from the mothership of philosophical endeavor, a set of topics then broadly referred to as "moral philosophy" was basically what remained. It was mostly about us as people, as selves, and about our main forms of engagement with the broader world, encompassing matters of ethics, epistemology, or the theory of knowledge, logic, the philosophy of language, social and political philosophy, metaphysics, philosophy of religion, aesthetics, and other such areas. In modern classrooms for the past century or so, an introduction to philosophy might tackle a variety of topics outside the range of issues addressed by the various natural sciences, but in some ways the methods of approach used by philosophers now could look quite similar.

When philosophy professors approach such things as the nature of knowledge, our understanding of goodness, or theories of political organization, they tend to engage in activities of conceptual exploration and technical argument that can seem much like the scientific pursuit of understanding that goes on across campus in the various science lecture rooms and labs, but without all the elaborate equipment and mathematical formulas. And yet, with a focus on theory and a strict formalization of investigation meant to arrive at accurate and helpful theories, philosophy during the past century unintentionally but increasingly moved farther away from such issues as meaning and purpose, or how best to live and be in the world, questions that we all eventually confront in our daily lives and that modern Stoicism takes as its focus. From ancient times, Stoicism had theories about the world and our lives, but the purpose of theory was to provide for practice, to suggest ideas for daily living.

TIP

We can make something like a rough division, running through the centuries, of two contrasting forms of philosophy:

>> Theoretical philosophy, which is about analysis, argument, and the advancement of our ideas

>> Practical philosophy, which is about analysis, argument, and the advancement of our lives

There's a sense in which the fruit of analysis and argument in the one case is an assessment that provides a new twist in our intellectual understanding, and in the other case, it's more like a new orientation or form of advice, which looks like a new twist on interpreting, feeling, and doing. But both endeavors count as proper philosophy, and each should relate to the other, because all is, in the end, somehow one.

And by the way, the best and deepest advice for living well will often look more like musings based on theory rather than like imperatives, nudges, or even helpful suggestions. The best theory advises us on new ways of thinking about something that puzzles us, which can then apply to the rough and tumble of daily life as well as to the theoretical conundrums of the seminar room. The founding Stoic philosophers did a lot of theorizing, but their ultimate intent and aim was practical. As Seneca writes:

> Philosophy is both theoretic and practical; it contemplates and at the same time acts. (*Letters* 95.10)

Philosophy and life

As an aside, we should point out that vocal critics of philosophy — who frequently don't really know what they're talking about because they've never been serious students of the discipline — often complain about the study of philosophy, and especially its theoretical side, for never making any progress throughout the centuries. But this is just false. Ancient thinkers, philosophers during the Middle Ages, Enlightenment figures, 19th- and 20th-century intellectuals, and many professors of the subject in our time have made tremendous progress in understanding very difficult matters, and in many ways. But there are of course some subjects and ultimate issues that make theoretical leaps forward extremely difficult. Marcus Aurelius says:

> Things are wrapped in such a veil of mystery that many good philosophers have found it impossible to make sense of them. (*Meditations* 5.10)

He then adds in the same passage:

> Even Stoics have trouble.

We all hit intellectual limits eventually. But Marcus quickly turns from a concern with theoretical understanding and its boundaries to the more practical side of philosophy, and says to himself, in his capacity as emperor:

> Don't be a Caesar drunk on power and self-importance — it happens all too easily. Keep yourself simple, good, pure, sincere, natural, just, god-fearing, kind, affectionate, and devoted to your duty. Strive to be who your training in philosophy prepared you to be. Stay in awe of your Source and serve humanity. Life is short.

The only good fruit to be harvested in this world requires a pious disposition and charitable conduct. (*Meditations* 6.30)

Many students for a very long time have signed up for a first philosophy course hoping to get their bearings in the world, and have discovered to their surprise that the professor seemed to spend most of the time talking about words like "Truth" or "Knowledge" or "Good" or "Justice" along with other bits of language that were then mined relentlessly for their conceptual content, to see precisely what ideas might lie behind them. But the Stoic teacher Epictetus, talking with one of his students who wanted to go give his own lecture on theory in such a way, focused on words, asks him:

Is it for this then that young men should leave their homelands and parents, to come and listen to you interpret words? When they get back home, shouldn't they be people who are tolerant, helpful, imperturbable, and serene? Shouldn't they be furnished with equipment for the journey of life that will empower them to endure everything that happens to them, and to endure it well and in a way that's a credit to them? (*Discourses* 3.21.8,9)

REMEMBER

We often think we need information when the real need is transformation. In the ancient world, philosophy was meant to be a transformative path, a way of life, and not just a mode of thinking, or the cumulative and codified results of such thinking. Philosophy was and is a particular embrace of life, along with a release of whatever gets in our way of living with inner peace, real excellence, and full flourishing in this world with others, while helping other people around us to do the same thing in a manner that's right for them.

The Stoics also dealt with words, of course, and the ideas encoded in those words, or else we wouldn't have their teachings available to us today. But they always used their words and ideas with a practical end in view. Elsewhere, Epictetus says:

What's the fruit of these ideas? There could be no better or more proper fruit for people who are receiving a real education than tranquility, fearlessness, and freedom. (*Discourses* 2.1.21)

He even indicates later that he wants to help his students become good people who, precisely because of that goodness, are in a sense invincible. And this can never come from just collecting, reading, and memorizing philosophical ideas. It will only result from living them. In another passage Epictetus says:

It's one thing to have bread and wine stored away, and another to use them. When you take something in, it's digested and distributed around the body and turns into muscle, flesh, bones, blood, a good complexion, and good lungs. Stored things may be available for you to bring out and display whenever you want, but they don't do you any good at all, apart from gaining a reputation for having them. (*Discourses* 2.9.18)

TIP

It's in the end not what we have collected or know, but what we do with what we know, and what we become because of it, that matters most.

PRESENT DAY PHILOSOPHERS ON STOIC PHILOSOPHY

Many philosophers in our own day have rediscovered Stoic wisdom. Here's a sample of what they say about it.

"Stoicism is a practical philosophy for everyday life. It's about being in control of your emotions and not letting them control you." —Massimo Pigliucci

"The Stoics believed that true happiness comes from within, not from external circumstances." —William B. Irvine

"Stoicism is the philosophy of courage. It teaches us to face our fears and overcome them." —Stephen Hanselman

"Stoicism is the philosophy of personal responsibility. It teaches us to focus on what we can control and let go of what we cannot." —Donald Robertson

"Stoicism is a philosophy of personal ethics informed by its system of logic and its views on the natural world." —Nancy Snow

"Stoicism is about finding inner peace and happiness through acceptance, not by avoiding negative emotions." —Tanner Campbell

"Stoicism is a philosophy that emphasizes reason, ethics, and personal responsibility." —Brad Inwood

"Stoicism is a way of life that emphasizes the development of self-control and the acceptance of what we cannot control." —John Sellars

"Stoicism . . . teaches how to live a supremely happy and smoothly flowing life and how to retain that even in the face of adversity." —Jonas Salzgeber

"Above all, Stoicism aims to make you skillful at life. . . . It sculpts your moral character into someone who is content, joyful, resilient, and able to take actions that make the world a better place." —Matthew J. Van Natta

Using Wisdom with the Stoics

In this section, we're going to stick with the quotable Epictetus for a moment more. He was often concerned over some of his young students who came to study with him to learn a bit of theory about the world, and perhaps even more theory about our ways of living in the world, and were enjoying themselves so much that they wanted to stay in school and stick with theory as a sort of refuge from the world, instead of taking their new insights back into the world. When you read Epictetus, you quickly realize what a good teacher he was — full of great stories, images, metaphors, analogies, and even jokes. He was vivid and memorable. He comments in an interesting metaphorical way on those students who get really excited about the study of philosophy and seem to want to live only in their ideas, books, and seminar rooms. Imagining a conversation about such a person, and with such a person, he says this:

> But what happens is that people behave like someone who's on his way back to his homeland when he passes a great inn, and it delights him so much that he stays there. "Man, you've forgotten your purpose. You weren't traveling *to* the inn but *past* it." — "But it's really nice." — "There are plenty of nice inns, and lots of pretty meadows, too, but only as places on the way. You have a different mission, to return to your home and put an end to your family's fear, and to engage in your duties as a citizen by getting married, raising children, and holding the customary offices. You didn't come into the world to go around finding pleasant locations to enjoy, surely, but *to live* where you were born and where you're a citizen."
> (*Discourses* 2.23.36–39)

We were born into this world to live in and with its challenges as well as its opportunities, with its discomforts and conveniences, its pains and its pleasures, and are meant to use philosophy as a way of doing so, across all circumstances, wisely and well. But how can we do this? We need some sound advice, some helpful guidance. And philosophy offers exactly that.

The prominent Stoic thinker and highly placed political advisor Seneca speaks about this to one of his friends and writes in a letter:

> Do you really want to know what philosophy offers humanity? Philosophy offers counsel. (*Letters* 48.8)

And in another place, he says even more succinctly:

> Philosophy is good advice. (*Letters* 38.1)

This is not always what we get in modern philosophy classes and academic philosophy books. Seneca saw the problem even in his time. He writes:

> We're taught how to debate, not how to live. (*Letters* 95.14)

There is of course nothing wrong with debate. Ideas are often developed through it. And people can discover truth or become persuaded of it through the reasoned presentation of ideas in the form of rational argument that is found in debate. But while debate can be a useful technique of philosophy, it's never the point of it.

Seneca makes the same point and expands on it in a latter correspondence. Our teachers can make mistakes in how they present philosophy to us, and we then often go on to repeat the same errors that we've been open to emulating because of our own inappropriate motives:

> There are indeed mistakes made through the fault of our advisors who teach us how to debate and not how to live. There are also mistakes made by the students who come to their teachers to develop not their souls but their wits. (*Letters* 108.23)

Young philosophy students recently introduced to the power of sound reasoning easily become arrogantly argumentative, intensely critical of others and their ideas, and simply insufferable know-it-alls. They can become exactly the wrong sort of ambassador for the philosophical life. Seneca wants to cut this off and writes to his younger friend who is making his way in the discipline of ideas, and is presumably proud of his progress:

> But you should never boast about philosophy, because if it's used with insolence and arrogance, it's been dangerous for many. Let philosophy strip off your faults, rather than helping you call out the faults of others. (*Letters* 103.5)

Happiness and freedom

Seneca is always bringing his initial reader and then all of us back to his view of what philosophy is all about:

> My advice is this: That all study of philosophy and all reading should be applied to the idea of living the happy life, that we should not hunt out archaic or outlandish words and eccentric metaphors and figures of speech, but that we should seek guidelines that will help us, statements of courage and spirit that may at once be transformed into realities. We should so learn them that words may become deeds. (*Letters* 108.35–37)

His correspondence partner is concerned about the many forces in life that he feels to be oppressive, and the difficult things we can't avoid, like disease and ultimately death. Seneca writes:

> You ask, "How can I free myself?" You can't escape necessities, but you can overcome them. It's said that: "By force a way is made." And this way will be given to you by philosophy. Go then to philosophy if you want to be safe, untroubled, happy, and ultimately if you wish to be — which is most important — free. There is no other way to attain this end. (*Letters* 37.4)

In another place he says about the ups and downs of life:

> The power of philosophy to blunt the blows of chance is beyond belief. (*Letters* 53.12)

And he writes:

> As much as you're able, take refuge with philosophy. She'll treasure you in her heart, and in her inner fortress you'll be safe, or at least more so than you were before. (*Letters* 103.4)

At a relatively advanced age, he says:

> Philosophy gives us this gift: It makes us joyful in the very sight of death, strong and brave no matter what physical condition we may be in, cheerful and never failing even if the body fails us. (*Letters* 30.3)

We often make fundamental mistakes in our approach to life that render us vulnerable to anxiety, worry, and fear. We sleepwalk through our days, far too often, and are surprised at what happens to us as a result. Seneca at one point concludes with this advice to his friend:

> Let us then rouse ourselves so that we can correct our mistakes. Philosophy, however, is the only power that can stir us, the only power that can shake off our deep slumber. Devote yourself wholly to philosophy. You're worth of her; she's worthy of you. Greet each other with a loving embrace. (*Letters* 53.8)

REMEMBER

Seneca has the view that, as long as we live, we should be learning how to live. And he's convinced that this will be provided by an ongoing training in philosophy. Epictetus and Marcus Aurelius seem wholeheartedly to agree.

When to go to philosophy

Marcus even expresses the idea that any situation is perfect for the study of philosophy, so no good excuses are ever available to anyone who would rather put it off until another time, and perhaps another situation. He basically says this to himself during a war, while he's leading the way in defending Rome: So you think you don't have time for philosophy because you're facing great pressures, perhaps exhaustion, and endless responsibilities? It's a surprising general truth that, because of the nature and universal applicability of philosophy:

> Clearly, no situation is better suited for the practice of philosophy than the one you're in right now. (*Meditations* 11.7)

At one point, the philosopher Seneca weighs in and suggests to his friend:

> Find a list of the philosophers. That very act will compel you to wake up when you see how many men have been working for your benefit. You'll want to be one of them yourself. For this is the most excellent quality the noble soul has within itself, that it can be roused to honorable things. (*Letters* 39.2)

He later adds this great thought:

> Philosophy did not find Plato already a nobleman; it made him one. (*Letters* 44.3)

TIP

We should go to philosophy for clear ideas and helpful principles, and the most useful of these are meant to lead to practices — habits and routines of thought, feeling, and action that will put the ideas into play in the tough and wonderful world around us, transforming us along the way so that we can become, be, do, and feel all that is our calling as alert, alive, conscious beings of reason. We are all on a journey that can often perplex us, but that will also develop and grow us when we let it. And philosophy can help us with that.

If you're intrigued by what these Stoics have to say about philosophy and its proper role in life, then read on. There aren't many schools of thought in our time that make such promises and offer such perspectives. You may find here much that you can use. You might even become a Stoic yourself. But the aim of the great Stoics of the past wasn't really to recruit and make other people Stoics, but rather to help us all become good people, ready for life and well prepared to live in all the best ways.

Chapter **2**

Socrates and the Beginnings of Western Philosophy

The story of Stoicism begins in ancient Greece more than 2,300 years ago. Before we dive into what Stoicism is all about, it's helpful to understand a little bit about how it got its start.

Socrates famously said that "philosophy begins in wonder." In ancient Greece, philosophical reflection first seemed to find its way into the world around 600 BCE when a small group of thinkers in the Greek cities of Ionia (now part of western Turkey) began asking new kinds of fundamental questions about our existence in the universe. Prior to this, efforts to explain reality were usually made in terms of religion or mythology (Zeus, Apollo, Athena, and all those other fun-loving deities). For example, eclipses and thunderbolts were commonly seen then as signs of divine anger. And then, by contrast, in certain areas of ancient Greece, systematic efforts were made for the first time to explain things substantially in terms of natural, observable, *physical* causes. This revolutionary step marked the beginnings of both Western philosophy and science.

As we'll discuss in this chapter, thinkers like Heraclitus, Socrates, and the Cynics set the stage for the Stoics. In various ways they had all sown the seeds for a distinctive philosophy that would later take root, grow, and blossom. The Stoics drew from all these earlier sages, as well as others, such as Plato and Aristotle, to create their own unique and fascinating philosophy and wisdom-centered way of life that continues to inspire us today.

Heraclitus the (Cranky and) Obscure

One important early Greek philosopher who greatly influenced the Stoics had the well-deserved name of "Heraclitus the Obscure." The man was apparently a curmudgeonly, "Hey-kids-get-off-my-lawn" kind of guy who lived around 500 BCE in Ephesus, a once thriving Greek city that is now in Western Turkey. People called him "The Obscure" because he wrote in pithy, cryptic sentences, and half the time nobody knew what the heck he was talking about. Scholars are still scratching their heads over many of his enigmatic sayings, though some are pretty clear and suitable for printing on T-shirts and bumper stickers, like "Everything is always changing" and "Character is destiny."

Heraclitus seems to have believed that the entire cosmos is *alive*, a gigantic living organism infused with a kind of divine "force" he called the *Logos*, a Greek word with numerous meanings, including "reason," "word," "rational utterance," and "really boring study of," as in modern phrases and words like *symbolic logic*, *physiology*, and *microbiology*. Just kidding about the "boring" part. (Sort of.)

Anyway, Heraclitus said that *fire* (not water, air, or tapioca pudding) was the basic stuff of reality, and he thought of the Logos as a kind of invisible fiery vapor that pervades all of nature and gives it purpose, direction, and rational order. According to Heraclitus, Logos directs and determines everything that comes to pass. Nothing in reality, he suggests, is truly permanent or stable; the cosmos is an ever-changing flux of ceaseless, kaleidoscopic change. Buddhists, in their notion of "impermanence" (*annica*), believe something similar. So do astute observers of the stock market.

Moreover, Heraclitus thought that everything in nature is "beautiful and good and just," though humans, from our limited and biased perspective, might call some things "bad" or "evil." The universe is also eternal, rather than made or created. Though Heraclitus held that the Logos is "an ever-living fire," he also believed, according to some scholars, that the entire cosmos is periodically destroyed in a giant conflagration. However, it is never completely obliterated. Instead, there is an eternal cycle of cosmic death, rebirth, and renewal.

THALES, THE FIRST KNOWN GREEK PHILOSOPHER

According to surviving sources, the first philosopher in ancient Greece was Thales (c. 625–c. 545 BCE), an astoundingly versatile thinker who lived in the bustling Ionian coastal city of Miletus, near the water. Thales wondered if there might be some basic "stuff" out of which everything in the universe is made, and decided there is. Everything that exists, he claimed, is either water or some transformation of water (like rocks and mud, which Thales thought were just compacted bits of water).

Later thinkers, following in the footsteps (or possibly chariot tracks) of Thales, offered different answers to the same question. One early philosopher suggested that the primal stuff of reality is actually air, not water. Another surmised that all things are actually made up of tiny little particles of matter that they called "atoms." (Bravo! Not a bad guess.) What's important here isn't the specific answers but the *kinds* of explanations that were being offered. Now, for the first time in history as far as we can tell, serious efforts were being made to explain the natural world substantially in terms of physical, humanly understandable causes.

"YOU CAN NEVER STEP TWICE INTO THE SAME RIVER"

Or whiz. For the same reasons. This quote above is Heraclitus's most famous saying and, perhaps not uncoincidentally, one of his least obscure. The thought is that in this world nothing is literally the same from one moment to the next, so the river you step into today is, in strict truth, a different physical object than the one you stepped into yesterday or five minutes ago. The waters you dipped your tastefully painted toes into before have flowed far downstream, and now all-new waters fill the banks. As we think we mentioned, Heraclitus was a curmudgeonly guy, so what he probably said was, "You can never *relieve* yourself twice in the same river." Or so a waggish friend of Greg's likes to joke, usually after drinking "a couple-two-tree" beers.

As we'll see, all of these ideas would later find echoes in Stoic thought, and especially in the writings of Emperor Marcus Aurelius, the last great Stoic philosopher.

Socrates: The Barefoot Gadfly and General Pain-in-the-Patootie of Ancient Athens

Heraclitus was one major influence on the Stoics. Another was the Athenian philosopher Socrates (c. 469–399 BCE), who influenced *every* thinker who followed him in ancient Greece. Socrates was the teacher of Plato (c. 428–c. 348 BCE), who in turn taught Aristotle (384–322 BCE). Together, these three giants of Greek philosophy powerfully influenced the course of Western civilization, and its many still existing philosophy departments.

In some ways, it's strange that Socrates should be such an iconic figure in Western history. He founded no state or religion, won no wars, created no great works of art, discovered no life-changing inventions, and wrote no books. He didn't even come up with any big new philosophical theories. He was a barefoot, paunchy, pug-nosed, scruffy-looking, famously ugly sidewalk philosopher who spent nearly every day of his adult life in public places prodding people about their basic beliefs, and then patiently demolishing those convictions with relentless, razor-sharp logic. Naturally, this made him very unpopular with some people, especially rich and powerful politicians who preferred that people think they knew what they were talking about at all times. As a result, he was eventually arrested on false charges, tried, convicted by a large public jury, and executed for his "subversive" activities by the leaders of the Athenian democracy.

Why did Socrates devote himself to this strange and often irritating life of public philosophizing? He defended it by saying that the gods had commanded him to assist his fellow Athenians to live what he called "examined lives," that is, lives of self-scrutiny, depth, curiosity, and enhanced self-awareness. He seemed to believe quite sincerely that this was his personal mission in life, and he never veered from what he saw as his divinely appointed task.

REMEMBER

Socrates never claimed to have discovered "The Way" or "The Truth," and he would have faced serious difficulty in being hired as a motivational speaker. He claimed only to be a humble seeker of wisdom and truth.

Though he said he knew nothing with certainty, he did seem to have certain bedrock convictions that he used as a personal life compass. Some of those beliefs struck his contemporaries as so unorthodox, and a few even seemed so nonsensical to others, that they came to be known as "Socratic paradoxes." These were some of the claims:

>> What's truly important in life isn't money, fame, or other worldly goods, as most people seem to think; it's wisdom and goodness, or what Socrates liked to call "care of the soul."

>> Goodness ("virtue," or "excellence," which the Greeks called *arete*) is all you need for true happiness. Virtue is sufficient for a fully happy life.

>> "No harm can come to a good person" (Plato, *Apology* 41d).

>> Virtue is knowledge. That is, anyone who truly and deeply *knows* what is good will always and necessarily *do* what is good.

>> No one does wrong willingly; all wrongdoing is, in an important sense, involuntary and based in ignorance.

All the ancient Stoic thinkers were greatly influenced by these Socratic zingers, so let's take a couple of moments to briefly unpack them.

Care for the soul

Like the great pre-Socratic philosopher and mathematician Pythagoras (flourished c. 530 BCE), Socrates claimed that our main concern in life should be for the health, moral fiber, and well-being of our soul (*psyche*), and not with money, fame, worldly success, or physical pleasures. In one dialogue, Socrates and a young philosopher-wannabe named Simmias are discussing how much importance we should give to drinking, sex, and other bodily pleasures:

> *Socrates*: Do you think that the philosopher ought to care about the pleasures of . . . eating and drinking?
>
> *Simmias*: Certainly not.
>
> *Socrates*: And what do you say of the pleasures of love — should he care about them?
>
> *Simmias*: By no means.
>
> *Socrates:* And will he think much of the other ways of indulging the body — for example, the acquisition of costly clothing, or sandals, or other adornments of the body? Instead of caring about these does he not rather despise anything beyond what nature needs?
>
> *Simmias*: I should say that the true philosopher would despise them (Plato, *Phaedo*, 64d-e).

REMEMBER

Physical pleasures, Socrates believed, are temporary, fleeting, and ultimately unfulfilling, and can often tempt us into immoral or self-destructive behavior that harms the soul. But your "true self" is your soul. Your thoughts, memories, character, and personality features — those are what most essentially make you, *you*. They are what will survive if there is any kind of life after death, as Socrates hoped and believed there probably is. So what matters most are not "externals" like money, power, or fame, but goods that are *internal* to the soul, like moral excellence and wisdom.

Virtue is sufficient for happiness

Nearly all ancient Greek philosophers agreed that the chief goal of life is happiness, though their actual term is *eudaimonia*, a hard to translate Greek word for overall well-being and well-doing that is sometimes rendered in English as "flourishing" "true fulfillment," "blessedness," or even "the ideal life." These thinkers often differed, however, over what makes a person truly happy, as well as in their accounts of what happiness really is. Some simply equated happiness with pleasure, saying that a happy life is one that includes lots of fun, excitement, and good times, with little pain or suffering. Others suggested that a happy life is one that combines important internal excellences of soul (e.g., wisdom and virtue) with various external goods, such as financial well-being, good health, and great friends.

Socrates had a different and unconventional view of happiness. He believed that *arête* — virtue, or the excellence of wisdom and goodness — is the most important thing in life. Compared to *arete*, other goods such as wealth, bodily pleasure, or fame are of little or no importance. For these reasons, Socrates maintained that virtue is "sufficient," or all that is necessary, for happiness. Although it's not clear exactly what Socrates thought about the value of "externals" (that is, things outside the mind or soul) generally, he might have agreed that externals like good looks or good health might slightly increase one's happiness and well-being, but are trivial in comparison with goods of the soul.

What is clear is that Socrates believed that *arete* (aka wisdom and goodness) is by far the most important *ingredient* of happiness and is really all a person needs to live a happy and successful life that's pleasing to the gods.

No harm can come to a good person

As the Bible reminds us, in this life rain falls upon both the just and the unjust (Matt. 5:45). And as Buddha said, life is full of suffering (poverty, sickness, injustice, grief, and unsatisfied longing, to at least begin our list). What possible sense does it make, then, to say that no harm can come to a good person? Isn't it obvious that this is a world in which "bad things happen to good people?" *A lot.*

Socrates's answer is to remind us that *arete* is the only *true* good and vice the only *true* evil. A good person can certainly be robbed or cheated, but as Socrates sees it, those are harms only if they make a good person bad, in which case that person wasn't truly and deeply good in the first place.

Truly good people can always preserve wisdom and virtue in the face of any adversity, and so long as they do, Socrates believed, no real harm can befall them. As long as their souls are healthy and morally sound, they're still "happy" and undamaged as people. This is admittedly a different way of thinking about personal happiness and well-being, but it can be an empowering one.

Virtue is knowledge

To know the path is one thing; to follow it is quite another. Or so common sense seems to suggest. But Socrates believed that if we look deeper, we can see that all wrongdoing, or wandering off the proper path for life, results from a kind of ignorance: a lack of a particular form of knowledge or awareness. Since virtue is the only true good, anyone who does evil is choosing, in actual fact, to give up what is good. To deprive oneself of anything that is good is to harm oneself. But no one, Socrates believed, would knowingly or willingly harm themselves — we all naturally and unavoidably desire what we think will benefit us. Thus, anyone who truly and deeply knows what is good will always do it.

No one does wrong willingly

This paradoxical claim is clearly linked to Socrates's view that virtue is knowledge. If I mistakenly take your nondescript black coat instead of mine when leaving a party, it wouldn't be fair to say that I "willingly" or "knowingly" took it. No one who acts from ignorance acts willingly or voluntarily. As we just saw, Socrates believed that all wrongdoing stems from a lack of knowledge of what is really good and evil. So no one truly does wrong willingly. If they knew all the relevant and important facts, they would not have done what they did.

Okay, we can guess what you're thinking. You're maybe saying to yourself, "But can't someone know something is wrong and still do it, because of the strength of temptation, for example? Can't we know something is wrong or bad for us and do it anyway, maybe because "though the spirit is willing, the flesh is weak," so "Hello, third chocolate donut?"

WARNING

No, sorry, Socrates would reply. We only do what we think is good, in the situation and at the moment we do it. And of course, we can be misled through a false belief or simple ignorance of what's really going on. And in that case, we don't do wrong willingly, just like you didn't take the wrong coat willingly or intentionally. I took your coat "by accident," not intentionally or deliberately.

As we'll see in the next chapter, the Stoics embraced versions of these Socratic paradoxes and added a few doozies of their own. For the Stoics, Socrates was the ideal *Sage*, a model of perfect wisdom and goodness, and he remained one of their chief inspirations and a big influence.

Diogenes of Sinope: Socrates on Steroids

Another huge influence on the Stoics was a group of wild and crazy guys (and girls!) called the Cynics. Who were the Cynics? They weren't actually cynics in the modern sense of the word. That is, they weren't scornful scoffers who always expected the worst in people and seemed to begin a lot of sentences with the phrase "Back in *my day*." They were called "Cynics" (from the Greek *kunikos*, meaning "doglike") because they were intentionally homeless and lived, in the eyes of their early critics, much like stray dogs.

The reported founder of Cynicism was a friend and student of Socrates named Antisthenes (c. 455–360 BCE), who after Socrates's death wrote several works of philosophy, all long ago lost, and proudly lived an impoverished and highly eccentric kind of life. What apparently impressed Antisthenes most about Socrates wasn't so much his teaching but his distinctive *character* — especially his simple, nonmaterialistic lifestyle, his scorn for conventional values such as money and power, and his unwavering devotion to wisdom and goodness, whatever the cost. However, Antisthenes and his even more famous pupil Diogenes of Sinope (c. 412–323 BCE) went far beyond Socrates in their contempt for civilization and conventional values.

They favored, in fact, a kind of radical "back-to-nature" approach to life that rejected most civilized norms as artificial, corrupting, and unnatural. Their goal was to achieve complete personal freedom and self-reliance by reducing their wants to a bare minimum and living as simply and as "naturally" as possible. For example, they rejected jobs, homes, possessions, politics, marriage, and even many ordinary decencies as "unnatural" and as forms of slavish dependency. They went so far in this extreme back-to-nature counter-culturalism that Plato once supposedly described Diogenes as "Socrates gone mad."

The Cynics came up with several ideas that greatly influenced the Stoics, and they're summarized in the sections that follow.

Virtue is the only true good

WARNING

Much in the spirit of their hero Socrates, the Cynics prized moral goodness above all other things. In fact, they seem to have held the arguably extreme view that all supposed "goods" other than virtue — including health, money, friendship, a free subscription to whatever the ancient Greek equivalent of NFL+ was back then — are literally worthless, *completely valueless*, or at best are only trifles that we shouldn't really care about much. Nothing is *truly* good, they said, except moral goodness. Only virtue has intrinsic value. So virtue must always come first.

Virtue is sufficient for happiness

Like most schools of Greek philosophy, the Cynics believed that everybody naturally wants to be happy and that happiness is in fact the main goal of life (the highest good, or *summum bonum*, as the barbarous Roman knuckleheads used to say while scarfing up most of the best Greek baklava). Since, however, the Cynics also held that virtue is the only good, they defined "happiness" (the Greek word, again, is *eudaimonia*) very narrowly. To them, a happy life simply *is* a virtuous life.

WARNING

Hunger, cold, sickness, and even extreme pain, they held, are not happiness defeaters, or even happiness interrupters. A person of true moral goodness, like Socrates, would be happy, or flourishing, even on the proverbial "rack," a tool of physical torture, which was all too real back in those tough and brutal times. Moreover, since *we* control how moral we are, we also control how happy we are. In other words, our happiness is completely internal, entirely up to us.

REMEMBER

The world does not determine either whether we're happy or how happy we are; we do, by our own choices and attitudes. This is the hard-core but inspiring Cynic (and later Stoic) ideal of complete "self-sufficiency" (*autarchia*, in case you want to know). Nothing that we truly need for happiness is outside our control. In everything that really matters in life, we are "masters of our fate."

"Follow nature"

As we have seen, the Cynics were strongly pro-nature and just as strongly anti-civilization. They drew a sharp distinction between what is "natural" (and therefore good) and what is "artificial" or conventional (and therefore bad, or else not worth caring about). In their view, nature was not simply a bunch of rocks, trees, bear droppings, flies buzzing around bear droppings, and the like. It was "normative," a moral norm or pattern of proper behavior. Nature, for them, was "the Way," the path of wisdom and goodness.

Temples, courts, laws, nice clothes, jumbo-sized gyros with creamy tzatziki sauce, and other trappings of civilization are artificial, not natural. They corrupt us, weaken our moral character, and create all kinds of harmful and unnatural dependencies and desires.

What should we do, then? What Diogenes and his Cynic friends urged is that we scrap civilization and return to a simpler, more primitive life that is "in accord with nature." Super-hard-core Cynics like Diogenes took this back-to-nature attitude to extremes, even performing both "the duties of nature" (aka defecation) and "the rites of love" (aka sex) in full public view. Had Heraclitus still been around in 350 BCE, he would surely have yelled at these guys to get off his rocky lawn.

Be a citizen of the world

As we discussed in the previous section, Cynics scorned the conventions and artificialities of civilization and had zero respect for governments, laws, or societal norms that they considered to be contrary to nature. But the Cynics did recognize a kind of higher loyalty. When asked where he was from, Diogenes reportedly replied, "I am neither Athenian nor Greek, but a citizen of the world" (*cosmopolites*). This is the origin of the influential modern idea of *cosmopolitanism*, the belief that all humans, in spite of everything that divides us, are actually part of a single human family.

REMEMBER

For Diogenes and his fellow Cynics, we are all equally children of God, or Nature, and our highest allegiance should not be to any particular city, state, or nation, but to humanity as a whole, and even to the larger and nobler community of the wise and good, both humans and gods.

Heraclitus, Socrates, Diogenes and his fellow Cynics — these are some of the fascinating ancient thinkers that prepped the stage for the Stoics.

Are there any modern counterparts of "mad" Diogenes still around today, outside of psychiatric wards and perhaps a few jails? In a way, the answer seems clearly to be: yes. Few responsible citizens run around half-or-mostly-naked like Diogenes was reported to have done, or intentionally make it their habit to violate basic cultural norms. But in other ways he has many descendants in our time. For instance, environmentally conscious followers of the modern voluntary simplicity movement seek to live as simply as possible, own few possessions, and generally try to leave as small a footprint on this beat-up and rapidly warming planet as they can. "Simplify, simplify, simplify!" Thoreau scribbled in the mid-19th century in his little hand-built cabin on the shores of Walden Pond. Bestselling authors now urge us to de-clutter our lives and get rid of all the stuff that's just suffocating us, and great numbers of people seem to respond enthusiastically. For many, it's an age-old message that resonates strongly today.

MODERN CYNICS

We're told that Diogenes was quite flamboyantly immodest in his public behavior, as in all his bodily functions being on full public view, but strikingly modest in his needs. The story is passed down to us that he gave away all his possessions except for a clay bowl for drinking water. And then one day he saw a young boy drink out of cupped hands, and he gave away the bowl. He liked to say such things as, "He has the most who is most content with the least." In a world where nothing seems to count as enough anymore, his is a voice that echoes down to our time and stands out. And yet, he was a very odd bird in many ways.

Chapter **3**

The First Stoics

S toicism was founded in Athens around 300 BCE by Zeno (c. 334–262 BCE), often called "Zeno of Citium," because he hailed from the town of Citium on the island of Cyprus. In those days, Citium was mainly a Greek city, but with a large Phoenician population as well, and it's possible that Zeno was himself of Phoenician (that is, Middle Eastern) extraction, as several early sources suggest. The biographer Diogenes Laertius (flourished c. 230 CE) tells a wonderful story about how this man who was to have such amazing influence on ancient and modern thought came to Athens and decided to become a philosopher.

Reportedly, Zeno was a merchant who sold expensive purple dyes, apparently working for his father in a family business. One day when he was still a young man, he was shipwrecked near the Athenian port of Piraeus. His ship and all his precious cargo were lost. Making his way to Athens, Zeno stopped by a bookstall. There he heard someone reading a passage about Socrates from Xenophon's *Conversations with Socrates*. Intrigued, he asked the bookseller where he could find someone like Socrates. Just then the Cynic philosopher Crates walked by. "Follow him," the bookseller said. And that's what Zeno did.

At that period, Athens was the undisputed philosophical capital of the world. There were three major schools of philosophy there, plus some less prestigious ones, such as Cynicism and Pythagoreanism. The three most celebrated organized schools were the Academy (founded by Plato around 388 BCE), the Lyceum (started by Aristotle around 334 BCE), and the Garden (founded by Epicurus just a few years before Zeno came to Athens). Each of these places for philosophical activity had its own unique flavor. Plato's school stressed math, Socratic "care for the soul," and training for political leadership. Aristotle's school focused a good deal on logic and science. And Epicurus's beautiful place just outside town emphasized the intelligent pursuit of pleasure and mental tranquility.

Zeno went on to study not only with the Cynic philosopher Crates, but also with several other leading thinkers of his time, including two heads of Plato's Academy. Sometime in his mid-30s, he decided to start his own school of philosophy. Because it was Zeno's habit to teach in the *Stoa Poikile* ("Painted Porch"), a sort of covered public colonnade in Athens' central marketplace, his school came to be known as Stoicism.

Zeno wrote around 20 books, but sadly none have survived. What we know of his teachings is based mainly on a few fragmentary quotations and secondary accounts of Stoic doctrines in later sources (many written by critics of Stoicism). From these, it appears that Zeno divided philosophy into three main branches:

>> Physics, which deals with God, the soul, the fundamental nature of reality, and what we would call natural science

>> Logic, which for the Stoics included not only the study of good reasoning ("dialectic") and good speaking ("rhetoric"), but also parts of what we today would call cognitive psychology, semantics, and the philosophy of knowledge

>> Ethics, which focuses on the ultimate goal of human life, sound moral conduct, political theory, and how to live a good and fulfilling life

The Basic Teachings of Zeno and His Stoic Followers

Zeno believed that philosophy should mostly be practical; it should help us solve real-life problems and live good and happy lives. But as the titles of many of his books make clear (see Diogenes Laertius, *Lives of Eminent Philosophers* 7.4), he also believed that knowing how to live requires a deep understanding of how the world works. For that reason, he and his followers worked out an elaborate worldview to support their ethical teachings. Let's begin with a sketch of that worldview. (A more detailed account will be provided later, in Part 2 of this book.)

Materialists through and through

Unlike Plato and Aristotle, Zeno and his fellow Stoics did not believe that anything spiritual or immaterial exists. They were strict materialists (though, as we shall see, they did admit that certain incorporeal things, like space, have a kind of "reality"). Everything that strictly exists, they believed, is some form of matter. To the Stoics, the notion of a purely spiritual being such as an unembodied god, an angel, or an immaterial soul made no sense. Whatever exists, they thought, must be capable of causing or experiencing some kind of change, and they believed that only bodies could do that.

Belief in Logos

Despite their strict materialism, the early Stoics were deeply religious. They believed in a kind of material God or higher power that they alternately called the Logos, nature, fate, or Zeus. In the mainstream Judeo-Christian tradition, God is conceived as an eternal, unchanging, and infinitely perfect spirit existing apart from the entire material universe that has been divinely created from nothing. By contrast, the Stoic God (the Logos) is made of matter, is ever changing, and exists entirely in the physical world. The Logos is supposed to be composed of a special type of matter — a gas-like mix of fire and air — that the Stoics described as a kind of "breath" (*pneuma*) interfused throughout the universe and that gives the cosmos and everything in it rational order, purpose, and shape.

The Stoics were "monists" who believed that only one thing exists: God (or nature). What we call nature or the physical universe is simply God in one of the divine phases. In fact, the Stoics thought of the entire universe as a living, rational being with both a body and a soul. The body of the world is passive, inanimate matter that God generates out of his own fiery substance; and the soul of this body is the active, intelligent Logos that lives and operates within the Cosmos, giving it order, beauty, and purpose.

"YES, VIRGINIA, THERE IS A LOGOS"

One major difference between ancient Stoicism and modern Stoicism involves religion. The ancient Stoics, both Greek and Romans, were highly religious, and many of their core beliefs (e.g., on fate, providence, radical acceptance, the soul, and life after death) make little sense apart from the spiritual or religious beliefs on which they were grounded. By contrast, as we'll see, many modern Stoics do not believe in God or any kind of higher power. Their brand of Stoicism is much more practical and doctrinally stripped down, so to speak. As Plutarch reports, the great Stoic thinker Chrysippus (c. 279–206 BCE) would never begin a book or lecture on ethics without references to the theological and "scientific" groundings of Stoic teaching.

(continued)

(continued)

The religious basis of ancient Stoicism comes out clearly in the famous "Hymn to Zeus" written by Cleanthes, who succeeded Zeno as the head of the Stoic school in Athens in 262 BCE. Here's a part of it in a modern translation by Brad Inwood and Lloyd Gerson:

Most glorious of the immortals, called by many names, ever almighty

Zeus, leader of nature, guiding everything with law,

Hail! For it is right that all mortals should address you,

since all are descended from you and imitate your voice,

alone of all the mortals which live and creep upon the earth.

So I will sing your praises and hymn your might always.

This entire cosmos which revolves around the earth obeys you,

wherever you night lead it, and is willingly ruled by you; . . .

Nor does any deed occur on earth without you, god,

neither in the aethereal divine heaven nor on the sea,

except for the deeds of the wicked in their folly.

But you know how to set right what is excessive

and to put in order what is disorderly; for you . . .

have fitted together all good things with the bad,

so that there is one eternal rational principle for them all. . . .

But Zeus, giver of all . . .

grant that they may achieve

the wisdom with which you confidently guide all with justice

so that we may requite you with honor for the honor you give us,

praising your works continually, as is fitting

for mortals; for there is no greater prize, neither for mortals

nor for gods, than to praise with justice the common law for ever.

Strict determinists

In addition to being materialists, the early Stoics were strict causal determinists. They held that all events have causes and that everything that occurs is the inevitable outcome of prior causes. So, they rejected any notion of "chance" or random events. They believed strongly in "fate," conceived as a kind of inexorable and rigidly determined sequence of preordained events. This makes it hard to see how human actions can be meaningfully free or responsible. And yet they talked often about "what's up to us," and of our freedom and "control," as if it's not only real, but vitally important to their philosophy. We'll see how the Stoics themselves tried to wrestle with this thorny problem of harmonizing fate and free will.

REMEMBER

Though the Stoics believed in fate, they did not think of it as blind. Instead, they held that the universe is providentially ordered by the all-wise, all-good Logos. Since there are no limits on the control, wisdom, and goodness of the Logos, the Stoics believed that whatever ultimately happens in the universe must happen "for the best," or at least in an extremely wise and well-ordered way. Though the world does contain some evils (namely, the immoral thoughts and deeds of human moral agents), the Logos ensures that even these work out for the long-term good of the universe as a whole. Thus, for the Stoics, despite all the suffering and evil that exists, this is "the best of all possible worlds."

Since everything in the universe is part of God, humans must be portions of God too. The Stoics, in fact, thought of us as being parts of God in a special way. They believed that we have a rational soul and that such souls are "sparks" or fragments of the Logos, the Divine Fire. Thus, the Stoics often spoke of "the God within." They also referred to us as "God's children," since we all were made from God and have minds that are parts of God. Beings that lack rationality, such as nonhuman animals, were thought of as inferior to humans and to exist solely for our benefit. So, the ancient Stoics were highly anthropocentric (human-centered) in their views of nature. As we'll see, this is one of many aspects of historic Stoicism that modern Stoics commonly reject, but usually without mention or comment.

Belief in an afterlife

WARNING

If humans have no spiritual souls but are entirely material creatures, it's hard to see how there could be any sort of afterlife beyond physical death. But the standard Stoic view was that humans do experience a limited afterlife (see Diogenes Laertius, *Lives of Eminent Philosophers* 7.156–57). After death, they believed, our souls leave our bodies and drift up into the starry regions, where they will continue to exist for some time, though not forever. Eventually, the entire universe, including all human souls, will be burned up in a huge cosmic bonfire ("conflagration") and nothing will exist except the Logos in its primordial fiery essence. Then the Logos will generate out of its own substance a new material universe. Since, on Stoic thought, the old universe was the best one there could be, the new universe will be exactly like the old one in every detail.

WARNING

And here's the unexpected benefit, the surprisingly good news in this Stoic idea of eternal recurrence: There will be another "you" just like before! With the exact same parents, same home, same pets, same schools! (Also, same acne, same braces, and same bad haircuts, so don't get too psyched up about it.) This cosmic cycle of creation, destruction, and re-creation will continue forever. It would be like watching the same movie over and over again for all eternity, except luckily you won't remember ever having seen the movie before. It will be like having total amnesia and watching "Groundhog Day" again and again — sort of like some golden-agers you may know.

Live rationally

The influence of Socrates and the Cynics is clearly apparent in Stoic ethics. The Stoics agreed with the core Cynic idea that we should "follow nature," but they gave it a radically new twist. For the Cynics, following nature meant renouncing civilization and living much like the stray dogs from which they were named, obedient only to one's instincts and conscience, and free of all artificial constraints and conventions. The Stoics agreed that we humans are animals, but of a higher and special kind. Humans are *rational* animals and contain a spark of divinity within. Hence, for the Stoics "follow nature" did not mean "live like animals," but rather "follow *human* (and cosmic) nature and live rationally."

Since humans are naturally sociable and can fulfill ourselves only as parts of organized communities, the Stoics did not favor ditching civilization and going back to the Stone Age. They believed in building and sustaining strong communities where people can fulfill their social instincts and develop their higher intellectual and moral capacities (more on this in Chapters 13 and 15).

The good, the evil, and the indifferent

REMEMBER

The spark of reason we have within us can clearly go wrong and fall into error, unlike its divine source. Like Socrates, Zeno thought that most people are deeply mistaken about what really matters in life. Contrary to popular belief, things like pleasure, wealth, fame, power, and social status do not lead to true or lasting happiness. The Stoics taught that something is truly good only if it is always and unconditionally good, inevitably contributing to a virtuous and happy life. Things like wealth and power can be misused and produce effects that are morally bad in our human responses to them. The only thing that is truly and unconditionally good is moral excellence. So, Socrates was right in thinking that virtue is the only real good, and vice the only real evil. All other things of value, such as health, knowledge, pleasure, and friends, are not strictly "good" in the exacting Stoic sense, though they can and should be pursued in many contexts.

In accord with this view of good and evil, the Stoics divided all objects of human choice into three categories: good, bad, and indifferent. What is good is virtue and things that "participate" in virtue, either as a means to virtue (e.g., good moral teaching), or as a necessary accompaniment of virtue (e.g., the "joy" Stoic sages feel in knowing they have achieved peak human well-being), or activities that contain virtue as an essential component (e.g., a good political system). What is bad is vice, or immorality, and the inner weaknesses or desires that contribute to vice. Everything else is to be classified as "indifferent," neither strictly good nor strictly bad.

REMEMBER

In a bow to common sense, the Stoics did admit that some indifferent things have more positive value than others. Health, for example, is better than sickness. Health, therefore, is what the Stoics called a "preferred indifferent." It has a form of positive value and should be pursued, but never at the expense of virtue. Things other than immorality that have negative value (e.g., pain, injury, and death) are "dispreferred indifferents." And, yes, in case you're paying attention, that phrase is so ponderous that it may itself be a dispreferred indifferent! We go over this in more detail later.

Only virtue leads to happiness

REMEMBER

Though preferred indifferents like health, life, knowledge, and friendship have genuine positive value, in the eyes of the Stoics they cannot in any way contribute to the ultimate goal of life, which is happiness. So forget what you've read in those last 27 magazine articles or heard in those latest 19 podcasts about happiness. Virtue is the sole "happiness-making" factor in life, the sole contributor to, and component of, human wellness. First of all, it's necessary for happiness: No one can be happy who lacks it. And it's also sufficient for happiness: Anyone who has virtue is guaranteed to be completely happy, even if they are in great pain or affliction. In short, for Stoics, virtue is a kind of priceless jewel. It cannot be bought or attained through the many external things in the world that we commonly chase with happiness in view. Those who have virtue are blessed and enjoy complete well-being; those who lack it are miserable and wholly morally bad (Diogenes Laertius, *Lives* 7.127). So, Socrates was right when he said that no harm can come to a good person, because those who are good possess everything that is truly good and nothing that is really bad. They have come as close as mortal beings can to the blessedness and invulnerability of the gods.

Elements of virtue

For Stoics, virtue is thus the one and only key to the good life. But what is virtue, exactly? What qualities does a completely virtuous person possess? Here the Stoics followed Plato in identifying four primary virtues:

>> Wisdom

>> Self-control

>> Courage

>> Justice

In ancient philosophy, these were considered the "cardinal virtues" (from the Latin *cardio*, meaning "hinge"). They were seen as foundational because all other moral excellences depend on them, or as with a hinge, turn on them. We'll see later in this book (Chapter 17) why the Stoics believed these four virtues were so critically important.

Emotional control

Zeno taught that one very important aspect of the virtue of self-control is self-command, or emotional control. Contrary to common belief, Stoics did not believe that all emotions should be repressed or avoided. But they did reject what they called the "passions," especially strong, agitating emotions and desires such as anger, fear, lust, greed, and grief. These they saw as irrational and excessive "disturbances" of the soul that are rooted in false beliefs and are inconsistent with the Stoic ideal of a serene and fully rational life.

REMEMBER

A perfectly wise and good person would possess the virtue of *apatheia* ("without passions," in the original Greek), which they conceived as a complete equanimity and perfect freedom from any negative or irrational emotions or desires. Later (Chapter 14), we'll take a closer look at what ancient Stoics thought about desires and emotions, both positive and negative.

Acceptance

Besides emotional control, Stoics attached great importance to the virtue of acceptance. This followed from their view of divine Providence. As we've seen, they believed that the universe is created and wisely governed by Divine Reason (the Logos). Everything that exists has been generated, shaped, and guided by the Logos, which pervades all of reality and rules all with goodness and justice. The Logos controls everything and is perfectly wise and good. From this, the Stoics deduced that whatever happens must happen for the best.

An all-good, all-wise, supremely powerful God would not permit any evil (or apparent evil) to exist unless it was necessary for some higher good. Whatever happens, therefore, must either be good or lead to some higher good that justifies it in the grand cosmic scheme of things.

REMEMBER

What attitude, then, should we take toward life's hard knocks and terrible tragedies? We should accept and even welcome them cheerfully and without complaint, agreeing with the choice made by the Logos. Though "bad" things may happen to us and to those we love, from a Stoic perspective they are good for the Cosmos as a whole, and thus, in a sense, not genuine evils. Stoics believe that even true evils (namely, moral mistakes) must ultimately serve a larger good.

With our limited minds, we may not always be able to see what that greater good is. But for Stoics, our basic attitude toward all events must always be one of trust, gratitude, and acceptance But as we shall see, this is a form of "acceptance" that many people today would struggle with or simply reject as unrealistic or undesirable. And yet the Stoic view was that if you can get yourself into this welcoming and accepting mindset, you will be much more at peace with yourself and with the world. And many people, it seems, would love that result.

Why Stoicism Had Its Moment in Ancient Greece and Rome

What you just read in the previous section, in broad outline, is the original and enduring Stoic worldview. What made it so consoling and attractive for so many in ancient times? Why for centuries was it the leading philosophy of the ancient Greek and Roman world? These are questions that may help us understand the major resurgence of Stoicism in our own time.

Stoicism arose at an especially turbulent time in ancient Greece. The basis of Greek political life, the city-state, had been destroyed by the conquests of Philip of Macedon (338 BCE) and his son Alexander the Great, whose armies went on to conquer Persia and most of the East as far as India. After Alexander's early death in 323 BCE Greece was kicked around like a football by his successors and later by the Romans, who conquered Greece and absorbed it into their growing empire. This was also a period when the old Greek religion of Zeus and his classic crew was collapsing under skeptical doubt and the influx of new mystical cults from the East, creating a moral and spiritual vacuum and a climate of existential confusion and disbelief.

Stoicism helped to fill this void and provide a sense of meaning, consolation, and (perhaps most importantly) *control* in an increasingly chaotic and unpredictable world in which self-rule and self-determination, for most inhabitants of the Hellenistic world, were at best fond memories. For reasons we will explore more fully in Chapter 19, these same attractions may help to explain some of the appeal of Stoicism today. We live in pretty confused and stressful times, too.

After Zeno's death in 262 BCE, his school in Athens continued to flourish under the leadership of hardworking, reliable, and yet likely less than brilliant Cleanthes (c. 331–c. 232 BCE) and then the very smart and perhaps even genius Chrysippus (279–206 BCE). Chrysippus was a first-rate thinker and a prolific author, writing over 700 works, none of which have survived. He did a great deal to restate, systematize, and defend Stoic teachings and was regarded as something like a second founder of the school by his followers.

Beginning around 150 BCE, Stoicism was becoming increasingly popular in Rome, where it had great appeal as a practical, demanding, and tough-minded philosophy of life. It was in Roman times that Stoicism achieved its greatest influence and popularity. In fact, the three best-known Stoic philosophers of all time — Seneca, Epictetus, and Marcus Aurelius — are all associated with Rome rather than Greece, though Epictetus was born as a Greek slave, lived for most of his life in Greece, and taught in Greek rather than in Latin. He did, however, arise as a philosophical voice first in Rome, and so is closely associated with the other Stoics who were affiliated with that great city.

These three philosophers, all known as Romans, had little interest in Stoic logic, metaphysics, or natural science; they were mostly interested in Stoicism as a practical guide to life. As we'll see in Chapter 4, their brand of Stoicism had a distinctive Roman vibe and differed in interesting ways from the original Greek brand of Stoic philosophy.

Chapter **4**

Stoicism Comes to Rome

Though Stoicism began in ancient Greece, it flowered in imperial Rome, becoming for many centuries the leading philosophy of the Roman Empire. The Romans were a tough, practical-minded people; they excelled as warriors, builders, administrators, and lawmakers, and generally had little interest in abstract speculation or subtle theorizing.

In Stoicism, educated Romans found a stern and demanding creed that provided guidance and consolation in an age of crumbling faiths, political despotism, and constant social upheaval. As rulers of a vast empire encompassing many diverse nations and ethnic groups, Romans also found Stoic teachings on universal law and world citizenship highly relatable. Much like Christianity, Stoicism had special appeal in Roman times to slaves and the poor, who found solace in its teachings about inner toughness, acceptance, managing negative emotions, and the essential connectedness of all humans.

What Romans valued most in Greek Stoicism was its ethics and practical art of living. In the philosophy of Romans like Seneca, Epictetus, and Marcus Aurelius, we can see concretely what it means to think and live as a Stoic.

Seneca and Epictetus

WARNING

Scholars divide the history of ancient Stoicism into three phases with less than breathtakingly creative labels: early, middle, and late. Early Stoicism stretched from the founding of the school by Zeno around 300 BCE to the death of Antipater, the sixth head or "Scholarch" of the Stoic school, in 129 BCE. It was in Early Stoicism that the basic principles of Stoic philosophy were worked out and stated in authoritative form. In Middle Stoicism (129–c. 50 BCE) classic Stoic doctrine was modified in significant ways, largely as a result of Platonic and Aristotelian influences. The two great figures in Middle Stoicism were the Greek philosophers Panaetius (c. 185–c. 109 BCE) and Posidonius (c. 135–51 BCE), both of whom spent considerable time in Rome encouraging the spread of Stoic ideas. In tailoring Stoic philosophy to Roman tastes, both Panaetius and Posidonius stressed ethics and the practical side of Stoic teachings, in effect offering a more moderate and less dogmatic brand of Stoicism than what was taught by Zeno and Chrysippus. Late Stoicism (c. 51 BCE–180 CE) was the period of the great Roman Stoics — Seneca, Epictetus, and Emperor Marcus Aurelius. The only complete works of Stoic philosophy we have date from this Late Stoic era.

The first major encounter Romans had with Stoicism occurred in 155 BCE, when Athens sent a political embassy to Rome. Not surprisingly, the Athenian delegation consisted entirely of philosophers: Carneades (a brilliant skeptic and head of Plato's Academy), Critolaus (an Aristotelian), and Diogenes of Babylon (head of the Stoa). About a decade later, Panaetius came to Rome, where he befriended Scipio the Younger (conqueror of Carthage) and did a great deal to promote the spread of Stoic philosophy in Rome.

An even more important transmitter of Stoic ideas to the Romans was the Roman philosopher and powerful statesman Cicero (106–43 BCE). Cicero studied philosophy in Athens and was a student of the Stoic philosopher Posidonius. Though Cicero was more of a Platonist than a Stoic, he drew heavily from Stoic ideas, especially on the importance of virtue and rationality, divine Providence, the need to control one's passions, universal moral law, and the ideal of public service, with a focus on the common good. Because he was such a brilliant writer and so many of his writings survive, Cicero was a major conduit of Stoic ideas in ancient times and remains an important source of information about Stoic teachings today.

Seneca: Wealthy but Frugal

The first great Roman Stoic was Lucius Annaeus Seneca (c. 1–65 CE). Born into a wealthy and well-connected family in Cordoba, Spain, Seneca studied Stoic philosophy as a youth and rose to become an important lawyer and member of the

Roman Senate. When he was exiled for eight years (41–49) to the island of Corsica by the emperor Claudius, Seneca used his enforced leisure to write a series of philosophical works, as well as some uber-bloody tragedies that were popular in antiquity and greatly influenced later playwrights such as Shakespeare and Racine.

In his late forties, he was recalled from exile by the empress Agrippina to become tutor to her 11-year-old son, Nero. Seneca taught Nero for five years, then became his close advisor after the young man became emperor. For several years during Nero's early reign, Seneca teamed with Burrus, head of the Praetorian Guard, to basically run the Roman Empire, and run it very well. During this period Seneca wrote several of his most important works on Stoic philosophy, including such appropriate titles for anyone in close proximity to this dangerous and psychopathic emperor as *On the Shortness of Life*, On *the Tranquility of the Soul*, *On Mercy*, and *On Anger*.

While serving as tutor and advisor to Nero, Seneca became incredibly wealthy by means of skillful investments, gifts, and insider connections. He owned lavish villas all over Italy and had 500 identical tables of citrus wood and ivory that he used in epic parties at his homes. Personally, however, Seneca lived a temperate and disciplined life, eating little, drinking only water, and sleeping on a hard mattress. When he died, he was emaciated from his very frugal diet.

Sometime around 62 BCE, Seneca finally succeeded in freeing himself from public duties under the increasingly bloodthirsty and erratic Nero. He then retired to his villas in the south of Italy, where he spent the last three years of his life in philosophical seclusion. It was during this brief period of retirement that he wrote his famous *Letters to Lucilius* (aka *Letters from a Stoic*), which in later centuries became important models for essayists such as Michel de Montaigne and Sir Francis Bacon. In 65, when Nero discovered a plot to overthrow him, he wrongly suspected his old tutor and ordered Seneca to commit suicide, which he did, bravely and without complaint, even though it was difficult and he had to try several times.

Seneca was not an especially original thinker, but he was a superb writer and warm, humane personality who expressed classic Stoic themes in timeless prose. Like most Roman Stoics, Seneca had little interest in Stoic logic or philosophy of nature. He saw Stoicism as a kind of medicine for the soul and a path to a happy and fulfilling life. In his letters and essays, Seneca returns frequently to a few major Stoic themes, which we'll explore in the next sections.

Philosophy as a therapy for the emotions

In ancient times, as classical scholar Pierre Hadot reminds us, philosophy wasn't seen as a "subject" or "field of study." It was a complete way of life, demanding commitment and a radical change of priorities. New enthusiasts "converted" to a particular philosophy much as someone today might convert to Christianity or

Buddhism. Philosophers in ancient times were readily identifiable by their distinctive styles of dress, facial grooming, and unconventional lifestyles. Philosophy was widely debated in marketplaces, plays, and around dinner tables. Wealthy families hired celebrity philosophers to teach their sons. Philosophy held the key, it was widely thought, to a happy, fulfilling, and successful life.

Seneca fully embraced this bracing view of philosophy. Like Socrates and the Cynics, he believed that philosophical reflection should be mostly practical. He defines philosophy as "the love of wisdom, and the endeavor to attain it." The "gift of philosophy" is the art of "living well." Philosophy molds our characters, disciplines our conduct, instructs us what is right or wrong, and steers us wisely and skillfully through stormy seas. Without it no one can lead a life free of fear or anxiety. Daily, we confront situations that call for wise judgment, and for that judgment we must look to sound philosophy.

In a sense, as Epictetus would later famously say, "the philosopher's school is a doctor's office." Our souls are sick with false beliefs, out-of-control desires, unruly emotions, and unnecessary worry. Philosophy, which is the love and pursuit of wisdom and proper perspective, provides the cure.

Coping with life's hard knocks

Why do bad things happen to good people? This age-old question was a major concern for the Stoics because of their strong belief in divine Providence. On their view, an all-wise, all-good, and very powerful God (the Logos) is in complete control of the universe and everything that occurs is ultimately for the best. Why, then, do bad things happen? If the Logos is fully in charge, fully "sovereign," shouldn't this be a completely just world in which the innocent never suffer, and where wrongdoers always get their deserved comeuppance?

Every ancient Stoic thinker wrestled with this classic "problem of evil." Some of the most thoughtful and detailed responses were offered by Seneca in his classic essay, "On Providence."

Bad things in fact never happen to good people

WARNING

Seneca begins by reminding us that, in the Stoic view, bad things, strictly speaking, never do happen to good people — that is, perfectly good people (that is, Sages; see "On Providence" 1.2). Certainly, Sages suffer pain, sickness, poverty, and death just as we all do, but for Stoics these are not truly or strictly "bad." The only true evils are vices — immoral thoughts and acts). And Sages, by definition, don't have any vices. Thus, starkly contrary to common appearances, this is not after all a world in which bad things happen to good people. Moreover, the world is fundamentally just and contains far fewer genuine evils than most people believe. That's the Stoic line.

Hardships can make us better people

TIP

Second, Seneca points out that hardships can benefit us, often in unsuspected ways. Adversities can test us, thereby showing us who we are deep inside and providing opportunities for better self-understanding ("On Providence" 3.3–4). Hardships can also toughen us and help us build inner strengths that can serve us well as we navigate the storms and stresses of life ("On Providence" 2.7). Finally, adversities provide opportunities for exercises of virtue, which for Stoics is the chief goal of life and the deepest form of happiness. Truly noble and heroic acts of courage, endurance, and self-sacrifice, for example, are possible only in a world of pain and hardship ("On Providence" 3.4). So, as Seneca famously remarks, "disaster is virtue's opportunity" ("On Providence" 4.6). Adversities and challenges provide essential fuel for the brightest flames of all.

Adversity can serve the greater good

TIP

Finally, some adversities that may be hard on us as individuals will be weaved by Providence into larger goods, such as the good of the community or even of the cosmos as a whole. For instance, a Stoic who suffers sickness or extreme pain bravely and without complaint can serve as a model for others ("On Providence" 6.3). In such ways, Seneca seeks to show that Stoics have both personal and philosophical resources for dealing with the problem of evil.

Controlling anger

REMEMBER

Stoics are commonly thought to be emotionally constipated kill joys, opposed to both feeling or showing emotion, but this is at best a half-truth. The Stoics had no word for the wide range of both healthy and unhealthy feelings or affective states we call "emotions." What they opposed were "passions" (pathē), which they defined as irrational and excessive mental disturbances, such as rage, terror, or depression. Stoics believed that passions should be avoided or suppressed because they hinder rational thought and are based on false value judgments. Take jealousy, for instance. Suppose we are jealous of Bill Gates because he has something good (e.g., a fancy private jet) that we lack. This judgment is based on a false assignment of value, because, for Stoics, nothing is truly good except virtue. According to Stoics, all negative emotions are rooted in false judgments of value.

The most harmful emotion

In his work *On Anger*, Seneca claims that anger is one of the most harmful and "inhuman" of all our emotions. Anger, he says, is a kind of "brief insanity," a blind and often ungovernable rage that stems from a perceived injustice or mistreatment. He notes that anger has caused countless wars, massacres, persecutions, and other terrible evils. It also disturbs our inner calm, hinders our powers of rational thinking, and can make us snarl and rage like a ferocious wild beast, thereby submerging our humanity into something low and animalistic.

Many philosophers, like Plato and Aristotle, argue that anger can benefit us in some contexts, for example by making us more aggressive in battle or in defense of our families. On this view, anger is not inherently harmful or irrational, and should be moderated rather than totally rooted out. Seneca rejects this view. He argues that anger makes it impossible for us to think clearly, and so does not actually make us more effective fighters. As he sees it, anger is always based on a false judgment of value (namely, that some perceived mistreatment is really worth getting irate and upset about) and should be totally avoided or suppressed, if possible.

Suggestions for mastering anger

But can anger be completely suppressed or bottled up? Seneca admits that early stages of anger are sometimes instinctive and involuntary. Imagine how you would react, for example, if you saw a stranger strike your child. Your face would flush, your heart rate would rise, and you would probably experience a hot flash of emotion and perhaps a strong desire to lash out at the offender. Seneca admits this, but then claims that such instinctive physiological reactions are only "preliminaries" of anger, not anger itself. True anger, he claims, always involves an "assent," or judgment, of the rational mind both that something is truly bad and that an agitated reaction would be a fit way to respond. Such judgments are always false, he claims, and so anger is never justified. The gods never experience anger, and neither should we.

How can we master our anger? Here Seneca offers a host of helpful suggestions, many of which jibe with advice offered by anger management therapists today. Often, Seneca's suggestions are examples of what modern psychologists call "cognitive restructuring." This is a psychological technique for replacing negative, irrational beliefs with ones that are more positive and realistic.

TIP

For example, Seneca notes that anger frequently arises from a sense that one has been seriously harmed or mistreated. But from a Stoic perspective, is that perception accurate? He suggests asking yourself in such a situation: Have you really been harmed — that is, injured in your ability to live wisely and ethically? If some genuine harm or mistreatment has occurred, is it as serious or as blameworthy as it may first seem? How certain are you that the offense was intentional? Could it have been inadvertent? Could you be misreading the situation?

TIP

Stoics want us to ask: Does anybody, at a deep level, really do wrong willingly or knowingly? And even if this can indeed happen: Is anybody perfect? Haven't you yourself sometimes been guilty of similar behavior? Is flying into a towering rage really a helpful or appropriate reaction to such conduct? Wouldn't it be better to take a breath, walk away, and calmly think about the situation, or else just to let it go? These are all useful reminders and good pieces of advice, in Seneca's day as in ours.

Epictetus: Slave Turned Philosopher

Seneca was powerful and immensely rich. Epictetus (c. 55–c. 135 CE) was born a slave and always remained poor. We know much about Seneca's life, but little about Epictetus's, not even his real name ("Epictetus," in ancient Greek, simply means "acquired"). We're told that he was born in Hierapolis, a major Greco-Roman city in what is today central Turkey. Probably a slave from birth, Epictetus was taken to Rome at an early age, where he became the property of Epaphroditus, a wealthy ex-slave and secretary in the court of the emperor Nero. According to some sources, Epictetus was unjustly tortured by one of his masters, breaking his leg and causing him to walk with a limp for the rest of his life. Later, referring to a common torture device of the time, he reportedly said, "I was never more free than when I was on the rack."

As a young man, Epictetus must have shown remarkable intelligence, because he was permitted by his owner to study philosophy with Musonius Rufus, the leading Stoic philosopher of his day. At some point Epictetus was freed from slavery and opened his own school of philosophy in Rome. In 89 CE, the increasingly paranoid emperor Domitian banished all philosophers from Italy. Epictetus then opened a new school in Nicopolis, a thriving city on the west coast of Greece, where he lived and taught the rest of his life. There, affluent young Romans flocked from all parts of the empire to study with him.

Though Epictetus, like Socrates, wrote nothing, some of his daily lectures and conversations were jotted down by his student Arrian, who later became a famous general, writer, and politician. These were later published as the *Discourses* (*Diatribai*, or "Informal Talks"), of which unfortunately only half have survived. Arrian also composed a smaller collection of Epictetus's best sayings known as the *Enchiridion* ("Manual" or "Handbook"), which became a bestseller in ancient times. Despite his growing fame, Epictetus continued to live a simple life with minimal possessions. As an old man, he adopted a child who otherwise would have been abandoned and allowed to die. To help him raise the child, he also took on a wife or partner to live with him and help with the child's upbringing.

Like Seneca, Epictetus was mainly interested in Stoicism as a practical guide to life (though we know from his recorded conversations that he did regularly teach logic and speculative theory by means of classic Stoic texts). While Seneca seems to have been influenced mostly by later Stoic thinkers such as Chrysippus and Panaetius, Epictetus looked back to the Socratic and Cynic roots of ancient Stoicism. He repeatedly praises Socrates and Diogenes the Cynic as great Sages and models of Stoic wisdom. What he admired most about Socrates and Diogenes was their contempt for money, power, and other worldly goods, and their single-minded devotion to wisdom and virtue. Though Epictetus makes no reference to Seneca, he certainly would not have been impressed by Seneca's immense wealth, numerous slaves, and luxurious lifestyle. Of all the great Stoic teachers, only Epictetus explicitly condemns slavery as contrary to human dignity and divine law (*Discourses* 1.13.5).

True freedom

As an ex-slave, Epictetus not surprisingly talks a lot about the value of freedom. The type of freedom Epictetus speaks of, however, has little to do with political liberty or legal freedom. Nor does it concern so-called freedom of the will in the common philosophical sense of a power to make choices that aren't strictly predetermined by prior causes. What he's most interested in is a special kind of psychological or moral freedom that is extremely rare and difficult to achieve, what we might call "true freedom" or even "Stoic freedom." This is a kind of freedom that only Sages — persons who are perfectly wise and good — can attain.

REMEMBER

Epictetus says that freedom in general is "the power to live as we like," free of external constraints or impediments to our wishes (*Discourses* 2.1.23, 4.1.1). This seems to imply that most of us can frequently be free. For example, you could probably read this entire book next weekend if you wanted to. There likely are no "impediments" that would prevent you. It seems to follow from Epictetus's definition of freedom, therefore, that you are free to read this book next weekend.

But this isn't the kind of freedom Epictetus has in mind. When he speaks of "the power to live as we like" he's thinking about the totality of our lives, the ability to *always* live as one likes and to achieve *all* our deepest wishes. This is Stoic freedom, and it is extremely rare. In fact, according to Epictetus, only two kinds of beings possess it: God and the Stoic Sage.

Why can the Stoic Sage always live as she likes? For three reasons,

>> First, the Sage is perfect in virtue and wisdom, and thus both possessed of complete well-being and totally free of fear, distress, and other undesirable emotions.

>> Second, the Sage has trained her will so that she approves of whatever happens to her as the decree of an all-wise and all-good God.

>> Finally, the Sage never desires anything that is in the power of someone else (*Discourses*, 4.1.64, 4.1.125). All she desires is what *she* can fully control, namely her own thoughts and acts of will.

So, even if a Sage is sick, impoverished, or in prison, she is living exactly as she likes, and so is free in the deepest sense of the word.

Clearly, this is a very demanding concept of freedom. Is it too demanding? Is it really possible to desire only those things that we can fully control? Would this be a good way to live even if it were possible? We'll delve into those important issues later in this book.

The dichotomy of control

In one of his most powerful passages, Epictetus states:

> Some things are within our power, while others are not. Within our power are opinion, motivation, desire, aversion, and, in a word, what is our own doing; not within our power are our body, our property, reputation, office, and, in a word, whatever is not our own doing. The things that are within our power are by nature free, and immune to hindrance and obstruction, while those that are not within our power are weak, slavish, subject to hindrance, and not our own. (*Manual* 1)

Epictetus goes on to note that if we care greatly about things that are not within our power, we will often be frustrated and inclined to blame and complain. A Stoic, therefore, will not place much value in things she cannot control, but only in things that are directly within her power, namely her own thoughts, beliefs, intentions, likes, and dislikes.

This is what scholars call Epictetus's *dichotomy of control*. According to Epictetus, all things fall into one of two categories: things we can control and things we cannot control. What things can't we control? Our health, our looks, our income, our reputation, our relationships — in fact, most things in life. What can we control? Only things in our minds (our opinions, desires, choices, and so forth). This distinction between things we can and cannot control is vital, Epictetus claims, because happiness and virtue depend entirely on things in our control. If we attach significant value to "externals" such as money, power, or fame we make our happiness hostage to changing fortune and will likely pursue goals that are unethical and contrary to our true well-being.

WARNING

Epictetus's dichotomy of control raises all kinds of interesting questions. Some critics have suggested that control is not an all-or-nothing matter and that Epictetus's two-part distinction is therefore itself a kind of *false* dichotomy. The contemporary Stoic William B. Irvine, for example, has pointed out that there are many things (for example, how well we do in school) that we can greatly influence but not completely control.

>> Irvine thus suggests that what we really need is a *trichotomy* of control, a three-part division into things that are (1) completely in our control, (2) partly in our control, and (3) completely out of our control.

>> Another option is to speak of a *spectrum* of control. On this model, control is a continuous sequence, ranging from total control on one end and zero control on the other, with some control in between and no clear dividing lines anywhere along the spectrum.

Which model of control is most helpful? We weigh in on that in Chapter 9.

Epictetus's dichotomy of control raises other thorny questions as well. For example, is he correct in claiming that we can fully control our opinions, motivations, desires, and aversions? Can you, right now, form the sincere belief that you are riding a roller coaster at Disney World? If someone threatens to torture you, can you honestly believe that the anticipated pain is an "indifferent" that lies outside your control and is therefore "nothing" to you, as Epictetus frequently states (*Discourses* 1.30.3, 3.3.15)? If you are suffering from a severe anxiety disorder, can you overcome your fears just by *deciding* that you will no longer experience them? Some parts of our mental life do seem to be more or less fully in our control, but many others don't. So, what parts of our minds can we completely control, and is Epictetus right in thinking that we should attach significant value only to those things? Those, too, are questions we'll explore later on.

Radical acceptance

As we've seen, the ancient Stoics were big believers in divine Providence. They held that God (the Logos) is perfect in wisdom and goodness, that the Logos fully controls everything that happens, that it has a plan for the world, that this is the best possible plan, and that nothing can alter or defeat this plan. From these premises the Stoics inferred that everything that happens must be (in some sense) "God's will," and furthermore that everything happens for the best. This is a view sometimes labeled "cosmic optimism." Given this hopeful, optimistic view of reality, how should humans respond to events in the world? The proper response, Stoics argued, is one of "acceptance."

What is it to "accept" a happening or event in the world? That's a little tricky, because there are different sorts and degrees of acceptance.

WARNING

Acceptance can vary, for example, by how pleased or displeased a person is with a given outcome. Some things we accept "resignedly" ("Yes, we lost the game because of a bad call, but it's not worth filing a protest over"). Other things are accepted "willingly" but without any great enthusiasm ("I'm fine working as a barista for now until something better comes along"). Still others are accepted "cheerfully" or even "joyously" as something truly good or wonderful ("I'm excited and proud to accept this new opportunity").

When Epictetus says we should accept whatever happens in life, what sense of "acceptance" does he have in mind? It's the last sense, the one of cheerful, wholehearted acceptance. This is the difficult and demanding Stoic ideal of *amor fati* ("love of fate") the ideal of positively welcoming and in fact actually *loving* everything that happens as coming from the hand of a perfectly good God, however "bad" it may seem by conventional standards.

Cosmic optimism and its implications

According to Epictetus, the idea that we should gladly welcome and embrace all events in the world follows from the Stoic doctrine of cosmic optimism. As Epictetus sees it, once we accept that the world is providentially governed and that everything happens for the best, four things follow:

» We should never complain about anything or anyone.

» We should never blame God.

» We should accept all events cheerfully and even joyfully.

» We should continually thank and praise God, whatever befalls us.

For Epictetus, acceptance means, first, that we should never gripe, whine, or complain. And you may know people for whom this would mean eliminating their single favorite activity. Thus, in a famous passage the philosopher says:

> I must die. But must I die bawling? I must be put in chains — but moaning and groaning too? I must be exiled; but is there anything to keep me from going with a smile, calm and self-composed? (*Discourses* 1.1.21)

Second, acceptance means that we should never blame God for anything. Instead, Epictetus says, your attitude should be much like this imagined conversation he hopes to have with God on his deathbed:

> Is there any way I violated your commands? . . . Did I ever blame you? Did I ever find fault with your administration? I fell sick when you wanted it: So did others, but *I* did not complain. I became poor when you wanted, again without complaint . . . Did you ever see me any way but with a smile on my face, ready to obey any orders that you had for me? Now you want me to leave the fair, so I go feeling nothing but gratitude for having been allowed to share with you in the celebration, to get to see your works and comprehend your rule. (*Discourses* 3.5.7)

Third, we should approve and even cheerfully welcome all events as well-ordered and flowing from the wise and holy will of God. So, Epictetus says:

> Realize that the chief duty we owe the gods is to hold correct beliefs about them: that they exist, that they govern the world justly and well, and that they have put you here for one purpose — to obey them and welcome whatever happens, in the conviction that it is a product of the highest intelligence. This way you won't blame the gods or charge them with neglect. (*Manual* 31)

Finally, Epictetus states that we should accept all events in a spirit of thankfulness and praise. Thus, he says to his students, chiding them on their inability to see and appreciate God's benevolent role behind the many things of the world:

> Well, since most of you are blind, I suppose there has to be someone who fills this role and will praise God on others' behalf. And what is a lame old man like me good for, anyway, except singing God's praises? If I were a nightingale or a swan, I would sing the song either of them was born to sing. But I am a rational being, so my song must take the form of a hymn. That is my job that I'll keep to as long as I'm allowed; and I invite any and all of you to join me. (*Discourses* 1.16.19)

This is clearly a very robust doctrine of acceptance — many would say much *too* robust. But as Epictetus sees it, an uncompromising view of this sort follows logically from the Stoic's highly optimistic view of reality.

Can we take radical acceptance seriously?

Of course, lots of questions can be asked about this teaching of radical acceptance. Is it realistic, or even psychologically possible, for us to respond to all events in the way Epictetus recommends (with approval, cheerfulness, and thankfulness)? Even if it is possible, is it healthy, proper, or ethical to approach life in this spirit? (How should a parent, for example, respond to news of their child's serious injury, or even death?) Is Epictetus serious when he says we should "welcome" whatever happens to us cheerfully and thankfully? Or might he be exaggerating for rhetorical effect?

Further, when Epictetus says we should accept and welcome "all" events, does this include acts of *moral evil*, including our own? Should we, in some sense, "accept" our own moral mistakes and misdeeds? If so, in what sense? With love, joy, and thanksgiving? Should we "accept" the crimes and immoral acts of others, even of moral monsters like Hitler? If so, again, "accept" in what sense? This can easily seem too extreme.

These are hard questions for any Stoic who, like Epictetus, embraces a strong view of acceptance. (As we'll see, religious believers who hold that literally *everything* is "God's will" run into similar issues.) Can something like Epictetus's radical view of Stoic acceptance be defended? If not, is there a more moderate view of acceptance that might make more sense and still do the job that Stoics want? We'll explore these issues more fully in Chapter 7.

Chapter **5**

Marcus Aurelius: Philosopher-Emperor

The last great Roman Stoic wasn't a slave or a professional teacher of philosophy, but the most powerful man in the world, the Roman emperor Marcus Aurelius (121–180 CE). Plato famously said, "Unless philosophers become kings . . . or those who are now called kings and rulers come to be sufficiently inspired with a genuine desire for wisdom . . . there can be no rest . . . for states, nor yet, as I believe, for all mankind." Though Marcus Aurelius certainly had his flaws, he may be the closest humanity has ever come to Plato's ideal of a perfectly wise and good philosopher-ruler. Because of his readability, his historical influence, and his central role in the rise of contemporary Stoicism, Marcus deserves a separate chapter of his own.

A Stoic Philosopher Comes to the Throne

Marcus Annius Verus (later known as Marcus Aurelius) was born in Rome on April 26, 121 CE. Though his father, a wealthy Roman official, died when Marcus was three, the boy generally had a very happy and privileged upbringing. His family was prominent and well-connected, and Marcus grew up in palaces and was educated at home by over a dozen elite private tutors.

One family friend and frequent visitor was Emperor Hadrian, who took a shine to the young man, admired his mind and character, and called him "Verissimus" (Latin for "truest," a play on Marcus's cognomen Verus, meaning "true"). Hadrian had no children and wished to appoint a worthy successor as emperor when he died. His first choice, Lucius Aelius, died not long after Hadrian adopted him and named him as heir. Hadrian then invited Antoninus Pius, a wealthy and well-respected Roman politician, to succeed him, on the condition that Antoninus adopt both young Marcus and Aelius's son, Lucius Verus.

Hadrian's long-term plan, it seems, was for Marcus to succeed his adoptive father as emperor, which happened. As a result of this wise succession plan, Rome had two outstanding emperors in a row following Hadrian's death in 138 and the Roman Empire enjoyed over 40 years of wise and competent rule.

Early influences

We know a great deal about how Marcus became interested in philosophy because he tells us in the opening pages of his famous private journal, the *Meditations*. When he was 11, he was taught "to practice philosophy" by his painting teacher, Diognetus. As we've seen, in ancient Greece and Rome philosophy was a way of life, not merely a subject one studied or a creed to be adopted. Marcus tells us Diognetus inspired him "to choose the Greek lifestyle — the camp-bed and the cloak." He's referring to the traditional "philosopher's cloak," the *tribon*, a thin, coarse, one-piece shawl made of undyed wool that was worn like a sheet draped about the torso and shoulder. It was inspired by the cheap, thin, and rarely washed cloak Socrates wore summer and winter to show his disdain for fashion and worldly possessions. Later, it became the official uniform, so to speak, of all self-professed philosophers in ancient Greece and Rome, particularly Cynics and Stoics.

Marcus's adoption of "the Greek lifestyle" was probably short-lived, but his love of philosophy proved lasting. As a youth, he received a first-class education from a kind of "dream team" of formal and informal teachers. For rhetoric (the art of effective speaking and writing), these included the two most famous instructors of his time: Herodes Atticus for Greek rhetoric, and Marcus Cornelius Fronto for Latin. The eager student idolized and became close friends with Fronto, and the two exchanged many intimate letters that have survived. His Greek teacher, Atticus, was a super-wealthy Athenian who, as it happened, detested Stoicism and blasted it as a "cult of the unemotional," whose followers "want to be considered calm, brave, and steadfast because they show neither desire nor grief, neither anger nor pleasure, cut out the more active emotions of the spirit and grow old in a torpor, a sluggish, enervated life." Ouch!

The immensely privileged young man was also lucky to have had a series of great philosophy teachers, some of whom were famous throughout the Greco-Roman world. These included, among others, Apollonius of Chalcedon; Sextus of Chaeronea, who was grandson of the famous biographer and powerful critic of Stoicism, Plutarch; and, most importantly, Junius Rusticus, a Stoic soldier and politician, who as Prefect condemned the Christian philosopher Justin Martyr to death and who apparently gave Marcus his own personal copy of Epictetus's *Discourses*.

Significantly, not all the teachers Marcus mentions with appreciation in the *Meditations* were Stoics. Claudius Severus was an Aristotelian. Alexander the Platonist was — big reveal — a Platonist. So too, probably, was Sextus, like his famous grandfather. And Atticus, as we mentioned, was a severe critic of Stoicism. Marcus's philosophical education was eclectic, and this is reflected throughout the pages of the *Meditations*, where he quotes Plato and Heraclitus more often than he does Epictetus or any other Stoic author. As we shall see, there are a number of recurring themes in Marcus's *Meditations* that reflect an eclectic borrowing from non-Stoic sources.

Conversion to Stoicism

Shortly after his marriage at age 24, Marcus seems to have had a kind of "conversion" to serious Stoic philosophy. It probably wasn't marriage that made him philosophical, though that has been known to happen. Rather, it was more likely the influence of his Stoic mentor, Rusticus. Marcus tells us in the *Meditations* that it was Rusticus who convinced him that he needed to "train and discipline his character," that is, to perfect his rationality and, more generally, to live, think, and act like a serious Stoic philosopher. And, as the *Meditations* reveal, that's what he did until his dying day.

Reign as emperor

After about 20 years of faithful service and apprenticeship to his adoptive father, the emperor Antoninus Pius, Marcus became emperor himself following Antoninus's death in early 161. Marcus clearly never wanted to be emperor. He would much rather have studied and taught philosophy, as Epictetus did. But, like any good Stoic, he also believed strongly in public service for the common good. He never had any illusions about being able to save the world or make fundamental, transformative changes to Roman society or imperial rule. He was, as historian Will Durant notes, basically a conservative who tried to preserve what was good in the ancient world, while working tirelessly and selflessly to make things a little better.

As soon as he was formally invited to become emperor, Marcus shocked the Roman world by insisting that his adoptive brother, Lucius Verus, share power with him as co-emperor. This was a lavishly generous gesture and clearly demonstrated Marcus's Stoic indifference to power. But as many historians have noted, it was probably unwise in that violent and power-hungry age, because it set a dangerous precedent of divided power and blurred lines of responsibility, as later Roman history would make all too clear with its frequent civil wars and clashes between parts of the empire.

During Marcus's 19-year reign (161–180), one disaster after another struck the Roman Empire. In 161, shortly after Marcus became emperor, there was a terrible flood and a famine in Rome. That same year, the empire suffered an invasion by Parthia in the east, leading to a long and bitter war (161–166) that Rome won. A deadly pandemic, the Antonine Plague (165–180), killed between five and ten million people, roughly ten percent of the population of the empire. In 167, an invasion of Italy by Germanic and Central Asian tribes along the northern Danubian frontier (now modern-day Hungary and Austria) resulted in the brutal and costly Marcomannic Wars (166–180). In 175, a major rebellion arose in the eastern provinces, led by Avidius Cassius, one of Marcus's most trusted generals. When the rebellion ended with the assassination of Avidius by two of his soldiers, Marcus characteristically refused to punish any of the rebels and successfully restored harmony by a Lincoln-like policy of malice toward none and charity for all.

Personal tragedies and death

During these same troubled years Marcus also experienced many personal sorrows and tribulations. He was constantly plagued by insomnia, frailty, and ill health. Of his at least 14 children (13 named in surviving sources), only six lived to adulthood (five were alive at his death). In 169, Lucius, his hard-partying adoptive brother and co-emperor, suddenly died, likely from a stroke. That same year, Marcus's seven-year-old son, Annius, whom he hoped would grow up to become co-emperor with his brother Commodus, died unexpectedly in a botched surgical operation. Then in 175 his wife, Faustina, passed away at the age of 45 while she and Marcus were traveling through what is today southern Turkey to deal with Avidius's rebellion in the East.

In 180, shortly before his 59th birthday, Marcus himself fell ill somewhere in present-day Serbia or Austria while leading an attempt to push back the tribes along the Danube that were constantly threatening the northern frontiers. Realizing his death was near, Marcus refused all food and water for six days, and died on March 17, 180. He was succeeded as emperor by what historians describe as his oddly worthless 18-year-old son, Commodus, who had served as co-emperor for the previous three years, and presumably could not have been replaced at that point — even given his known incompetence — without a grave threat of civil war. Commodus in fact turned out to be one of the worst Roman emperors ever, rivaling even Caligula and Nero in cruelty, depravity, and megalomania. Among other things, Commodus claimed he was the reincarnation of the god Hercules; ordered the deaths of countless men and women of high rank; regularly fought in rigged gladiatorial fights in the Coliseum; commanded that the city of Rome and all the Roman months to be renamed after himself; and according to the often-unreliable *Historia Augusta*, kept 300 women and 300 boys in his personal harem. After Marcus, Rome rarely knew good rule and went into a slow death spiral that resulted in the final collapse of the Western Roman Empire three centuries later.

By our lights, Marcus was no marble saint, but unsurprisingly shared many of the cultural biases and moral blind spots of his age. For instance, he seems to have planned to expand the Roman Empire northward into Germany by annexing the lands of the tribes that lived there (Anthony Birley, *Marcus Aurelius: A Life*, p. 183). According to Dio Cassius, he also planned, as part of this war of conquest, to exterminate the Asiatic Sarmatians entirely. The famous second-century Column of Marcus Aurelius in Rome's Piazza Colonna shows bound tribal prisoners being beheaded, possibly as part of this campaign of mass slaughter and forced removal.

Some historians also fault Marcus for dividing imperial rule; for being a poor judge of character, twice picking grossly unqualified co-emperors, Lucius Verus and Commodus; for his generally conservative legal rulings that often benefited the ruling classes and sometimes worsened the plight of slaves and reduced the political rights of former slaves; for deifying both Lucius and Faustina after their early deaths; and for apparently doing little to learn about Christianity or mitigate its persecution, which was severe during his reign.

Whatever we may think of such alleged faults, the near-universal verdict of history is that Marcus was, on the whole, an exceptionally good emperor and a remarkably wise and virtuous human being. Though hating war, he spent more than half his reign as a soldier living in military camps, defending Rome's embattled frontiers and advanced civilization itself. Amid great pomp and splendor, he allowed himself no luxury and embodied the simple virtues modeled by his heroes, Socrates and Epictetus. When the Roman treasury was nearly empty during the Antonine Plague, Marcus sold all the ornaments in his imperial palaces to raise funds to defend Rome against the northern invaders. Though living in an age of violence and privilege, he labored ceaselessly to create what he believed was a just "society of equal laws, governed by equality of status and of speech, and of rulers who respect the liberty of their subjects above all else" (*Meditations* 1.14).

After his death, Marcus's ashes were returned to Rome to be laid beside those of his wife and deceased children in the great brick mausoleum, now the famous Castel Sant'Angelo, built by his adoptive grandfather, Hadrian. He was deified by the Roman Senate and his loss was mourned on the banks of the Thames, the Danube, the Nile, and the Euphrates. And, of course, his notes to himself, written down as he could snatch a bit of time here or there, continue to inspire people around the world after all these centuries.

Two Themes in Marcus's Philosophy

Most of what we know about Marcus's Stoic philosophy is based on his private journal, written in Greek, that today we call the *Meditations*. (The original manuscript was probably untitled.) Written toward the end of his life, when he was fighting on Rome's the northern frontier, the *Meditations* is not a diary in the usual sense, but rather a series of philosophical memoranda that Marcus seems to have used as spiritual exercises to center himself, regain composure and perspective, exhort himself to greater efforts, and remind himself of what really matters in life.

As classical scholar Gregory Hays notes in his superb introduction to the Modern Library translation of the *Meditations*, Marcus was in some ways an atypical Stoic, He drew from many philosophical traditions (especially Heraclitus and Plato), had little apparent interest in Stoic logic or physics, and seems to have had real doubts about some traditional Stoic teachings (e.g., whether we can know for certain that there is any kind of providential higher power or any kind of afterlife, or whether it's really true that everything happens for the best). We find in the *Meditations* many of the stock themes of Stoic thought (the primacy of virtue, following nature, accepting whatever befalls one, the existence of a universal divine law, the natural sociability and kinship of humans, the emptiness of fame, the importance of fulfilling one's social and personal responsibilities, and so forth), but also notes of pessimism and wistful sadness that we don't usually encounter in Stoic writers. In later chapters, we'll look at Marcus's Stoic philosophy of life in detail, but here let's briefly explore two themes that recur frequently in the *Meditations*: the impermanence of all things and a form of philosophical pessimism.

Impermanence: Reality is flux

As we noted in Chapter 2, one important influence on Stoic thought was the pre-Socratic philosopher Heraclitus, who lived about two hundred years before Stoicism was founded. A central idea the Stoics borrowed from Heraclitus was the notion of transitoriness or impermanence. Heraclitus said that reality is "flux," a process of constant change, creation, and destruction. "Change alone," he famously said, "is unchanging."

Though some things, like the pyramids, appear to alter very little over decades and even centuries, they are in fact changing constantly, by means of erosion and other slow processes. Although Plato believed that some things in reality are eternal and unchanging (e.g., the mathematical truth that $2 + 2 = 4$), he agreed with Heraclitus that all things in the physical world are in a state of continual flux. The Stoics took up this Heraclitean and Platonic idea, holding that nature is constantly changing, always in a state of "becoming," and never in a state of stable or complete "being." Marcus returns to this idea of impermanence over and over in the *Meditations*. For example, in *Meditations* 5.23, he writes:

> Keep in mind how fast things pass by and are gone — those that are now, and those to come. Existence flows past us like a river: the "what" is in constant flux . . . Nothing is stable, not even what's right here. The infinity of past and future gapes before us — a chasm whose depths we cannot see. So, it would take an idiot to feel self-importance or distress. Or any indignation, either. As if things that irritate us last.

And in an especially vivid passage (*Meditations* 2.17), Marcus writes:

> The body and its parts are a river, the soul a dream and mist, life is warfare and a journey far from home, lasting reputation is oblivion.

REMEMBER

We might be tempted to read such passages as altogether gloomy and pessimistic, but Marcus believed that ongoing reflection on the transience and ever-changing nature of reality can be a source of consolation and strength.

We naturally feel less attached to things we view as fleeting and smoke-like, and we feel their loss much less when they are gone. A mindset of transience will also help us avoid the common obsession with lasting fame that seems to drive so many talented people to excess and ruin. A keen sense of flux and evanescence can be liberating. We see much the same type of thinking in Buddhism, which views attitudes of attachment and unhealthy desires as major sources of human suffering and dissatisfaction (*dukkha*).

By reducing attachments to things like wealth, fame, and power, Marcus hopes to focus more clearly on what ultimately matters in life, which he believes is wisdom and goodness.

Pessimism

As classicist Gregory Hays notes, "there is a persistent strain of pessimism" in the *Meditations* that is not seen, or at least is not as evident, in other Stoic writers. In the introduction to his Hackett translation of the *Meditations*, classics professor G. M. A. Grube refers to the *Meditations* as a "strange, noble, and sad book." But why sad? What exactly are these strains of pessimism and melancholy that Hays and Grube claim to detect here?

"Pessimism," of course, takes many forms. People are often said to be pessimists if they see the world as being generally "bad" (full of suffering, sin, and dissatisfaction, for example) and have few if any expectations for a better world in the future. In philosophy, the term "pessimism" is often used to describe some extreme form of "negativity," such as the view that life is totally devoid of meaning, a view sometimes called "existential nihilism," or that our world is inevitably and thoroughly *pervaded* by suffering, pain, struggle, and disappointment, which is a view often associated with the German philosopher Arthur Schopenhauer, as well as some strands of early Buddhism. The modern American film writer Woody Allen parodies such extreme forms of pessimism in one of his bittersweet lines, "Life is full of misery, loneliness, and suffering — and it's all over much too soon."

World-weariness

Clearly, Marcus is not a radical gloom-and-doom guy of this Woody Allen sort. Though he drew ideas from many philosophical traditions, especially Platonism, he was primarily a faithful Stoic who believed that the world is rational, providentially ordered, and good. He also clearly believed that life is worth living and that the world has value and purpose. So, again, why would anyone speak of Marcus's "pessimism" and the *Meditations* as a "sad" book?

The short answer is that many passages in the *Meditations* display a kind of "world-weariness" and disgust with earthly concerns that scholars tell us was increasingly common in Marcus's day. Not long after his death, Stoicism took a nosedive in popularity and faded out as an organized movement. In its place arose a host of "otherworldly" philosophies and religions, including Platonism, which saw a resurgence in late antiquity. A medley of anti-matter, anti-body movements also grew in popularity at this time, including Gnosticism, neo-Pythagoreanism, Orphism, and a number of Eastern mystery cults.

To some degree, certain strands of Christianity also fed into this otherworldly trend. In the New Testament, for example, Christians are urged not to "love the world or the things in the world" (I John 2:15) and to see their earthly lives "as a mist that appears for a little time and then vanishes" (James 4:14). A similar strain of thought appears in the Old Testament book of Ecclesiastes, which proclaims that "all things are full of weariness" and that "everything that is done under the sun . . . is vanity and a striving after wind."

Though Marcus appears to have known little about Christianity, he does seem to have been influenced by the general anti-worldliness of his period. As the distinguished Christian historian Henry Chadwick notes, Marcus's *Meditations* displays "a markedly individual, introspective, brooding mood" that is not typical of most earlier Stoics, who, as we have seen, were cosmic optimists who rejoiced in their sunny conviction that, as Alexander Pope would later put it, "whatever is, is right" (though compare Marcus's similar statement in *Meditations* 4.10).

Anti-body themes

Like Epictetus, Marcus often speaks of the body in negative terms. His body, Marcus says, is a "battered crate," made of "earth and garbage" (*Meditations* 3.3). Stoics should despise their bodies (2.2) as nothing more than "rotting meat in a bag," full of the "stench of decay" (8.38), a "corpse" (4.41). It's easy to hear the voice of the character Pee-wee Herman here saying, "I know you are, but what am I?" Then, "Things that happen to the body are meaningless," Marcus says (6.32). The mind is far superior to the body and "should remain unstirred by the agitations of the flesh — gentle and violent ones alike" (5.26). Anti-body themes of this sort are more characteristic of Platonism than they are of early and middle Stoicism, where the notion of "following nature" (aka following virtue and reason) was emphasized and was not generally seen as implying that one should despise the body or bodily goods. Here Epictetus and Marcus are both really channeling Socrates, Plato, the Cynics, and then-current anti-body movements like Orphism and Gnosticism, not Stoic tradition.

Life is a sewer

Along with this hostile attitude to the body, Marcus often expresses pessimistic views of earthly life in general, which he once described as a "deep darkness" and a "sewer" (*Meditations* 5.10). As translator Gregory Hays notes, two of Marcus's most persistent themes in the *Meditations* are "the vanity and worthlessness of earthly concerns" and "disgust and contempt for human life and other human beings." These gloomy themes, so clearly at odds with Stoic belief in a benevolent providence which ensures that all things turn out for the best, largely drop out of sight in contemporary Stoicism, but they undeniably appear again and again in the *Meditations*.

Detachment and apathy

It's not hard to see why a Stoic might be inclined to minimizing views of the body and of earthly existence in general. As we've noted, Stoics seek both moral excellence and inner calm (*ataraxia*, for those keeping score in Greek). Achieving inner serenity is difficult if you tend to worry a lot about your health, your appearance, or other bodily goods. Mental tranquility can also, of course, be disturbed by wars, natural disasters, economic depressions, and other negative events in the news or on social media. The physical world is indeed a metaphorical minefield of troubles and challenges.

What's the solution?

>> Well, you could try to *stop caring at all* about things like cancer, wars, and storms, to "extinguish all desires and attachments" regarding them, as some

Eastern philosophers seem to urge. As we'll explore, however, total apathy or nonattachment of this sort is for many reasons neither possible nor desirable, as thoughtful Stoics have always acknowledged.

>> A better solution would be to try to *care less* about the body and supposed "indifferents" such as health, relationships, famines, and other earthly concerns. You could try to be more detached about such matters, less emotionally invested in them, as modern psychologists might say.

And that, of course, is precisely the coping strategy ancient Stoics like Marcus recommend. They urge us to become emotionally detached from externals like the body and the vicissitudes of earthly affairs. This is the ideal of Stoic "apathy" (*apatheia*), which they saw as an important form of freedom from all disturbing passions and excessive desires. We'll take a closer look at the often-misunderstood idea of Stoic apathy in Chapter 14.

Psychological depreciation

But how can we achieve a healthy and appropriate level of detachment? One way, Marcus suggests, is to adopt a mental practice that modern Stoic Donald Robertson calls a strategy of psychological "depreciation." By this, Robertson means a kind of coping strategy that involves attaching less value to things, and thus coming to worry or care less about them, by a process of "deflationary" reductive analysis that allows us to see things objectively, "as they really are," rather than as how they may present themselves to the imagination. Marcus uses such a depreciatory "X is really just Y" strategy frequently. Thus, the body is just "earth and garbage" (Meditations 3.3), the soul is just "a dream and mist" (2.17), change is just transformation from one thing into another (8.6), fame is just emptiness and oblivion (4.3), history is just an endlessly repeating cycle in which nothing really new ever occurs (2.14, 7.1), and death is just a natural process (2.12) in which bits of matter combine, split apart, and recombine into something new (4.5).

There's no doubt that reductive strategies of this sort can be effective — as can alcohol, which Dave Barry reminds us in his satirical book *Live Right and Find Happiness (Though Beer Is Much Faster)*. Buddhism, Hinduism, and many other spiritual traditions endorse a wide variety of deflationary psychological practices as a means to reduce harmful attachments.

Psychological depreciation works. It's a proven technique for reducing suffering, numbing our sense of loss, anesthetizing our pain, and protecting us from emotional risk and affliction with a kind of psychological armor. In this way, it can produce more inner calm or tranquility. But at what personal and moral cost? That's a crucial question we'll tackle later in this book.

The Demise of Ancient Stoicism

Why did ancient Stoicism kick the proverbial bucket not long after Marcus Aurelius? Several factors seem to have played a role. Let's briefly glance at four causes in the following sections.

The demise of "the old gods" of paganism

As is especially evident in Cleanthes's famous "Hymn to Zeus" and in the works of Epictetus, Stoic philosophy was widely seen as tied up in complex ways with the old pagan mythology of Zeus, Apollo, and their colorful and nectar-loving Olympian friends. When pagan theology waned in Hellenistic Greece and Rome and eventually died out for good in late Imperial Rome, Stoicism as an organized system of thought and belief died along with it. When the Christian emperor Justinian closed all the philosophical schools of Athens permanently in 529, it was justified to Justinian's Christian subjects as the final nail in the coffin of Greek and Roman paganism.

The rise of competing philosophies

As we saw earlier, in Marcus's time and for centuries after, otherworldly philosophies and religions such as Platonism, Christianity, Gnosticism, Orphism, and various Eastern mystery religions were becoming increasingly popular. Often, these next-world-oriented creeds were seen as providing greater hopes and consolations, along with a firmer grounding for real long-term optimism than older philosophies and faiths such as Stoicism, pagan theology, and Aristotelianism. Christianity, for example, offered its followers eternal life, posthumous justice, a God who answers prayers, divine aid in living a moral and religious life, and eternal happiness in a heavenly paradise, none of which Stoicism could promise.

Failure to appeal to the masses

As Victorian literary critic Matthew Arnold astutely notes in a classic 1863 essay on Marcus Aurelius, in ancient times Stoicism had a kind of public-relations problem. It was widely seen by the masses as a cold, stern, demanding, and rather gloomy creed for the strong and the few. Christianity, by contrast, seemed to offer "a ray of sunshine" and "the glow of a divine warmth." As Arnold remarks elsewhere, if one is looking for "a binding force and a power to transform and save" someone who sees himself as sorely needing redemption, a religion like Christianity has an emotional appeal and a consolatory message that Stoicism might well seem to lack.

Attacks by rival philosophical schools

Finally, ancient Stoicism clearly suffered from attacks by other philosophical schools. A fair bit of the surviving evidence we have about the teachings of ancient Stoicism is contained in works by pagan and Christian authors that were mostly critical of those ideas. From these attacks we can see that for centuries the Stoics were hammered repeatedly on many of their core teachings, especially by Platonists, Aristotelians, and Skeptics.

Down but not out

Despite the factors just discussed, it's misleading to say that Stoicism "died" in late antiquity, because much of its thought survived through other channels. As is clear in writers like Plutarch (around 110) and Boethius (around 500), vital bits of Stoic teaching were absorbed into Neoplatonism and Christianity. Throughout the Middle Ages and into the modern era, Stoic ideas on the four cardinal virtues, natural law, divine Providence, the problem of evil, the reconciliation of divine foreknowledge and human free will, and the importance of Stoic/Christian virtues such as fortitude, endurance, patience, constancy, and resignation continued to have a major impact.

As long as Western thought and culture was predominantly Christian, there seemed to be little hope that Stoicism could make a comeback in any big way. After all, historic Stoicism teaches materialism, pantheism, the divinity of the human mind, virtue as the sole good and the goal of life, the achievability of that goal without divine assistance, and no eternal life — all ideas directly opposed to traditional Christianity And yet, by roughly the middle of the 20th century, as Western culture gradually became more secular, conditions grew more favorable for a potential revival, a "modern Stoicism" that might again bring this ancient wisdom into the everyday lives of millions. For that exciting story, stay tuned for later chapters!

2

The Stoic Worldview

Discover the big-picture Stoic view of reality.

Explore Stoic ideas of fate and free will.

Chapter **6**

The Stoic View of Reality

The ancient Stoics developed a complex theory of reality to support their moral teachings and conception of the good life. Many aspects of this larger worldview are mostly ignored by later Stoics such as Seneca, Epictetus, and Marcus Aurelius, all of whom focus mostly on practical questions of ethics and how to live a great human life.

Many contemporary Stoics bypass that original worldview entirely, perhaps because they think it's outdated or mostly irrelevant to everyday problems and concerns. Yet, to understand Stoic teachings on wisdom and virtue, it's important to grasp the broader view of reality that underpins them.

Classic Stoic teachings on such matters as fate, radical acceptance, following nature, becoming wise, imitating God, cosmic citizenship, human solidarity and kinship, universal moral law, true freedom as obeying reason and God, and life after death don't make a lot of sense apart from this wider worldview.

For those interested in a deeper dive into Stoic teachings about the Logos, nature, and humanity, F. H. Sandbach's book *The Stoics* (2e 1989) offers a clear, comprehensive, authoritative, and readable guide for beginners.

Everything Is Made of Matter

Like the Epicureans, the ancient Stoics were physicalists or materialists. Everything that exists, they held, is made of some type of matter. Contrary to thinkers like Plato and Aristotle, they did not believe in disembodied spirits or minds. Even God (the Logos), they held, is made of a special kind of very fine and invisible matter.

REMEMBER

Why did the Stoics believe that everything is material? Because they agreed with a suggestion floated by Plato (*Sophist* 247e) that something is real only if it has a capacity to causally affect other things or to be affected by them. The Stoics could not conceive how something that was totally incorporeal could have any causal effects or be causally impacted by other things. For example, to cause a ball to begin rolling across a floor seems to require that some sort of physical force be exerted on it. But how could something immaterial exert any physical force? Conversely, how could a purely spiritual being (an angel or disembodied ghost, for example) be causally impacted by a rock, a stick, or anything else made of matter? For such reasons, the Stoics sought to explain everything in the cosmos in purely physicalistic terms.

WARNING

Interestingly, the Stoics did recognize that we can talk and think intelligibly about certain things that do not seem to be made of matter. Space and time are two examples of what they called "incorporeals." Another is the infinite void that the Stoics believed surrounds the cosmos and is the only "thing" that "exists" outside the universe. The void contains no matter and is not itself made of matter, yet it does have certain properties like emptiness and infinity. Finally, there is a diverse class of incorporeals the Stoics called *lekta* ("sayables"). Verbal meanings are one kind of *lekta*. Consider two sentences:

The sky is blue.

Le ciel est bleu.

These are different sentences in different languages (English and French), yet they have the same meaning. That meaning, the Stoics recognized, is real but does not seem to have any size, shape, weight, or to be composed of any form of matter. It is abstract, like the property of being kind, or not being a rectangle. Thus, the Stoics were not strict or "reductionistic" materialists in the sense of totally dismissing all talk of immaterial things.

REMEMBER

Like some later philosophers, the Stoics qualified their materialism by saying that while incorporeal things like space and the void have properties and "subsist," only material things strictly "are" or "exist." It's a fine distinction that many contemporary philosophers reject or find puzzling.

God and Nature

As we saw in Chapter 2, ancient Stoicism was grounded in a deeply religious view of reality. The Stoics believed in a kind of God or "force" or higher power that they, like Heraclitus, called "the Logos." Here are some of its characteristics:

>> Unlike Zeus, Hera, Apollo, and the other fun-loving and easily-ticked-off gods in traditional Greek mythology, the Logos was not conceived in anthropomorphic (that is, humanlike) terms.

>> The Logos does not have anything like human form. It has no face, no arms or legs, no beard, no toga, throws no thunderbolts, and has no interest in mating with mortals. Rather, the Logos is a sort of intelligent invisible gas or vapor that permeates the cosmos and animates all things.

>> Like Heraclitus, the Stoics believed that the Logos is made of fire (or, later, of a mix of fire and air). This fire, however, is not a flame but a special kind of fire that produces heat yet can't be seen.

>> The Logos is the Primal Reality out of which the entire physical cosmos is generated. What we call "the universe" is a combination of inert, formless matter (the passive principle in nature) and *pneuma* (literally "breath"), the "world-soul" or active principle in nature. Sometimes the Stoics use the terms "God" or "Zeus" or "Logos" to refer to the whole shebang, matter *plus* world-soul, i.e., everything that exists. But more commonly they refer only to the world-soul or active principle in nature.

>> Out of its own fiery substance the Logos produces the four basic elements (air, earth, fire, and water) and then through a complex process of condensation (compaction) and rarefaction (expansion), stars, trees, rocks, animals, and other familiar physical objects.

>> The Logos thoroughly pervades the material universe, filling it completely. Matter itself is purely shapeless and passive and has no qualities until acted on by the indwelling Logos. Whatever qualities a thing possesses (for example, the redness, sweetness, and roundness of an apple) are entirely due to the causal activity of the immanent Logos.

Stoic pantheism

Since Stoics believed that God is everything and everything is God, they embraced a form of pantheism. Pantheists are monists or "cosmic holists" who believe that only one substance exists and that that substance is divine. What may appear to be individual substances (for example, a rose, or a dog) are really just parts or modifications of the one reality, parts of God's body, so to speak. This is very different from classical theism, which views God as a transcendent Being distinct from the physical universe he has created.

Like the God of classical theism, the Logos is not just an impersonal "force" or "energy field" like The Force in the *Star Wars* movies. It is a *person* (or at least person-like) in the sense of having consciousness, self-awareness, sentience, rationality, moral awareness, the ability to act and make plans, and so forth. Also like the God of classical theism, the Logos is caring, provident, and perfect in wisdom, goodness, and happiness, though perhaps not all-powerful in the way the Judeo-Christian God is thought to be. It seems unlikely, for example, that the Logos could cause things to exist or cease to be simply by willing it, as the Judeo-Christian God is conceived able to do.

As we saw in our discussion of Epictetus, for Stoics the proper human response to the Logos is one of reverence, gratitude, obedience, acceptance, and a zealous and lifelong attempt to imitate its perfect wisdom, goodness, and happiness, and thus become a Stoic *Sage,* a kind of Stoic saint or model human being.

The Earth's place in the universe

Like Plato and Aristotle, the Stoics believed in a geocentric (earth-centered) universe. The earth is a sphere surrounded by concentric layers of water, air, and fire, with divine beings dwelling in the fiery outermost sphere of the fixed stars, which are themselves intelligent and divine (as are the sun, moon, and planets). The cosmos as a whole is spherical in shape and alive, an enormous rational organism with both a body (matter) and a soul (*pneuma*). Like human beings, the cosmos has an intellective "command-center" or directing mind, which some Stoics located in the sun and others in the starry regions of the sky.

In portraying the cosmos as a living animal, spherical in shape and animated by a world-soul, the Stoics were clearly influenced by Plato, who sketched a somewhat similar view in his great dialogue *Timaeus.*

Stoic arguments for God

The Stoics' belief in a pantheistic God was not based merely on faith or guesswork. They offered a series of rational arguments for God's existence, many of which have been preserved in ancient sources such as Cicero and Sextus Empiricus. Sextus, a Greek philosopher who flourished in the third century, was a skeptic and generally critical of the Stoics. However, scholars, believe that he usually reported Stoic teachings accurately.

A faulty one

Zeno, the founder of Stoicism, seems to have offered several such arguments for divine reality, expressed in compact, syllogistic form. Here is one:

> One might reasonably honor the gods. But one might not reasonably honor the nonexistent. Therefore, gods exist.

Since no one would agree that it is reasonable to honor the gods who did not already believe that the gods exist, this argument is clearly circular and therefore faulty. It essentially assumes what it tries to prove.

Universality of belief

Another Stoic argument for the existence of the divine was based on the near-universality of belief in the gods. The Stoics claimed that it is unlikely that such a widespread, persistent, and perhaps inborn belief could be false.

A proof from motion

Another Stoic argument for God involves the source of motion in the heavenly bodies and other parts of the cosmos. Since matter does not move itself, it must have a cause of motion. This cause must in turn have a cause. But any such series of causes cannot go back infinitely, since everything must have an explanation and there would be no explanation for the fact of motion if it's eternal and has no cause. Thus, God must exist as its ultimate source.

Rationality and intelligence

The Stoics also supported belief in God by appealing to human rationality and intelligence. What is the source of such rationality? Could rational beings have been produced by blind chance? Their rivals, the Epicureans, believed this to be true, but the Stoics said, "Not a chance!"

The design argument

Probably the best argument for God offered by the Stoics centers on the great beauty and orderliness of the cosmos. Cicero gives one such argument:

> If you see a large and beautiful house, you could not be induced to think that it was built by mice and weasels, even if you do not see the master of the house. If then, you were to think that the great ornament of the cosmos, the great variety and beauty of the heavenly bodies, the great power and vastness of the sea and land were your own house and not that of the immortal gods, would you not seem to be downright crazy? (*On the Nature of the Gods* 2.17)

Here we see a type of argument that is now often called the argument from design. The basic idea is that the world displays too much order, beauty, and apparent purposefulness to have been a product of mere chance. It must have an intelligent designer. From the surviving sources, it is unclear why it was thought that such a designer must be a pantheistic God, as the Stoics supposed. It may be that they assumed that only a pantheistic god would have the requisite, all-pervasive power to ensure that the world was fully providentially ordered. By being embodied in the entire cosmos, God is able to exert full control over it and see to it that everything happens for the best.

Stoic belief in divine Providence was rooted in their conception of the inherent nature of God. If God is all-good and all-wise and fully in control of the universe, then this must be the best of all possible worlds. This is the basis of the Stoics' cosmic optimism and their belief in radical acceptance of all that happens. These are topics we'll explore more fully in the next chapter.

Stoic belief in periodic conflagrations

One Stoic teaching that drew sharp attacks from critics and that some later Stoics even rejected was belief in eternally recurring world-cycles ending in "conflagrations," or all-consuming infernos, that marked the destruction of one universe and the start of another. The idea of a fiery end of the cosmos (*ekpyrosis*, for those who like to show off at parties) was grounded on the Stoic belief that the sun and stars require fuel to burn, which they believed was supplied by water that was "exhaled" from the earth. Eventually, it was thought, this fuel would run out, and the earth and its surrounding spheres would be burned up in its place. Since God is good and wishes to share his goodness eternally, a new cosmos would be created to replace the one that was destroyed. Because God must necessarily create the best of all possible worlds, the new cosmos would be identical in absolutely all details to the old one. This sequence of cosmic fires and renewals is eternal, without beginning or end. Marcus Aurelius speaks of this idea of eternal recurrence:

> To bear in mind constantly that all of this has happened before. And will happen again — the same plot from beginning to end, the identical staging. Produce them in your mind, as you know them from experience or from history: the court of Hadrian, of Antoninus. The courts of Philip, Alexander, Croesus. All the same. Only the people different (*Meditations* 10.27).

Some later Stoics, such as Panaetius, rejected the idea of periodic cosmic conflagrations. Apparently, he thought it was more pious to suppose that the world is eternal and indestructible. The idea of a fiery end to the cosmos also made it impossible for souls to be immortal, since the Stoics believed souls are made of matter and all matter is destroyed in the final inferno. Its's also a bit depressing to think, as the biblical Book of Ecclesiastes puts it, that

> What has been is what will be; and what has been done is what will be done; and there is nothing new under the sun (Ecclesiastes 1:9)

Woody Allen captures the gloomy aspect of eternal recurrence when he jokes:

> And Nietzsche, with his theory of eternal recurrence. He said that the life we lived we're gonna live over again the exact same way for eternity. Great. That means I'll have to sit through the Ice Capades again. It's not worth it.

REMEMBER

Nearly all contemporary Stoics drop the idea of a periodic cosmic bonfire as based on outdated Stoic physics. But it's interesting to note that modern science leaves open the possibility of some kind of cosmic destruction and renewal. If the universe contains enough matter to slow and eventually reverse its current expansion, it may collapse on itself again and another Big Bang occur, leading to the creation of a new cosmos. In fact, it may be that there is an eternal cycle of Big Crunches and Big Bangs. If so, the Stoic idea of an eternal series of world-cycles would have some correspondence to fact.

The Place of Humanity in the Cosmos

The Stoics gave human beings a very important role in the cosmos. They held that all things are in a sense divine, since all are parts of the divine Logos. But humans were thought to have a special role and status in the universe.

An anthropocentric view

Only gods and humans have rational souls, which the Stoics believed to be "sparks" or "fragments" or "emanations" (see *Meditations* 2.1, 2.4) of the Logos's ruling faculty or directive mind. Like the *pneuma* that pervades the cosmos, human souls are composed of fire and air; they are not purely spiritual or immaterial as Plato had taught. Our souls are present in every part of our bodies, but the Stoics believed that the seat of human rationality and consciousness lies in the heart, in what they called the *hegemonikon*, a kind of rational "command-center" of the soul, which is the human counterpart of the Logos's directive mind. It is this central core of the soul that is responsible for all higher functions of the mind, including perception, impulse, assent, and reasoning. In virtue of this bit of God's mind within us, the Stoics saw no sharp separation between humans and gods, and in fact held that "every man's mind is god" (*Meditations* 12.26).

Stoics thought of the human soul as a single undivided entity; there are no lower parts of it responsible for bodily appetites and emotions, as Plato and Aristotle had taught. Our having rational souls distinguishes us clearly from nonhuman animals, none of them with "minds" exactly like ours. Stoicism held a highly anthropocentric view of the place of humans in the cosmos. Not only is the earth at the center of the universe, but the whole cosmos was designed for human and divine benefit. So, Cicero, echoing Stoicism, writes:

> Here someone will ask: "For whose benefit was such a complex system created?" For the sake of trees and plants, which despite their lack of sense-perception are nevertheless sustained by nature? But surely that is absurd. For the beasts then? It is no more likely that the gods should have worked so hard for mute animals that understand nothing. So, for whose sake will we say the cosmos was made? Surely for the sake of those animals which use reason, and those are gods and humans. Surely, nothing is better than they are since reason is superior to all other things. So, it turns out to be plausible that the cosmos and all in it were created for the sake of gods and humans. (*On the Nature of the Gods* 2.133)

One important implication of the idea that all humans possess souls that are fragments of God is a strong sense of human kinship and solidarity. So, Seneca writes:

> I can lay down for mankind a rule, in short compass, for our duties in human relationships: all that you behold, that which comprises both god and man, is one; we are parts of one great body. Nature produced us related to one another, since she created us from the same source and to the same end. She engendered in us mutual affection, and made us prone to friendships . . . Through her orders, let our hands be ready for all that needs to be helped. (*Letters* 95.52)

And Epictetus, speaking of slaves to his students from wealthy families, says:

> Won't you keep in mind who you are and who these people are whom you're ruling over? That they belong to the same family, that they are by nature brothers of yours, that they are offspring of Zeus? (*Discourses* 1.13)

REMEMBER

Though few today would agree that human souls are literally fragments of God, the Stoic belief in human solidarity has proved one of their most enduring contributions to our progress. Belief in the inherent and equal dignity and rights of all members of the human family is a pillar of modern human rights law.

Belief in a (temporary) afterlife

Although Stoics believed that human souls are made of matter, most accepted the idea of some kind of personal afterlife (see E. V. Arnold, *Roman Stoicism*, pp. 263-70 for details, or just trust us on this, which is much easier). Most Stoics believed that human souls, in virtue of their divine nature, have a special kind of "tension" (*tonos*) or cohesiveness that allows them to survive the death of the body. This may be surprising to readers who know Stoicism mainly through the writing of Epictetus and Marcus Aurelius, because neither says much about a possible afterlife. Seneca, however, reflects the mainline Stoic view, though with a Platonic twist, reflected in his belief in the pre-existence and literal immortality of souls, when he writes:

> The human soul is a great and noble thing; it permits of no limits except those which can be shared even by the gods . . . The soul's homeland is the whole space that encircles the height and breadth of the firmament, the whole rounded dome within which the upper air that sunders the human from the divine also unites them, and where all the sentinel stars are taking their turn on duty. Again, the soul will not put up with a narrow span of existence. "All the years," says the soul, "are mine; no epoch is closed to great minds; all time is open for the progress of thought. When the day comes to separate the heavenly from its earthly blend, I shall leave the body where I found it, and shall of my own volition betake myself to the gods" (*Letters* 102. 21-23).

Seneca is here expressing the traditional Stoic view (see Sextus Empiricus, *Against the Professors* 9.71) that at death, the soul contracts into an invisible sphere, leaves the body, and floats up to its natural homeland in the starry regions of the skies, where it may be able to commune with the gods, much as Socrates had speculated at his trial (*Apology* 40c-41c) and Seneca himself indicates in the above-quoted passage. Stoics did not believe in anything like the Christian notions of heaven or hell. They seem to have held that there are no divine punishments or rewards after death.

As noted earlier, the Stoics generally did not believe in strict immortality. They maintained, as Epictetus says, that "all that comes into being must also perish" (*Discourses* 4.7.27). Nothing, not even the celestial gods, can survive the fiery destruction of the universe at the end of the current world-cycle except the Logos itself, which is eternal and imperishable. The Stoics seem to have disagreed about how long souls survive after death. Cleanthes apparently thought that all souls continue to exist until the conflagration, but Chrysippus held that only the souls of the wise last that long (Diogenes Laertius, *Lives* 7.157). As we noted, later Stoics such as Panaetius and Marcus Aurelius seem to have doubted or denied that souls can survive death at all, while Seneca seems to follow Plato in affirming that souls are strictly immortal and exist forever. As we shall see, many contemporary Stoics question or reject any sort of afterlife.

Finding truth in outdated notions

REMEMBER

A great deal of Stoic theology and philosophy of nature is clearly outdated. For instance, no informed readers today will accept the Stoic doctrines of fire as the primordial element, the four basic elements, an earth-centered universe, the divinity of the sun and stars, or the heart as the seat of human consciousness. In addition, many of the core teachings of Stoicism about focusing on things we can control, the priority of wisdom and virtue, managing negative emotions, recognizing the impermanence of all things, keeping earthly concerns in perspective, and learning to roll with life's punches are at least largely independent of such outdated notions.

However, some key Stoic beliefs can only be understood by grasping the metaphysical and religious teachings on which they rest. This is true, most obviously, of the Stoic doctrines of divine Providence, radical acceptance, and true freedom as perfect obedience to God, which clearly make little sense apart from the Stoic theology that undergirds them. Understanding the ancient Stoic worldview is also important for seeing how widely those original forms of Stoicism differ from the variants of contemporary Stoicism that are now being promulgated in popular books, newsletters, and podcasts. This difference will emerge even more clearly in the next chapter, where we will explore the fascinating Stoic views of Providence, fate, free will, and moral responsibility.

Chapter **7**

Providence, Fate, and Free Will

A s we've seen in earlier chapters, the ancient Stoics were strong believers in a higher power that they called the Logos. They believed that the Logos was the all-wise and all-good ruler and director of the cosmos who created the best possible universe and governs all things for the ultimate good of rational beings (gods and humans) and the cosmos as a whole. The Stoics were thus firm believers in what religious thinkers call divine Providence: God's foreknowledge, design plan, benevolent care, and faithful governance of the universe as a whole, and of human beings in particular (Cicero, *On the Nature of the Gods* 2. 73-162).

The Stoics, in fact, held a very robust view of divine Providence, believing that God foresees *everything* that happens in the universe (including the so-called "free" choices of human beings) and even predetermines or foreordains whatever comes to pass (Plutarch, *On Stoic Self-Contradictions* 1049f) in such a way that everything that happens is entirely fixed and unalterable, even by God himself (Seneca, "On Providence" 5.8). The Stoics' term for this fully determined and unchangeable sequence of cosmic events was fate (*moira*). All the great Stoic teachers held that "everything happens by fate," (Diogenes Laertius, *Lives* 7.149). According to some sources, some leading Stoics, including Chrysippus, the greatest Stoic thinker, even held that human crimes and evil deeds are also fated and necessitated.

These two Stoic teachings — theological fatalism and a very strong form of divine Providence — have both attractions and potential problems. Let's begin with Stoic fatalism, then turn to Providence.

"Everything Is Fated"

In modern English, "fate" can refer to both "whatever happens to a person or thing" ("The fate of the missing ship is unknown") and "a power or agency that predetermines things to occur in a way that cannot be changed." Everybody, of course, believes in fate in the first sense. As the Eagles sing, "time keeps on slippin, slippin', slippin' into the future," and things do happen as time flows on. But the second sense of "fate" is more controversial. In ancient Greece, it was widely believed that many or all events were destined or unalterably predetermined by the gods, the stars, or other agencies (Long and Sedley, *The Hellenistic Philosophers*, p. 392). This can be seen in Greek mythology and tragedy, where the Fates were personified as three divine sisters — Clotho, Atropos, and Lachesis — whose job was to spin the thread of human destiny from birth to death.

For the Stoics, belief in fate flowed from their conception of God, the providential Logos. Like Plato (*Republic* 381b), they conceived of God as a nearly perfect being, infinite in wisdom and goodness, immensely powerful, and free of any possible evil or defect. Such a being, they believed, would wish to share his goodness by creating other good things — in fact, a whole created universe infused with reason, goodness, beauty, and ordered harmony.

REMEMBER

Such a universe would not be haphazard and left to luck and happenstance; it would be planned meticulously, in complete detail. This plan would be the best possible plan, as befits a planner of infinite wisdom and goodness.

Moreover, since God is so wise and powerful, he cannot suffer any harm, defeat, or setback. His plan for the world can't be derailed or obstructed by anyone or anything. His will must be fulfilled. God's will *could* be defeated if rational agents such as you or me could do things — for example, steal a lollipop — that God forbids and were not part of his preordained order. So, whatever happens must happen inevitably and in accordance with God's will and design. This unalterable causal nexus of divinely foreknown and predetermined events is what the Stoics call fate. The Stoics, sometimes, in fact, use the terms "fate" and "God" interchangeably.

Fate in this religious sense raises obvious questions about human freedom and moral responsibility and may seem to imply that God is in some sense responsible for sin and evil. We'll see how the Stoics wrestled with these and other objections to their belief in all-encompassing fate. But for people who, like the Stoics, value virtue and mental tranquility above all things, there are real attractions to theological fatalism. These include:

>> Radical acceptance of whatever comes to pass (a key Stoic virtue) as reflecting the will of an all-wise and benevolent God.

>> A sense of comfort and consolation that flows from the sense that whatever hardships and sufferings one meets with in life were unavoidable and will eventually turn out for the best.

>> A sense of optimism that whatever the future may bring, God is in control and all will turn out well.

>> A sense of self-acceptance and self-gentleness that stems from belief that whatever faults or weaknesses one struggles with were predetermined and could not have been otherwise.

>> An attitude of tolerance and forbearance toward other people's shortcomings, which are likewise preordained and unavoidable. (As the French proverb says, "To understand all is to forgive all.")

>> A lack of pride or self-conceit resulting from the realization that one's accomplishments and good deeds were fated and not really "up to you" in the "libertarian" sense that you could have failed to perform them. The glory belongs ultimately to the Logos, and not to you.

REMEMBER

In short, from the Stoic perspective, faith in an all-encompassing divine fate fosters moral strength and inner peace and helps one avoid a wide array of negative emotions.

Despite these attractions, there are pretty obvious worries with this idea of all-controlling fate. These include:

>> It seems to rule out any free will and moral responsibility.

>> It seems to make God responsible for sin and evil.

>> It seems to encourage a kind of what-will-be-will-be passivity toward evils in the world.

Let's look at how the Stoics addressed these concerns.

Fatalism gone rogue

In contemporary philosophical discussions of fatalism, one sometimes sees it defined as the extreme view that fated events must necessarily occur no matter what you or I or anybody else might do to avoid them. A vivid illustration of fatalism in this radical sense is provided in the classic Arab tale "Appointment in Samarra," as retold by the British writer Somerset Maugham. The speaker is Death:

> There was a merchant in Bagdad who sent his servant to market to buy provisions and in a little while the servant came back, white and trembling, and said, "Master, just now when I was in the marketplace I was jostled by a woman in the crowd and when I turned I saw it was Death that jostled me. She looked at me and made a threatening gesture; now, lend me your horse, and I will ride away from this city and avoid my fate. I will go to Samarra and there Death will not find me." The merchant lent him his horse, and the servant mounted it, and he dug his spurs in its flanks and as fast as the horse could gallop he went. Then the merchant went down to the marketplace and he saw me standing in the crowd, and he came to me and said, "Why did you make a threating gesture to my servant when you saw him this morning?" "That was not a threatening gesture," I said, "it was only a start of surprise." I was astonished to see him in Bagdad, for I had an appointment with him tonight in Samarra.

On this view of fatalism, the future is already written and completely unalterable, and we are like actors in a completed disaster movie, oblivious to our inevitable doom.

WARNING

Fatalism in this extreme sense can seem attractive at times — like when you're wondering whether you might be "fated" to eat that second chocolate cupcake at your friend's party — but it's actually quite nutty when you think about it for two seconds. Consider what's implied, for example, in saying that you're fated to eat that second cupcake *no matter what you or anybody else might do*. That means that if you got run over by a bus on the way to the party and were squashed to jelly, you *still* would have eaten that second cupcake. That would be a neat trick even for a serious chocolate lover like you. In short, extreme fatalism conflicts with our common-sense "modal" or counterfactually hypothetical beliefs about what would have happened if things had turned out otherwise than they did.

REMEMBER

As the philosopher Richard Taylor argues, very few people subscribe to fatalism in this extreme no-matter-what sense. Instead, fatalism is better understood as the view that what is happening at any given moment is unavoidable, that neither you nor anybody else has any actual power to prevent it, though the event was not *absolutely* necessary and would not have occurred if other possible events had occurred.

For the Greeks, fatalism was essentially connected to religion. What happens by fate, they thought, is deliberately *fated* or made to happen by some powerful, divine agent (see, for example, Aeschylus, *Agamemnon* 1085 – 88). This is the core meaning of fatalism, though philosophers sometimes talk about forms of fatalism that supposedly flow from the weblike causal order of nature or even from the basic laws of logic (especially, as Cicero notes, the so-called Principle of Excluded Middle that says that every proposition must be either true or false, including all propositions about the future like "You, dear reader, *will* eat that second chocolate cupcake tomorrow.").

REMEMBER

In general, few philosophers or religious thinkers today accept any strong form of fatalism, although many do endorse universal causal determinism, the claim that all events have causes and that everything that occurs is totally determined by prior causes. Some philosophers classify determinism in this sense as a form of fatalism, but most do not, because they can seem to have very different practical implications.

Free will and responsibility

Humans are social animals. We are also — uniquely, so far as we know — *moral* animals. We give *weight* to moral reasons and judge things to be ethically good or bad, and right or wrong. We *praise* people for what we think is good ethical behavior (kindness, fairness, and so forth) and *blame* them for bad ethical behavior (lying, cheating, etc.). For really serious acts of unethical antisocial behavior (murder, robbery, etc.), we *punish* people by putting them in jail or imposing other forms of hard treatment. Yet, interestingly, we don't praise or blame all forms of antisocial behavior.

As Aristotle (384–322 BCE) pointed out, our common practices of moral praise and blame are based on certain assumptions. For example, if somebody steals your car, we wouldn't blame them or put them in jail if we found out they were suffering from some severe mental disorder or were forced to do it by someone holding a gun to their head. We praise and blame people only under certain conditions. What conditions? It's not easy to say precisely, but generally we praise and blame people only if we think they *deserve* praise or blame. And when does someone deserve praise or blame? Common sense and most legal systems say: Only when they act freely and responsibly (meaning here that they alone are ultimately responsible for the act).

As a rule, we don't put people in prison unless we believe they acted "culpably," that is, willingly, knowingly, and without an adequate justification or excuse. In short, both ordinary morality and law presume that people can at least sometimes act freely and responsibly. They presuppose a human capacity for free choice and morally responsible action.

Does free will exist if everything is fated?

But *can* people, in fact, ever act freely and responsibly? Here the ancient Stoics ran into a ginormous problem. They believed that everything is fated and that all events are the inevitable outcome of prior causes resulting from God's fully pre-scripted and unchangeable design plan.

As Cicero, Plutarch, and other ancient critics of Stoicism pointed out, this form of fatalism seems to rule out the possibility of meaningful free will and moral responsibility. Why? Imagine that you're in a cafeteria, trying to decide whether to have an apple or an orange with your lunch. Suppose you reach for an apple, but then decide at the last second that an orange would be sweeter, so you grab that instead. Did you choose the orange freely? For strict fatalists like the Stoics, it's hard to see how you could have. The nub of the problem can be put like this:

1. If God knows in advance that I will have an orange for lunch, then it *must* be the case that I will have an orange for lunch. (Reason: God, as a flawless being, can't have any false beliefs; whatever he believes about the future will *definitely* come true.)

2. If it *must* be the case that I will have an orange for lunch, then it's not in my power to refrain from having an orange for lunch.

3. If it's not in my power to refrain from having an orange for lunch, then I'm not truly free to decide whether I will or will not have an orange for lunch.

4. So if God knows in advance that I will have an orange for lunch, then I'm not truly free to decide whether I will or will not have an orange for lunch. I had no power to do otherwise, so the choice was fated, not genuinely free.

In short, free will and moral responsibility seem to presuppose a capacity for *acting otherwise than one did*. Stoic fatalism implies that no one can ever perform any act other than the one they did. So Stoic fatalism seems to rule out free will and moral responsibility, and it make humans beings, in effect, mere puppets of powers beyond our control. If we're puppets, even of the divine Logos, then we aren't really free.

Needless to say, this *isn't* an argument the ancient Stoics wished to accept. Stoics like Seneca and Epictetus talk constantly about things that are or are not "up to us" and "within our control." Epictetus speaks of our faculty of volition or deliberative choice (*prohairesis*) as being completely "free, unrestricted, unhindered." But how can that be? How can we be free and responsible if all our actions are totally pre-scripted? In short, how is strict and inexorable fate compatible with free will?

Compatibilism

We know that great Stoic thinkers like Chrysippus wrote lengthy treatises on fate and Providence and wrestled deeply with this problem. Sadly, those works are all lost, but luckily a good chunk of Cicero's book *On Fate* survives. From that and a few other surviving sources, we can get a pretty good idea how the Stoics tried to square their seemingly conflicting beliefs in fate and free will.

The gist of Chrysippus's ingenious strategy was to deny that free will, properly understood, requires either an uncaused choice or an ability to do otherwise. A free act, he claims, is what Stoicism scholar Suzanne Bobzien calls an *autonomous* act, that is, an act that is uncoerced or unconstrained, and springs from one's own wishes, desires, and settled character (Bobzien, *Determinism and Freedom in Stoic Philosophy*, p. 279). Free will, in the sense relevant to moral responsibility, is thus simply *the ability to do as one likes*, free of any kind of external constraint or compulsion, such as brainwashing, or physical restraint, or coercion. Fate then most operate on a different level from such things as compulsions or constraints.

So, Chrysippus would say, even though I may have been fated from all eternity to have an orange for lunch today, my choice to do so is still free because no one around me is coercing me or somehow controlling my will. Like all events, my choice to have an orange has a cause (in this case, my desire to eat a sweet and healthy fruit), and my choice is what Chrysippus calls a "complete and primary" cause that, though sufficient to produce the effect, is in no way itself either coerced or constrained. In other words, Chrysippus argues, fate negates free will only if it acts as a *coercive* cause; but fate doesn't act as such a cause — it's only an antecedent "auxiliary" cause; so, fate does not negate free will. In other words, fate is a kind of cause, but not of the sort that can eliminate free will (reported in Cicero, *On Fate* 39-43). Whew! Anybody got an aspirin, or three?

As Epictetus would later say, our power of assent is by its very nature entirely free and "up to us." Not even Zeus, he believed, can force you to assent to, or believe, what you see to be false, or to have an immoral intention or an irrational belief if you are firmly determined not to (*Discourses* 1.1.23). But then of course all our beliefs, intentions, and states of inner determination are themselves fated to be what they are, and yet not in a coercive way. Your mind, as Marcus Aurelius would say, is "an inner citadel" that only *you* control (yet, on Stoic doctrine, only in the ways you were fated). Thus, Chrysippus and later Stoics argued, acts of free and responsible choice are possible even though all of our acts and choices are strictly fated and determined by God to be what they are.

REMEMBER

This view — that free will is consistent with theological fatalism and strict causal determinism — is called "compatibilism" (or sometimes "soft determinism"). Most philosophers today are compatibilists of one stripe or another, right or wrong. As far as we know, the Stoics were the first philosophers to defend compatibilism in a systematic way.

As we saw in Chapter 4, Epictetus describes a higher kind of freedom that we labeled "Stoic freedom." This is a form of psychological freedom or autonomy achievable only by the wise after lengthy spiritual and moral training. As Chrysippus said, freedom involves an ability to do as you like, but Epictetus believed that what people would *really* like, deep down, is to be perfectly wise and good, like Socrates, or the gods. Hence his oft-quoted remark that "no bad man is free" (*Discourses* 4.1.3).

Strict Stoic freedom (a.k.a. desiring only what we truly like and being able to do those things without external constraints or obstacles) is not necessary for moral responsibility. Though Epictetus often talks of not blaming people for their faults, he clearly does not want to deny moral responsibility and the legitimacy of all praise and blame. Epictetus believes people are accountable for their behavior, and he praises people like Socrates for their good deeds and faults people like his slacker students for their lame efforts. But true Stoic freedom (being able to do as you like but liking to act wisely and virtuously) is definitely the Stoic ideal.

Ancient Stoics thus believed that humans possess free will and that free will is compatible with universal causal determinism in the form of divine fate. They believed that free will is consistent with universal fate because we are free when we are able to do as we like, and we can often do as we like regardless of whether our acts are fated or necessitated by prior causes of any sort over which we have no control. But there's a question we need to ask: Does such a "compatibilist" solution really work?

Sadly, no. As many contemporary critics of compatibilism point out, being able to do as you like without external hindrance is not sufficient for free will. People who are psychotic or totally delusional, or completely ignorant of what they are actually doing, or suffering from severe dementia, or subject to some irresistible psychological compulsion, are not acting freely and responsibly, even if they are able to do as they please. So contrary to the Stoics, there must be something more to free will than simply the ability to do as we like, free of external hindrances or constraints. What else is required? That's a thorny problem philosophers and legal theorists have debated for centuries and continue to bat around today. Compatibilism may be true, but unfortunately not the rather simplistic form embraced by the ancient Stoics.

Why is age-old debate about the compatibility of free will and fate, or any other form of determinism important? It's because practices of praise and blame are pervasive and deeply embedded in our institutions and in our everyday lives. Moreover, if humans lack a true and robust free will and responsibility, we seem diminished, mere puppets manipulated by forces over which we have no control. So, any doubt about our freedom and responsibility threatens our self-image, our sense of our own inner worth.

Much to their credit, the Stoics were among the first philosophers to think deeply about the complexities of human freedom. Even if they didn't get the answer quite right, they made a real contribution to ancient discussions of free will and responsibility and gave us something of lasting value to ponder. Many contemporary defenses of compatibilism, in fact, use strategies along roughly the same lines as those offered by the Stoics.

Is God to Blame for Evil?

If the world is ruled by a powerful and benevolent God, then why is there so much suffering and injustice in the world? This is what philosophers call "the problem of evil." On this topic, too, the Stoics were among the first Western philosophers to wrestle deeply with a big problem. The solutions they came up with greatly influenced later Christian thought on why God permits evil.

If there is no God and the universe is nothing but "atoms and the void," it's a piece of cake to explain why evil and injustice exist: In a godless world, of course sh*t happens. Who's to stop it? Gravity for example causes rocks to fall; humans have evolved to feel pain; nature is blind and indifferent, and sometimes rocks fall on decent and innocent people, causing pain and even death. *Voila!* A bad thing has happened to a good person. Not rocket science, or even rock science. It's simple and unavoidable.

But suppose there is a God. And imagine this is no flawed and limited Olympian god with a bad attitude, but by contrast a perfect being, infinite in wisdom, goodness, and power. Then you have a really hairy problem of evil, because as the great 18th-century philosopher David Hume pointed out:

>> If God is all-powerful, it seems he must have the *power* to eliminate all evil.

>> If God is all-wise, it seems he must have the *wisdom* to eliminate all evil.

>> If God is perfectly good and just, it seems he must have the *desire* to eliminate all evil (or at least all "gratuitous" or "pointless" evil that leads to no higher, redeeming good).

So why then does evil exist? Or put slightly differently, why is there *so much* seemingly *pointless evil* in a world ruled by a just and powerful and caring God? And in fact, in the face of such evil, why should we not conclude quite decisively that there *is* no such God? This is Hume's argument in brief.

Seneca's response

The Stoics faced this classic problem of evil in an acute form, and they addressed it head-on. The most detailed and thoughtful surviving Stoic response is contained in Seneca's insightful essay "On Providence." There, as we briefly noted earlier, he basically argues that God allows evil as a *test*, a kind of character-building obstacle course for the human race. Good people suffer and encounter adversities because God wants to:

>> Harden and strengthen them, thereby promoting the ultimate goal of human life (wisdom and virtue).

>> Allow them to test themselves, so they can see what they are really made of deep inside.

>> Permit them to serve as role models, teaching others how to endure hardships with patience and courage.

>> Promote the common good by developing good, battle-toughened leaders who have learned wisdom from the harsh realities of life.

>> Achieve and display for others extremely high-order virtues, such as heroic endurance of pain or self-sacrifice for the good of the community.

>> Use lower-order evils, such as the unjust execution of Socrates, to achieve higher-order goods, such as the spread of Socrates's wonderful teachings and example throughout the world.

In addition, as we've seen, Seneca argues that there is a good deal less actual evil in the world than is commonly believed. The only true evils, on his Stoic philosophy, are immoral thoughts, desires, and acts. Since evil desires, acts, and thoughts result from an ignorance of true philosophy, and people often can't be (strongly) blamed for lacking knowledge of true philosophy, there is less true evil in the world than is widely supposed.

Finally, God uses vices as pathways, or means, to bring about higher goods. Such "evils" are therefore in fact, and despite any initial appearances to the contrary, instrumental *goods*, and thus, in a full sense, not evils at all. When Marcus Aurelius states, "All's right that happens in the world" (*Meditations* 4.10), he is likely thinking about how the Logos is able to weave the threads of fate together to bring good out of evil, and triumph out of tragedy.

Natural evils and animal pain

Seneca makes some good points in his discussion of evil, sketching insights that great Christian thinkers like Augustine (d. 430 CE) would later use to develop their own influential responses to the problem of evil. But there are two key aspects of the problem that the Stoics never adequately addressed. One deals with so-called natural evils, such as natural disasters or animal suffering that don't seem to result in any obvious way from any kind of moral fault or wrongdoing, but rather from we call "the forces of nature." The other has to with God's responsibility, however indirect, for sin and evil.

Consider, first, animal pain. There's a lot of it. Sentient nonhuman animals like antelopes and chipmunks have been living, fighting, suffering, and struggling to survive long before humans evolved on the African savannah a few million years ago. Scientists tell us that higher-order animals like horses and deer have pain centers in their brains very similar in structure to our own. In nature, few animals live to adulthood; most struggle to survive and live short, pain-filled lives. So why does the Logos permit — and, for Stoics, in fact cause — such immense animal suffering?

To this, the Stoics had a simple and simply awful answer: God doesn't care much about animal pain. Animals, they said, exist entirely for human benefit. Animals lack rational souls and were created by God solely to serve human needs for food, clothing, and other purposes. In fact, as we've seen, the Stoics believed that the entire cosmos was created solely as an orderly, beautiful, and healthful "Great City" for gods and humans to inhabit (Cicero, *On the Nature of the Gods* 2.133). Whatever pain animals feel isn't an evil (only vice is evil), and like slavery, which most Stoics also accepted, animal life serves its just and allotted purpose simply by being a resource for beings of superior value. Like Aristotle, most ancient Stoics believed that nature is an ordered hierarchy and that inferior beings exist for the sake of superior ones (see, e.g., *Meditations* 5.16). So, for Stoics, animal pain is justified because it is part of a just natural order and contributes to the good of rational beings and the overall good of the universe.

REMEMBER

Needless to say, few scientifically informed or moral people would accept such a view of animals today. It is baldly anthropocentric, scientifically outdated, and premised on a form of self-serving hierarchy (a view that inferiors, by nature and divine intent, should serve superiors) that very few of us would now find convincing. For those reasons, the Stoic account of why God permits animal pain doesn't work.

This is a problem for Stoics. Another problem involves what philosophers call "moral evil" (a.k.a. unethical acts and thoughts and all the bad things that flow from them). If, as most ancient Stoics believed, absolutely everything is foreknown and fated by God, then mustn't human crimes and immoral acts be foreknown and fated too? That seems to have been Chrysippus's view (Bobzien, *Determinism and Freedom in Stoic Philosophy*, p. 32). But then isn't God in some real sense responsible for sin and evil? And if so, mustn't all religious attempts to "justify the ways of God to man," in Milton's famous phrase, go down in flames?

The idea that God is in some significant way responsible for sin and evil seems blasphemous to many religious believers and seems clearly inconsistent with the Stoic conception of God as holy and perfectly good. So how might a good Stoic try to resolve the apparent contradiction?

Are sin and evil caused by God?

Some early Stoics, like Cleanthes, refused to admit that human wrongdoing is in any sense willed by God, in effect denying that all human choices are fully predetermined. Others took the bold step of denying that there is any genuine evil in the universe at all. Epictetus leans in this direction, as does the Christian Platonist Boethius (d. 524), in his hugely influential *The Consolation of Philosophy*. "If you could see the plan of Providence," Boethius argues on largely Stoic grounds, "you would think there was no evil anywhere" (4.205).

WARNING

Later Christian philosophers would try to deny God's responsibility for whatever evil there is by distinguishing different senses in which God does or does not "will" sin and evil. One common solution was to distinguish God's "perfect will" (roughly, what he ideally desires to happen), his "efficacious will" (what he causes to happen), and his "sovereign will" (what God ordains to occur, either by way of permission or positive approval). On such an account, it can be claimed that God does will sin in his sovereign will (he permits and ordains it for the sake of some larger good, while neither directly causing it nor approving of it), but does not will sin in either his perfect will (ideally, God would prefer that creation be completely sin-free) or his efficacious will (God is never the direct cause of sin, though he does sometimes permit it and, in fact, causally "concurs" in it by maintaining the physical conditions necessary for the sin to occur). Whether distinctions of this sort succeed in exonerating God from all responsibility for sin and evil is a matter of continuing debate. How would you weigh in, dear reader?

In "On Providence," Seneca hints at one strategy that some might find attractive. Perhaps God does will and even cause certain kinds of evils, but for fully justifiable reasons such as to provide opportunities for moral growth. Perhaps a perfect God would not merely allow, but directly cause, certain kinds of evils as long as those evils were needed for the achievement of higher-order goods, such as the attainment of Stoic Sagehood. Philosopher John Hick (1922–2012), in his influential "soul-making" solution to the problem of evil, offers an account along those lines. According to Hick, evil exists to allow for the possibility of moral and spiritual growth through our own freely chosen responses to struggles, hardships, and dangers. This universe seems pretty poorly constructed if it was designed to be a pain-free, pleasure-filled paradise. But if it was designed as a theater of "soul-making" in which free beings potentially can grow, both ethically and spiritually, by grappling with real challenges and adversities, it seems far better designed. Or so Hick and Seneca propose.

Stoic Fate and Passivity

One final knotty question: Does the Stoic doctrine of fate, as some have suggested, encourage a dangerous kind of passivity? As Cicero notes, one common objection to the Stoic view of fate was that it saps motivation and implies, or can easily induce, a kind of unhealthy do-nothing resignation or passivity. How so? Suppose you're worried you might have a fast-growing, fatal brain tumor and wonder whether you should see a doctor. Then you reflect that everything in the future is fated, including whether or not you will soon die of a brain tumor. So, you reason like this:

1. Either I'm fated to die of a brain tumor or I'm not.

2. If I am fated to die of brain tumor, then going to the doctor will be pointless. (I'll kick the bucket regardless.)

3. If I'm not fated to die of a brain tumor, then going to the doctor will also be pointless. (Since then, there'd be no tumor for her to cure.)

4. So, either way, it's pointless for me to go to a doctor.

5. Therefore, I'm not going to a doctor; I'll just lie in bed, eat some munchies, and see what fate brings.

Here we have a version of what the ancients called "The Lazy Argument," and it's clearly a lame bit of reasoning that would, if sound, justify a kind of a slug-like passivity in all areas of life. But where exactly does the argument go wrong?

As Chrysippus points out, the Lazy Argument confuses Stoic fatalism (the view that all events are predetermined by divine selection and foreknowledge, and the causal nexus of fate) with the extreme form of fatalism discussed earlier that claims that fated events will occur *no matter what anybody does to avoid them*. As Stoicism scholar Donald Robertson notes, "Events are not predetermined to happen in a particular way, *regardless* of what you do, but rather *along with* what you do." Chrysippus expressed this point by saying that some things — like going to the doctor and hopefully finding out that you don't have cancer — are "co-fated" to occur.

Recognizing this, the ancient Stoics did not favor lazy, inactive, do-nothing lives. They strongly encouraged energetic and dedicated lives of service for what we think of as the common good. As they saw it, labor for a better world, not Jabba-the-Hut-like passivity, is what "the Fates" decree.

Divine Providence

For Stoics, fate is closely connected to the idea of Providence. As we saw in Chapter 6, they believed that the Logos has not only generated the material universe out of its own fiery substance, but that it actively, wisely, and benevolently guides, rules, and pervades the cosmos in order to fulfill its beneficent and wise plan for the entirety of things. This is what the Stoics called Providence, and it includes three basic parts: The wise and good Logos . . .

>> Foresees all things

>> Actively governs and controls all things

>> Beneficently cares for all things for the overall, long-term good of the cosmos

So defined, Stoic Providence sounds a lot like Stoic fate, but the Stoics seem to have thought of them slightly differently. As Boethius explains in his classic Stoic-inspired discussion of fate, foreknowledge, and free will in *The Consolation of Philosophy*, fate, as the ever-evolving causal nexus, is constantly changing and deals only with changeable things, whereas Providence is immutable and applies to things that are eternal and immutable (like God's knowledge of mathematics) as well to as objects that change and come into and go out of existence (like snowflakes and people). Speaking somewhat loosely, we might say that Providence is a kind of blueprint that exists eternally and immutably in the mind of God, whereas fate is the ever-changing actualization of that blueprint in time.

As noted earlier, the ancient Stoics were cosmic optimists who believed that God's providential plan for the universe is the best possible plan there could be. We live in a world in in which all that comes about happens for the best, and all evils (if there are any true evils) are necessary means to higher goods that fully justify them. Such is the sunny — some might say pollyannish — vision of Stoic Providence. Is it believable?

We know from Cicero that the Stoics argued at great length for their claim that the universe *must* have been created by a benevolent Intelligent Designer. Look how orderly and beautiful the cosmos is! Look at the starry heavens, the smiling fields, the wholesome air, the sparkling rivers, the wonderful abundance and variety of living beings! Consider the lowly pig, how easily it is raised and how quickly it can be fattened up into juicy pork chops! Earth is a garden and the cosmos a shining temple of awe-inspiring order and beauty! Who can deny that all of this was the product of a supremely good and wise Divine Designer?

Here the Stoics are offering a version of an argument for God's existence that later came to be called "the argument from design." In broad strokes, the argument goes like this:

1. The universe displays great order, beauty, harmony, and apparent design.

2. The best explanation of this great order, beauty, and so forth is that the universe was made by an Intelligent Designer (God).

3. So an Intelligent Designer (God) probably exists.

Though many religious believers today find such arguments convincing, most philosophers think that they have been fatally weakened by the progress of modern science, especially by Darwin's theory of evolution. Even before Darwin, however, Stoic-like theories of cosmic optimism were powerfully critiqued by Enlightenment thinkers like Voltaire (d. 1778) and David Hume (d. 1776). In his classic *Dialogues Concerning Natural Religion* (1779), Hume points out that all theories that we live in "the best of all possible worlds" founder on a close examination of the actual course of nature and human affairs. Look closely, Hume writes, at what actually occurs in those "smiling fields" of which the Stoics spoke:

> A perpetual war is kindled amongst all living creatures. Necessity, hunger, want, stimulate the strong and courageous: fear, anxiety, terror, agitate the weak and infirm. The first entrance into life gives anguish to the new-born infant and its wretched parent: weakness, impotence, distress, attend each stage of that life: and 'tis at last finished in agony and horror . . . The stronger prey upon the weaker, and keep them in perpetual terror and anxiety. The weaker too, in turn, often prey upon the stronger, and vex and molest them without relaxation . . . And thus on each hand, before and behind, above and below, every animal is surrounded with enemies, which incessantly seek his misery and destruction.

And this is, of course, to say nothing of wars, plagues, droughts, floods, earthquakes, and other mass disasters in human affairs. For such reasons, the literary historian Basil Willey has aptly said that cosmic optimism of the robust Stoic sort is "almost impossibly hard to attain, and can never be long sustained by flesh and blood."

There is also a deeper, less obvious reason to be skeptical about Stoic Providence. Stoics claim that our cosmos is the best there could possibly be. Yet how much good does the cosmos actually contain? According to the Stoics, the only true good is virtue, so we can ask a simpler question: How much virtue does the cosmos contain? Very little, it seems. Only Stoic Sages possess actual virtue, and such Sages are extremely rare. At best, the Stoics claimed, one comes along only as often as the mythical Phoenix, that is, every few centuries. Moreover, they held, virtue is an all-or-nothing deal. Virtue and vice don't come in degrees. Only complete or perfect virtue is true virtue, and all immoral acts, no matter how minor, are totally heinous. Thus, anyone who lacks perfect virtue (that is, almost certainly everybody alive today) is totally lacking in virtue and, in fact, wholly vicious. The upshot: Our universe contains immense amounts of evil (because every living human is completely evil) and little if any good. If so, how can this possibly be the best possible world? By claiming that virtue is the only good, and then that virtue is practically nonexistent, the Stoics seem to completely undercut their belief in cosmic optimism. Their teachings seem to be self-contradictory.

In response, Stoics might claim that, actually, *plenty* of virtue exists in the universe, but only among the gods, all of whom possess complete virtue. So how much virtue exists in the cosmos as a whole, including humans and gods? That depends on how many gods there are, which even ChatGPT-4 doesn't seem to know, though the Stoics clearly believed there were tons of them (every star, for example, is a god, they thought, proving that they could indeed get some things very wrong). But regardless of how many gods exist and how blissful and virtuous they are, we can easily imagine a world in which *human* virtue was much more abundant and more easily attained. So, again, it's very difficult on Stoic premises to see how this could be an unsurpassably good world. From a human standpoint, a world in which no living human has ever done a single truly good act or even witnessed one, does not seem like a very good world. It's almost as if we're fated to think the Stoics had some revising of their views to do that they never quite got around to. But maybe that's our fate, too.

As we'll see in later chapters, most modern-day Stoics drop all talk of fate, Providence, and cosmic optimism. For reasons we have discussed, that's probably a good thing. On such matters, a less speculative and dogmatic Stoicism is a better Stoicism and likely makes for a better world. Maybe if we could just get them to loosen up a bit, we'll have some great wisdom we can use. So stay tuned and read on.

3 Stoic Ethics

Chapter **8**

Virtue as the Goal of Life

The ancient philosopher Heraclitus (c. 500 BCE) was one of the chief guiding lights for the Stoics. Among his most famous statements is the stark declaration that "Character is destiny." The Stoics agreed and put issues of character at the center of their thought. A core belief in Stoicism related to this is that nothing is truly good and always beneficial to us except moral *virtue*, which is the positive foundation of character. Virtue is deemed to be a quality or state of being that alone provides for the peak of human excellence.

A corollary belief is that nothing is genuinely bad and harmful to us but moral *vice*. This is then taken to be an attribute or state of being that represents the worst of human imperfection. The main choice in life as the Stoics see it is between virtue and vice. Everything else is secondary. In fact, nothing else matters at all in their view except as it connects with one or the other of these moral opposites.

This issue is the touchstone for all of life. It's crucial to grasp such a key principle because it will then shed light on much else that we find in Stoic thought. In this chapter, we explore the nature of virtue and the crucial role it plays in Stoicism. We look at the concept itself and examine the way it has been developed to fill out what Stoic philosophers have felt to be of the utmost importance for living a good and happy life.

Virtus and Arete

There are many common words that nearly everyone seems to think they understand, but when asked what such a word means, they'll find it hard to give a good definition. One of those words is surely "virtue." If you ask people what it signifies, they may say things like "decency," or perhaps "modesty," or a bit more broadly, "goodness." For a very long time, since at least the days of Shakespeare, many have associated the word with a carefully guarded attitude toward sexuality, almost as if it was a synonym for chastity or even something like a "hypervigilant virginity." But in our time, it's not at all used in that way. And in a world full of uncertainty, we're virtually certain of this — which we could not resist saying, because there's an odd connection between the virtual and the virtuous, one that we'll explain in a second.

Virtus

The English word "virtue" is derived from the ancient Latin *virtus,* a term that meant strength, power, or prowess. That in turn derives from the shorter Latin *vir* that meant, simply, a man. The word virtue is used in this tradition as conveying all those qualities that are distinctive to being a good, strong, or complete man. And later in history, it came to denote everything needed to be a complete human being, regardless of gender. But the original connotation had to do with the qualities required at the time, particularly in men, to attain peak effectiveness in such challenges as military battle. In warfare, a man needed to be honest with himself and his comrades about their difficulties and options, courageous in the face of danger, fair and just in treatment of his fellow soldiers, and moderate in his desires and needs. His overall virtue was the complete cluster of such qualities that made him strong.

Over centuries, the sense of a person's "effectiveness" in various pursuits and in meeting challenges grew to be an ever more important connotation of *virtus* and, in the later tenth century, this was also true of the derived French term *vertu* or *virtu.* Something was viewed as "virtuous" if it had the needed effects. And it was then only a short hop to using a twist on the root word to give us the terms "virtual" and "virtually." An elected president who was said to be a "virtual dictator" acted in such a way as to have the effects of a dictator, or autocrat, in his methods. And in our time, the ideal form of "virtual reality" is meant to have some of the power, or at least many of the effects, of a physical environment. Likewise, the "virtual meetings" that we attend now on our online platforms have in principle enough of the feel and effects of in-person meetings to be judged effective. They have that power.

It's interesting that as the word "virtue" has fallen out of most ordinary conversation (except perhaps in the odd, flippant use, like the wine drinker's "Ah, to enjoy the virtues of the vine!"), other terms with the same etymology, such as "virtual" and "virtually," have ascended to common use.

Arete

The even more ancient Greek word that the later Romans translated as *virtus* and that we also typically read as "virtue" is the philosophically very important term *arete* (AH-reh-TAY), which was used by Greek philosophers generally to refer to the ideal of peak human excellence. *Arete* is also often described as denoting a maximum of ability or even a superior potency for proper action. It's meant to involve excellence in all things essentially human, from the moral and intellectual to the physical. The reference of the term encompasses the full range of qualities thought to facilitate the highest form of human potential and achievement.

Even though it was a major philosophical term in the ancient world, *arete* had associated with it only a minor goddess by the same name, who was said to be the divinity of both knowledge and virtue. And that's an apt combination, since Stoics view virtue to be a form of knowledge and vice to be a sort of ignorance, or cognitive error. The ancient term was also employed to describe both nonhuman objects as well as human beings, and in that usage was always associated with the fulfilling of a natural or intended purpose, or else with some performance at peak excellence. *Arete* could then be used of a horse or hammer to convey appropriate forms of excellence or performance.

One of the authors of this book has an amazing friend, Brian Johnson, who spreads wisdom in the world and has the transliterated Greek word ARETE tattooed in thick block letters on the inside of his forearm, one inch tall and four inches across (see Figure 8-1). Throughout each day, he's reminded by the bold ink of the vital importance of this concept for his life as the founder and CEO of the Heroic Public Benefit Corporation — teaching ancient and modern practices of excellence in our lives — and as a man, husband, father, and productive citizen who deeply cares about others. Arete counts. Virtue matters.

FIGURE 8-1:
A not-so-subtle
reminder that
virtue matters.

Courtesy of Brian Johnson

Virtue at the Center

One quick characterization of virtue, also known as "moral virtue," is that it's the overall cluster of strengths or personal powers we can bring to any challenging situation. Another description would be that virtue is the innermost set of positive habits or dispositions of any human being that help bring out the best in us as well as in others as we interact with them and the world around us. Think of the few people you may have met along the way who seem to represent the ideal of what a person should be — gracious, kind, brave, resourceful, rational, resilient, generous, and strong, to mention just a few peak qualities. These are virtuous individuals.

May the Force be with you

The ancient Stoics saw virtue as a key characteristic of God, or Zeus, properly understood as the Logos or rational guiding Force of the universe. So, "May the Force be with you" is for Stoics no mild expression of blessing. It's the invocation of a great power for good. Traditional Stoics believe that by the proper use of our reason, a sort of divine spark and force implanted within us, we can discover that virtue is what best links us with the workings of the Logos, the logical goodness behind all things, as well as connecting us deeply and appropriately with all else. Reason will also show that virtue alone helps us live boldly and properly in this world, which is a complex reality that's undergirded at the deepest level by both reason and virtue. Remember the claim that "Character is destiny." We could express the Stoic view of virtue with a parallel claim that "Virtue is victory." What that means will become clear as our analysis proceeds.

It should be pointed out of course that in addition to "virtue" in a singular form, we can also properly speak of "the virtues" in the plural, using this phrase to refer to the full range of individual properties like honesty, fairness, justice, compassion, and courage that are all forms of virtue, are often known as individual virtues, and so are each virtuous to embody or have. A virtuous person will then be an individual who has and lives the full array of human virtues. And that's what the Stoics considered to be virtually divine.

Classic Stoics also believed in what has been called "the unity of the virtues," a conviction that you can't truly have any individual virtue without having them all. So, if a person seems to be brave but is not also honest, just, and compassionate, he or she is not genuinely courageous after all, but is merely exhibiting a counterfeit of that virtue. Likewise, you can't truly have the virtue of honesty without embodying courage, self-control, and so on. The idea is that the moral life at its finest is not just a hodgepodge of varied characteristics but a tightly woven fabric of essentially connected qualities. We return to this intuitively fascinating view of virtue in another part of this book (Chapter 17).

Vice: The opposite of virtue

Vice is correspondingly to be understood as something like the opposite of virtue, and as the moral weakness that prevents people who are mired in it from attaining any overall version of proper human excellence. The vices would then be those individual qualities that detract from our divinely intended purpose, and can encompass such things as deceitfulness, unfairness, unkindness, a lack of self-control, and cowardice.

Stoics believe that it's in the end entirely up to you whether you live a life of virtue or vice, and that this result is brought about by your choices every day. Virtue cannot be given to you or taken away by any power other than your own soul or mind, the governing element of your deepest self. It's always an inside job.

Can you progress toward virtue?

The Stoic ideal of a perfectly wise and virtuous person is an individual known as a Sage. And as in the case of all ideals, the founding Stoics admitted that it's hard to find a true Sage in the world. But they liked to suppose that, even though such a person might be as rare as the mythical Phoenix, a bird said by legend to be found only once every five hundred years or so at most, it's still possible to be a Sage, and it's an ideal worth striving for in any case, despite any strong headwinds of improbability.

For those of us who fall far short of the absolute ideal envisioned by the Stoics, there is an assurance that we can still make progress in its direction by thinking and doing the right things as a matter of course. But as a side note, any progress toward ideal virtue or in the direction of perfection in the virtues was not understood by the founding Stoics as a matter of growing in wisdom, or justice, or courage, for example, from one level to the next. They didn't think that individual virtues had degrees or levels, but rather that they are more starkly all-or-nothing affairs. You can't be a little courageous, a bit just, or partially moderate. You either are in fact brave, or you're not. You treat others justly, or you don't. You approach life in a spirit of moderation, or not.

REMEMBER

While progress cannot then be made within a virtue from one degree to the next, it can be made toward a virtue. Stoics with this view can then say of someone, sensibly, "Well, she's not courageous yet, but she's well on her way." Or "He's growing in the direction of moderation." And growth in the direction of a virtue shows that you're on the right path.

VIRTUE SIGNALING

In the 21st-century public square, especially online, the term "virtue" has recently received a surprising new life, but not in a particularly virtuous way. We have in mind the phrase "virtue signaling." It's typically defined as "the public expression of opinions or sentiments intended to demonstrate one's good character or social conscience, or the moral correctness of one's position on a particular issue." Most definitions give the impression that virtue signaling is a matter of showing off to political friends and irritating opponents by a pretense of moral concern. The phrase is a label that tends to be used more by one side of current political debates than the other whenever issues of justice, fairness, or goodness arise. It's typically meant to undercut a discussion by attributing to the other side a form of insincere "moral showboating."

Any activity or statement portrayed as virtue signaling is being characterized as a piece of rhetorical "performance art" intended to convince others that the person sending the signal is enlightened, morally astute, superior, and on the right side of history. The problem with this usage of such a core ethical word is that any quick check of political debates on social media where controversial moral issues arise will reveal that most honest attempts to address such topics in a sensitive way are now too easily dismissed by the demeaning charge of virtue signaling. And the allegation is typically from someone who dislikes a moral position as being economically inconvenient or personally disturbing, but rather than raising a serious objection merely uses this charge as a quick tactic to change the subject from whether a position is true to whether the motives of the person who made the statement of concern are themselves worthy.

Real virtue signaling, as an insincere or hypocritical and manipulative activity, is of course not virtuous at all, and ought to be discouraged. But the danger in our time is that the increasingly common claim that someone is engaged in such behavior is often itself used manipulatively for non-virtuous purposes. Its widespread employment has made many people more reluctant to discuss real issues of moral virtue in public. And in a deeper irony, those who most frequently lodge the charge of virtue signaling are often themselves displaying such vices as anger, hostility, and unfairness in their own rhetorical performance, in a sort of "vice signaling" that strangely upends the typical moral calculus to encourage qualities more involved in moving toward social disruption and "power politics" than in arriving at moral truths and sensible policies. The Stoics would find this to be decidedly unvirtuous. On their view, all issues of moral concern ought to be assessed rationally, on their merits. A proper engagement over virtue is at the center of what's required for a good life together in flourishing communities. When we allow any tendencies in public political discourse to flip these things around, we court serious trouble.

Happiness and Virtue

Virtue is power. It's an inner source of effectiveness in the outer world. And according to several ancient philosophers, including the Stoics, it alone brings us the great gift of true happiness, or peak flourishing. The Greek word for that gift was *eudaimonia* ("you-day-MON-ee-a"). Etymologically, the word means a "good or flourishing (*eu*) spirit (*daimon*)." It's most often translated into English as "happiness," but given common modern assumptions about what it is to be happy, that can be a bit misleading.

WARNING

Eudaimonia is not merely an inner sense that all is well in your soul and your immediate environment, nor is it simply about positive feelings of pleasure or delight, or even a temporary touch of giddiness. It doesn't require a smile on your face or a lightness of being in your heart, and it isn't necessarily manifested by a cheerful tone of voice and a bounce in your step. A few modern translators render *eudaimonia* as "well-being" and a couple of others as "flourishing," or even "blessedness," but most stick to "happiness," and some explain that this is simply because there's an easily available related adjective, which is of course "happy." It was important to the Stoics that we be good and that we be happy, and they believed that the former alone could guarantee the latter. But modern thought has tended to be a bit different.

TIP

There are serious research centers, bestselling books, podcasts, and internet sites dedicated to understanding happiness and identifying its components and causes, or what can lead to being happy. The advice they give is well known:

(1) Cultivate great relationships; (2) Craft a sense of meaning in your life; (3) Exercise regularly; (4) Eat well; (5) Sleep properly; (6) Find purposeful work you enjoy; (7) Spend quality time in nature; (8) Have a pet or hobby you love; (9) Learn

to relax; (10) Try to eliminate anger and worry from your life; (11) Keep a gratitude journal, or just spend time being grateful; (12) Pursue interests and goals that are right for you.

Do these things and maybe you won't have to buy so many of the various happiness books or visit the numerous websites on human felicity. You might not even need to go on that happiness retreat you may have been considering. But then again, it can't hurt, and it's likely in a beautiful place, so feel free to sign up after all. And send us a postcard. We'll be happy for you.

We know the things that happy people tend to have in their lives, as well as the things they regularly do, and we have reason to believe that these things can function either as causes of happiness or as components of it. But do we have a more general understanding of what happiness is? We may, indeed.

First, though, you might have noticed that the list of things to do if you want to be happy, the list we've just given as a framework of 12 Steps summing up most of the current research and recommendations, doesn't mention things like great wealth, fame, social status, or power. And these relatively rare possessions are oddly often thought of by those who lack them to be among the very few actual guarantees of happiness. Yet, many who have chased these things and seem to have them well in hand aren't happy at all and will often confess in private to their unhappiness, or even to a measure of misery.

But most of these rich, famous, high-status, and powerful people, rather than realizing they were on the wrong path if their real quest was to be happy, and as a consequence then dismissing wealth, fame, status, and power as either causes or components of happiness, will rather surprisingly often conclude that they clearly just don't yet have enough of these things, and so they gear up and launch out to get even more in their lives, in an endless cycle of what will turn out to be a completely futile endeavor, a treadmill to nowhere.

MONEY, FAME, AND HAPPINESS

The rich and famous did not have to wait until now to discover the disconnect between wealth, celebrity, status, or power and the deep goal of happiness. Pursuing the former to get the latter is a mistake that's long been understood. Marcus Aurelius reminds himself:

Up to now, all your wanderings in search of the good life have been unsuccessful. It was not to be found in the intricacies of logic or in wealth, fame, worldly pleasures, or anything else. Where, then does the secret lie? In doing what nature seeks. But how? By adopting strict principles for the regulation of impulse and action, such as rules regarding what's good or bad for us. So, for example, the rule that nothing can be good for a man unless it helps to make him just, self-disciplined, courageous, and independent, and nothing can be bad unless it has the opposite result. (*Meditations* 8.1)

The emperor may be the only person in history to have sought the good life or happiness "in the intricacies of logic," and it's not at all a surprise that this path failed, along with wealth, fame, and pleasure. At the end of the passage here, he talks about having come instead to see the importance of seeking virtue and avoiding vice. We keep chasing the wrong things and hoping they'll work, even when it becomes clear they don't. The Stoics wanted to get us off this false path and onto the right road of virtue. Marcus says to himself in another passage of his journal:

It's perfectly possible to be godlike, although unrecognized as such. Always keep that in mind and remember that the needs of a happy life are very few. (*Meditations* 7.67)

In fact, he ends up agreeing with other Stoics that the needs of a happy life may just come down to one thing. And what that thing is, we'll explore fully and soon. But first, a big picture may help.

The surface complexity of happiness

In the estimation of many philosophers who have been influenced by classic sources like Aristotle, happiness isn't just a subjective *feeling* that may result from several contributing factors, but also an objective state of *being* in the world that encompasses *doing* and *becoming*, along with perhaps even a modest measure of proper *having*. One way of analyzing it in this way would be to identify various components of happiness, like:

>> Contentment: an acceptance of the present, without negative feelings

>> Fulfillment: a progressive realization of your positive potential

>> Enjoyment: an ongoing, regular experience of both pleasure and love

The idea is then that these are either individually necessary and jointly sufficient conditions for happiness (meaning that they are each needed for happiness, and together they fully deliver it), or else that they are at least strongly facilitating conditions and normal components of it that may involve or be cultivated by the various things in our 12-Step happiness list presented above. Where then is virtue? The surprise is that it may lie behind each.

Contentment

In this brief three-part sample analysis, contentment is meant to be an entirely subjective inner state of accepting the broad present moment as being what it is, and encompassing as it does the now set past from which it arose. Contentment in the precise sense intended does not require liking what's going on in the present or wanting it to continue as it is, or as it might naturally develop. The form of acceptance is simply a recognition of the present as being what it is, along with a releasing of all negative emotions and resistant attitudes about it, such as irritation, frustration, regret, resentment, bitterness, disappointment, despair, dismay, fear, anxiety, or worry.

REMEMBER

Much of wisdom is in knowing what to embrace and what to release. A form of contentment of the relevant sort here is perhaps less about embrace and more about release. It's a releasing of inner negativity and a freeing of yourself from any pressures of outer circumstances that could otherwise result in bad feelings. It's about an attitude that says, "All right. This is how things are. Now let's try to help make them what they could be."

Fulfillment

Fulfillment is very different, and yet connected. It's difficult to be fulfilled as a human being without a foundation of contentment. If contentment is about a release, fulfillment is focused on an embrace. It's about embracing a process for living in the world that yields positive results. While contentment is wholly inner and subjective, fulfillment is by contrast partly outer and objective, and then also partly inner and subjective. We should explain.

Fulfillment in its objective side involves being engaged in outer activities and relationships both at work and in your personal life that involve a progressive realization of your potential for good, both in your own growth and in your contribution to the world around you. Is your work fulfilling? Do your relationships help fulfill you as? Do they encourage you and involve a progressive realization of your positive potential? If so, you're then also likely to experience the inner and subjective side of the process, which is simply an accompanying sense or feeling of fulfillment in your life.

Enjoyment

Enjoyment is next. And it can be thought of as involving first and most readily a range of pleasures and delights, from the simplest to the more complex, subtle, and acquired. Do you enjoy your work? How about your life outside of work? Do you take pleasure in a beautiful morning or a great sunset? Do you relish any of the routines of your day, and perhaps experience a measure of joy in small things? This can be an important ingredient in living a happy life. Plus, the greater issue of love will also arise here as involving a deeper form of enjoyment, one tied in with an interplay between embrace and release, both of which are involved in genuine love, along with a vulnerability and an inner victory in your commitment to the flow of life.

This brief but complex analysis of happiness would suggest that if you regularly experience a basic contentment in the present and an ongoing process of fulfillment in your life, while enjoying a suitable sense of pleasure and love along the way, you're a happy person, flourishing and blessed. And this is a philosophical analysis that's relatively simple to grasp. But if it still seems too complicated as an understanding of happiness, Stoicism has something much more basic to offer. And it may be a big surprise.

The Stoic simplification of it all

On the classic Stoic analysis, *eudaimonia* requires just one thing. One single item alone is both necessary and sufficient for happiness. And that is virtue. If you want the ultimate and all too elusive state of maximal flourishing or deep well-being in your life, *arete* will do the job. It will suffice. You can't be happy without being virtuous, on this view, and if you are indeed virtuous, you're also guaranteed to be happy. *Eudaimonia* merely tracks *arete* and nothing more really needs to be said. But of course, that won't stop us.

REMEMBER

Do you want to be happy? Be good. Embrace virtue. That's the beginning and end of the story, according to our Stoic advisors.

Virtue and happiness coincide

Perhaps more should in fact be said, because this is not the sort of recipe for happiness that most people eventually seem to discover on their own. At least it's not a common formula discussed or recommended in our time. It's in fact initially quite stunning as an answer. It appears to circumvent the 12 Steps revealed by recent research and avoid altogether the notions of contentment, fulfillment, and enjoyment. And that seems odd. Furthermore, we should notice that the Stoics aren't just suggesting that many good people are happy and that many happy people are virtuous, and so if we want to be happy, we should likely give virtuous living at least a try. They're claiming that virtue and happiness are functionally equivalent in some deep way. To have one is an absolute guarantee of the other, almost as if they are two sides of one spiritual coin. And the side always up and in our sights is virtue.

The background of this claim is an interesting one. To the founding Stoics like Zeno, the broadest purpose for any human life is to "live in accord with nature," and by that phrase they seem to have meant both of two things. First, they believed there is a deep rationality and goodness to be found within nature in the broadest sense, and that we're to seek to live in accord or harmony with that. But then there is also a distinctive constitution within each of us, by and through which we are human beings, a more narrow *human nature* to be respected and harmoniously embodied in how we live.

Our distinctiveness as humans is our specific kind and level of reason and rationality, as will be elaborated in Chapter 13 of this book. So to live in accord with our nature is to respect and honor the guidance of reason and the reasonable requirements of healthy relationships, in which alone we can flourish. It turns out that for Stoics, reason and virtue are essentially united. To live in accordance with reason is to embrace all those qualities known as virtues, the various strengths available for flourishing in a distinctively human life. So, in this way, reason and virtue naturally track together. As we mature, we grow in our capacity for following the lead of reason and thus of virtue, unless something interferes and blocks our development. Notice that virtue as strength, or as a range or connected cluster of strengths, is all about flourishing, or well-being in the world, and this is *eudaimonia*, or happiness.

Only virtue is good, and only vice is bad

As mentioned earlier, Stoicism embraces a surprising principle that only virtue is truly good, and vice genuinely bad. The Stoic contention is that everything else that could seem to be good in some circumstances, or under certain conditions, can appear just as strongly to be the opposite in other situations. Wealth can certainly seem good. But it can also warp people's values and ruin their lives, making a wider array of temptations available and luring the newly rich to destruction. And in that case, it's bad. The same is true of fame. It can be a great resource for getting beneficial things done. But it can also be a prison, a trap, and a bad psychologically warping force in a person's life. Recent research also shows that felt power and perceived high status can have results that are functionally equivalent to limited brain damage, causing people to become more impulsive, less empathetic, oblivious to long-term consequences, and more prone to take irrational risks.

The Stoics argued that nothing can be both truly good and genuinely bad in different settings. So, their conclusion was that only those things that can be judged good and never bad can indeed actually be good. And the reverse also holds. But here's the rub. Classic Stoics seem to say that this guarantee of stable value, always the same, holds only for inner things, or interior mental states. Any external thing that can seem good in some situations can also appear bad in others. But inner things like prudential wisdom, moral care, benevolence, a concern for justice, and a sense of moderation, along with real courage, can only be strengths or goods. And the contrary or opposite vices can only be bad. There is no situation in which a genuinely unjust attitude is a good thing. All else that we typically think to be good or bad must then have instead another status, quite different, which is our next topic. But first we should consider a problem, and then tie a few threads together here.

The problem is obvious. Consider an external event like the murder of innocent civilians in wartime. That surely seems bad across all possible broader circumstances. So why not assign the moral category of bad to that external item? If we do, then not all moral good and bad is about inner things. But Stoics have an answer that we examine in Chapter 16 on the fear of death. Stoic philosophy rejects the idea that death is ever a morally bad thing. Their simplest argument is that bad things ought to be avoided, and death can't be, so death is not a bad thing, but a natural part of our life cycle in the universe. The mass murder of civilians in wartime, or any time, will involve moral badness, even true evil, but in the hearts and minds of the perpetrators, in their vices, rather than in the events of deaths themselves. That's the argument and the conclusion. And we'll scrutinize both later. But let's get back to the main claims about happiness and virtue for now.

REMEMBER

Here's the Stoic line of thought. Happiness, as an exemplary good thing, surely can't essentially depend on things that are bad. And it would make just as little sense to see it as depending on things that are neither good nor bad. So, then, happiness must depend only on other good things. But we've just seen that, according to the Stoic view, nothing is good except certain internal matters, or states of the mind or soul. We call these internal good things virtues, or in a collective sense, virtue.

It very well could be that the virtue required for happiness, the virtue that is guaranteed to produce the rare and wonderful state of *eudaimonia*, is needed for, as well as cultivated, supported, or facilitated by, matters of contentment, fulfillment, and enjoyment. It could also be that it's encouraged by some, or even all, of the 12 Steps to be found in modern happiness literature. But in the Stoic view, there is a pure simplicity beneath all this complexity: Virtue alone can guarantee happiness. So if you want to be happy, don't seek that goal by chasing external things that can't do the job, but rather by working on the inner virtue of your own soul. That is the only true and reliable path.

The Good, Bad, and Indifferent

If the original Stoics concluded that only virtue is good, and only vice is bad, this leaves us asking what the status of everything else might be. And the initially perplexing or even shocking answer is that literally all other things in the world merit the label of "indifferent." But wait. We naturally think that being alive with a measure of physical health is good, that friendship is, as well, that properly attained success in life is good, and that a reputation for trustworthiness has the same status. We think of children as a blessing, and so of course good. In fact, people even label "baked goods" as such, as well as advertising "goods and services." We say things like "You got the job you wanted? That's good, very good!"

We view meaningful work as good, but we also appreciate pleasant vacations as good. You may have a good dog, and a good, reliable car. Indoor plumbing is surely good to have, and so is electricity and a dishwasher, as well as a microwave and maybe a big-screen TV. But the Stoics are right now frowning and shaking their heads. They believe we misunderstand what it is to be good.

And consider those things in life that we believe are bad and so naturally seek to avoid, and even to eliminate from the world. We tend to consider many things other than vice to be bad and even very bad indeed, like dire poverty, poor health, forced unemployment, storm damage to property, pandemic disease, debilitating accidents, and premature death. But again, the Stoics would correct us quickly, saying we're wrong about all of this. None of these things that aren't virtues or vices are either good or bad, but rather fall into a very large and in fact enormous category of "indifferent" things.

When you first read the Stoics on this topic or come across anyone making such a claim, it's natural to suspect that they can't really mean what it seems like they're saying. How can disease or death be indifferent things, in themselves, or to us? How can good health, by contrast, or friendship, or a great job be a matter of indifference? Did the Stoics just hang around too many Cynics who perversely seemed to pride themselves on rejecting most normal values? Or is something deeper going on here?

We may be able to understand the motives and reasons behind this categorization and what exactly it is that Stoics are telling us with it by looking a bit more into what the category of "indifferent things" seemed to mean to them from early on in their thought. The word "indifferent" is nowadays defined in many but related ways. *Merriam-Webster* starts off by specifying a meaning having to do with the attitude of a human being, "marked by a lack of interest, enthusiasm, or concern for something: apathetic." But then the second definition right after that is "being neither good nor bad," and later we see "characterized by lack of active quality: neutral." Vocabulary.com throws in "lacking importance." And we should mention one other source simply because it's reliably so good (sorry, classic Stoics, as we persist in our error): *The Compact Oxford Dictionary* reinforces the objective meaning of "neither good nor bad."

There are clearly many facts in the world, like whether the number of hairs on your head right now is even or odd (an example even Stoics oddly love), or how many grains of sand happen to exist right now on American beaches that, as true realities, are presumably neither good nor bad, and so are in that precise sense indifferent. And then, correspondingly, we can and probably should take the attitude toward those facts of being ourselves indifferent about them. But disease and death, as well as friendship and health, can seem very different from the properly indifferent.

What's different about the Stoic indifferent

We can reasonably suppose that when the early Stoics introduced the category of indifferent things, calling them "indifferents," (*adiaphora*), they clearly meant in doing so to label all things external to the mind as neither good nor bad. The Greek *adiaphoron* and its plural *adiaphora* come from the privative *a* ("without") and *diaphora*, which meant "difference" or "differentiated," as in "cannot be morally differentiated," or "making no difference to happiness." It's clear that in their use of the term the Stoics were talking first about things themselves rather than our attitude toward those things. Yet the two category assignments do track in parallel. Attitude should reflect reality.

If you see something, an object or option, as indifferent, categorizing it as such, then that's exactly what you're most likely to be or feel in response to it. But it is also possible to leap beyond indifference and take a keen interest in something prior to knowing whether it's either good or bad or indifferent.

Imagine that you've read about poisonous spiders in your part of the country, have sometimes found spiders in your bedroom, and worry about the confluence of these two facts. Now, suppose that tonight you notice a dark insect of some sort on the ceiling of your bedroom right above your pillow at bedtime, just before turning out the light. You can certainly leave any attitude of indifference behind and take a keen interest in this little thing before you come to know whether it's something you'd naturally want to think of as good or bad. Is it a cute ladybug just visiting, or a dangerous arachnid ready to drop onto your soon-to-be-sleeping head? The Stoics think that in terms of your own peace of mind, it should really make no difference what insect it is. The answer is indifferent, meaning, neither good nor bad. It's up to you to dismiss it from the realm of your concern and to be untroubled by whatever a closer look might reveal. It's literally without a significant difference whether the insect is harmless or harmful. But that just sounds wrong.

TIP

Here's a key to what they meant: What the Stoics had in mind with this category is that the things they label as indifferent lack *moral value*, or importance relative to ultimate issues of happiness, or *eudaimonia*, which they see as strictly about inner things like courage and justice.

That's why all external objects and facts are said to be neither good nor bad, because both those evaluative categories in Stoic thought are intended to refer strictly to moral status. Things are good if and only if they are virtuous or are inner states that can help you with virtue, or yet are inner matters that result from an exercise of virtue. And things are bad if they are vicious, or are inner matters that cause vice or result from it, or can harm you regarding issues of virtue and vice, negatively influencing whether you are virtuous. No poisonous spider can force you to abandon virtue in favor of vice, so no such thing is bad. That's the Stoic view. But looking for a safe device of insect transport to the great outdoors is another issue altogether.

The preferred and dispreferred

There's a crucial twist to be added. Most ancient Stoics came to concede that, whether external matters have anything intrinsically or essentially to do with virtue and happiness or not, there are many such things that seem to protect or support our natural physical existence and deserve a special value category. In so far as a proper concern for self-preservation appears to be reasonably implanted by God or nature in every living creature and is discoverable by our reason to be of value in that sense, we have a reason to value and seek these things that tend to provide safety rather than not caring about them.

The Stoics who recognize this truth, and so this further category of things, which would surely include such matters as physical health, bodily strength, safe living conditions, and other resources that help to sustain life, add the important idea that some morally indifferent things can properly be thought of as naturally "preferred" and others as naturally "dispreferred," or "to be rejected." A poisonous spider poised over your pillow ready to drop on your sleeping head could then rightly be thought of one of the many "dispreferred indifferents" in our world. It's perfectly reasonable to take an interest in such things and seek to avoid them. And yet, while the phrase "dispreferred indifferents" may strike you as itself a dispreferred indifferent that you'd very much like to reject rather than carry around in your normal vocabulary, it does seem to acknowledge, along with its sister phrase, some sort of value, positive or negative, to be seen in a great many external things.

TIP

The category of a preferred indifferent is tailor-made for recognizing a positive value for things that support or enhance life, whether they connect in any direct way with virtue and vice, or whether they are strictly required for the elevated form of happiness, or *eudaimonia*, that the Stoics hold up as the supreme goal of human life. So you can be a Stoic without feeling like you'd end up without any rational decision-making tools if offered a choice between drinking a glass of pure cold water or a tumbler of deadly poisoned wine. You wouldn't have to think, "Well, it makes no difference whatsoever." And that's surely a good thing, or at least a preferred indifferent.

On Stoic physics, or their comprehensive account of our world, we're meant to be reasonable beings. This is why we have the divine spark of the Logos, or Divine Reason, in us. And we're designed by Zeus, or the Logos, to be social beings as well, ideally to live together in harmony. The additional evaluative categories of the preferred and dispreferred are intended to capture the positive or negative value of the otherwise morally indifferent things in the world that might help or hinder our experiences of, or a properly dutiful behavior around, both our use of reason and our participation in positive relationships. So, it's proper to pursue such things as safety, health, and bodily fitness as preferred indifferents for yourself and others. It's rational to avoid bodily harm and physical diseases as dispreferred indifferents.

But all such external things have a value category of their own other than strictly "good or bad," to reinforce the determination by Stoic thinking that they are not intrinsically relevant to or necessary for happiness, for which, again, virtue is said to be sufficient. Stoics insist that you can possess heaps of naturally valuable preferred indifferents and yet not be happy, or else exist without most such things and still experience happiness. There can be misery in a palace and happiness in a prison.

REMEMBER

Those who chase externals aiming for happiness are pursuing things that are literally indifferent and strictly irrelevant to their goal. We should learn from their experience, redirecting our own efforts to where they can count, refocusing on what sort of people we are inwardly, in our character, in the matters of thought, feeling, and choice that count as instances of virtue rather than vice. This is where the ultimate game of life is played well or badly. This is where our supreme state is to be discovered, and it's also interestingly where our autonomy and a form of self-sufficiency are to be found.

TIP

On the Stoic view, we are to hold tightly to the good within; release the bad thought, emotion, or impulse to action that tempts us; and approach the outer world around us with a lighter touch of commitment and feeling. Some externals can be helpful, if used properly. Others can be quite inconvenient, but even those can be used well to test and grow our virtue. Seneca once went so far as to say about even the most difficult of externals, "Disaster is virtue's opportunity." When we are properly armed with a new sense of what's most important, we can grapple productively with everything in the world, growing in our own closeness to the ideal of virtue and helpfully providing for others to do so as we enjoy a sense of liberation, or freedom from worry.

One of the most prominent and almost revered of books about Stoic philosophy in recent decades may be *The Inner Citadel* (Harvard University Press), by the late Pierre Hadot, a French historian of philosophy who was fascinated by the Stoics. It's in many ways a complex and classic academic reading of Marcus Aurelius's

Meditations, along with a few related Stoic philosophers. At one point in the book, Hadot writes something about the concept of indifference as quite central to Stoic thought:

> The principle of all Stoicism is, moreover, precisely indifference to indifferent things. This means, in the first place, that the only value is moral good, which depends on freedom, and that everything that does not depend on our freedom — poverty, wealth, sickness, and health — is neither good nor bad, and is therefore indifferent. (71)

Our only warning about this sentence is in a sense just a bit of a semantic concern, but one that should not be allowed to muddy the waters of our understanding. The Stoics don't exactly mean to say that "the only value is moral good." But they do mean to say that moral good or bad — namely, virtue or vice and any inner states closely related to them — are matters that are so different or distinctive in value, and are of a unique importance to us, that they cannot be weighed in value with any other items in the world. A preferred indifferent can be said to have a value, for example, regarding human survival and social duty, but that sort of value can't be weighed against the very different sort of value to be found in the moral matters of virtue and vice. That's why it can't make sense to think that if you pile up enough external things in the world, their cumulative value could be sufficient to defeat the call of virtue, or to justify any action based in vice.

Virtue and vice

Virtue and vice are in a unique category of their own. Either

A. They are, in a technical sense, strictly "incommensurable" with external things — the two sorts of matters literally cannot be compared, in terms of more-or-less on the same scale of value, or

B. The inner and the outer can be compared, but only in theory, because the inner is so far superior to the outer that no cumulative amount of positive or negative values in the realm of indifferent externals could ever equal or outweigh our higher commitment to what is truly good.

It's not altogether clear which of these alternatives traditional Stoics would endorse, and yet they're functionally equivalent for our attitudes and actions. In either case, we can assign a sort of rational use-value or preferability to external things that are labeled as "indifferent." Some are useful and reasonable to pursue, and others aren't.

But Hadot goes onto say one more thing that may cause confusion, and to clear it up can be helpful. As his very next sentence, he writes:

Second, it means that we must not make any distinction between indifferent things; in other words, we must love them equally, since they have been willed by universal Nature.

But of course, as we've just seen, many of the Stoics have indeed made a distinction between what they call indifferent things, sorting them into the two categories of preferred and dispreferred. One thing Hadot says here is correct. Stoics believe that all things in the world around us, all external events and objects, in some sense come from Nature, the Logos, or the Divine Benevolent Reason, and so are to be accepted by us as proper parts of a universe that is designed and guided by goodness and for the best. Some Stoics even go so far as to say that all things that happen or come to be are worthy of being equally loved by us, as coming from a good God. We'll look at this in more detail later. But it's important to draw another distinction here that Hadot seems to miss in this passage.

How we react to external things that happen apart from our freedom or control is one issue, but what we reasonably decide to seek or pursue is another quite distinct issue. We can perhaps learn to accept equally all that happens in the world, in one sense, without thinking that everything is equally to be sought or pursued by us as freely willing beings. Most Stoics do want to make distinctions between indifferent things, and precisely because it seems to be a requirement of reason that we distinguish those things we are reasonable in seeking from those we are more rational to avoid. When something happens outside our control that causes us dismay, the Stoics would remind us not to consider it bad, but only a dispreferred indifferent, and not to let our emotions get too worked up about it. We should learn to accept whatever is, even if we may reasonably have preferred it to be different, and however much we may want to make things better in the future, along the scale of value appropriate to such matters.

Inner and outer things

The Stoic view is that we should concern ourselves with our own inner state and emotionally accept whatever external things may happen. The extreme version of this is to embrace and even love whatever happens external to our own free-willed choice, as indeed given by God for the overall best value of the world. So even if someone punches you in the face, you're to accept that, embrace it, and even seek to love it as both allowed and somehow brought to you by the Rational Benevolent Force behind all things. The punch itself is in the category of dispreferred indifferents. You rightly and reasonably ought not to form the sort of inwardly bad intentions toward another that would result in a punch thrown out of anger or disgust. But once morally bad intentions have caused an external event — a fist hitting a face — that event is, in relation to your mind and judgment, or any other person's, merely a dispreferred indifferent, and not itself morally bad or evil. That's the view.

Moral badness characterizes an inner intention and choice, not any external deed or event. Once an act occurs in the world, once it enters the realm of externals, it has no proper moral status, though the intent and the agent behind it does. So when we naturally say of such an action, "That was a bad thing to do," all we can properly mean on the Stoic view is that it was the result of a bad intention or a bad choice on the part of the agent, or doer.

While the Stoics may never convince you to love being punched in the face, being insulted, lied to, cheated, evicted from your apartment, or forced from your job, their line of thought may help you to let go a bit, loosen up your emotional reactions and attitudes toward such things, not to resent them or worry about them, and not to become bitter over them, and so retain some measure of inner peace and happiness even in the midst of such challenges. And that alone could be a good thing. But in the end, you'll have to decide whether to go all the way with the Stoics, or just adopt some of their perspectives from the whole package of conclusions they offer. Maybe they are introducing us to some shocking truths, very different from our normal perspectives, or perhaps they had some good ideas that they may have taken too far, but that can be helpful if we borrow parts of their thought. We'll see.

The classic Stoics often say surprising things. But in the end, they're most often simply seeking to express bits of deeper wisdom that are found in many other world traditions of philosophy as well. And here the main lessons are simple. The inner is more important than the outer. We'll never get external things right until we first get internal things right. It can't be reasonable to sacrifice inner goods to get outer results. No accumulation of external things, however massive, can justify abandoning virtue and embracing vice on any occasion and however temporarily. Happiness happens within.

A good person can't be harmed

One more issue should be addressed in this connection. Among all the most puzzling Stoic pronouncements throughout their classic statements, one of the most surprising on initial exposure, at least to many people, may be their claim that a good person cannot be harmed by any other individual or force in the world. Others can certainly damage your body, which in the Stoic view is a prime possession of yours, or even kill you, ending your journey in this world by separating you from your body. But you are not simply your current body. So, what harms your body doesn't necessarily harm you.

You are the inner controlling self, will, or intelligent volition (power of choice), indwelling and enlivening the organic physical object that you rightly consider your body. The body clearly can be harmed by physical force, but you cannot. And this is because of a conclusion Stoics draw about what harm is. Harm is the degradation of an object from being what it naturally is. To harm the body is to damage or degrade it in some physical way. To harm the mind, soul, or true self, which is essentially a moral agent or doer, would require damaging it in some moral way, taking away its virtue or forcing on it some vice. But that's impossible for any external source to accomplish.

Our minds are free to embrace virtue and reject vice under any possible circumstances. Even amid severe pressures, threats, and physical dangers, the self can choose virtue and remain unharmed. Other people can spread awful rumors about you so that you lose your job and perhaps your reputation, as well as your livelihood and even lifestyle, but those rumors and losses cannot harm the core self that is you. What can? Only your own wrong choices.

REMEMBER

On a Stoic view, harm to a person, to a self or mind, always consists in moving that self from virtue to vice, and nothing outside your own free will can force that on you. No one else has that power. You can be tempted into vice, and lured into bad conduct that you freely choose through ignorance of what's best, but no one can harm you by forcing you into what's morally bad. The temptations, pressures, and threats that enter your life are then not to be feared, because they are nothing more than dispreferred indifferents that you are free to pass by or ignore. It's up to you how you choose to react to them.

Use and value

For the Stoics, the true value of most things resides not in what they essentially are, but in how we view and use them. Many things appear to us to be good or bad, but we must learn to manage those appearances, which the Stoics call "impressions." It's our "use of impressions" that constitutes a chief strength or weakness of our inner life. Most people are misled by impressions most of the time. The wise and virtuous are not. Impressions come to us, then we judge what to make of them.

Epictetus in the *Handbook* is famously reported to have said:

> It is not things themselves that disturb men, but their judgments about these things. (5)

He goes on to explain in the same passage:

> For example, death is nothing dreadful, or else Socrates too would have thought so; but the judgment that death is dreadful, this is the dreadful thing. When therefore we're hindered, or disturbed, or grieved, let's never blame anyone but ourselves, and that means our judgments.

Many of the ancient Greek and Roman philosophers, as well as wise people from other cultures, seem to have believed that the value of most things in the world should be assessed not just in general, or even regarding their potential role in our lives, but in terms of how they actually function for us. The real question then ends up being not about what things are but how we choose to use them, whether badly or well. Accordingly, Stoics stress the importance of how we "use appearances," or "use impressions." External things in the world impress themselves on our senses and our minds. What will we do with these impressions? How should we judge them? Do we run with first appearances, which is how most people act, or by contrast slow down and consider the deeper matter of how they relate to our freedom, virtue, and happiness?

Be wary of judgments

Most of us are too quick to say of developments in our lives, "This is terrible!" or "This is wonderful!" What seems awful or great may end up being very different from its first appearance, and that may in the end turn on how we choose to use the thing or occurrence. You might have heard someone in your life at some point say, "Losing my job was the best thing that ever happened to me." It's a surprisingly common judgment often given in retrospect by people who have been through that initially hard experience. They may have felt only panic, fear, and discouragement at the time they learned of their sudden unemployment, but years later they say it was the best thing that ever happened to them. Maybe it helped them break some old habits or become more creative or brave in their lives. It could have opened them to the possibility of new opportunities they otherwise would have missed.

Epictetus wants us to consider how our initial judgment of things, rather than the things themselves, can cause us distress or even, on the other hand, ecstatic enthusiasm. And the resulting agony or ecstasy can unhinge reason from its proper operation. How many major lottery winners initially exuberant about their "great luck" have come to realize five or ten years later that because of the windfall and the way they handled it, they've lost their marriage and their friends, and then also are completely broke? It's a strangely common fact. Epictetus, along with his fellow Stoics, wants us to take a breath, calm down, and free ourselves from the roller coaster of emotion that easily knocks us off a proper and reasonable path. He wants to help us rise above the rough and tumble of unpredictable fate.

But the opening statement of section 5 in the *Handbook* just quoted may present us with what philosophers call a false dichotomy. Epictetus says that it's not things themselves that disturb or bother us, but merely our judgments about those things. And you may easily find yourself wondering whether this is always and exactly true. Take a terrible, imagined case of tragedy as a test. Someone murders a good friend of yours, and you naturally feel distraught. Is it, as Epictetus says, not the murder, the objective event itself, but only your judgment about the event, that's bothering you? Is he really suggesting that if you were to take away your own negative evaluation of the event, there's nothing intrinsically wrong or negative about the event itself, and so there would be no reason at all for anyone to have an emotional reaction like dismay? Really? Or suppose a young child is harmed intentionally and grievously, and you naturally recoil in disgust at both the perpetrator and the deed. Is it only your judgment that's causing you distress and not the actual event itself? Scholars say that Epictetus often uses hyperbole in his rhetorical efforts to make a point. And here in his words we might have a major case of that. But then again, maybe not. It could be that he's completely serious and means what he says quite literally. He sometimes seems that odd a duck.

The philosopher claims that it's not things but our judgments about things that bother us. But if the thing naturally causes the resulting judgment, if the event has the inherent characteristics or qualities that naturally yield a strongly negative assessment within us, and then that negative judgment naturally causes a correspondingly emotion, how can we be told with any measure of insight both that we should live in accord with nature (a basic Stoic view) and that it's just our judgment and not the thing itself that has caused our disturbance, and so our natural judgment should be rejected?

Achieving freedom from external matters

When we read Epictetus thoroughly and carefully, there in fact seems to be more going on here than mere hyperbole. One of the reasons he may urge us to characterize all external things as "indifferent," and one of the motives he may have to seek to convince us that it's literally our typical assessments of things rather than the things themselves that trouble or disturb us, is that he seems to want to provide us with a philosophy of absolute liberation, one whose use will allow us to free ourselves completely from depending on external matters in any way for our own virtue and happiness. If it's just our judgments that trouble us, well then, we can deal with that problem by simply changing our judgments. But if external things are really at fault, namely, things and events that are literally outside our power, then we can't do much about that, unless we so diminish the perceived value of those things that it no longer makes sense to allow them any power over our emotional lives.

In fact, this concern over the idea of power is at the core of the next stage of our adventure in this book (Chapter 9). As you'll see there, Epictetus will take up the issue of power and control directly, and in line with his predecessors in Stoic thought, he'll counsel us that we should not concern ourselves with things that are outside our power, and he will make it clear that this means all external things. It will be vital for us to understand and critically evaluate this famous claim of his.

As you've seen in this chapter, he also advises us, apparently independently of considerations about what we have power over, that since externals can't in themselves deliver or destroy happiness, then for this distinct reason, we should not concern ourselves much with outer things or events. And the reasoning is clear. If our emotions depend at all on externals, we can't absolutely guarantee an avoidance of troubling emotions, feelings that might hinder or unhinge our reason and so affect our virtue and happiness. The Stoics believe that virtue ultimately depends on reason. So Epictetus, among his fellow Stoics, wants to urge us in more than one way that we need to release externals, or not consider them important enough that they can hold us hostage regarding our own happiness and supreme freedom in the world. But perhaps, with a noble goal in mind, he simply takes things too far.

Did you ever see the classic feminist movie *Thelma and Louise*? There's a famous final scene where (spoiler alert!) the title characters intentionally drive their car at high speed off the edge of a cliff. The classic Stoics can sometimes seem to be doing the same thing. They have a great idea, an important concept, and give us a needed insight about something that can be very helpful, and then they go on to drive the idea at high speed off the edge of a cliff, taking it too far. Is it mere hyperbole to get our attention? Or is there a flaw within the philosophy itself, at least in its most extreme, strict and absolutist form? Are the Stoics after all giving us powerful tools we can use every day, or rather some impossible standards that we can't live up to, and perhaps should not even attempt to meet? The answer here could go either way. Or we might decide that the answer is: both. In order to preserve your own inner freedom to be the judge, you may want to read on.

IN THIS CHAPTER

» **Understanding the dichotomy of control**

» **Digging deeper**

» **Assessing the problem of external goals**

» **Creating an alternate strategy**

Chapter **9**

Things We Can Control

D o you ever feel stressed out, anxious, or worried? And in case that question made you smile, even inwardly, maybe we don't have to ask how often you feel those emotions. But let's narrow it down for a moment to just the inner activity of worry. Assuming you do sometimes worry about things, and maybe more often than you'd like, consider this question: What do you tend to worry about the most? If you went around to your friends and asked them the same thing, you might get many different answers.

There are almost uncountably many things that spark worry in our hearts. People worry about money, health, safety, the future, their kids, their parents, their jobs, their friends, the economy, the environment, politics, pandemics, world power conflict, the weather, their travel plans, bee stings, snake bites, their reputations, accidents, their pets, the challenges of aging, the threat of AI, the possibility that their favorite stuff will get stolen, and on and on.

The American writer Harlan Ellison is often quoted for his witty and timeless observation that the two most common things in the universe are hydrogen and stupidity. The third just might be worry. The number one thing that stands between most people and some measure of inner peace seems to be exactly that: worry. It's clearly not a foundation for happiness. Add to it the inner pressure of stress and the more general state of undefined anxiety, increasingly common in our day, and you have a real mess of inner turmoil. But this is not just a modern difficulty. People worried a lot in ancient Greece and in Rome. The Stoics noticed, and it was a problem they wanted to solve.

This chapter explains one of the simplest and most powerful Stoic ideas involving a distinction that many have found liberating to consider and use in their lives. But how we use it may be a bit more complex and controversial than the idea itself. We're on the verge of something that's very interesting and helpful, and perhaps even very powerful. So let's dive in.

The Dichotomy of Control

A dichotomy is any distinction or contrast between very different or even opposite things. One of the chief Stoic ideas, sometimes even considered their main idea, is often called the "dichotomy of control" and is occasionally referred to as the Stoic fork, because it's like a fork in the road of how we should categorize things in the world. And related to this, it's also a fork in the path of potential mindsets, or attitudes of focus. One path of focus is the main way of most people; the other is the Stoic way.

This idea, or claim, will draw a vital distinction that's at the core of the great practical value to be found in Stoicism. The famous short *Handbook* of sayings by Epictetus begins with a memorable passage that presents this big idea as a vital reminder we all need. The philosopher says:

> Some things are under our control, while others are not. Under our control are judgment, choice, desire, aversion, and, in a word, everything that's our own doing. Not under our control are our body, our property, reputation, office, and in a word, everything that's not our own doing.

He goes on to suggest here and elsewhere that the things strictly under our control are by their very nature, "free, unhindered, and unimpeded" by any force outside ourselves, while the things that are not under our control are essentially vulnerable to every sort of happenstance, misadventure, interruption, external power, and hindrance. Because of their vulnerability to many other forces, the things outside our control can then spark in us such emotions and attitudes as worry, frustration, irritation, anxiety, fear, anger, disappointment, and even deep grief. They can disturb us in many ways.

TIP

Our guide then makes the suggestion that the things that are within our control are genuinely our own, our true possessions, while the many things outside our control are not. Even when we gain or attain them, they can be taken away. Consider wealth, fame, status, and power. If they ever do come to us, they can be lost. Reversals happen. And we worry about that. The very fragility of such things shows that they don't ever fully belong to us, and so our Stoic advisor is convinced that they shouldn't serve as a focus for our emotions and attitudes. His advice then is simple. We should be concerned about only the things that are within our control, while the many things outside our control should not hold our focus. We should let them go.

First, it needs to be mentioned that this is a distinction not unique to Epictetus, but one embraced by all traditional Stoics. And it's an important foundational point for much that is yet to come throughout their philosophy. In this passage that opens the *Handbook*, our advisor goes on to point out that when we confuse these two categories of things, the things we control and the things we don't, or when we act toward the latter in a way that's appropriate only to the former, we set ourselves up for big trouble.

REMEMBER

The surprise to many readers is then this simple insight: All worries, all stresses, and perhaps even all forms of anxiety depend on wanting something that isn't in our control. If we wanted only those things that are fully in our control, we could just take care of them with no worries, no stress, and zero anxiety. All these negative emotions arise when we have desires about things that aren't wholly in our power to attain or avoid. And something that's beyond our control is in that category precisely because it's inherently subject to forces that might damage it, destroy it, or keep us from either attaining it, or else avoiding it if we don't want it. And even if we have what we desire with such a thing, whether possession or avoidance, outer forces can take that away. All of this is what worries us and causes stress.

Your Wants and Your Power

You may want to be the wildly successful founder of a new start-up company. Or you want a great job. You could want to be liked by someone you've met. You may even crave a romantic relationship with this person. You might hope your podcast will hit paydirt and bring wealth and fame. You likely want to avoid all the deadly diseases and fatal accidents that happen to people every day. But none of these things is wholly within your control, so you may feel anxious in connection with one or more of them, maybe stressed, possibly worried. Epictetus wanted to offer you and all of us something better than this. He knew it wasn't within his control whether we'd take him up on the offer, and so he wasn't stressed about it. But he sought to share his advice just in case. And it's simple: We need to learn when to let go.

Think of the list of common worries that started this chapter. How much control do you have over matters of money, health, your safety from disease, accidents, violence, the future, the integrity and sustainability of the environment, the potential for world power conflict, or the weather? Epictetus wants to convince us that such things are all outside our control and that because of this important fact, we should take a very different attitude toward them than the one we properly take toward things that are genuinely and firmly within our control. Since the former are a multitude without number and the latter are few, following his advice would simplify our lives a lot. And maybe we'd have more peaceful days as a result. If the dichotomy of control can bring us a change of perspective, we might come to feel completely different about the many vicissitudes of life.

POWER AND CONTROL

In times of radical uncertainty and frequent turbulence, people often seek for some sense of control or power in their lives. This need for a feeling of power or control may be innate in us, granted by nature as an aid for our survival in the world. Babies love to see and feel themselves make things happen, however small, as a result of their own agency or power to act. It first seems to give them fascination, then delight. By making things happen, they grow in their sense of being doers in the world and not just passive observers. These are the small seeds of a need for power that we all feel early in life. Some people appear to have a much stronger need for power and control than others. This can develop from various forms of childhood deprivation or damage. A great spectrum of personalities can result from how we respond to this early need. Some people become control freaks, always seeking more power, and others seem largely to give up that quest, choosing instead to go with the flow and allow life to surprise them. But most of us are scattered somewhere in the middle of the spectrum.

We live in a world that's both supportive and dangerous. So, we most often intuitively search for where our actual power might be, among our various talents and within our circumstances, looking for the places where we can have some control to push back the fog of uncertainty, or to pull aside the thick, heavy curtain of the unknown. It's typical for a loss of control or power to spark intense anxiety, a rash of worries, and even various forms of fear, as well as other negatives like low self-esteem. A healthy measure of feeling some degree of control over our lives tends, by contrast, to ease stress and allow more of a natural inner peace.

But a few philosophers and religious thinkers have worried about our felt need for power and control. Some have even speculated that the need to feel in control may be the "original sin" represented in the beginning of the Bible through the portrayed actions of a rebellious first pair of humans who apparently felt a need for their own independent agency, along with a desire to take control and exercise their own power, even in the face of prohibitions from their Creator.

Those who are not content with the power they are naturally given, but who always seem to seek greater power over others as well as over their circumstances, often appear to degrade their own souls, corrupting their sensibilities and setting themselves up for the consequences of *hubris*, or the excessive, haughty pridefulness often pictured in ancient cautionary tales, from the *Epic of Gilgamesh* through the myths in Greek poems and plays. When the Stoics write about control and power, they typically seek to caution us about our most basic limits in the world, and what those limits should mean for how we govern our lives. They had seen plenty of *hubris* all around them, as well as the disturbing results of thinking we have power when we don't, and they wanted to help us understand the most basic issues of power and control in a liberating way.

The dichotomy of control, or the Stoic fork, this distinction first drawn between two very different kinds of things in our lives, is presented by various ancient and modern philosophers in several verbally different but roughly equivalent ways. They often distinguish variously between things in terms of the categories of:

» Things that are in our control, and things that are not

» Things that are in our power, and things that are not

» Things that are up to us, and things that are not

» Things that are our own doing, and things that are not

» Things we can totally take care of, and things that we can't

And this distinction seems to track another quite different one:

» Things that are within our minds, and things that are not

Or

» Things that are within our choice, and things that are not

Choice is here understood as the power of the will, or our ability to decide or select freely, without constraint or impediment. When we think of all the stuff that isn't under our control or power, it's always a long list involving external things outside our own minds, issues that are not wholly within the tight circle of our unhindered freedom of choice, or volition. By contrast, what is within our control is a very short list of things wholly in the mind, like the examples given by Epictetus of judgment, choice, desire, and aversion. Nothing can make us judge something to be true or good that seems to us false or bad, or the reverse. No power external to us can force a choice on us that we don't decide to make. According to the Stoics, we have control over these inner things, and not outer stuff. But is it this simple? Are they right?

Exploring the Concept of Control

Let's begin to dig a bit deeper, first with the concept of control, and especially with the extreme idea of complete control. What is complete control over anything? Maybe we can begin to get our minds around this notion by specifying that to have full control over something means

>> If you want it, there is nothing that can keep you from getting it.

>> If you wish by contrast to avoid it, there is nothing to prevent that either.

>> This thing over which you have complete control will have no feature or quality you want it not to have.

>> It will not lack any characteristic you prefer it to have.

>> It's not something that's either subject to or vulnerable to any power or force outside your explicit desires and determinations.

In other words, something within your complete control is not also within even the partial control of another person or any other kind of independent power outside you. It's totally up to you and nothing can interfere. You decide. You choose. You can make it happen or not. It's firmly within your free action and can't be changed against your will by any other force.

For example, you can choose to imagine a bright red tomato right now, and nothing can interfere with your conjuring up that mental image. It's completely within your control. It's up to you. You can make the image large or small. You can imagine moisture drops on the skin of the tomato, and nothing can change what you have conjured before your mind's eye. Your imagination is protected territory, as is the entire circle of your total control.

WARNING

These are high standards for what it means to have control over something, but they seem to be what Epictetus and other Stoics require when they talk about what's in your control, or up to you. The result of these standards is that very few things will turn out to be within your control, and because of that, you need to know what they are and use them well.

On reflection, you will quickly discover that indeed nothing satisfies such strict standards except certain things in your own mind, those mental items that are wholly up to you, like that image of a red tomato you may have formed as you read about it, but didn't have to form, however much our words seemed to suggest it. We're all suggestible, but Stoics insist that we're free to resist any suggestion in our innermost thoughts.

Value judgments, desires, and goals

The Stoics also pointed out that our judgments are ultimately up to us, meaning the interpretations or values we assign to things, whether they're internal mental items like thoughts or else external objects, people, or facts in the world. For example, we can't control what other people say but we can control what we make of it. We can't control the weather, but we can decide how to value rainy days. A travel delay that irritates or frustrates most people can be judged by a Stoic to be a chance for meditation or reading, or for having a chat with a stranger. As has often been said, we can't control what happens to us, but we can control our reactions to what happens. It's up to us how we think of things in the world, and how we then respond to them.

Epictetus suggested that your desires can also be wholly up to you, in the sense that whenever a new desire crops up in your own mind, you can choose to hold on to it and pursue it, or let it go and not follow it. He says the same thing about aversions, or those preferences of avoidance you may feel. You can come to realize that you don't like certain things, and so as a result you wish to avoid them. On realizing this about yourself, you can then freely choose whether to stick with those aversions or work to eliminate them from your mind. The first time you sampled coffee or beer, you may have had an instant aversion to the taste, as many people do, especially at a young age, but like lots of them, you may later have decided to override that reaction, or else through repeated exposure, you might have found that your tastes gradually changed and you ended up with a liking or desire for both of those beverages. It's up to you what you cultivate or resist among your desires and aversions. No one else can force you to continue with one or to drop it.

Some modern Stoics also suggest that our goals, as formed choices, are wholly up to us, understanding personal goals to be what we aim at and intend to accomplish, the things we set as a target to attain by our efforts. We don't all pursue the same things, and it does clearly seem up to us which paths in life we'll decide to follow and which we'll leave aside. Some goals, of course, may be implanted in us by nature, general aims regarding our survival needs like getting and taking in food and water. But just as obviously, there are people who go on hunger strikes, or at the end of their lives refuse even water, overriding a very strong influence and showing us the full extent of the freedom we have regarding even such naturally implanted general goals.

So, assent, value, desire, and the choosing of goals seem to be within your control. But what about those things that are not? How do you identify them? It's easy. They can be described simply as "everything else," which means all the things that exist or occur in the world outside the inner freedom of your own mind. And that's a lot more stuff, to be sure. The implications of this vast disproportionality are then extreme because our Stoic advisors tell us to focus on the things we can control and not on the things we can't, or to concern ourselves with only the former and not at all the latter. But are we really supposed to ignore in some sense everything outside our own minds, just to avoid any possible worry, anxiety, or fear? That sounds impossible. So maybe we should examine the Stoic advice here a bit more carefully.

More options about control

Some modern Stoics have pointed out an obvious complication that seems to have been overlooked by Epictetus and other classic Stoics: There aren't just two kinds of things in the world in relation to our control or power — simply the few things over which we have total control, and the other things over which we have no control at all. What about all the stuff that seems to be at least partly in our control? Maybe we need more distinctions. And, accordingly, some contemporary Stoic philosophers are now talking about "The Stoic Trichotomy," which may sound a little too much like a painful surgical procedure, but nevertheless, we can after all distinguish three different sorts of things in the world in connection with the issue of control:

>> Things completely in our control or power

>> Things completely outside our control or power

>> Things partly within our control or power

And ultimately, then, following this way of thinking a little farther down the road it's opened up to us, we can come to suspect that what we may need isn't as simple as even a threefold list of categories, but something more like a broad spectrum of real possibilities, beginning at one extreme and ending at an opposite yet equal extreme. All things in the world may fall somewhere along a spectrum that looks like this, relative to your personal power:

>> Total control

>> Partial control

>> Direct influence

>> Indirect influence

>> No control or influence

We can even imagine this spectrum as being even more nuanced and having many more gradations along the way, both in terms of what's possible and what we have evidence to think is possible:

- » Things completely under my control
- » Things partially under my control
- » Things I can't control at all but may somehow affect
- » Things I can't directly affect but might indirectly influence
- » Things I can at least try to do that might have some small relevance
- » Things wholly outside my control and I should just give up

Maybe there are many things over which we don't have complete control, but only a form of partial control. And philosophers enjoy crazy examples, so consider this. Bob would like it to be true that two people are very soon thinking about the brilliant color of his new shirt, which is a bright, scintillating blue. Since he's only one person and not two, he doesn't have complete control over this desire coming true. He can completely see to it only that one person is thinking soon about the color of his shirt — he himself. But if he can persuade his friend Susan to think about it too, he'll get his wish. And yet, as persuasive and influential a guy as he may be, he doesn't have anything like control over what Susan thinks. He can have a chat with her and point out the amazing color of the new shirt and try to get his wish to come true that two people will be thinking about it, but especially if the chat is by phone or text and not in person (where the shirt would be right in front of Susan, properly placed for her desired attention), he can't guarantee that result. And complete control is about guarantees.

Imagine, though, that Bob wants to do what he can, and so he tries hard to work his magic quickly on Susan with all his wily ways of persuasion, vividly describing the shirt to her, and he thereby actually convinces her to think about the striking color of the shirt for a bit, while doing such thinking too. Then he's gotten his wish, and yet it's a situation over which he didn't have full control, but only a partial control that had to be augmented by a measure of weaker direct influence. It's a good example of silly made-up stories whose only value is to help make a philosophical point.

There are many other things over which Bob, and you, and the rest of us, may have no version of control, but only direct influence, or even some version of influence weaker than that, a more indirect form, in which, for example, you seek to convince your friends to try to persuade their friends (people you don't even know), to go and get a copy of this book at their favorite bookstore. And if you're successful, we the authors will be grateful for the enhanced sales. It's a result that you did not and could not literally control, but you can have some influence over the matter, and seek to use it, for which we thank you. And you can succeed with that effort, to our great delight.

This may be a model for a lot of our activities in the world. We don't in fact control very much at all, but we often can have more influence than we think, as others exercise their own freedom to choose how to respond to our efforts at persuasion and influence, perhaps going on to use their own. We operate all over the spectrum of control and influence every day. So, it's important to get clear on why Stoics like Epictetus would advise us to back off, retreat within, and concern ourselves only with the few things we can completely control.

The inner citadel or fortress

The Stoics want us to have a place of peace and power inside ourselves, a spiritual fortress or inner citadel within our souls that cannot be breached. In most of the world, there are very few actual guaranteed certainties — some say just death and taxes, but there are a few Silicon Valley billionaire tech founders now working on how to eliminate even those. Our Stoic guides want to help us find some true guarantees that will help us have better and happier lives, and especially a form of stable comfort and assurance amid the craziness of fate or fortune. They'd love to convince us there is available deep within us a safe retreat, a place of peace and power.

And to be sure, these things — emotional peace and inner power — are both important in life and far too neglected in our busy time. They are wonderful things that can be the source of many other great benefits as well, and they both seem to be at the core of a good and happy life.

We all need a sense of agency or personal power, and also a measure of inner tranquility in order to feel, do, and be our best. We need to find our proper source of power for good, and to avoid the many distractions and emotions that would impede our best use of it. Far too many people seem to be distracted by things over which they have no control or influence, endlessly worried by them, and prevented by this from doing what they actually could be accomplishing for their own benefit and the greater good of the world.

A fixation on externals outside your full control may seem to be the path of the peak achiever and the world conqueror, but ironically it can be extremely disempowering in its side effects. An obsession on external results can actually erode your effectiveness while all too often taking away a more powerful and natural state of mental and emotional calm. Why indeed should anyone spend so much time worrying about what they can't do much about? Why not fix our attention instead on what we can achieve? And if that's entirely or even mostly inner stuff, well, then so be it. We'll turn within and enjoy some serenity while the rest of the world goes nuts. But maybe, just maybe, we don't need to go to such an extreme here to get the job done.

NEEDLESS WORRY

"Nothing in the affairs of men is worthy of great anxiety." —Plato (*Republic*, Book 10)

One of the co-authors of this book had been invited to be the featured keynote speaker at a big celebration held by a financial services company. The day before the event, in the large auditorium where all the festivities would take place, the CEO of the organization seemed to be in a state of high anxiety about all the last-minute preparations going on, as he made his way from one responsible person to another. His tone of voice and face conveyed big worries. So, when he came over to his just-arrived and now smiling philosopher to offer a terse greeting, some cheerful words intended to help calm him were confidently spoken with a smile: "One thing you don't have to worry about for tomorrow is me." The CEO replied, "Whenever anybody says something like that, I really worry." In the fun conversation that followed, this highly successful leader explained, "It's my job to worry. That way, everything gets taken care of, and things go well."

Many people have that same belief. It's their job to worry. But on analysis, what's really their job is to plan, prepare, focus on details, double-check on the people and planned events, perhaps triple-check on everything rather than making any assumptions, see to it that everyone involved has a shared understanding of what's required and when it's expected, leave as little to chance as possible, and then oversee things as they transpire in a calm but careful way. And all those things can be done utterly without worry. It adds nothing positive to the mix. It can be eliminated without the loss of anything needed. And that will be a major gain for the otherwise worried person, while also reassuring everyone else that things are fine and they need not worry either.

A retreat within can seem to be the best retreat from worry. But perhaps we should be cautious about fully withdrawing into our inner circle of control. Friendly critics of the Stoics, and many people who find themselves both greatly influenced by these ancient philosophers and deeply grateful to them for their liberating ideas, can still sometimes think they've brought us some truly great perspectives that they themselves tend to take too far.

It's one thing to agree that we think too much about things that are outside our control, and maybe even obsess over them, but it's a bit extreme to say we should not focus on them at all, nor even concern ourselves with them and, as many ancient Stoics say, instead view them as literally "worthless," or without any value that could justify our time or attention. That's one way to avoid worry, but you may find yourself rightly worrying that it goes too far.

Another spectrum

There may be another relevant spectrum here in our proper reaction to the concept of control and its related ideas, instead of a strict either/or dichotomy or even a trichotomy of attitude. Perhaps we can consider something like a range of potential time investment, or even of intensity for our focus and emotional concern over external things, a spectrum represented by a wide range of gradations whose major milestone markers might be as simple as

>> Obsess and worry over

>> Concentrate on a lot

>> Give some attention to

>> Utterly ignore

And it could be that this spectrum should closely track the other spectrum of control and influence, with even more gradations of commitment regarding time and emotional energy. The more control or influence we may have regarding something, the more this may justify a given magnitude of time and attention, along with a degree of emotional energy devoted to that thing. It's not like a classic two-position light switch, on or off, but perhaps more like a dimmer switch in the dining room where we can turn up the light or bring it down a lot for an ultimate romantic dinner ambiance.

The standard Stoic view is the strict either/or: Either something is in your full control or it's not. So either you should concern yourself with it or you should not. There are no other salient options.

The Stoics had a precise reason for this stark view. If you begin to extend your focus and concern to things that fall beyond your complete control, you render yourself vulnerable to negative emotions like disappointment and discouragement that can be associated with such an attachment and its aligned expectations, just like that romantic dinner for which you had such high hopes that sadly were dashed, despite your adroit use of that dimmer switch.

REMEMBER

The Stoics want to help us find a place of invulnerability and complete security in this tumultuous and fragile world. They keep pulling us back from anything that might set us up for negative consequences within ourselves.

The Problem of External Goals

There is a subtle hidden tension in Stoic principles that we should bring to light at this point. Stoics value both inner peace and also unhindered power that's used virtuously. Their advice about control and concentration — that we should focus on and concern ourselves about only those things that we can fully control — seems to arise out of an effort to help us use our divine gift of reason in an uninhibited and untainted way.

When we instead focus on things we can't fully control, we make ourselves vulnerable to forces that can disturb us with negative emotions like irritation, frustration, anger, fear, disappointment, and despair. And it's precisely such emotions that most frequently unhinge our use of reason. They trouble us and push us into irrational thoughts, feelings, attitudes, and actions. To honor reason and keep our access to it pure, Stoics want to avoid all such emotional forces. They notice that we stress out, worry over, or feel anxiety about things that we don't control. So they tell us to avoid focusing on such things, to shirk any real emotional concern about them, and even to let them go completely as nothing more than distractions from our core task of living consistently in accordance with reason.

But classic Stoic thought wants us to follow reason in all ways and at all times because it's a core part of our nature, and "follow nature" is one of their basic guidelines, properly understood. It turns out that when we look deeply into human nature, we find that we all do seem to have a measure of reason granted to us, an ability to think logically, but that it isn't the whole story about our essence as human beings. We are also born with an innate relationality, a tendency to respond positively to other people, to form friendships and partnerships, and to enter into forms of interdependency within those relationships. It's only in community with others that human beings flourish. We take up this important Stoic theme in all its wonderful detail in Chapter 13, but will now point out something deeply relevant to our present issue of control and concern.

WARNING

Stoics believe that relationships among human beings bring with them both amazing opportunities and also important duties. Spouses have duties to each other. Parents have duties to their children, and children have their own set of duties toward their parents, to each other, and to their friends, as well as toward others in their broader community. And these outer obligations create a tension that may amount to a strict inconsistency with the separate Stoic recommendation to retreat into an inner fortress of control.

Relationships, reason, and common good

We all live well and flourish only in community with each other. The many social and moral responsibilities that weave the fabric of healthy community demand that we not just attend to our inner thoughts, judgments, desires, aversions, and other mental items over which we may, in principle, have complete control, but that we also concern ourselves with each other and tend to one another, caring for each other with love and consideration, whether in the circumstance of family love, neighborly love, real friendship, or romantic love. That means, of course, reaching out beyond what we can strictly control and involving ourselves in the notorious messiness of human relations. It means having personal aims, intentions, hopes, dreams, and ambitions for our relationships with each other. It requires working on those relationships, and also collaborating in partnership with others for goals that we share.

There can be no healthy society or real community among people without any engagement around shared goals. The Stoics in fact believe that we have an obligation, based in reason — as all moral obligation is — to care for each other, to concern ourselves with each other, and to work toward what we call "the common good" that depends in part on each of us. It's no surprise then that so many ancient Stoics were active in their communities as teachers or counselors or government officials, with one even serving as an emperor.

To Stoics, reason is the most basic foundation for a good life. And yet, to work well, it has to be used well. And so our reason needs to be protected from disturbing forces that would keep us from using it properly. Because of this, reason itself seems to require that we attend to the dichotomy of control, or trichotomy, or spectrum, and choose only one of the options to focus on, concern ourselves with, or care about — the things we completely control — in order to avoid entanglements of concern that would make us vulnerable to all those negative forces that degrade, erode, or contaminate our use of reason. And yet at the same time, reason also tells us that we can flourish and be happy as fulfilled beings only in relationships that, to be healthy, require us to go beyond the tight circle of things we can control, and venture out from this safe zone to tend to the legitimate and important social needs we all have.

We need to concern ourselves with each other and care for each other. And that makes us vulnerable to things like disappointment and its attendant feelings. So what actually should we do? Should we stay in the safe zone of control in order to protect reason? Or do we venture out beyond this protected area in order to obey reason? We seem to have on our hands a bit of a conundrum, or paradox. Reason appears to require two different, opposite, and even contradictory paths. And while the Stoics were known for often saying paradoxical-sounding things, they weren't known for believing or recommending inconsistent things, because that would not be in accord with the principle of reason they so rightly value. So we have a problem to solve.

A modern Stoic's strategy

As a building block for addressing this problem that few current fans of the Stoics seem to notice or ever talk about, we can usefully shift our focus for a moment and attend to something that may help position us for a breakthrough idea. There are contemporary Stoics who have taken to heart the ancient advice about not focusing on things we can't control and have applied it to the important activity of goal-seeking in the world. For example, William Irvine, one of the best philosophically credentialed of recent advocates for Stoicism as a helpful philosophy of life in our time, has written on this in his excellent book *A Guide to the Good Life*. He wants to suggest that Stoics can have some concern over things they can't control, but must be careful in this.

The Stoic tennis player

Irvine uses the example of tennis and whether it's acceptable for a Stoic to want to win a game or a match. He writes:

> I think that when a Stoic concerns himself with things over which he has some but not complete control, such as winning a tennis match, he will be very careful about the goals he sets for himself. In particular, he will be careful to set *internal* rather than *external* goals. Thus, his goal in playing tennis will not be to win a match (something external, over which he has only partial control) but to play to the best of his ability in the match (something internal, over which he has complete control). By choosing this goal, he will spare himself frustration or disappointment should he lose the match: Since it was not his goal to win the match, he will not have failed to attain his goal, as long as he played his best. His tranquility will not be disrupted. (95)

This certainly sounds sensible. Irvine then goes on to say:

> It is worth noting at this point that playing to the best of your ability in a tennis match and winning that match are causally connected. In particular, what better way is there to win a tennis match than by playing to the best of your ability? The Stoics realized that our internal goals will affect our external performance, but they also realized the goals we consciously set for ourselves can have a dramatic impact on our subsequent emotional state.

Irvine seems here to have come up with a way for a Stoic tennis player to get all possible benefits. And it's quite a racket: The player doesn't set any external goal that he could fail to meet, and so he avoids the possibility of disappointment, frustration, or racket-throwing temper tantrums as a result of such a failure, or even as a reaction to any mistakes along the way that might lead to that result. And these avoided states of mind are of course emotions that could impinge on his capacity for the most pure and proper use of reason. Yet, this Stoic tennis player with the right inner goals as his only aims on the court also thereby engages in precisely the goal-structured activity that will set him up potentially to win the match after all. Of course, he shouldn't actually care, since winning isn't one of his goals, right? And we note this of course with an inner smile because, really, how likely is it to be or find a tennis player who is so completely taken up with inner goals as not to have at least the hope of an actual win? Is it possible to play both sides of the mental court like this after all? If you wouldn't at least like to win, or want in your hidden heart of hearts to win, at least a point or game if not a set, then why is it so important to play to the best of your ability? Is it simply a love of the game, a game whose external outcomes ought oddly never to matter? Maybe so, but we'll have to look at a second example and take this to another level.

The Stoic husband and wife

Irvine claims that Stoics will always be cautious about the goals they set for themselves, and seems to think that a Stoic will not chase externals, precisely to avoid the possibility of disappointment that could endanger his serenity and threaten his reason. But in another passage, he also seems to have in mind the importance of our relationships within Stoic philosophy, and he concedes that he thinks Stoicism would recommend that he, William Irvine, should concern himself with whether his wife loves him, although it's something over which he lacks full control. And yet in fact classic, strict Stoics would likely suggest more carefully that he concern himself rather with his own contributions to the relationship by focusing on how loving he is with his wife. The health of such an intimate partnership would indeed seem to be a proper item of care for any Stoic who rightly values relationships. But Irvine's attention in the example is also still on the issue of control, so he then reveals his thinking that he shouldn't actually set it as a goal to get his wife to love or keep loving him, but rather just to act so as to *be* lovable, since with this more modest goal, he doesn't set himself up for disappointment and a disturbance of his inner peace. He says his goal should just be an inner one.

But there's a problem. Have you ever sought to act in a loving and lovable way and yet had your actions misinterpreted? According to the strict Stoic view, how anyone, including a spouse, interprets your attempts to be loving should not be a matter of your concern. It should not be a goal to have your loving intentions interpreted as such. So when your spouse misreads your best intentions, that shouldn't be a cause for disappointment or frustration. But this just seems wrong. No, we can't control how others see us or view our actions. And yet when we're working hard to express and live truly loving intentions, then to have them misunderstood and rejected as the opposite of what they're meant to be should surely be a matter of care and concern. Wouldn't we indeed care so much that we'd want to focus on the situation very seriously, figure out the cause of miscommunication, and work hard on changing the external fact that's admittedly not within our complete control?

A broad issue arises here. Despite suggesting that we endorse a trichotomy of control rather than a simple dichotomy, Irvine seems in the end not to want to take advantage of the additional category of partial control. But does he really mean to suggest that a modern Stoic should have no external goals? If you're a Stoic, you really can't set it as a goal on a hot day to get a cool glass of water? You should only have as your aim to try your best to act in such a way that water might be available to you? Are you merely to aim to line up your desires, beliefs, and intentions as you would if you were to have the forbidden external goal of actually getting a sip? This seems like tying yourself into mental knots to escape a problem that may have a better solution.

The aspiring Stoic novelist

One more example may help us find a way out of the maze. Irwin finally considers the example of a young writer who wants to be a novelist, and he does here seem to endorse some actions involving partial but not total control. He says the aspiring novelist will need to fight two battles: to master the art and craft of writing, and then to deal with a lot of rejection, because that's what the world of publishing involves. Many experience one rejection and then give up, unwilling to endure more disappointment. But Irwin thinks there's a solution. He offers what he takes to be a Stoic strategy, and lays out an alternative to having the external goal of being published. The earlier tennis example is clearly an inspiration here, because he writes (on page 98):

> How can the aspiring novelist reduce the psychological cost of rejection and thereby increase her chance of success? By internalizing her goals with respect to novel writing. She should have as her goal not something external over which she has little control, but something internal over which she has considerable control, such as how hard she works on the manuscript or how many times she submits it in a given period of time.

We'll pass by the question of why, on Irwin's own views, this Stoic strategy should include any care at all about "her chance of success" in an external way and merely note that he admits that, even though this internalizing strategy may not fully eliminate the emotional toll of rejection and satisfy the strict Stoic concern for an utterly serene inner life, it could reduce the sting of disappointment and perhaps prevent the author's giving up.

Silly mind games

Now, Irvine is an experienced, senior philosopher, so he anticipates some pushback on the part of readers, in the form of a complaint that this recommendation amounts to nothing more than a "mind game" of pretending not to have an external goal, so as to diminish the emotional consequences of such a goal's not being attained.

His first answer is that if this process of reorienting to the inner is done long enough and effectively enough, we could perhaps get ourselves to the place where we aren't just playing a mind game and pretending not to have the relevant objective external goal, but where we do indeed wholly internalize our motivations and aims, and so have no focus on objective results.

He then concedes that if this is not fully possible, it's still legitimate to use a mental trick or a "mind game" to subdue our emotions and protect ourselves from the many disappointments we otherwise might face. In fact, he says that the Stoics were not at all averse to mind tricks by which to reframe a situation, switch perspectives, gage a desire or difficulty by a different measuring stick, or divert their attention from troubling features of what they face, to focus on other facets of the situation instead. If seeking to internalize our goals and avoid external ones can work to reduce or eliminate stress, worry, and discouragement, there's nothing wrong with it at all, he concludes.

But then he surprises us by offering "a confession" and admitting he can find "little evidence" that the ancient Stoics actually did this internalizing trick or technique. He says he attributes the move to Stoic philosophy simply because it's the "obvious" thing to do, in his words, "if one wishes, as the Stoics did, to concern oneself only with those things over which one has control and if one wishes to retain one's tranquility while undertaking endeavors that might fail (in the external sense of the word)."

Imagine the aspiring novelist in Irvine's example has thought up a great story and produces an entire manuscript without ever having set an actual goal for completing a book or getting it published. She's really excited about it, and in any other situation she'd begin to look for ways to submit the work to publishers, with the goal of getting a contract for publication. If she had external goals, they might include having her story beautifully printed and sent out into the world through bookstores of all sorts as her first published novel. She'd hope to be on podcasts and get the book favorably reviewed, and perhaps make author appearances to promote its sales. It's a great dream and a powerful vision. But she's read some books by the ancient Stoics and maybe one by William Irvine, and so she knows not to set such outer goals at all, only inner ones. And yet, on Irvine's portrayal of what can be fine to do, she begins to submit her manuscript to agents or publishers without having the external goal of getting it accepted or published. And when it gets turned down, no problem; she stuffs a copy into another envelope and sends it to another publisher and does this repeatedly.

But why? If she doesn't actually have the outer goal of getting her manuscript published, why is she sending it to publishers? Well, maybe she just wants them to read and enjoy it, even without publication. But she could be disappointed in even that. And yet, if she's suitably cautious and really sharp about internal goal setting, she won't aim at even that, but will simply align her desires, beliefs, and intentions as she would if she had such a goal.

But again, we have to ask why she is going through all this if she lacks even the outer goal of having any other human being read the story. On Irvine's strictures, could she just have set the modest goal of getting it typed into a computer, then printed out? Those are all external things too. Can she set the tiny goal of getting the manuscript to the post office across town, stamped, and mailed? More outer things: The printer could jam. She could have a flat tire on her way to the post office and be intensely disappointed. So she obviously could not have even such small external goals if she has a strict Stoic concern for avoiding here the possibility of all negative emotions.

This strategy ends up sounding both convoluted and forced, and admittedly a bit silly, doesn't it? Certainly, a modern Stoic and careful thinker like Irvine doesn't intend this consequence. It's almost as if we've become engaged in a massive charade due to a fear of failure and the emotions any failure could cause. To then avoid any possibility of that, we're advised to shun all goals about external things, things not wholly in our power, and concentrate only on things over which we have total control. But they turn out to be very few, and to be entirely mental, and so we end up with a puzzle: Why in the world would we be doing these internal things unless we wanted or hoped for them to have the obvious external results toward which they would ordinarily aim? And if we know anything at all, we know that even hopes can be dashed and fail, just like working with desire and confidence toward an outer goal. So this seems to be less than successful as a Stoic strategy. What then is left?

Trying Our Best

Many of us have had parents who generously said to us in our school days, "You don't have to get top grades, we just want you to try your best." And that seems both sensible and liberating. Irvine's tennis player decided to just seek to play his best, without the goal of winning. And we can all understand this, if rooted in a sheer love for the game. But when other examples are considered, such activity seems less naturally motivated, if at all. And even the tennis player in setting his modest goal of "going out there and playing my best" can be disappointed, strictly speaking, since playing his best is not always in his control. He could have a muscle cramp so persistent as to prevent this, or a severe stomachache from a virus, or he could suffer heat exhaustion, or have a heart attack mid game. In order to guarantee avoiding failures and disappointments, he'd have to pull back all his goals to merely mental items, and even those, as our medical disaster examples indicate, can be interfered with by forces outside of his control, and so end up in failure. It seems we do need another option.

Irvine is right to say that if we hope for big wins in life like being victorious in an important tennis match or getting a book published, we need to set more intermediate and immediate goals, smaller goals over a longer time period in advance of that particular challenge, or there is little hope of attaining such a result, and disappointment is nearly guaranteed. But that just means operating in a broad swath of the spectrum of control starting with what we do have some control over, which is indeed the mental game, and yet then stretching out to what we have less control over but is always involved in the cultivation of a skilled behavior. And this means activities where some risk is present.

If we were able to safeguard our lives in such a way as to eliminate all risk, we'd be eliminating the need for and even the possibility of courage, and courage has been seen as a prime human virtue from nearly the beginning of philosophy. In fact, it's one of the four cardinal virtues recognized by the Stoics. And courage requires risk. But there is strategy for dealing with the problem of negative emotions that allows for the exercise of this key virtue in the face of real risk.

An Alternate Strategy

At the outset of this book, we suggest that half of wisdom may consist in knowing what to embrace and what to release, and that most of us get this wrong much of the time by embracing what we should release and releasing what we should embrace. Perhaps we can satisfy both elements in Stoicism's paradoxical pair of concerns regarding reason if we approach the tension in a different way. Maybe the solution is not about avoiding external goals, but how we approach such goals and think about external things more generally.

The classic Stoics keenly recognized that negative emotions can interfere with or degrade our use of our most precious endowment, reason. And they wanted to protect us, to help us guard our use of reason against these defeaters. So they drew our attention to the issue of control, because they knew that when we venture too far out onto the limb of things we can't control, and do so with a strong desire or excessive emotional commitment in operation, we endanger our emotional life and also our ability to reason well.

As we've seen, one possible response to that problem is to pull back from things we can't control and seek shelter in our inner citadel, feeling secure in the fortress of our souls by embracing only the things over which we have complete control, while releasing all else. But, as we've also noted, that seems to clash with the implications of another major Stoic commitment and the deliverance of reason itself that we should seek to flourish in our lives, and that we find by using reason well that we cannot flourish without being in healthy relationships with other people like spouses, tennis partners, and occasionally publishers. And this is possible only by upholding reasonable responsibilities and duties regarding those relationships. That means venturing out and acting beyond the inner fortress of total control, risking an engagement with goals and various, different activities with others where negative emotion is not only possible but perhaps inevitable.

Yet there may be a mitigating strategy that will work to reconcile these two concerns, and that doesn't involve convoluted mind games of releasing outer goals and embracing only inner processes that then seem wholly unmotivated. It won't require any tricks, and can be as successful as it is sensible.

Our emotional relationship to goals

We'd like to suggest that for a Stoic, external goals can and should be fine to have, as long as our emotional relationship to those goals is proper and satisfies legitimate concerns about protecting the integrity of reason. You can set an external goal like winning your tennis match, shooting under par on your favorite golf course, sparking love from your spouse or partner, or getting your first novel published. The bigger and more challenging such a goal is, the more your desire to attain it will then depend on starting a process involving intermediate and more immediate goals. There will then be means for attaining these subordinate targets that will begin in every case with things that are closer to your circle of total or partial control than the more remote stages it might later take to achieve each outer goal.

The ancient Stoics were concerned that too much attachment to external things, or the wrong sort of attachment, can set us up for terribly disturbing emotions. And it's not just emotions that feel bad that can disturb reason. When you're too attached to a goal, thinking of it as far too important, and you do manage to attain it, you can be as unhinged by irrational exuberance or extreme giddiness as someone who just as wrongly craves to realize a goal, fails at it, and is plunged into despair. In either case, the problem isn't the goal, but the kind and level of emotional attachment to it.

There's a lot of good advice in Eastern philosophy, especially within the Buddhist and Hindu traditions, about our proper relation to external goals. And it's simple: Such goals are fine, but as we pursue them, we should emotionally embrace the process and release the results. If we embrace the process well enough and in the right ways, we can begin to take such a joy in the journey itself that it will matter less whether we attain the destination for which we'd set out. Maybe another destination will be just as good. Perhaps in the end, life is mostly about the process, the journey, the adventure itself, guided by goals as giving us basic directions, providing paths forward, but not emotionally holding us hostage over potential results.

WISDOM FROM THE EAST

Eastern philosophy has great wisdom on the relationship between our actions and their results that can inform a Stoic perspective. A central text of Hindu thought, *The Bhagavad Gita*, says:

> You have a right to your actions, but never to the intended fruit of your actions. (2.47)

> The wise man lets go of outer results, good or bad, and is focused on the action alone. (2.48–52)

> This is how actions were done by the ancient seekers of freedom. Heed their example: Act, while releasing the fruits of action. (4.12–16)

And in the Buddhist *Dhammapada* we see:

> Whoever is in touch with the infinite, free of attachment, without craving, is the highest among men. (7.8)

> Releasing both victory and defeat, serene minds dwell in happiness. (15.5)

> Sorrow springs from craving. Fear also. Whoever is free from craving knows neither sorrow nor fear. (16.8)

The proper path of action

TIP

We attach our sense of personal identity and value far too often to the outer things we accomplish and what we receive into our lives as a result in the form of financial rewards. We also have that same attachment to matters of reputation or social status. But our identities and our value as human beings are not dependent on such things. Those results can be valued and preferred, but they don't define us or establish our personal value. We can release them in our hearts, or at least hold them much more lightly and loosely. When we learn the secret of a light touch or a gentle hold, we free our emotions from the ups and downs that the vicissitudes of life can otherwise impose on us.

REMEMBER

We can care about external things, but with a concern that's moderate, flexible, agile, and resilient. Having outer concerns need not in itself endanger us or our reason. How we hold those commitments can make all the difference. And that insight is consonant with much Stoic thought. As Seneca wrote in "On

Tranquility," about our goals: "The pang of disappointed wishes is necessarily less distressing to the mind if you have not promised yourself sure fulfillment." We can be resilient by being realistic. We can moderate our emotions with proper mindfulness. We can balance embrace and release.

And if we set a goal we think right, judging it a better outcome than any available alternative, and we then pursue it amid risk and finally find that our efforts fall short, we can train ourselves to simply accept the result as the will of God or the Logos, as better than or equal to what we had in mind. We're not omniscient or infallible. And we have at least learned, and perhaps grown. In fact, one common Stoic technique is to set any goal with the qualifier "if God wills." I'd love to win the match, have a loving spouse, or get my book published . . . if God wills.

One door closes and another opens. It's a big part of Stoicism to accept what we can't fully control and agree with God, without insisting on understanding the reasons for everything. Wisdom isn't to be unhinged by unexpected events. It can transcend disappointment and move forward, even with a smile.

WARNING

The Greek and Roman Stoics who were the originators of such a potentially powerful philosophy of life did seem to believe that we have total control over our affirmations and denials, our value judgments, our desires and aversions, and many other mental states. And yet the psychology of the past century or more has strongly suggested the existence of unconscious powers and forces that render the conscious mental realm far less under our direct control than we might think. Even more recent research has shown that our degree of self-control can vary greatly depending on the time of day or the nature of our activities that deplete available nutrients for our brains. It's also well known that issues of self-control can become problematic with too much alcohol consumption, or the use of certain other substances. So, even though the distinction between things we can control and those we can't is useful, it may not be as solid or precise as the original Stoics assumed, or even as some contemporary followers of theirs seem to take for granted. And this new realization can even further deepen our considered reticence to think that we must keep our hopes, commitments, and goals within the smallest circle of things we can control. We can and do properly venture outside that circle all the time. But as we do, we need to govern our emotions accordingly.

The farther something is from the envisioned inner circle of our seemingly direct control, the more loosely and lightly it should be held. Imagine again a spectrum. As we move out from the circle of more control, our embrace should be easier, gentler, and more casual, until it properly gives way to full release. This is a skilled behavior, or else everyone would be good at it. We need to practice various levels of engagement and disengagement, ranging across the spectrum from a tight hug to empty arms. We don't need to restrict our goals and concerns to things that are internal to our own minds. But we do need to govern our desires, aversions, and associated emotions properly, so that outer goals are held and handled well, our outer activities enhance our lives rather than being a constant threat, and we have plenty of room for that virtue of courage that takes into account both the great value and the risks that we do sometimes need to experience as we seek to do what's right.

As it happens, the Stoics also have some other tricks up their tunic sleeves to help us deal with external events better than we often do. And we examine each of them in this book.

Chapter **10**

Desire and the Happy Life

S ome analysts of the human condition think that our capacity for having desires is among the best things in life. Desires get us up in the morning and get us going. They give us ambition and a motivation to do and be. Other commentators view our desires as among the worst things. They say that our desires enslave us to doing more and getting more and never allow us to be satisfied with who we are or what we have. Who's right? What do you think?

In this chapter, we explore the distinctive and surprising Stoic views on desire, putting them into our modern context and examining the issue in detail. The Stoics have some unexpected perspectives for us here, as in other aspects of their thought. And to many contemporary readers of their work as well as users of their ideas, what makes them different is exactly what makes them attractive for our time. Of course, it's our keen desire that you will find what we have to say here helpful as you dig more deeply into Stoicism itself and its understanding of the happy and fulfilled life we all seek. Sometimes, Stoicism gives us answers. At other times, it simply helps us to grasp the right questions. A philosophy can be useful either way.

Getting Clear about Desire

What exactly is desire, anyway? What role does it normally play in your life? Is it a proper and helpful element for you? Or does desire cause you trouble? What do we generally tend to desire and why? Of course, this last question is a very general one and may be too abstract. Yet when doing philosophy, we often find that general questions can get us started on a path of discovery that will bring us a new form of very specific understanding.

A standard philosophical model for our action in the world roughly specifies that we have beliefs, desires, and commitments that together tend to produce our actions by way of influencing our choices. Beliefs are convictions about how anything in the world is, was, or will be, including ourselves and how we fit into the big picture. Desires are often classified as a form of positive and potentially motivating emotion, or a kind of pro-attitude toward something believed to be valuable, such as an object, event, or a state of affairs like "getting married" or "starting a successful business." These examples are of things that Stoics classify as neither intrinsically good nor bad, and so as "indifferents" that can have their own sort of value to us, but not the kind relevant to the Stoic understanding of happiness, inner flourishing, or ultimate personal well-being (a view we explore in Chapters 8 and 9).

Commitments

If you believe that something is useful or in some other way valuable, or that it would be enjoyable, and is thus to be preferred over available alternatives because of this, and so you find yourself with a desire for it, we often think that's enough to explain the subsequent fact of your acting to get it. But there is perhaps one more element that can be involved, which we think of as a commitment. Our commitments include our broad assessments of importance that we normally call our basic values, along with our many promises to others as well as to ourselves, and the responsible roles we have agreed to play in the world, along with any duties involved in those roles.

Our basic values as commitments are the general and firm approaches to life that we think of as important for living well. They involve mindsets, attitudes, or ongoing intentions like honesty and generosity, justice, and courage. Our promises are more specific commitments based on declarations or assurances we've made to others that we will be or do certain things in the future, or else refrain from certain things. Those promises can be either explicit vows or implicit understandings conveyed more indirectly that both generate and support an expectation and form of trust. Our responsible roles involving commitments include that of son or daughter, husband or wife, parent, citizen, employee, coach, team athlete, business owner, manager, government representative, or church official. Our roles as well as our promises and basic values rightly have a function in suggesting and generating proper actions in the world, as well as in ruling others out. Now let's illustrate what this means.

Suppose for the sake of an example — even though we're sure this isn't going on in your life at all, but just entertain the possibility — that you've been imagining a future romantic relationship with your favorite film or music celebrity. In your fantasy, it's a wonderful development involving lots of travel to beautiful places, luxury hotel suites, great meals at top restaurants, and, overall, a life to be envied. But we're going to suppose further that you don't really have any solid belief that the realization of this fantasy would in real life be a good thing. In fact, you're wise enough to know better. You've heard plenty about the difficult realities of celebrity life and the way their relationships so often collapse under all the crazy demands of living in public view. You realize that you have just a harmless ongoing daydream, despite the amount of time you may spend mesmerized by those photos online. Yeah, we know but won't tell.

Such a fantasy alone won't move you to action. A fantasy is just a nice mental picture or video, or a streaming series to enjoy. It dwells in the imagination. But a firm desire is different. It's usually thought of as an inclination of the will. And it typically arises only in relation to some positive beliefs and supporting values. If you come to have a firm belief that your favorite icon of pop culture is just the person for you, and that if you were introduced, magic would result, plus that you could avoid all the negatives typical to such relationships, you just might begin to desire it, perhaps enough to try to find a way to meet. You'd be poised for action — unless you had prior solid commitments that made this impossible, in which case you'd realize that you needed to calm down and drop this vision. But in a context where everything did fall into place, with firm supporting beliefs, a strong desire, and a range of commitments that gave a green light to it all, then some form of action most likely would result, even if it sadly ended with a restraining order.

We're inclined to choose those things around which positive beliefs, proper desires, and our commitments align. Then we act. This is a nice, simple, rough sketch of what we tend to think is normally behind our actions, but the full truth is a little more complex. Our beliefs, desires, and commitments don't exist wholly independent of each other. What you strongly desire can affect what you're able to see in the world, how you interpret what you do notice, and the exact beliefs you form as a result.

Thought, desire, and action

Rational emotions can help our perceptions, interpretations, and thoughts, while irrational feelings tend to degrade the process. We often see the latter on a large scale in politics and on a small scale in personal life. Likewise, your various commitments — involving the full range of your values, promises, and roles — can affect what you believe it might be right to do, and in that way encourage or discourage the rise of a particular desire in your heart connected with that belief. And of course, your beliefs as to what's good, useful, convenient, proper, or fun obviously can influence your desires and commitments. There's a dynamic interaction between these distinct but inseparable elements within each of us. And this complexity of our inner lives can make it hard to predict what another person will do unless you know them well or have observed the group dynamics in which they normally participate.

Stoicism sees these distinguishable but entangled elements of the mind, or of the person moving through the world, as crucially important for personal happiness and meaning. In his classic book *The Inner Citadel*, the French philosopher Pierre Hadot identified three spiritual disciplines as central to Stoic philosophy, and as ongoing needs we have for living well in the world around us. He distinguished disciplines as shown in Table 10-1.

TABLE 10-1

Three Spiritual Disciplines

Thought	Desire	Action
What you believe	What you want	What you do
Your judgments	Your attractions	Your deeds
To believe rationally	To embrace rightly	To act virtuously

On this perspective, the Stoics wanted us to get our thoughts right so that we could get our desires right, and then also our actions. Thought is primary, because our desires and actions arise out of how we view and interpret the world, or from the mental judgments we make due to our sense perceptions and the inner representations of the world to which they give rise. For example, you may sense sounds coming your way from another person, and your mind represents those sounds as words spoken to you. If you interpret the words as insulting, demeaning, or in any other way offensive, that can generate certain emotions and related desires that result in an impulse to act in a particular way. But when we discipline our thought well, we remove the tendency to interpret certain words and tones of voice as a personal attack that requires a response. We remove our inclination to take offense at what's said in those tones or with such words, as well as to interpret other things that happen around us as bad or terrible. That allows us to better discipline our desires and our actions that most often go along with our desires. Such a discipline will prevent the rise of unhealthy, irrational desires to retaliate, and actions that would fit the same description.

When you exercise proper discipline in all three areas of thought, desire, and action, you're better prepared to remain inwardly calm and conduct your life virtuously, no matter what seems to be going on around you. Your inner self is strengthened by each of these disciplines and can operate in more emotional independence of the ups and downs of the world. You won't share the needless roller coaster ride of extreme feelings that most people seem to experience. You can come to agree with the late psychologist Richard Carlson that "Life is not an emergency." You can stay calmer and be more at peace to think, feel, and act well.

Managing desires

From the Stoic perspective, the ideal goal for the management of our desires is for all of us to desire only that things be exactly as they in fact are at any given time, like the present moment. Epictetus, for one, joined his more ancient colleagues in thinking that inner peace, tranquility, or serenity is necessary for the full and unfettered use of reason in our lives. He says:

> Instead of wishing that things would happen as you'd like, wish that they would happen as they do, and then you'll be content. (*Handbook,* 8)

His concern was that if we ever desire anything other than what already is happening, exists, or is in our possession, we'll be vulnerable to discontent, disappointment, and other negative attitudes toward any failure of the world or God to satisfy that desire, and this would be an attitude contrary to virtue, in effect an act of impiety toward the gods, which is always to be avoided.

There's one qualification and exception to be made here. According to Epictetus, we're free to desire inner things that aren't yet true, such as to be morally better, because ultimately that's entirely up to us, within our power, and so not vulnerable to external force or disruption, and thus to the sort of disappointment that could lead to our blaming God. Inner gaps can be crossed with desire, but no gaps in external matters not wholly in our control.

Whatever should be will be

In the Stoic worldview, everything that happens is directly or indirectly a result of the Logos, God, "the gods," Zeus, Providence, or Benevolent Nature having planned at or before the birth of this universal order what best should be and will be. So everything that happens in the world comes about for the best, whether we can see that in our own limited perspective and particular judgments or not. We simply know from first principles about the governance of God over all that it must be so. Under this theory, it would make no sense for desire to be a want or wish that crosses a bridge between what is and is not — or is not yet and could come to be.

Here's the reasoning. Imagine something you might desire, like winning a huge lottery. Either you will win such a prize, or you will not. Whichever will be true is the absolute best result for the universe, and so too, at least indirectly, for you as a part of what whole. In case you will win, the same is true of the timing. Next year may be better than tomorrow. Or 20 years from now could be best. So, there is no unfortunate gap between what is and what should be. Whatever should be will be, in the best way and at the best time. Everything is in place for the proper unfurling of cosmic and worldly events, and so is as it should be. Because of this, the emotion of desire has no useful reaching forward to do, no need for crossing gaps. There is no sensible wishing for something that is not or is not likely to be, something that could be better than either what is, or is to be, because there can be no such thing.

Desiring only what is true

If desire for anything external to the mind is then to play any role in human life, in the Stoic worldview, it must be as an emotional embrace of exactly what is, was, or will be. The wise and virtuous person desires whatever comes from the hand of God, whatever results from the Logos, whatever Nature provides, and nothing else at all. We should then desire everything about our current circumstances, however delightful, difficult, or even disastrous they may seem to be. We ought to embrace everything that is true of the world and should wish for nothing different than what is, or is to be, because to do so would be to imply that God got things wrong, which would be impious and morally bad, as well as inevitably false.

REMEMBER

Moreover, to desire anything different from what is or is going to happen would render us vulnerable to negative emotions and attitudes like worry, fear, anger, irritation, resentment, bitterness, and disappointment toward life and its creator, all inner states that are as difficult for us as they are contrary to God's will. That is the classic Stoic viewpoint.

Think about this for a moment. If you could manage to embrace emotionally all that is, accepting it completely and having no desire that it be different, then your life would be much easier, calmer, and more peaceful. You'd avoid inner dismay and the turbulence of negativity. You could have a smile on your face and a glow in your heart all the time, trusting in the ultimate as providing whatever you truly need, exactly when you need it. You'd live in an attitudinal paradise of positivity. But there is a big problem with this.

Consider the things in the world around us right now that seem the most horrible — the chaos and carnage of war, the terrible accidents that maim or kill, the sudden onset of debilitating or fatal disease, the morally horrific actions of the deranged toward innocent victims, racial injustice, gender oppression, sexual violence, and on and on. These things are all viewed by Stoicism as somehow coming from the overarching long-term plans of the morally perfect Logos, or

God, and so as providing a part of the cosmic weave that will, ultimately, be best for the cosmos, and in that way for us all as parts of it. So if we were to have a repulsed aversion rather than an embracing desire toward any of these apparently terrible things, we'd be judging God to be wrong and the rational flow of events to be grossly flawed and suboptimal. We'd be impiously cutting ourselves off from the divine reason behind it all, dangerously separating ourselves from the universal body that includes the Logos, to which we rightly belong as valued members.

The starkness of the Stoic view of desire results from their determination that, to be virtuous people, we ought to embrace — and not with just a form of acceptance but of actual love — whatever is in this moment and all moments past, as well as encompassing all that will be in what is now yet the future. We can still work for what we think of as a good future, seeking to alleviate the suffering of others around us in the next moments, or as soon as possible, and to help make the world the sort of place it's capable of being, as a part of our virtuous intentions and impulses to act, but at the same time remaining able to accept and love whatever happens, either due to or despite our actions.

The problem of evil

This is a lot to get your head around. And it brings us into the area of what's called "the problem of evil" in relation to a belief in a good and powerful God as the ultimate creator of the physical universe or multiverse in which we created beings exist. Much more is said on this in Chapter 7 of this book. The question that arises around such a belief is how or why a perfectly good and powerful God could have created a world in which there is so much evil — facts or events involving tremendous pain and suffering on a massive scale. To the Stoic, of course, no external events are literally evil at all. Evil, like true good, occurs only within the thoughts and choices of the human heart or mind. It's always an inside job. The worst that can be said of war, disease, disaster, apparently untimely deaths, and all bodily pain intentionally inflicted on innocent people is that these are all from a general human point of view severely "dispreferred indifferents" that God, or the Logos, allows for the overall greater value of the cosmic scheme. Perhaps God knows that someone will respond in a massively virtuous way to a vicious act or a case of terrible suffering, the reaction outweighing the pain and rendering it justified within a greater good. But the alleged moral duty to "love" these things, while yet remaining free to prefer their alternatives, seems to be a demand that's psychologically hard to meet, if possible at all.

How do we love what is, as being somehow the best, and yet rationally determine to work to eliminate or moderate what is now for what comes next? If we value the opposite of much that happens in the world — peace over war, kindness over hate, safety over injury — how can we equally or even more greatly value all that does take place?

REMEMBER

Yet Stoic philosophy will insist that a genuine love for what is, an embrace of the realized moment, if we can attain it, is fully compatible with a preference to make things different in the next moment, or in most moments to come. But that preference must always be geared only to the future and should itself progressively evaporate like fog in the morning sun as what was future becomes present, and can then only shift forward again to what is yet still future, if it is a virtuous preference, as we come to see in the ongoing unfolding present what events the Logos has decreed for us to embrace instead of any alternative we've had in mind.

The Stoics are clearly right that we're happier and likely stronger, more empowered to do good things, if we're not all balled up in negative emotions and attitudes about the world or our present circumstances, and if instead we can in some way accept the present as being what it is. But does that require *loving* everything that's now going on in our lives or in the world more broadly? Do we have to agree with Stoic doctrine that God has chosen *everything* that happens and so, to be negative about anything is to rebel against our creator and source? Or could it be that the creative force behind it all set into motion the best that was initially possible for a physical universe and that this includes some slippage, some gaps, and ample room for us to get busy and help? Do the classic Stoics have some insights here and yet again drive their collective car off a cliff in being too extreme in applying them?

Desire and Happiness

In classic Stoic thought there is an idealistic absolutism, or an absolutist idealism, that lies behind much of what we read in, say, Epictetus about desire and action. The philosopher wants to liberate us from everything that chains down our spirits. Among those things from which he seeks to free us, to protect our inner peace or serenity, are the frustrations and disappointments we suffer. He doesn't want for himself or for us to desire anything we might not have or attain from the hand of God, and he takes this stance as an absolute protection against discouragement and grievance, the latter of which could well be described as the fuel for modern dystopian politics.

He also hopes we won't seek to avoid anything and yet end up facing it. He realizes full well that nobody among us has the superpower to make the world conform to their wishes in all ways and all times, so he advises us to seek rather to conform our wishes to the world. And in taking this position, he differs dramatically from what we can call the mainstream view of desire and happiness, while yet oddly sharing a version of the assumption that lies behind it. Let us explain, which we now desire to do, to your satisfaction.

The Desire Satisfaction View of Happiness

A widespread assumption in our day, as well as in eras past, mostly unconscious but operating under the surface of many worldviews, can be broken down into a pair of simple equations:

Unhappiness = Unsatisfied Desires

Happiness = Satisfied Desires

Let's call this "The Desire Satisfaction View of Happiness." It could also be called "The Spoiled Child View of Happiness." But let's not prejudge. We can picture this common perspective in a simple and vivid way. As shown in Figure 10-1, imagine a row of drinking glasses sitting side by side along a table, all the same size. The size or capacity of the glass represents the number of desires you have. All your desires are included: your wants for such things as a certain degree of success, wealth, status, respect, power, love, comfort, adventure, a stable supply of pistachio ice cream, a car or spouse that will turn heads and elicit admiration — or else one that's simply great, good, fun, and reliable — a nice cold drink right now, a week at the beach, a good movie to see tonight, or just about anything else at all that you'd like to attain, have, or experience.

The degree to which an individual glass is filled or empty will then represent the degree to which your desires are satisfied or unsatisfied, either at present, through a stretch of your life, or across all your years up until now. Your life at any given time will be represented by some such desire glass, with its overall ratio of content to capacity.

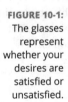

FIGURE 10-1:
The glasses represent whether your desires are satisfied or unsatisfied.

© John Wiley & Sons, Inc.

Glass empty

Picture now the first glass on the left as completely empty. This will represent the theoretically possible condition of a person whose many desires are all unsatisfied, an utterly miserable wretch leading a totally empty life. This poor soul is unhealthy in more ways than we could say. He desperately dreams of wealth and fame without any hope of either. He has no job, and no prospects. He has no home, and is completely without friends. You can fill in more details. But you get the picture: utter misery with no glimmer of happiness.

Glass quarter full

Next along our spectrum will be a desire glass that's one-quarter full. This second glass stands for the overall life condition of a person who has only a few of her desires satisfied, an individual who is very unhappy, three-quarters frustrated, but not utterly and absolutely defeated. She's extremely frustrated and not at all happy. Again, you can fill in other details as desired, or just move on. The person whose life is represented by this mostly empty glass has a long way to go before experiencing, on the viewpoint we're examining, anything remotely like most common portraits of happiness.

Glass half empty

Next, imagine glass three being half empty or, of course, half full. For our purposes now, this represents the life of a person much farther along the scale of desire satisfaction. It's anyone's guess whether such a person would be inclined to pessimism or optimism, and whether he would feel pretty good about his life overall, or rather seriously discontented. This would vary with personality and the choices we are always free to make about the attitudes we'll embrace, regardless of circumstances. But, apart from any inner heroism or a delight in small things that's completely outside the borders of the view on happiness we're now analyzing, we can imagine such a life well enough. This person has a decent job with acceptable coworkers, a more-or-less convenient place to live, a few friends, and a marriage that seems good about every other day, or at least every other week. He has some significant satisfaction, and yet considerable worry and unfulfilled dreams, too. He also has about half the savings he'd like. For every ambition he's attained, there's another that's out of reach. He sometimes contemplates his frustrations, but at other times counts his blessings. This is clearly not a miserable soul. But he's not exactly the ultimate popular ideal of a happy and fulfilled person either.

Glass three-quarters full

Glass four, to the right of center, will be three-quarters full, standing in for the person who has had most of his desires in life come true. He's in a good marriage with a couple of fine children, has a nice job in a field of interest, and enjoys a basically rewarding work life. His children are doing fine in school as well as in other interests, and they have nice friends. He's in decent physical shape and lives well in most ways. His income could be higher, the house could be larger, but he's in a neighborhood he likes and he even drives the sensible car he always wanted. Most of his desires are satisfied. He feels very lucky. On the common view of happiness we're considering, this is thought to be a very happy life indeed. Who could legitimately complain?

There are some people in this position, however, whose nagging awareness of still other good things they don't have, and whose worries that perhaps some of these things are simply out of reach, sadly keep them from enjoying what they have as much as they should. You may know someone like this. Or you may be someone like this. This sort of person is the envy of many, but in turn may envy at least the image of the next person who seems to have it all.

Glass full

Glass five, the positive end point of our spectrum, will be full to the brim, representing, on the view we're considering, the utterly blissed-out individual, the ideally happy human being whose desires are all completely fulfilled. She has a perfect mate who's loved, admired, and held in high regard by everyone who knows him, and he adores her. She also has the greatest possible career, enjoys the company of wonderful, generous, and accomplished friends, maintains a flawless physical appearance, has a face that could launch a thousand ships, a keen intellect, a heart of gold, a home that's the envy of all, and successful yet well-balanced, kind, and loving kids who view her as their best friend and confidant, with their dad a close second. She drives her dream car, oversees an investment portfolio that amazes even her top financial advisors, and has done astonishing good in the community. She's managed to study and master every subject that interests her. She is even a black belt in three martial arts. Did we mention that her clothes and accessories are perfect for her? And there's this thing about her skin — it somehow glows with health, a preternatural youthfulness, and a form of beauty that seems to emanate from within and yet find its perfect expression on the outside. We could go on. But we really shouldn't. You get the idea.

There is nothing this blessed individual desires and yet doesn't already have. Mail-order catalogues go straight into the very stylish trashcan in her breathtakingly attractive kitchen. Advertised sales are no lure. She has it all. In addition, there's nothing she wants to accomplish that she hasn't already done. There's no place she hopes to visit that she hasn't already gone. She's bathed in an utter completeness of satisfaction. Her radiantly smiling face and almost supernatural Zen-like calm say it all.

Don't we all just hate her? We're kidding, of course, because we haven't ever met her, and we won't likely any time soon. Most of us might not want to. But the very idea of her is enough to cause some people distress, unease, and tremendous jealousy. The fact that there could even theoretically be such a person can be perceived as a judgment on those of us who don't measure up. Her idealization typifies the theoretical maximum of bliss that the most common assumptions about happiness seem to imply. Fortunately for the rest of us, this view of happiness has a serious problem. It's completely bogus.

Finding the real flaws here

There are at least two serious problems, or deep flaws, with the belief that happiness ideally is just a matter of having all your desires satisfied.

What you desire matters

First, it matters what your desires are. Any satisfaction of the wrong desires will just get you farther from true happiness. As Seneca wrote:

> Whenever you want to know what should be avoided or pursued, consider its relation to the Supreme Good, to the purpose of your entire life. Whatever we do should be in harmony with this truth: no one sets in order the details unless he has first set in his mind the chief purpose of his life. (*Letters*, 73)

And in another place, he makes this remark about having the wrong desires:

> Some objects are superfluous, and others aren't worth what they cost. (*Moral Essays* 1, 281)

In the fourth century, Saint Augustine wrote down a series of conversations about happiness that he had enjoyed with a group of good friends and relatives. At one stage, he asked the group whether they thought that everyone who has everything he wants is happy. He writes about what happened next:

> At this point our mother said: "If a person wishes and possesses good things, he is happy; but if he desires evil things — no matter how many of them he may possess — he is wretched."

> I smiled at her and said cheerfully: "Mother, you have really gained the mastery of the stronghold of philosophy. For, undoubtedly, you wanted to express yourself like Tullius [aka Cicero], who has also dealt with this matter. In his *Hortensius*, a book written for the defense of philosophy, he said: 'Behold, not the philosophers, but only people who like to argue, state that all are happy who live according to their own wishes. This of course is not true; for to wish what is not fitting is the worst sort of wretchedness. And it is not so deplorable to fail of attaining what we desire, as it is to wish to attain what is not proper.'"

A noble failure is unfortunate, in this perspective, but it's not as bad as pursuing an improper form of success. There are people who want all the right things and don't get them, Augustine says, and there are others who aim for the wrong things and attain them. It's the latter we should pity most. And this is not just a matter of what's good and evil, to use Augustine's terms, but also of what's right or wrong for a particular person. It can be a matter of what's appropriate or not, given an individual's talents, personality, commitments, potential, and circumstances. Not all desires are worthy to be pursued and fulfilled, and not all generally acceptable desires are right for all people. Whether satisfying a desire will get you closer or farther from a good and happy life will on this view depend crucially on what that desire is, and on the question of how it fits with who you are. The point is that happiness cannot be simply a matter of getting all that you want, regardless of what your desires might be. Some desires should be pursued and fulfilled, while others are best left to wither on the vine. Some may bring expected delight. Others might produce unanticipated pain. It matters what your desires are.

The gap between desire and satisfaction

But this is not the only difficulty with what we're calling "The Desire Satisfaction View of Happiness," the claim that happiness consists in getting what you want in life. The second problem for this common view is just as interesting and instructive. Between even a proper desire and its satisfaction, the existence of a gap is not always a negative that detracts from happiness. The common view we're examining assumes otherwise. And the common view is again wrong. We can go even farther and say that a gap between desire and satisfaction can be a very positive, healthy, and important element in life. Rather than diminishing or eliminating happiness, it may even be essential for it, a secret sauce, or a needed spice for the stew.

First, and this is basically a small issue but it's still important to point out: We're often saved from huge mistakes by a time gap between the formation of a desire within us that we intend to pursue and its possible satisfaction. That gap gives us a chance to reflect further, gain new insight, change our minds, and be very glad we didn't immediately get what we wanted after all. At times, as we've just seen, we want the wrong things, things that would be bad for us, and possibly disastrous for those around us. But we might not realize that at first. A gap of time between desire and fulfillment, a territory of unsatisfied desire, may save us from calamity more often than we realize. So rather than being a bad thing, a gap between desire and satisfaction can be a very protective and good thing.

There is, however, a much more important and deeper reason that a gap between the formation and satisfaction of a desire is not a bad thing, but rather perhaps a necessity. And this is something on which we need to get clear. It may be that maintaining a running gap between what we want and what we attain is one of the best things about being human. The perceptive American novelist John Steinbeck once remarked:

> For it is said that humans are never satisfied, that you give them one thing and they want something more. And this is said in disparagement, whereas it is one of the greatest talents the species has and one that has made it superior to animals that are satisfied with what they have.

Perhaps any theoretical individual who had every desire already satisfied would lack something vital that he or she should have desired and will be unhappy without — the great good chance of having hope.

An Opportunity for Hope

Let's think for a minute about a claim that's central to the common view of happiness. Could it really be true that we would all be better off, completely fulfilled, and blissful if we had no unsatisfied desires whatsoever, but rather had already attained all that we ever would want? Let's call that assumption *The Perfect Satisfaction Axiom* and state it simply:

> Full happiness requires that all desires be satisfied.

Suppose for a moment that all our desires were both good and appropriate. That way, in theory, we can avoid running afoul of the point made earlier by St. Augustine's mother. But there are still at least two decisive problems with this axiom. First, it may assume a literal impossibility. It may just be impossible to have all your desires satisfied. A new day might necessarily bring new ones — a new desire for a nice breakfast, and for a good word from a friend sometime today, and on and on. Plus, and this is a crucial point, the more we live and learn, the more we come to know what's available in life, the more we may also begin to want. New knowledge breeds new desire.

Once you tasted a brand of rare chocolate, or gourmet doughnuts, or that incredible crispy pizza, you instantly and perhaps permanently had a new craving, a desire for more of that specific sensation. The result of a new experience was a new desire or range of desires. This is the way luxuries become felt necessities. What we encounter can create new wants and felt needs to an extent that can take us completely by surprise and make our formerly satisfied lives seem to be lacking in what we really might require for peak happiness. And this is an ongoing dynamic for life in the world.

As long as we live, there is the ongoing possibility for new experiences, new learning, and along with it, the development of new desires. And since there is no magical mechanism for the instantaneous satisfaction of desire, despite what some popular gurus of success may claim to the contrary, new desires will mean new satisfaction gaps generated by the fact that these wants are yet to be fulfilled. Are we to conclude that what necessarily happens as we live and learn is tragic and blocks us from ever being fully happy? That would yield the paradoxical conclusion that experiencing great new things — things that could and should presumably contribute in at least some small way to our happiness (sorry, Stoics) — are all on the contrary experiences that end up robbing us of the possibility of happiness by instilling in us new desires we haven't yet satisfied. And that's what philosophers like to call absurd.

It may simply be an unavoidable fact about life that the gap between our desires and their satisfaction will not go away. Like a geometer's abstractions of a perfectly round sphere or a completely straight line, a real life of total desire satisfaction may be a logically describable "ideal" that is just not possible to realize in the actual world. And then again, it may not be so ideal after all. This is the important point: As Baltasar Gracián, a 17th-century philosopher once wrote, "Croesus was rich but not wise; Diogenes, wise but not rich. Who has ever had it all? The day that one has nothing left to desire, he will be unhappy." The famous 20th-century philosopher Bertrand Russell once went so far as to say, "To be without some of the things you want is an indispensable part of happiness." And there may be a deep insight lurking in these paradoxical-sounding words.

Most of us have had the unexpected experience that seeking can be sweeter than finding, hoping to have even more exciting than having, and aspiring more pleasurable than actually attaining. Hope itself is a joy that nothing else, including its own fulfillment, could replicate. The 18th-century English essayist and poet Joseph Addison once remarked along these lines that, in his considered view, "The grand essentials to happiness in this life are something to do, something to love, and something to hope for."

The gap is good

So let's assume that we solve Augustine's problem and have only appropriate desires. And let's even assume, against all evidence we have to the contrary, that it is really possible to satisfy all our desires. There is still a huge problem remaining that alone shows the common view of happiness and its axiom to be false. If we somehow managed to get ourselves into the state of having absolutely everything we ever had wanted and ever would want, we would surprisingly find ourselves in a stifling and stagnant position. It's almost as if, when we really think about it, life is intended as much for pursuit as possession, for hoping as well as having.

We are built for a greater dynamic of challenge than just to perfectly have and hold. George Bernard Shaw once put it starkly when he expressed the sentiment that "As long as I have a want, I have a reason for living." He even added to this philosophy the judgment that "Satisfaction is death." And, of course, this might be a bit strong. Or it could be that at least for the sort of total satisfaction we're talking about here, the full realization of your every desire with nothing at all left to pursue, Shaw was right on the mark. It's both false and even dangerous to think that having all our desires satisfied would be complete bliss. There's good reason to think that we are essentially hopers and dreamers, strivers and achievers, and that to be engaged in such a quest is a vital part of the whole point of the adventure. We seem made to travel and not just to arrive.

A gap between our desires and their satisfaction is then perhaps not at all unfortunate but completely healthy and, in addition, genuinely necessary for real happiness. A gap is not a formula for frustration, or bitterness toward God for allowing us to be disappointed now and then, or even frequently, but rather it's simply a broad space and foundation for hope. The gap is good. We all need something to propel us forward. We need unrealized possibilities, dreams that have not yet come true. We need goals to reach toward, and goals are always rooted in desires yet unsatisfied. As the bestselling author Paolo Coelho puts this insight: "It's the possibility of having a dream come true that makes life interesting."

Augustine's mother, of course, was right, as mothers most often are. We don't just seem to need desires and goals. We need the right desires and goals. Wanting is important in life. And it's part of a happy life to have proper desires. The right desires for you to have will propel you forward on your best adventures in the world. You are here to grow and become and to make a difference. So are we all. We are in this world to use our talents to create good for other people as well as ourselves. We're not here to ever get to a point where we just lie back and swing in the ultimate hammock of perfectly satisfied desire. That would be death to the spirit and the opposite of the good and happy life we need. Unsatisfied desire keeps a fire going within us, provides the basis of hope, and steers us forward in life like nothing else possibly could. So, we conclude at this point that the popular Desire Satisfaction View of Happiness is just false, and even dramatically so.

Can you rid yourself of desires?

There is one more thing that we should mention. The common view of happiness that we can now see is false, but that nonetheless maintains its grip on so many people, holds that any gap between desire and satisfaction creates unhappiness, and so if you want to be happy, you should eliminate that gap. But we can look around the world and see people acting in very different ways in response to this judgment. And there is an important reason why. In principle, there are two very different ways for getting rid of any gap between your desires and their satisfactions. One is obviously the attempt we've been talking about — satisfying all your desires. The other is just as radical, and likely to be equally impossible. It's getting rid of all your desires, extirpating them, rooting them out, just ceasing ever to desire anything. If you had no desires at all, then of course you'd have no unsatisfied desires. There would be no desire-satisfaction gap and so no disappointment in your life.

People often understand certain versions of Buddhism to be recommending this. The Buddhist diagnosis of life, as commonly interpreted, is that life is suffering.

Suffering is then said to be the result of unsatisfied or thwarted desire. We should eliminate all the suffering we can. It's typically easier to give up desires than it is to guarantee their satisfaction. In the case of any given desire, this seems within our power, at least in principle. Therefore, we should seek to eliminate every one of our desires, including, eventually, even this desire to engage in such a program of elimination.

The philosophical problems with this understanding of Buddhism are, interestingly, the same as the problems we have raised against the more western recommendation for dealing with the alleged connection between happiness and satisfaction. Much suffering arises out of inappropriate desire. Some suffering arises in connection with natural and appropriate desire. It doesn't follow that all suffering arises out of desire, or that suffering arises out of all desire. It matters what form your suffering takes and what your desires are, as well as how you hold those desires and view them.

As we write these words, we can say truly that even the Dalai Lama has long desired a free Tibet. He may be free of an unnecessary degree of craving relative to this desire, but it is clearly something he wants to see happen. Good Buddhists have attained a level of emotional detachment with respect to many things precisely because they have desired and set out to attain this end, that of detachment. And many desire to spread the word to others, otherwise they would not write books and give talks on the virtues of their path in life. So maybe somewhere between fulfilling all your desires and eliminating them all, there is a middle ground of having proper desires and holding them loosely, with a wise measure of detachment as well as of hope.

It would be most likely impossible to eliminate all our desires, even if it were somehow desirable to do so. But it seems to be a more insightful judgment that it wouldn't be helpful to do that even if we could. Desire fuels life. Without desire, we spiritually die. Then we physically die. The right desires held in the right ways can give rise to hope and positive action. And both these things seem to be important parts of any good and happy life. If our desires are appropriate and are held gently, with a measure of proper detachment or a lightness of embrace, they can be healthy to have and can function in a contributive role within the sweep of a happy life.

Desire may be among the strongest inner things we experience. And it seems to be an inherently prospective, or goal-directed inclination of the feelings. To use an ancient Greek word, *telos*, which meant a purposive inclination or an overall goal-orientation, we appear to be hardwired for a teleological enterprise. We seem to be created for an ongoing adventure of desiring unrealized goals and seeking to attain them across various dimensions of our lives. We're not intended to achieve a static completion of perfect satisfaction as long as we're in this world. It seems mistaken to suppose otherwise.

The many facets of happiness

The ancients thought of happiness as primarily a state of being. Modern people tend to conceive of it as a state of feeling. Those who haven't thought about it enough wrongly construe it as a state of having. It may instead be more like a process of becoming. It is a dynamic, progressive state involving the setting, pursuit, and sequential episodic attainment of goals, or else unexpected alternatives to those goals that are discovered only in the pursuit and found to be right for you and the people around you in ways that allow you to flourish and enjoy the process along the way. It's an extended endeavor that is ongoing as long as you're alive. It involves not just satisfying the desires you have, but shedding some, rising above others, deepening a few, pursuing those that are right for you with courage and hope, and finding in the process new ones that you never had before. But, through all this, it is a process of acting, adapting, discovering, and becoming.

Happiness is not a simple and seamless thing. It seems stitched together from contentment, fulfillment, enjoyment, and love. It's deep, complex, rich, and ever changing in its specific embodiment within a life. But there are basic aspects of it that are universal. You can be happy with or without much money. Happiness can happen with or without much health. But you can't be happy without any degree of virtue, or of satisfaction, or of hope. And just like virtue and satisfaction, hope comes in many forms. Life is an adventure, or better yet a series of adventures, each preparing you for the next one, and often in ways you can't imagine. When we come to understand that insight, we come closer to understanding the good and happy life we need.

Desire for that which is

And this is where we loop back to the Stoics and the details of their view, whom we haven't ever really left, although we've ventured far, to put them into perspective. Epictetus seems to have had some measure of agreement with the assumptions behind the common view that "Happiness = Satisfied Desires" and "Unhappiness = Unsatisfied Desires," at least to the extent of holding that any stable form of happiness *involves* satisfied desires, and unhappiness the opposite. He seems to accept or assume the Perfect Satisfaction Axiom, and then he treats it in a wholly surprising way.

Epictetus of course viewed happiness through the lens of virtue as itself being both necessary and sufficient for that desired condition. It is precisely virtue, he would maintain, that requires us not to be dissatisfied with our lot in life as it is right now, or with anything about this world, whose details come from God, or the Logos. Yet he wanted to avoid the widespread strategy for satisfaction by which we strive to satisfy our desires by getting possession of the many external things we may prefer to attain or achieve, things he thought of as "indifferents" that, in his view, it seems we happen to favor too often and too much. And yet he equally shunned the very different philosophical approach by which we seek to eliminate any gap between our desires and reality by simply extinguishing our desires.

He apparently thought of some desires as appropriate emotions, but he also believed all outer desires, desires for anything outside our own future mental states, should be bound to what in fact is, if we are to be fully liberated from the troubling quest for what is not, along with any disappointment or bitterness in our hearts at what happens to characterize our world in a way that might be in conflict with contrary desires. And so he directed us to desire one and only one external thing: *that which is.* Don't seek to satisfy such desire, don't eliminate all such desire, but rather transform all outer desire into what it ought to be, which is: *an embrace of all that is.*

And that's a big twist. Classic Stoics like Epictetus ask of us a complex balancing act. We're to desire, accept, and embrace — even to love — everything that is, as a dutiful act of piety toward the gods who have brought it to us. But we're also to live in accordance with nature in the additional sense that we naturally and rightly believe certain things to be preferred for our existence as beings in a physical world who flourish only in healthy and positive relationships. But what is it to prefer if in some sense not to desire?

REMEMBER

It seems that from a Stoic point of view, we can in some sense desire and hope for any relevant preferred indifferents, and that, accordingly, we not only properly have impulses to act in pursuit of such things that are not yet real and existent for us, but that we also properly engage in suitable actions that follow from these preferences as we seek to gain valuable indifferents for ourselves and others, and that we can rightly desire to have such impulses as we experience them. But in addition, we ought to desire whatever results of those actions the gods also decree, whether they seem successful satisfactions of our impulses and acts or not. We can desire or embrace what is true now, while we rightly can strive for something different we desire *next*, but always at the same time maintaining a general desire for *whatever happens*, whether it's in accordance with our own sense of preferred indifferents, or not.

There's an old Christian hymn with the lyrics "Trust and obey, for there's no better way." And those words may well sum up the Stoic attitude. We're to trust whatever happens as ordained by the Logos for the greater good of the whole of which we all are parts, and we're to obey the demands of reason and virtue to act to attain whatever we take at any moment to be for the sake of the good of the whole, in so far as we can discern what that might be. And yet, whatever our desires about our own moral improvement, and the preferred indifferents that may or may not come into our lives, we're to fall back, always and everywhere with the fundamental unshakeable desire for whatever already is.

Happiness comes from within

The big surprise the Stoics have in store for us is their distinctive claim that the many external or outer things, the preferred indifferents, that we desire and even properly seek to attain for our own bodily and social flourishing — like some positive measure of heath, wealth, and respect — have nothing at all to do with whether or not we achieve happiness. Their view is that happiness is determined entirely within, in the realm of our governing element, our freedom to pursue virtue. If we choose virtue in its many forms, committing to wisdom, courage, justice, and self-mastery, happiness will follow along, like a good dog at our heels, regardless of the externals we have in our lives.

Stoicism remains consistent with something like the axiom behind the common view of happiness in holding that any gap must be eliminated between desire and its fulfillment. To Stoics, the purpose of this elimination is to preserve our inner peace from any potential negativity a gap might rouse, and thereby allow happiness a safe perch in our souls. And the Stoics uniquely seek to secure that elimination by their recommendation that we desire only the actual course of what is and was and is to be. That way, there's no satisfaction gap at all. But on this picture, there also seems to be no room for hope and its distinctive benefits. Yet the Stoics stand firm, apparently torn between oddly hoping the rest of us will grasp the power of their view, and yet accepting that most of us won't.

REMEMBER

The Stoics are convinced: If we can come to desire all that happens, if we are able to embrace and love the flow of events we're actually given, however they may seem, we're positioned for happiness to follow us through life. But this happiness will then come only as the result of our own inner virtue.

The real question is: Are we convinced by this Stoic insistence? Do we need to accept, embrace, and even love all that happens in the world, desiring that it be exactly as it is, just to secure a place for virtuous happiness in our hearts? Or might it be enough to hold more lightly to many contrary desires, seeking to improve the world around us as well as our inner selves, yet not feeling an undue attachment to these desires, or a deep craving for any of our desires to be satisfied in our own preferred time and way, as we continue to move forward with that essential element of hope in our hearts, an element that classic Stoics seem not to have recognized or acknowledged as important for a happy life? It's a question they never asked. But we should.

Chapter **11**

Pleasure and Pain

I t gives us great pleasure to bring you this chapter, which we hope will be in no way a pain to read. If we can succeed in making this topic a pleasant journey, it may irk some of the true Stoics among our readers who seek to avoid unnecessary pleasures, even those provoked by their own ideas. And they won't like being irked either, since it's not an emotion they endorse.

In this chapter, we examine Stoic views on a basic feature of life that needs to be addressed by every practical philosophy. Some things give us pleasure, others cause us pain, and many things do both. What are we to make of these fundamental facts? How do you, or should you, react to pleasure and pain in your efforts to create a life worth living? What's the best way to think of these powerful forces that pull and push us along?

The Epicurean Pull of Pleasure

In the ancient world, the Stoics thought of the Epicureans as their main rivals. It wasn't exactly a mixed martial arts cage match, but there was a keen and extended competition for hearts and minds. Scholars think Epicurus built his garden retreat for philosophical conversations right outside Athens just a few years after Zeno began gathering Stoic followers in the heart of the city. The men shared a few ideas in common but disagreed vigorously on other things.

The Epicurean worldview was simple and clear, as developed by Epicurus himself and later elaborated by the Roman poet Lucretius, among others. These thinkers believed that the reality in which we live is infinite and eternal and composed of nothing but irreducible, indivisible physical atoms and the void surrounding those tiny particles of matter. Atoms have combined in random ways to form all that now is. There is no logic or purpose behind anything, no God decreeing, creating, or guiding it all. Any meaning or purpose is wholly up to us to achieve in our own choices, endeavors, and acts. We can make meaning but never find it waiting for us. Death is our end.

REMEMBER

To the Epicureans, ethics is all a matter of humanly constructed rules for making our lives easier. Our notions of good and evil as well as right and wrong correspond to no ultimate realities woven into a hidden fabric behind the appearances of the physical world. They are merely useful tools that we've made for our convenience. Morality, like politics and law, is just about smoothing the flow of human interactions and articulating rules of the road that aren't any more deeply rooted in the stuff of nature than, say, parking regulations or governmental requirements on banks and amusement parks.

Epicurus on pleasure

The Epicureans also had distinctive views about the topic of pleasure that were noteworthy in their time and that have given them a misleading reputation in our own day. Their founder Epicurus was convinced that pleasure is in fact the supreme good for human beings and that it also is and should be the central motive for all our actions. He said:

> Pleasure is our first and kindred good. It's the starting point of every choice and aversion, and we return to it as we make feeling the rule by which to judge every good thing. (Diogenes Laertius, *Lives*, 10:129)

In another passage he goes on to say that he would not know what to think of goodness or "the good" without all the pleasures of, for example, taste, hearing, seeing, and sex. But so that we don't misunderstand his philosophy of pleasure as being one of extreme and mindless indulgence, or even opulently sybaritic revelry, we should mention that he also adds an explanatory or cautionary note to these statements, saying:

> It's impossible to live pleasantly without living prudently, honorably, and justly, and impossible to live prudently, honorably, and justly without living pleasantly. (*Principle Doctrines*, ER 32)

To this philosopher of enjoyment, pleasure is and should be our proper focal goal in life, and even the guiding purpose behind all that we do. But there's a twist. Epicurus didn't have in mind a purely selfish pursuit of pleasure. On the contrary, in his estimation we best pursue not just our own pleasure but pleasure in a more general sense, seeking to increase the overall quantity of it to be found in the world — the more, the merrier — and so we try to expand the amount to be experienced by others as well as ourselves, so long as that's consistent with our own need of a pleasant life. For this reason, the pursuit of pleasure should not be considered a selfish, egocentric path. This focus of Epicureanism on increasing pleasure for all was deeply influential on later European ethical theories, such as utilitarianism.

TIP

It's a surprise for many to learn that Epicurus viewed inner peace, or the tranquility of soul that results from an absence of pain, suffering, and emotional turbulence, as in fact the highest and greatest of pleasures, and one that can be enjoyed for extended periods, even in principle perhaps without limit during our earthly sojourn, while yet being invulnerable to surfeit or satiety. True inner serenity has no expiration date and bears within itself no requirement for a pause. You can't have too much tranquility at your core.

He also believed that, while all pleasures are good in themselves, not all are equally worthy of being chosen and enjoyed at a particular time, or in just any situation. Discernment is needed. This philosopher even held pleasures of the mind to be higher in value than those of the body, although he heartily approved of the lower delights. He also preferred simple pleasures over those that can be considered luxuries, and proudly claimed to live on bread and water, with sometimes the addition of a small pot of cheese. He believed that, among our felt needs for pleasurable activities, some are natural and necessary, like eating bread and drinking water; some are natural but not necessary, as perhaps a warm bath for some or frequent sex for others; and that various of our felt needs are neither natural nor necessary, such as feasting on rich and rare foods in great quantities, or collecting lavish homes and gardens for a more elaborate enjoyment of diverse experiences.

And of course, this threefold categorization was thought to bring with it a useful measure for judging potential delights. Nature normally has made more easily available what we most naturally need, and more difficult what's not natural or needed at all. Epicurus also pointed out that some pleasures will bring greater pains in their wake and because of that should not be chosen, just as some pains will yield the possibility of greater pleasures and should therefore be embraced. Think about the difficulties and ordeals we undergo in the gym to train for accomplishments that can bring a great delight otherwise unattainable without those struggles and pains that alone made it available.

REMEMBER

So the Epicurean ideal isn't at all the debauched, heedless hedonist, but a prudently judging and wise person finding and enjoying higher pleasures as well as proper lower ones, with a sustainable balance of experiences along the way that allow, overall, for a relatively peaceful life.

Stoic objections to Epicureanism

You can easily see why Epicureanism, sensibly understood, was an attractive picture for many people in the ancient world, as well as in subsequent times. It obviously holds a strong allure in our own day. But the Stoics took it to be both wrong and dangerous as a worldview and life orientation.

First, the Stoics objected to Epicurean physics, or the overall description of nature in their philosophy as a purposeless realm ruled only by the arbitrary randomness of chance. The Epicureans shared with Stoics a materialist or physicalist account of ultimate reality, where there weren't believed to be any nonphysical souls, spirits, or gods in addition to the material things that exist. All minds, souls, or deities were held by them to be fully physical, though perhaps composed of a simpler or subtler form of matter than most. To the Epicureans, the gods of antiquity, if they existed at all, may have been impressive beings, but they weren't our creators, our governors, or even our guides. They did not actually intervene in our lives and could offer no larger purpose or value for our existence. They were just as governed by chance and the meaningless powers and debilities inherent in atoms and space as the rest of us. We are therefore on our own with our pleasures and pains.

The Stoic universe, while fully physical, and so a thoroughly material realm like that of the Epicureans, was yet in important ways radically different from the Epicurean vision, being pervasively infused with intelligence, meaning, rationality, and goodness from a divine source and dimension that governs all and decides all. In the god-drenched world of Stoicism, divine portions of reason and virtue are our highest, greatest, and most motivating attributes. Stoics believed that virtue, not pleasure, is the supreme good for human beings and that it both is and should be the central motive for all our actions.

For Epicureans to suggest that pleasure rightly leads the way instead, even with an enlightened and relatively subtle view of what this means, was to the Stoics an abomination and a reversal of the right order among things. Virtue at the center of life is pleasant, delightful, and brings joy when lived and embodied properly. But that's not why it's so valuable as to be the ultimate choice-worthy item of all. Pleasure does not lead the way and endow virtue with its goodness, but rather virtue is the only thing that can make pleasure proper and valuable in any way. Alone, pleasure is a danger.

PHILOSOPHICAL ASSESSMENTS OF PLEASURE

Analysts of our condition hold widely different views on pleasure. A sample easily shows this:

Pleasure is the greatest incentive to evil. —Plato, in Plutarch's *Life of Cato the Censor*

Pleasure may perfect us as truly as prayer. —W. E. Channing, *Notebook: Joy*

Pleasure is an inciter to vileness. —Cicero, *De Legibus*

Please is the only thing one should live for, nothing ages like happiness. —Oscar Wilde

He that loves pleasure must for pleasure fall. —Christopher Marlowe, *Doctor Faustus*

This debate about pleasure continues into our time. Is it a wonderful thing, or dangerous? Does it enhance our lives or distract us from what matters more? Some think it can go in either direction, depending on how we use it. And that, much more than a simple rejection of pleasure, would be a more Stoic view. Its value is up to us and our use of it.

REMEMBER

Stoicism insists that pleasure is at best a side effect of the virtuous life and should never be given priority in our thinking. Virtue can give us pleasure, but pleasure can't give us virtue. To the Stoics, pleasure in fact is often quite treacherous and holding it close is a bit like keeping a wild tiger as a pet.

Pleasure and Pain with the Stoics

We take great pleasure in quoting the classic Stoics in this section to give you a sense of the range and drift of their comments on pleasure, first, and then by extension pain, which is discussed less often in our sources for their views but was also important to them. We base our quotes on popular translations, but also modernize, using the original languages, lest thee be grievously bedeviled by abstruse phrasings of yore perforce bequeathed unto us.

Epictetus has his say

There are places where the Stoics give very reasonable advice about the pleasures of the world and the many desires that we tend to have for them, even sometimes with a measure of intensity. Epictetus says something very commonsensical and memorable in *The Discourses*, where he's talking about people who already enjoy ample possessions that give them pleasure, and yet are never satisfied and are always seeking and grasping after new delights:

> The same thing happens to children who put a hand down into a narrow-necked jar and try to take out figs and nuts — if they get their hand full, they can't get it out and then cry. Drop a few and the hand will emerge. And so, you too should release your cravings. Don't set your heart on too many things and you will have what you want. (*Discourses* 3.9.22)

This can sound like sensible advice of moderation concerning our desire for pleasures. If we're not too greedy, we can get what we want. But of course we live in a time when few people ever seem to have an operative sense of what's enough. Greed is more pervasive than we realize, even in our own hearts. Epictetus lived in such a time as well. And this vivid little story about children with a jar of figs and nuts illustrates how even modest self-restraint can avoid problems and yield positive results. Epictetus here sounds a bit like Epicurus. But this simple imagery of moderation also can conceal a deeper and more extreme view visible elsewhere, as for example when the Stoic philosopher says this quite starkly about our common desire to possess and enjoy more and more things, along with the pleasures they may bring:

> Freedom is not acquired by the satisfaction of craving, but by its suppression. (*Discourses* 9.1.175)

Some translators prefer "destruction" to "suppression." And of course, that's not a matter of dropping a few figs and nuts, but of eliminating any strong desire to have figs, nuts, or anything else, and keeping your hand out of every such jar. So, in one passage, we seem to be counseled to moderation toward any desire for delight, or pleasure, and in another, abstinence.

In the *Handbook*, Epictetus tells his students and us:

> Whenever the idea of a pleasure occurs to you, guard yourself, just as with all other ideas, that you don't get carried away by it. Let it wait. Take a pause. Then think about two periods of time: the one when you'll feel the pleasure, and a later one when you'll regret it and criticize yourself for it. Compare both together to the gratification and self-satisfaction you'll feel if you refrain totally. But if you think the time has come for indulgence, then be careful not to be overwhelmed by its

enticement and charm. Weigh against all this the thought of how much better the consciousness would be of having won a victory over it. (34)

Does our guide mean to imply here that all pleasures are somehow regrettable and will spark a self-critique and even a measure of self-accusation in their aftermath? Does he also believe that refusing or avoiding an available delight will never in itself cause regret and remorse? And if so, he seems to view our psychology with his own confirmation bias. We often regret the road not taken, whether it was a path of delight or of resisting temptation. There's no clear justification for either assumption he's making here. But perhaps we'll find his underlying reasons for this thinking in other places.

TIP

To provide a hint for what's to come, it could be that Epictetus is concerned in this passage not simply with pleasure itself, but with those situations in which we envision a potential future pleasure that's likely to be experienced if we engage in certain behavior, but is one we're not yet undergoing, and we have to choose whether to pursue it. He doesn't want us ever to get "carried away" by such a prospect. But he still might be fine with the pleasures that come our way without any explicit choice or pursuit of them. We'll see.

Later in the *Handbook*, Epictetus says this about some of the physical activities that, presumably, he thinks many people find to be pleasurable, although he includes one odd example:

> It's a sign of coarseness to spend a lot of time on bodily functions like exercising, eating, drinking, defecating, and copulating. These are things to be done only in passing, while your full attention is devoted to the mind. (41)

Good luck explaining this to your dinner companion, or romantic partner. "Sorry, my full attention is on Stoicism. What? Wait. Don't leave." In other words, Epictetus is saying here that basic bodily functions, and even those associated with pleasurable sensations, can be engaged in properly as long as it's not with your full attention. Despite their being normal and often needed actions, you can't allow them to distract you from a proper focus on more intellectual matters, like pondering, or reading a book such as this.

As much as we might wish to acknowledge and encourage the joys of pondering, as well as of reading, at least in this book, we should also point out that these recommendations are clearly not coming from a man who relishes the reality of embodiment, including the activities and sensations of physicality, or what are sometimes referred to as "the lower pleasures" of the senses. Why? Perhaps he worries that physical sensations of all sorts tend most powerfully to pull us away from our properly spiritual focus on reason and virtue, and so is convinced that the less we lend our attention to these sensations, the safer we'll be in keeping to our proper concerns.

As a former slave, Epictetus is always keen on liberating the rest of us from anything that might enslave us, however metaphorically yet genuinely. He prizes freedom and personal autonomy. He wants nothing to hold us back or chain us down. And he's concerned about how widespread the trap of either pleasure or pain seems to be for enslaving people in different ways.

He appears to reason that if the door is opened too wide to any concentration on the physical domain, our bodily experience can easily displace the mental side of who we most intimately are. With the door to our inner life carelessly thrown open to pleasure, the delights of the flesh can take over, distracting us from reason, duty, and virtue. That's the philosopher's concern, based presumably on such ample evidence as we still see all around us. And pain can chain us down in different ways — through fear or worry and even with a distaste, resentment, or a hatred of its presence and place in our lives.

So pleasure can turn us away from the gods, and pain can turn us against them. That's the diagnosis. Epictetus is especially concerned that those who spends most of their waking hours chasing pleasure and fleeing pain are not able to be fully wise, courageous, just, and self-controlled. Such individuals have rather locked themselves in chains that quickly become hard to break, and so have given up the autonomy that's rightly theirs by nature.

Marcus Aurelius weighs in

Emperor Marcus Aurelius, who was greatly influenced by the recorded conversations and concerns of this one-time slave, seems to agree with Epictetus, and writes in his own journal:

> The human soul degrades itself . . . when it is overpowered by pleasure or pain. (*Meditations* 2.16)

A few lines down from this statement he asks:

> Then what can guide us? Only philosophy. Which means that the power within us stays safe and free from assault, superior to pleasure and pain.

There is here the same sense that both pleasure and pain are dangers to the proper functioning of the greatest inner power in the soul. And yet in another place, while mentioning the many hidden beauties that can be seen in animals and in nature generally, Marcus says in a more positive mood:

> Anyone with a feeling for nature — a deeper sensitivity — will find that it all gives pleasure. (*Meditations* 3.2)

This statement is clearly not a warning about a danger to be found in nature, but is meant more as a reminder to approach nature with an open heart and mind to notice its wonders, experiences that will bring a healthy pleasure. Marcus does not seem to think that this sort of pleasure is a threat at all. No cautionary words are added to this observation and no concerns are raised about how such pleasure might trouble reason or virtue, or our inner freedom.

Then, however, sentences later, he coaches himself in what his ordinary thoughts ought to be like through the day, so that if anyone asked, "What are you thinking?" he could truthfully answer without hesitation or shame. He reflects on what should result if he's managing his thought life well, and his reported thoughts would be proper, from a Stoic point of view. He says to himself in commentary (with the emphasis here and below being ours):

> And it would be obvious at once from your answer that your thoughts were straightforward and considerate ones — the thoughts of an unselfish person, one *unconcerned with pleasures* and with sensual indulgence generally, or with arguing, or with slander and envy, or anything else you'd be ashamed to be caught thinking. (*Meditations* 3.4)

Notice that he groups pleasures here in a category with slander and envy. Elaborating in the next lines, he continues motivating himself to be more thoroughly philosophical in his approaches to the daily challenges of life, and reminds himself of the strengths to be attained by anyone who rigorously applies a wise Stoic point of view at each present moment in all his thoughts:

> Someone like that — who refuses to put off joining the elect — is a kind of priest, a servant of the gods, in touch with what's within him, and what keeps a person *undefiled by pleasures, invulnerable to any pain*, untouched by arrogance, unaffected by meanness, an athlete in the greatest of all contests, the struggle not to be overwhelmed by anything that happens. (ibid.)

He later writes in the same passage again, as always, addressing himself:

> The mind is the ruler of the soul. It should remain unstirred by *agitations of the flesh*, gentle and violent alike. Not mingling with them but fencing itself off and keeping those feelings in their place. When they make their way into your thoughts, through the sympathetic link between mind and body, don't try to resist the sensation. It's natural. Just don't let the mind get involved with making judgments, calling it "good" or "bad." (ibid.)

In the ending words of this reflection, Marcus connects with an opening passage in the recorded sayings of the Musonius Rufus, the teacher of Epictetus greatly respected by Marcus. Musonius is considering the role of arguments, or "proof" in life, saying that many things don't require proof because they're just obvious to us, as everything is to the gods. But he then points out that when things aren't obvious, a proof or argument can often be constructed that moves from what is clear to what was otherwise obscure, illuminating what may have been a hidden truth. He then illustrates how this works, using as an example a well-known Stoic claim about pleasure:

> Take for example the statement that pleasure is not a good. At first exposure, we don't recognize it as true, since in fact pleasure ordinarily appeals to us as a good. But starting from the generally accepted premise that every good is desirable and adding to it a second equally accepted claim that some pleasures are not desirable, we succeed in proving that pleasure is not a good. That is, we prove what was otherwise unknown or unrecognized by means of the known or recognized. (From the lecture, "That There is No Need of Giving Many Proofs for One Problem.")

Even though in this passage Musonius is merely seeking to establish something about how useful arguments work, his example shows some classic Stoic reasoning about pleasure, which we can restate in three simple steps:

1. Every good is desirable (meaning: at all times and in all circumstances),

2. Pleasure often is not desirable (because of its circumstances), so

3. Pleasure is not a good (despite how it often seems).

It still may be true, from a Stoic point of view, that in the right circumstances, pleasure can qualify as a preferred indifferent. But it's never to be thought of as a true good. Nor is pain to be appraised as an evil. And a parallel argument or proof can be constructed for that equally important Stoic assessment.

Yet we still have a way to go to appreciate these views more fully. In addition, what we've said so far about the reasoning Musonius gives still leaves open the theoretical possibility that in Stoic thinking, pleasure is somehow to be viewed in most instances as dangerous, or as a generally "dispreferred indifferent." But let's get back to Marcus Aurelius.

One evening Marcus does something like a quick life review, first asking himself how he has behaved to the gods, and then to the most important people in his life, and then he says, pondering the end of his earthly life:

> Consider all that you've gone through, all you've survived, and that the story of your life is done, your assignment complete. How many good things have you seen? How much pain and pleasure have you resisted? How many honors have you declined? How many unkind people have you been kind to? (*Meditations* 8.31)

In this musing, he's putting resistance to both pain and pleasure on a moral level with being kind to the unkind, surely a praiseworthy achievement. Later, he grows impatient about how he's using the limited time he has left, saying:

> No time for reading. For controlling arrogance, yes. For overcoming pain and pleasure, yes. For not feeling anger at stupid and unpleasant people, even for caring about them; for that, yes. (*Meditations* 8.8)

We've so far seen the emperor talk about being unconcerned with pleasures, undefiled by them, protecting the mind so that it's unstirred by "agitations of the flesh," keeping such sensations or feelings in place, "resisting" pain and pleasure, and "overcoming" them both. Yet we also saw him speak positively of the pleasures to be found in recognizing beauty within nature. And in fact, that was not a sheer anomaly for his reflections. He's not otherwise always negative about pleasure. In another later passage, he says:

> People find pleasure in different ways. I find it in keeping my mind clear.
> (*Meditations* 8.43)

This is a mental pleasure, for sure, but it is in fact a pleasure he seems to endorse. Yet, there is a complication. Marcus begins Book Nine of what has been called his "spiritual exercises" by reminding himself that any injustice is a form of blasphemy against God, who has formed us for better and more ethical relations with each other. Then he characterizes lying as another form of blasphemy, a kind of spitting in the face of what's real and provided for us by God. Even stumbling into falsehood unaware will cut us off from what is, and is intended by God. Then Marcus writes something very revealing for our current topic. He says:

> And to pursue pleasure as good and flee from pain as evil — that too is blasphemous. Someone who does that is bound to find himself constantly reproaching nature, complaining that it does not treat good and bad people as they deserve, but often lets the bad enjoy pleasure and the things that produce it, while making the good suffer pain and the things that bring it. And even to fear pain is to reject something that's bound to happen, the world being what it is, and that again is blasphemy. While, if you pursue pleasure, you can hardly avoid wrongdoing — which is obviously blasphemous. (ibid.)

He goes on in finishing the passage to remind himself that nature seems indifferent to some things, and that if we want to follow nature, as Stoic philosophy recommends for us, we need to be indifferent to those same things as well, sharing nature's attitude. And so, he concludes:

> To embrace pleasure over pain, life over death, fame over anonymity, is clearly blasphemous. (ibid.)

REMEMBER

Perhaps the key to this passage is in the concept of embracing. Maybe it's fine to experience pleasure, and even to prefer it to pain, but to embrace it is to grab and hold it tightly as a strong preference, and perhaps with a strength that's unbecoming in our response to the variety of what God gives us.

To grasp his point here is a bit tricky, since most classical Stoics have in some way acknowledged a proper natural sense in which such contrastive things as pleasure over pain, life over death, health over sickness, modest wealth over poverty, and perhaps even fame over anonymity can be viewed as preferred indifferents — not as intrinsically or morally good, or always and essentially beneficial, but rather as potential resources for the positive roles we're to play in the world, as given to us by the Logos, or God. But it's as if Marcus sees us too commonly going beyond a wise and modest preference in these matters and instead chasing such things or embracing them tightly, rather than yielding to whatever God or nature may have in store for us.

Here's the balance: If we're sick or poor today, we can seek health or more resources tomorrow, perhaps as partners to the Logos, but it would be rebellious to God to be bitter or resentful about our condition now. We can have wise and natural preferences in making our own choices for the future but should never strongly prefer a contrary reality at any given realized moment over what God has brought us at that moment. That's what Marcus sees as blasphemous, or impious. And it may be a clue to the full Stoic view on pleasure and pain. We're not there quite yet, but we're getting close.

In the last place in his meditations where the topic of pleasure arises, Marcus evaluates himself and reminds himself that:

> You'll never stop complaining until you feel the same pleasure that the hedonist gets from self-indulgence — only from doing what's proper to human beings as far as circumstances, inherent or fortuitous, allow. Enjoyment means doing as much of what your nature requires as you can. And you can do that anywhere. (*Meditations* 10.33)

Here we seem to have an acceptance of proper pleasure, enjoyment, or a state of feeling good, in its essence, as a nice potential side effect of acting right and living well, which means acting and living in accordance with nature, or virtuously. The hedonist feels a keen need for pleasure and wrongly chases it. The Stoic warmly accepts it whenever it comes along as a frequent but unneeded secondary feature of doing the right thing.

We've presented all these passages from the emperor to show two things: first, how often the issues of pleasure and pain come up in his reflections on his life, aspirations, and struggles; and second, the variety of thoughts and feelings he has about the role of such sensations in our lives more generally.

A brief recap may be helpful so that we don't lose the thread of thoughts here. Marcus has talked about the soul "degrading" itself when it allows itself to be "overcome" by pleasure or pain. He's spoken of the power within us as "superior to pleasure and pain." He proposed an ideal of being "unconcerned" with such sensations, "undefiled" by pleasures, "invulnerable to any pain," and affirms these attitudes as important for what he thinks of as "the contest of life" in which we're engaged. He talks about being "unstirred" by these things and "resisting" and "overcoming" them. He calls chasing pleasure and fleeing pain "blasphemous" to God. And yet he finds pleasure in nature and in keeping his mind clear. He sees pleasure as a natural side effect of virtue.

So what should we conclude from all this? It may help to go back a few years before Marcus was writing and see what the earlier Stoic Seneca said about these things. He's often thought of as more moderate than Epictetus, more certain than Marcus, and so more straightforward as to what his views are.

Seneca joins the fray

One thing we notice repeatedly in Seneca's writings is that he's especially keen to distinguish pleasure from what he considers to be a deeper and more resilient mode of human experience that we call joy. In a letter to his friend Lucilius, *Letters* 59, "On Pleasure and Joy" we find an extended statement about this. We'll quote it here in three segments with a few comments provided along the way. Seneca begins with a line that hopefully brought a laugh or at least a smile to the face of his correspondent:

> I should now show you how you may know you are not wise. The wise man is joyful, happy, and calm, untroubled; he lives on a level with the gods. Now, go ask yourself if you're never down, if your mind is not bothered by any fear, anticipating what's to come; if your soul keeps on a balanced straight path day and night, upright and content with itself, then you have attained the greatest good mortals can have. If, however, you chase pleasures of all kinds in all directions, you need to realize that you're as far short of wisdom as you are of joy. Joy is the goal you're after, but you're wandering from the path if you expect to attain that amid riches and official titles, or in other words, if you seek joy in a crowd of cares. Those things that you chase so eagerly, as if they could give you happiness and pleasure, are merely causes of grief. (*Letters* 59)

He goes on to detail the many ways that people pursue pleasure, deep down hoping for joy and often finding jeopardy or harm instead:

> Think then on this, that the effect of wisdom is a joy that's unbroken and continuous. The mind of the wise man is like the area beyond the moon, eternal calm pervades it. You have then a reason for wishing to be wise, if the wise man is never

deprived of joy. This joy springs only from the knowledge that you possess the virtues. None but the brave, the just, the self-controlled can experience joy. (ibid.)

Our Stoic advisor then imagines his correspondent, or else another skeptical conversation partner, pushing back here and saying, "What do you mean? Don't the foolish and wicked also feel joy?" And he answers that, no, they never experience true joy, but only many agitating sensations that ultimately weary them, in his words, "when the pleasures that they've heaped on a body that's too small to hold them begin to rot." He adds:

Pleasure-lovers spend every night amid glittering counterfeit joys, as if it were their last. But the joy that comes to the gods, and to those who imitate the gods, is never broken off short. It doesn't cease. And it surely would come to an end if it was borrowed from the outside. (ibid.)

In a different letter, addressed again to Lucilius, Seneca writes:

We've reached the heights if we know where to find joy, and if we've not placed our happiness in the control of external things. (*Letters* 23.2)

External things may bring us plenty of pleasure, but only inner things bring us joy, a much more stable, durable, and uplifting gift to the soul, with a deep positive underlying tonality for all our experience. Seneca later says in the same letter that real joy is not a superficial, cheery, and sparkly sensation easy to reap from the surface of things, but that it's rather like a deep vein of rich ore far down in a mine that must be worked to attain its "bountiful returns," the deeper sensibility and felt sense of goodness that will endure through any situation, however challenging it might be. He counsels his friend to avoid those shiny surfaces full of passing delights that lure most people into harm instead of happiness. And then he sums up:

This is what I mean: Pleasure, unless it has been kept within limits, tends to flow headlong into the abyss of sorrow. (*Letters* 23. 6)

The key is how it functions in our lives. In another letter, however, Seneca urges as he often does the importance of embracing virtue and avoiding vice in all its forms, and then writes these more extreme sounding words:

Above all, banish pleasures from your sight. Avoid them above all other things, for they are like the bandits Egyptians call "lovers," who embrace us only to strangle us. (*Letters* 51.13)

It's a vivid image that portrays our pleasures as ready to hold onto us in what we mistakenly take to be a lover's hug, but that's intended only to immobilize us so that we can be killed and robbed of anything precious. In a different letter, he goes even farther in the same direction, saying this of our common tendency when we go astray with worldly delights and lose our bearings:

> We have bound over our souls to pleasure, whose service is the source of all evil. (*Letters* 110.10)

In language here that's very much like what we often find in Epictetus, evoking the bondage of enslavement, Seneca speaks now of being bound to pleasure and living in service to it. The message seems to be that if pleasure is looked to for an easy and desired self-indulgence, it rather transforms itself and becomes a harsh and capricious master that leads us in a direction opposite to the path we need to follow. Again, we read this:

> The soul is our king. If it is safe, our other functions stay on duty and serve us obediently. But the slightest lack of balance in the soul causes them to waver along with it. And when the soul has yielded to pleasure, its functions and actions grow weak, and any undertaking comes from a nerveless and unsteady source. (*Letters* 114.23)

The "other functions" referred to here will most likely include such things as our ability to form beliefs, or judgments, our capacity to have proper emotions and reactions of attitude and action based on our thoughts, our imaginings, and the events of the world. When the soul, our guiding force, yields or gives way to the allures of pleasure, then all our inner functions are damaged and become unreliable. That's the claim.

And then Seneca surprises us. Among all these dire warnings about pleasure and its potentially damaging effects, we can still come across a passage like this that seems to be blown on a breeze from another place:

> People set a narrow limit to their enjoyments if they take pleasure only in the present. Both the future and past serve for our delight, the one with anticipation and the other with memories, but the one is contingent and may not come to pass, while only the other is set. (*Letters* 99.5)

This is a double surprise, since philosophers like the Stoics often counsel us to focus on the present rather than the past and future, and Seneca here wants us to relish all three times. He's recommending pleasure and delight, not of course as lures to bondage of any kind, but as something to be felt well.

Throughout these many and very different statements about pleasure, a lesson begins to emerge that we can apply both to it and to its counterpart of pain. And it's not just a bit of guidance involving moderation or releasing a few nuts in a jar.

Using Sensations and Situations

In a classic and characteristic passage, Seneca writes wisely about what is required for genuine happiness:

> Nature intended that we should need no great equipment for living happily. Each one of us can make his own happiness. External things are of slight importance and can have no great influence in either direction. Prosperity does not exalt the wise man, nor does adversity cast him down, for he has always endeavored to rely entirely on himself, to derive all his joy from himself. (*Moral Essays II*, "To Helvia on Consolation" 4.1)

Seneca sees "external things" as having hardly any importance in themselves for whether we experience happiness or its opposite in our lives. And by external he means anything outside the total control of the will, our ability of free choice, and our own reason. So, perhaps surprisingly, pleasure, even the inner felt aspect of it, would be classified in the main if not entirely as an external thing that comes to us. So too could pain be classified, even though it's also experienced within our minds. It's still as an occurrent event to be considered as outside, or external to, the will, the part of us that is the seat of vice or virtue, the circle populated only by the thoughts, emotions, attitudes, and impulses toward action we choose. Anything outside the will and its productions of virtue or vice have, in Seneca's words, "slight importance" to us. When we're wise, delightful externals won't lift us up, and difficult externals won't cast us down. Nor will any such feelings within our minds. We instead will remain calm, stable, and free.

Some of the Stoics will say now and then that externals are "nothing to us," as if they never have any form of value at all. But even those who occasionally state such a thing usually recognize in other contexts an instrumental usage of externals, an employment of them by the will that, as used well, can be said to have some sort of derived value in our fulfilling of our proper roles and duties in the world.

In the *Discourses*, Epictetus says:

> Material things are indifferent, but the use one makes of them isn't. (*Discourses* 2.5.1)

He then gives an example that in a ball-based game of catch among skilled players, the ball itself is in a sense neutral or indifferent — so long as it has the most basic qualities needed for play, it doesn't matter what ball is used — but the ways the players skillfully choose to catch and throw it are what matter. We call a throw or a catch good when it uses the ball well. It would just be awkward in the middle of a game to see a great catch and shout out, "Vastly preferred indifferent catch!" A simpler "Good catch!" will do.

We clearly can use externals, such as a ball in a game. We must and should. That's a part of why we're here in a physical world. It seems that we're to use externals in our own self-development as well as for other purposes, such as in aid of others. And so, how we use them can matter.

There's a philosophical principle to be found in the neighborhood here. Not just Stoics, but many other philosophers through history and across cultures have agreed that very few things in life are intrinsically good or bad, or essentially either valuable or worthless apart from how we relate to them. The values of most things consist in how in how they function in our lives, in how we put them to use. In fact, let's call this *The Functionality Principle*: The value of most things depends on how we use them, how they function for us.

A wise person uses all things well. He or she doesn't crave or avidly seek wealth or fame, power or status, or pleasure. A wise soul doesn't chase and embrace pleasure, or fear and flee pain, but uses either of these sensations well whenever they arrive. The point for Seneca seems not to be that we should refuse all pleasure, but that we should closely monitor how we think of it and use it. We shouldn't avidly seek it or wholeheartedly invest in it. And in certain times and moods of vulnerability, we may even have to banish it from our lives to the extent that we can, pushing it away as a danger. But to the Stoics, pain by contrast is a thing we should never push away, as we undergo it. We should accept it when it comes, without fright or flight. We can then certainly seek to alleviate it and even remove it in the next moment, prudently trying to steer clear of its likely sources in the future. But the Stoic attitude is that in the time we undergo it, we should accept it as properly given to us in the moment of its presence, as coming from the gods, or the Logos, who would know all things best.

For the classic Stoics, everything in the world is to be accepted as a gift from God, the gods, the Logos, or Nature. But when we take strong attitudes, pro or con, toward anything other than virtue and vice, we endanger our inner peace, and our obedient service or piety toward the divine reason and benevolence behind all that appears in this world. The only thing that should always be acclaimed, pursued, and embraced is virtue, and the only thing that should always be condemned, avoided, and refused is vice. Without a focus on virtue as our overarching purpose, we're vulnerable to weakness, corruption, and an inner collapse that renders us unable to serve God and do our proper duty in this world throughout our existence. When we live wisely and virtuously in accordance with our true nature, using impressions well and seeking to act with goodness in all things, pleasures may attend us, just as pains may visit, but a deep joy can also be found within that helps us to handle and manage both. We can use well whatever comes our way. Without this wisdom, we're lost. When we embody it consistently, we can live in a sense above the turbulence and at peace.

The most fundamental idea in Stoicism may be about how we use impressions — the sensations, perceptions, and ideas that appear to us throughout our lives in the world. Epictetus even employs this idea of use or usage in our relation to God, as he offers these words in advising a student on how to be obedient to the divine:

> Be bold to look up to God and say: "From now on, use me as you wish. I am of one mind with you. I'm yours. Whatever you decide is fine with me. Take me where you want. Dress me as you choose. Do you want me to hold public office, or to steer clear of politics? Do you prefer me to stay here or go elsewhere, to be poor or rich? Everything you do, I'll explain to people. I'll show them the true nature of everything that happens." (*Discourses* 2.16.42)

He then comments, as if in a life review imagining the end of his own journey here in the world as he faces his departure:

> Speaking for myself, I hope to be overtaken by death at a time when my attention is focused exclusively on my will — when I'm trying to make it undisturbed by passion, unimpeded, unconstrained, and free. That's what I'd like to be occupied with, because then I can say to God: "Have I ever disobeyed your orders? Have I ever used the resources you gave me for needless purposes? Have I ever misused my senses or my preconceptions? Have I ever accused you of wrongdoing? Have I ever found fault with your governance? I fell ill when you wanted me to — as did others, but I did so willingly. I became impoverished because you wanted me to, but I did so gladly. I didn't hold any public office, because you didn't want me to, and I never missed it. Did you ever see me downcast because of that? Didn't I always come before you with a joyful countenance, ready for whatever you might ordain or command? Now you want me to leave the festival, and I do so full of gratitude for the fact that you found me worthy to share the celebration with you, see your works, and understand your governance." (*Discourses* 3.5.7–10)

Epictetus thought of himself as having been used well by God, and as using well whatever God chose to bring to him. That is the Stoic path, using well whatever comes our way. And this applies to pleasure and pain as to all other more obviously external things. Epictetus says about using adversity:

> A person's caliber is revealed by difficult circumstances and so, when a difficulty occurs, think of it as God pitting you against a tough training partner. "To what end?" someone asked. To help you become an Olympic victor, which takes sweat. Anyway, it seems to me that no one has ever had a better difficulty than the one you have now, if you're prepared to use it as an athlete uses a training partner. (*Discourses*, 1.24.1)

And in one of his brief sayings that have come down to us, he tells us:

> Anyone who's dissatisfied with the circumstances assigned him by fortune is unskilled in the art of living, while anyone who nobly endures his circumstances and makes reasonable use of what they have to offer deserves to be called a good person. (*Epictetus: The Complete Works, Fragment* 2)

TIP

Everything that comes our way is a potential tool for use in self-development and in improving the world. But it depends on us whether those things function for us as tools and are employed well. Seneca writes:

> Tools lie idle unless the workman uses them to perform his task. (*On Benefits*, 5.25.6)

REMEMBER

What matters is how we use the things that enter our lives. Seneca has a magnificent image, a fiery metaphor for how we can use our troubles, whether pains, sufferings, setbacks, obstacles, or hugely tempting pleasures that threaten to lure us off the proper path of life. He says:

> When the governing power in us is true to nature, it stands poised and ready to adjust to every challenge and use each new opportunity. It's ready for anything and pursues its own aims and embraces whatever it confronts, finding advantage in even opposition. It's like fire in this way. While a small flame can be extinguished by trash that's dumped on it, a big enough fire will just use and consume anything dropped on it. The more that's thrown at it, the higher it rises and the hotter it burns. (*Meditations*, 4.1)

For a wise and strong person, everything is just fuel for the inner fire. So, to the Stoics, we don't properly seek for pleasure or run from pain, but rather wisely develop our ability to use either well when they come into our lives. And like a strong flame, we then grow and prosper and rise higher from whatever we confront.

Chapter **12**

Natural Law

W e live in a doubting age. Many ideas that were once seen as rock-solid certainties are now widely questioned or disbelieved. We see this in religion, politics, the economy, in social life, and especially in ethics and values.

Lots of people today deny that there are any objective or absolute or universal moral truths. They either believe that there are no moral truths at all, or if there are, that they are based only on feelings, opinions, or cultural norms that vary from society to society. As they see it, morality is subjective, a purely human invention.

The ancient Stoics rejected such forms of moral skepticism or subjectivism. They believed that there are real moral truths that are "objective" (i.e., not based on mere opinion or taste) and rooted in basic, unchanging features of reality. They called this objective moral reality *natural law.* Later thinkers developed this Stoic idea and made it the foundation for modern beliefs about universal human rights, equal human dignity, and basic principles of international law. In this way, the idea of natural law has proved to be one of the most enduring legacies of Stoicism.

What Is Natural Law?

The Stoic concept of natural law is rooted in ancient Greek thought about divine or higher law. The earliest forms of Greek law (*nomos*) were based in custom or tradition. Later these customary laws were codified, supplemented, or replaced by written laws. Each Greek city-state had its own set of customary or written laws; these constituted the set of "civil" or "positive" laws that applied in a particular city-state (*polis*), which of course varied from state to state. But the Greeks were generally a religious people and believed that all basic law and morality must ultimately arise from a divine source. Hence the idea of a "higher law" that derives from the gods, is always right and just, and applies in all nations and states.

Early hints of the Greek idea of higher law can be found in Heraclitus's saying that "all human laws are nourished by one divine law," and in the poet Pindar's line that "law is the king of all, of mortals as well as immortals." But a far more famous account is found in Sophocles' classic play, *Antigone* (c. 442 BCE). There Antigone, the daughter of Oedipus, defies the decree of King Creon that the body of her brother Polyneices must lie unburied. Antigone buries the body and justifies her action by invoking the eternal "unwritten and unfailing statutes of heaven" that override all human laws or decrees that might conflict with them. At his trial, Socrates would later express a similar view of higher law, declaring "Men of Athens, I honor and love you; but I shall obey God rather than you." Aristotle taught that in addition to written laws, which are changeable, there is a "universal law," the law of nature, that is unalterable and always just and equitable.

In addition to thinkers like Heraclitus and Socrates, Stoic teaching on natural law was greatly influenced by the Cynics. As we have seen, the Cynics were hostile to civilization and drew a sharp distinction between what exists by custom or convention (*nomos*) and what exists by nature (*physis*). They held that nature is the proper standard of human behavior. In their view, "nature" essentially means what is primitive, primal, and animalistic, as opposed to what is artificial or based on human conventions and creations. They thus rejected all the trappings and values of civilization, including laws, courts, schools, temples, and human-made customs regarding marriage, sex, and child rearing.

REMEMBER

As we saw in Chapter 2, the Stoics agreed with the Cynics that "follow nature" is the most basic rule of morality. But the Stoic view of nature was very different from theirs. For the Stoics, "follow nature" meant 'follow reason," which they equated with following the rationally discoverable will of the Logos that guides and pervades all of nature. So, higher law for the Stoics means the law of God, or the divine dictates of reason that apply to all rational beings, including ourselves.

Both Zeno and Chrysippus seem to have written a great deal on law, but unfortunately their works have been lost except for a few fragmentary quotes. Our main source on Stoic views of natural or higher law is Cicero, who in works such as *On Laws* and the *Republic* provides a clear picture of Stoic teachings on law.

Cicero on natural law

According to Cicero, the Stoics defined "law" as "right reason in harmony with nature," which calls people "to their duty by its commands," and deters them "from wrongdoing by its prohibitions."

By "right reason" Cicero means using our minds or intellects correctly, as they were designed to be used. By "in harmony with nature" he means both "in agreement with human nature," as rational, sociable animals with distinctive biologically-based needs, inclinations, and vulnerabilities, and "in agreement with cosmic nature," meaning the universe as a whole, conceived as the Stoics did, as a rational, purposive, divinely-ordered hierarchy directed to the good of the Whole.

WARNING

The Stoics apparently did not believe that principles of natural law must be "self-evident," or utterly obvious and requiring no proof, as many later natural law thinkers have claimed. Nor did they seem to think that natural law applies only to humans; it also applies to the other members of the cosmopolis, or cosmic city, the gods. Marcus Aurelius states that as a member of the human race he is "an intelligent and social being, sharing one law with god" (*Meditations* 8.2). Does this "one law" — natural law or right reason — apply in exactly the same way to both humans and the gods? That seems far-fetched because humans and gods have very different natures and hence presumably different moral virtues and duties. (Unlike humans, for example, gods have no duty to nurture and educate their offspring, because they have no offspring and require no education.) As Cicero explains, humans and divine beings such as those that Stoics believed steer the stars share the same law — the law of right reason — because "they possess the same rational faculty," a faculty that "recommends what is right and rejects what is wrong" and enjoins basic values such as fellowship and civic harmony and the virtues required to sustain those goods (*On the Nature of the Gods* 2.79). It would be a tricky business to try to spell out, from a Stoic point of view, what ethical duties and virtues humans and gods share in common. And this is probably why most later natural law thinkers limit natural law to human beings, restricting "the law of nature" to *human* nature.

In a famous passage, Cicero says this about natural law:

> It is spread through the whole human community, unchanging and eternal . . . This law cannot be countermanded, nor can it be in any way amended, nor can it be totally rescinded. We cannot be exempted from this law by any decree of the Senate or the people; nor do we need anyone else to expound or explain it. There will not

be one such law in Rome and another in Athens, one now and another in the future, but all peoples at all times will be embraced by a single and eternal and unchangeable law; and there will be, as it were, one lord and master of us all — the god who is the author, proposer, and interpreter of that law. (Cicero, *The Republic* 3.33)

So, natural law, according to the Stoics, is a set of rationally knowable moral commands and prohibitions issued by God that is eternal, unchangeable, and binding all over the world. It is "right reason" (correct reason) about ethical duties and prohibitions that flow from God and apply to rational, sociable beings with the kinds of minds, bodies, and natural constitutions we possess. What makes natural law "natural?" The fact that it's rooted in basic features of human nature and is knowable through natural reason. Natural law applies to *all* humans in *all* societies because it's not something we have to be taught; we can discover it just by using our intellects correctly, that is, by "right reason." Because, by definition, natural law is naturally knowable, it differs from "divine law," which can be based on revelation as well as unaided reason. So, when Marcus Aurelius thanks the gods for help they provided him in dreams and oracles (*Meditations* 1.17.9), this might be a case of learning about "divine" or "higher" law, but not of natural law, since it is not knowable by the use of natural reason alone.

REMEMBER

The basic idea of the natural law is that what is a good for a thing depends on what kind of thing it is. The good for an acorn is to grow into a big, flourishing oak tree, and the good for a lion cub is to grow into a large, healthy adult lion living a great leonine life. What's good for a human, the Stoics believed, depends on our nature as rational, sociable, and moral animals.

What are our basic human needs, drives, and inclinations? What are our distinctive modes of flourishing or excellence (*arete*)? Like Aristotle, the Stoics believed that what counts as a good life for a human must be keyed to fundamental features of our natures. If humans had very different minds and bodies — for example, radically different ways of reproducing our species and raising our young — we would have different rights and duties, different modes of flourishing or ideal well-being.

Basic elements of natural law

At this point a question naturally arises. What *are* the basic commands and prohibitions of natural law? And here's something interesting, since natural law is being presented as something that's so important for us: Neither Cicero nor the Stoics seem to have ever attempted to provide anything like a complete list of natural law precepts. But Cicero does offer some helpful specifics, which is good, because, as the famous twentieth century architect Ludwig Mies van der Rohe is often quoted as saying, regarding almost anything, "God is in the details." And so should be the law of God, or natural law.

Self-preservation

One fundamental human drive, the Stoics noted, is self-preservation. Much of what we do on a daily basis — eating, drinking, staying warm, avoiding stepping in front of buses, and so forth — we do in order to stay alive, healthy, and pain-free. So, one basic principle of natural law will involve a duty of self-care, an obligation to pursue one's own good, live temperately, and preserve our own lives and health.

Sociability

Another basic human drive is our sociability. Humans are naturally social animals and usually flourish only in healthy families and communities. Parents naturally love their children and seek to promote their happiness and well-being. From such fundamental facts flow basic natural law principles such as "avoid harming those among whom you must live," "act justly," "tell the truth," and "nurture and care for your children."

Like Aristotle, the Stoics believed that as humans our highest and most distinctive capacity is our intelligence and ability to reason. This is what most obviously sets us apart from nonhuman animals, aside from all the trendy clothes. Humans have a natural drive to seek truth, reason well, and pursue understanding. Accordingly, other basic commands of natural law will involve the proper use of our minds, such as "seek truth," "avoid error," "think logically," and "live rationally."

The Stoic ideal of "living in harmony with nature" seems very vague, but the Stoics believed that a great deal can be learned about proper moral conduct by reflecting on our natural or conventional social roles and responsibilities. As Epictetus remarks, "duties are broadly defined by social roles" (*Manual* 30). A father, a son, a teacher, a doctor, or a police officer each have certain responsibilities that flow from those particular social roles. Epictetus famously compares life with acting in a play:

> Remember that you're an actor in a play, which is as the playwright wants it to be: short if he wants it short, long if he wants it long. If he wants you to play a beggar, play even this part skillfully, or a cripple, a public official, or a private citizen. What is yours is to play the assigned part well. But to choose it belongs to someone else. (*Manual* 17)

In Cicero's *On Duties*, the most detailed discussion of Stoic ethics that survives from ancient times, the importance of social roles in the ethical life is repeatedly emphasized. Of course, such roles differ over time and across societies. Does this make Stoic ethics "relative"? Not really, because it's reasonable for societies to have various social roles (e.g., farmers as well as teachers), and for social roles to vary over time and different cultures. Thus, "right reason" dictates that reasonable and legitimate social roles and responsibilities be performed and performed well. As contemporary Stoic Ryan Holiday likes to say, "Do your job. Do it right."

For the Stoics, living in harmony with nature means not only living virtuously, which is the only true good, but also performing what they called "appropriate actions" or "proper functions" (*kathekonta*). These are activities that "befit" a living being's nature, as growing toward the light befits a sunflower and building a nest to raise its young befits a songbird. Appropriate actions for humans include not only virtuous or morally right actions (which only Sages can perform since only they possess the proper motivation), but also, in appropriate circumstances, acts aimed at "preferred indifferents" such as life, health, friendship, and avoidance of pain. Nature has implanted in us instincts for things such as self-preservation, sociality, and curiosity. So, it is rational and in accord with nature for us to prefer life over death, friendship over solitude, and knowledge over ignorance. Although preferred indifferents are not strictly good in Stoic thought, they do have value and so may fittingly be pursued unless they conflict with virtue.

Remember that the Stoics believed there are four basic moral excellences: wisdom, justice, courage, and self-control. According to Cicero, all particular duties arise from these four general virtues. Because of this, they are central to Stoic accounts of natural law. So, for example, "return borrowed goods" is a natural law precept because it is a rationally knowable dictate of the cardinal virtue of justice.

Acceptance

Another key Stoic natural-law virtue is acceptance, which Stoics saw as a form of piety. According to Epictetus, the gods placed humans on earth "for one purpose: to obey them and welcome whatever happens, in the conviction that it's the product of the highest intelligence." Obeying the gods and welcoming what happens constitute our purpose precisely because by embracing whatever happens, we obey the gods who have decreed these things for the greater good. We ought to will whatever they will and "try to resemble them as far as possible" (*Discourses* 2.14.12). The Stoics saw this alignment of our will with the will of the gods as a primary command of right reason and the path to inner peace and true freedom.

Common law and citizenship

As we've seen, the Stoics further speak of natural law as a "common law" that is shared not only with all fellow humans but even with the gods. This common law is the law of reason. This shared reason provides a common bond and even shared citizenship between humans and gods. So, Marcus Aurelius writes in *Meditations* 4.4:

If mind is common to us all, then we have reason also in common — that which makes us rational beings. If so, then common too is the reason that dictates what we should or should not do. If so, then law too is common to us all. If so, then we are citizens. If so, we share in a constitution. If so, the universe is a kind of community . . . From there, then, this common city, we take our very mind, our reason, our law . . .

Notice the repeated phrase "if so," which signifies how Marcus Aurelius and other Stoics infer or reason from one truth to another, to get eventually to what might have been a surprising conclusion to many — that we share citizenship, not only with all fellow humans, but with God, or the gods. For Stoics, natural law is in this way the basis for a worldview of cosmopolitanism, the notion that all humans are kin and members of one family and one community.

If true law, as Stoics claim, is right reason and thus invariably rational and just, what should we say of laws and legal systems that are seriously oppressive or discriminatory? Cicero argued that "inherent in the very name of law is the sense and idea of choosing what is just and right." Unjust laws are therefore not true laws, but exercises of force masquerading as law. This idea that *"lex injusta non est lex"* ("an unjust law is not law") would later be popularized by great Christian thinkers like St. Augustine and Thomas Aquinas, and in modern times it would be echoed by critics of Nazi law and in Martin Luther King Jr's philosophy of nonviolent protest expressed in his famous "Letter from Birmingham Jail."

Natural Law in Roman Law

Stoic thinking on natural law was not simply idle theorizing. It was incorporated in Roman law and later into European and other legal systems based on Roman law.

Roman law distinguished between the laws that applied only to Roman citizens (the civil law) and the law of nations (*jus gentium*) that applied to foreigners or to foreigners and citizens alike and that later evolved into what we call international law. Following Cicero, some Roman lawyers tended to identify the law of nations and natural law. For instance, the second-century jurist Gaius described the law of nations as "the law that natural reason establishes among all mankind." However, another influential Roman lawyer, Ulpian (c. 190 CE), distinguished natural law from the *jus gentium*, holding that natural law is "what nature teaches all animals," such as an instinct for self-preservation and for procreation. This confusion between the law of nations and the law of nature persisted into medieval and modern times.

Roman lawyers who distinguished between natural law and the law of nations recognized that the two could conflict. Echoing Epictetus, Ulpian declared that "by the law of nature all men are equal," and that slavery was therefore inherently unjust. The only legal basis for slavery under Roman law was human-made law, which was not generally thought to be invalidated by its conflict with natural reason. So far as we know, no Stoic in ancient times argued that slavery is *legally* invalid because it violates natural or higher law.

Modern Stoicism and Natural Law

As we noted in the Introduction, in recent decades there's been a major revival of Stoicism. As we shall see, however, current versions of Stoicism often differ in major ways from ancient Stoicism. One big difference involves natural law. Nearly all leading modern Stoics either quietly ignore or reject natural law, and many state that ethics is a purely human invention, answerable to no natural or higher law.

In ancient Stoicism, natural law has its source in the reason and will of the Logos. Its principles were thought to have the force of law because they were commands issued by a wise and good Lawgiver and Ruler of the universe. Many modern Stoics reject the concept of natural law because they deny the existence of a God or any kind of higher power. So, Lawrence E. Becker, author of *A New Stoicism* (rev. ed. 2017), argues for a thoroughly secular form of Stoicism that rejects all ancient

Stoic cosmology and theology and places ethics on a purely humanistic basis. William B. Irvine, author of *A Guide to the Good Life* (2009), offers a "modernized" version of Stoicism based in evolutionary science, not religion. And in his *A Field Guide to a Happy Life* (2020), Massimo Pigliucci proposes a version of Stoicism he calls Stoicism 2.0 that rejects any notion of God and sees ethics entirely as a human invention.

There are advantages to dropping all talk of God and natural law from Stoicism. Stoicism has wider appeal if it can formulated in a way that can be accepted by religious believers and doubters alike. And the idea of natural law is controversial both because it presupposes the existence of God and because, as we shall soon see, there are problems with treating "nature" as a moral standard. But without God, many key Stoic ideas, such as providence, fate, radical acceptance, an afterlife, universal moral law, and a cosmopolitan kinship and citizenship based on a shared "divinity within," appear to be ungrounded. What emerges seems to be a very stripped-down Stoicism with a very different flavor.

Natural law: Pros and cons

The concept of natural law was widely accepted from Hellenistic-Roman times up until around 1800. Since then, the idea has been much less popular, though it continues to play an important role in Roman Catholic ethics and the thought of many cultural conservatives. One reason for the decline of natural law ethics is waning belief in God. But two other factors should be noted. One is doubt about whether ethics can be based on facts about nature or the world, as natural law ethics apparently tries to do. The second involves ambiguities with the idea of "nature."

Can ethics be based on facts?

On its face, natural law ethics seems to infer or derive certain values (e.g., that we should care about our health) from alleged facts about nature (e.g., that we naturally or instinctively desire to be in good health). Many modern ethicists question this sort of inference. Logically, it doesn't seem to follow that "we ought to do X" from the fact that "we have a natural desire to do X." More generally, many modern ethicists claim, no "ought" can be derived from an "is." That is, no value statement can be inferred from any set of statements that talk only about facts, not values. One common criticism of Stoicism is that it commits this ought-from-is fallacy (also called the naturalistic fallacy). Is this a sound criticism?

There are two ways Stoics can avoid this charge. One is for Stoics not to infer values like life, health, and knowledge from any facts about human nature, but simply take them as "givens," that is, obvious truths that require no reasoned support. The value of health, for example, can simply be "intuited," not derived from any prior knowledge of human nature. Alternatively, Stoics can avoid any illegitimate attempt to infer an "ought" from an "is" simply by building a plausible "ought" principle into their reasoning. For instance, they might argue as follows:

1. The Logos is an all-wise, all-good Creator. (factual, conceptual statement)

2. Any basic instinct an all-wise, all-good Creator implants in his creatures has value. (value statement, not derived from (1), but taken as "basic" and conceptually, intuitively obvious)

3. The Logos has implanted a basic instinct in humans to love and care for their children. (factual statement)

4. Therefore, it's valuable for humans to love and care for their children. (value statement)

Here, there's no attempt to infer a value statement from facts that make no reference to values. Instead, a value statement (proposition 4) is inferred from a set of factual, conceptual, *and* value statements. No "ought" is inferred from a mere factual "is."

A more serious problem with natural law ethics lies in the highly vague notion of acting "in harmony with nature." For the ancient Stoics, "nature" here means both cosmic nature and human nature. Both senses are problematic. The Stoics held that humans should follow cosmic nature because the cosmos is orderly, harmonious, beneficent, providential, and pervasively rational. Modern science, however, does not seem to support such a rosy view. Charles Darwin, the discoverer of evolution, described the evolutionary process as "wasteful, blundering, low, and cruel." Nature may seem benevolent in the genial, sun-drenched climes of southern Europe, but in the tropics, as Aldous Huxley notes, "the life of those vast masses of swarming vegetation" seems to be "foreign, appalling, fundamentally and utterly inimical to intruding man." As philosopher John Stuart Mill wrote about "following nature":

> In sober truth, nearly all the things which men are hanged or imprisoned for doing to one another are nature's every-day performances. Killing, the most criminal act recognized by human laws, Nature does once to every being that lives; and, in a large proportion of cases, after protracted tortures such as only the greatest monsters whom we read of ever purposely inflicted on their living fellow creatures . . . Nature impales men, breaks them as if on the wheel, casts them to be devoured by wild beasts, burns them to death, crushes them with stones like the first Christian martyr, starves them with hunger, freezes them with cold, poisons them by the quick or slow venom of her exhalations, and has hundreds of other hideous deaths

in reserve . . . All this Nature does with the most supercilious disregard both of mercy and of justice, emptying her shafts upon the best and noblest indifferently with the meanest and worst . . . Such are Nature's dealings with life.

Ouch. Then, if we shift our gaze from life on earth to the universe as a whole, modern astronomy shows us a mostly cold, dark universe in which massive stars explode, asteroids bombard planets, black holes suck up whole star systems, planets grow cold and die, and the second law of thermodynamics works relentlessly to produce greater disorganization and disorder. Nature on the biggest picture doesn't quite resound with the clear message, "You're great. God bless. Have a nice day."

What's natural?

The idea of living in agreement with human nature also raises problems. What is "natural" human behavior? At various times, slavery, the subordination of women, polygamy, racial supremacism, the domination of nature, and an economic subordination of the poor by the rich have all been defended as according with nature. In Roman Catholic ethics today, suicide, homosexual behavior, sex outside marriage, same-sex marriage, sex-change operations, artificial insemination, and birth control are seen as contrary to nature, and hence God's will, and thus immoral. In Stoic ethics, strong emotions such as grief, fear, passionate sexual desire, empathy, pity, elation, and anger are condemned as anti-rational and so contrary to human nature, despite being adaptive psychological responses apparently instilled in us by evolution, or nature. In short, human nature seems to be a vague and dubious touchstone of good moral behavior. In many cases, "nature" seems something we should seek to rise above, rather than follow.

At the same time, there are undoubted attractions to the idea of natural law. It affirms the reality of fundamental moral truth and objective moral standards, and so avoids the many problems of moral skepticism and subjectivism. It recognizes a source of moral values above and beyond what you or we happen to think at a given time, and distinct from what our culture happens to endorse. It correctly recognizes that morality must be grounded in some sense on basic features of human nature, such as our natural inclinations and vulnerabilities. And natural law, as a form of higher law, provides a standard, in principle independent and objective, for criticizing human laws or widespread behaviors that are unjust or otherwise morally defective. Historically, the idea of natural law unquestionably helped to improve legal systems by insisting that true laws must be fair, rational, and just.

On balance, there are probably good reasons to drop the idea of natural law from modern versions of Stoicism. Most of the attractions of natural law, including moral objectivity and a grounding of ethics in human nature, can be achieved without opting for a full-blown natural law ethics. The central Stoic goals of greater emotional resilience, inner calm, and a more rational and virtuous life do not seem to depend on any kind of natural law ethic, as modern Stoics such as William Irvine and Massimo Pigliucci, who reject natural law ethics, maintain.

Framing Stoicism in a way that does not require belief in God or some kind of higher power will increase its appeal in an increasingly secular world, regardless of what the ultimate truth might be on such issues. And yet, at the same time, we can understand the attraction of natural law to religious Stoics such as Zeno, Seneca, Epictetus, and Marcus Aurelius. To feel that there is a binding law, laid down by a wise and good Lawmaker, directing us to our proper good and ultimate end, is a powerful backdrop and incentive for a life of felt purpose and meaning. It clearly seems to say that our desire for justice, fairness, and goodness aren't just empty and futile protests in a bleak and uncaring universe. So, is Stoicism better with a commitment to natural law, or without one? You make the call.

ZENO'S WILD AND CRAZY REPUBLIC

Philosophers who endorse the Stoic idea of "following nature" and the idea of natural law can still differ quite a bit on what those two things imply for our actual conduct. Even if you believe that nature has built into it a demand for wisdom and justice, for example, the question still arises: What would a truly wise and just state be like? Plato offers an answer in his book the *Republic*, which is widely considered one of the greatest works of philosophy ever written. But then, like many great works of philosophy, it's as controversial as it is stimulating. And with this greatness, Plato spawned many imitators. Diogenes the Cynic wrote a *Republic*. So did Chrysippus and, later, Cicero. And so did Zeno, the founder of Stoicism and at its outset. In their authoritative study, *The Hellenistic Philosophers*, Long and Sedley call it "the most renowned book written by any Stoic." The content of such a treatise offers a fascinating case in point about how tough it can be to determine what an ideal life "in agreement with nature" and nature's laws would be like.

Zeno argues in his *Republic* that there would be no need for any kind of general education in an ideal state, which would be populated by the otherwise rare Sages. Nature dictates that virtue is the sole good, so there is no need to study math or poetry or any anything that doesn't directly contribute to living a simple and self-sufficient life of moral rectitude. We of course realize how dangerous this is to report, as we may court the conversion of far too many people to an original version of Stoicism for all the wrong reasons. "No math? Sign me up." But wait. There's more. There wouldn't be any marriage either, or what we know as a classic and common form of family life. Everyone would be free to sleep with whomever they liked (including any willing teens, at whatever stage, according to the original Stoics), and children would be raised by the whole community. Even incest and cannibalism would be permitted, since such ordinary taboos involve indifferents that, apparently in Zeno's view, in no way impinge on virtue, the sole good. And yet, it's not like, if Zeno invited you over for dinner, you'd have to worry about making it back home alive. But if you happened to have a tragic accident on the way to his house, he might have had the attitude, "Well, the grill's still hot." Protein is, after all, naturally a main nutritional need and, let's face it, you're carrying a lot around with you wherever you go.

According to Zeno, everyone in the ideal society would wear unisex clothing, but no part of the body could be completely concealed (yeah, including those body parts), which he thinks would make it easier to pick out the partners you might enjoy most. And no, we're not making this up. There would be no money, or police or law courts, which probably made some of the other Stoics of the time breathe easier, in light of some of the other stuff.

Does this all sound "ideal" or "natural" to you? Reportedly, Zeno took a lot of heat in his day for proposing such unconventional ideas, obviously influenced by Cynic thought, though the otherwise and reportedly brilliant Chrysippus seems to have defended them. Clearly, Zeno and his most accomplished successor believed that "following nature" can lead to some very adventurous places. A modern Stoic can value natural law and following nature without following these influential early Stoics into their conclusions about what that involves.

IN THIS CHAPTER

» Consulting philosophers on
  sociability

» Understanding the human drive
  for community

» Unmasking Plato and Aristotle
  behind the scenes

» Using concentric circles to explain
  it all

Chapter **13**

Building Strong Communities

All forms of human community have been challenged throughout history and often shattered by both external threats and internal disruptions. The present time is no different, except that our communities at every scale may face more kinds of danger and at a greater level of severity than ever before.

The Stoics have some important insights about family, friendship, community, and the proper role of politics in life that can be immensely helpful now. Their wisdom on these topics can bring you some new and vital perspectives for sociability and community and a saner sort of politics. In this chapter, we present some of their groundbreaking thoughts and suggestions for creating great communities and making the most of our lives together.

Philosophers as Social Advisors

You may initially be surprised at the idea of going to philosophers for insights about being sociable and building community. After all, the most famous visual representation of philosophy is most likely August Rodin's sculpture *The Thinker*, a depiction of one guy sitting alone on a rock, staring into space, presumably pondering deep truth. And in case you've never noticed, he's completely naked. It's not exactly a portrait of social conviviality, but more like a guy who needs a little solitude. And pants.

You may also be one of the many people who had a course in philosophy at some point with a professor who was the kind of odd duck that, if you passed him in the hallway early in the day and made the mistake of saying, "Good morning," he might have scowled and stopped to prove you wrong, arguing with you about your cheery sentiment for long enough to convince you that, yeah, maybe you had been a bit hasty in your conclusion. Philosophers aren't particularly known for being warm and sociable, but rather are too often seen as disagreeable grumps who are quick to tell you that you've given a bad argument in support of an indefensible position, and that whatever you've just made the blunder of saying aloud in their presence is simply and inexcusably false. But please be reassured that it's not just you. In the history of philosophy, all the most famous thinkers seem to have believed that most of the other great minds before them and in their own time were badly, sadly, pathetically wrong about most things. Dogs bark. Philosophers disagree.

Indeed, it was the British philosopher Thomas Hobbes who claimed that in our most natural condition, what he saw as "the state of nature," human beings are all enemies to each other and at war. The French existentialist Jean-Paul Sartre is even known for the bold statement that "Hell is other people." But on the other side of the issue, there may be some positive evidence of philosophical sociability to consider.

The *New York Times* did a study years ago to determine the most popular spot in Manhattan to hook up, or meet someone new and get a date with romantic possibilities in mind, and the paper subsequently surprised the world by declaring that the number one pickup spot by far was a big bookstore in midtown, and in particular that the most social action was to be found in the precise area of the store at and around the philosophy section. It's true. But then again, maybe that's just because anyone you meet there is probably not doing anything Saturday night, or Friday night, or any other night. This may not be evidence connecting philosophy with sociability at all. Still, the Stoic philosophers in particular seem to have been decently friendly with others, and they also had some of the greatest and most enduring insights ever about our relationships and our communities.

Everywhere in our world right now we see a hunger for community and belonging. Psychologists and sociologists speak of "an epidemic of loneliness" and of a "permanent recession" of close friendships and nurturing social connections. Many of the traditional sources of social and community bonding and inclusion — family, work, neighborhood, school, local and national governments — seem now to be fraying and fragmenting. Increasingly in cubicles, Zoom rooms, and living digital lives, we feel like social atoms existing in our lonely cocoons. We hear much of individual rights and entitlements, but all too little about social responsibilities, healthy communities, and sacrifice for something larger than the self.

The Stoics were well aware of the dangers of social isolation and fragmentation. As we note in the first few chapters of this book, the earliest Stoics lived when the Greek city-state (the *polis*), the basis of all Greek community life and political self-determination, had been destroyed and forcibly swallowed up in huge new foreign empires (first Macedonian and then Roman). Out of this shattering loss of self-rule and cultural identity, the Stoics created powerful new ideas for both community building and coping with political problems and stressors that are beyond our personal control. We'll benefit from diving into their perspectives.

The Two Roots of Community

From the very beginnings of Stoicism, its prominent founding thinkers said that the two most important and distinctive characteristics of human beings that set us apart and define us are our reason and our relationality.

>> **Reason** is our ability to live with a clarity and continuity of logical thought. We're apparently able to think in more complex ways than any other natural creatures on earth, responding in various degrees to things like evidence and logic, discovering new ideas, testing them, and tracing out their connections, while assessing them for usefulness and truth. We've discovered mathematics, and our use of reason has given birth to science. Our capacity to reason, or having the crucial activity of reasoning available to us at nearly all times, is one of our chief strengths.

>> **Relationality** is just as important a human attribute. We seem to have a natural disposition for community, flourishing best in relationship to others. Our inborn reason, used well or badly, gives rise to our mindset and character, and our innate relationality naturally produces a mutuality with others that can create healthy forms of community.

We cogitate and we connect. Both abilities are central to who we are.

Reason and relationality

Reason is what allows us to see structures, patterns, and connections of all kinds among concepts, behaviors, statements, people, events, and things. It helps us understand, evaluate, and discern such matters as harmony and disharmony in the world around us. Our capacity for reason is necessary for our disposition toward relationships to serve us well. And our innate tendency to see and seek proper connection in community can help us to reason better. We often think more creatively together than alone. Our inclinations toward reason and relationality work best when they serve and support each other.

Of course, according to the Stoics, as well as other groups of philosophers throughout history, one of the fundamental truths of existence is that, ultimately, everything somehow connects with everything else. All of life is interconnected in vital and fascinating ways. It's not just human beings who have a drive and a tendency to join and interact with each other. The interconnections between trees and other plants beneath the forest floor can be astonishing. Everything in the earth's environment seems entwined in surprising interactions. Animals relate to each other and depend on each other as well as on their environment in a great many ways. But human beings connect and unite with a complexity and a scope not otherwise seen in nature.

We build houses for our families, neighborhoods of homes, towns with many neighborhoods, and sprawling larger cities, states, and nations. We connect our different nations through international political, economic, and health organizations. We build businesses and other types of structures to bring people together, along with networks of friends, associates, and the like-minded that can span the globe. This scope and complexity of intentionally created community isn't found anywhere else in nature. And our capacity to reason is deeply involved in that immense variety of relationality. In fact, the Stoics saw our remarkable reason as not only a gift from God, but even as a little bit of divinity planted within us. It's that special in its creative power.

A distinctive sort of reason and a certain level of reasoning allow for such sophistication and reach in the human desire to connect. In fact, reason and relationality are themselves inwardly connected. We first learn language and thought, and how to reason with words and ideas, from our parents or adult guardians, from our early teachers and other people around us, and in many ways from the complex matrix of social institutions and other relationships that nurture us into the world. And in turn, reason itself structures our relationships with beliefs, attitudes, plans, promises, norms, customs, expectations, and laws so that the relations in which we stand to others will more likely be safe and healthy for us. We come into the world because of relationships, and we learn and grow through them, becoming capable of making our own mark in life through various forms of connection with others.

REMEMBER

Relationships rock the world. And our capacity to reason allows us to figure out how to create great relationships. It also helps us to partner up with others to do things together that we never could have accomplished alone.

The self and society

At a time when selfishness can seem to be more widespread than ever and we're all encouraged to be focused on the rights, opportunities, achievements, and material rewards possible for the individual, the Stoics offer us good advice for squaring our natural and healthy self-interest with broader social concerns. They acknowledge that we all come into the world with a strong tendency to care for our own individual safety, health, and flourishing. We're apparently hardwired for self-care at the center of our desires and motives. But the Stoics also believe that when we realize we don't need to compete constantly with others for wealth, power, fame, status, or any external things to be fulfilled and happy (their reasons are found in Chapter 10), when we then come to see that other people can be our friends and aren't inevitably enemies or rivals for what matters most, we can be liberated from a certain sort of pervasive worry and then feel free to become positive contributors to society rather than just selfish users of it and manipulators of others.

Emperor Marcus Aurelius begins his now famous personal journal of meditations with statements of gratitude toward family members, teachers, and friends who have given him a wealth of benefits throughout the years of his growth and maturation, as well as into adulthood. His recitation of these many gifts from others reads a bit like an author's acknowledgments at the back of a book, thanking everyone who has helped him. But the emperor's private meditations were never meant to be a book, and these thanks are at the outset rather than the end of his manuscript. It's as if he's just remembering for his own sake the many benefits he's received from others in his life and that he's doing this to enhance his own thankfulness, or gratitude, for the many gifts he's been given by other people. And now his words of appreciation can remind us what we also owe to others.

His opening line is "Courtesy and serenity of temper I first learned to know from my grandfather Verus." He then mentions other gifts of temperament and insight from his father, his mother, his great-grandfather, and various teachers, mentors, and assistants along the way, finally thanking heaven for his wife and even the tutors who have taught their children. In all this, he's reminding himself of the importance of other people in his own life, and in our lives generally. We live and grow best in community. If he had indeed been writing a book intentionally for us as later readers, it's almost as if he'd here be reminding us to begin anything we do with positive thoughts of others and gratitude for the good things they've brought to our lives. Then we're better positioned to do the same for them.

In an extended essay entitled "On Benefits," the Stoic philosopher Seneca had years earlier described the helpful deeds we often do for each other out of an attitude of goodwill, and the gifts we give to others as "the chief bond of human society." Much closer to our own time, the well-known children's television host Fred Rogers, identified on his show as "Mister Rogers," once reflected on his own childhood and said that when, as a young boy, he'd see scary things on the news — disasters, accidents, or scenes from a war — his mother would comfort him by saying, "Look for the helpers. You will always find people who are helping." From ancient times to now, helpers benefit us all. And by remembering our own helpers, we are encouraged to become helpers for others along the way.

To Stoics like Marcus and Seneca, we're all to be inspired by the helpers among us to join their number and be helpers ourselves in all times, good or bad. And others in our lives have already helped us to play this role, if we keep them in mind and respond to their best examples properly. This is a natural expression of the innate connectivity we are born with and bring with us into the world as a part of our natural inheritance.

The emperor had no misgivings about human beings. He didn't think of everyone as a positive benefactor. He was quick to spot virtue, but he was just as realistic about the flaws and vices of many around him. He begins the next chapter of his journal of reflections with some very useful advice to himself, and from which we can all benefit, based on this realism. He writes:

> Begin each day by reminding yourself: Today, I'll be meeting with interference, ingratitude, disrespect, disloyalty, ill-will and selfishness, all of these things being due to the offenders' ignorance of what is good or evil. (*Meditations* 2.1)

He then expresses his properly Stoic view that the people who surely will speak to him badly or treat him poorly are still, despite it all, brothers of reason and members of his extended family within the divine scheme of things, and that their mistakes about what's truly good and evil can't injure him in his own soul or degrade him in any way. He need not and should not react to any of them with irritation, anger, or rage.

In this big-picture view of life that Marcus held as a philosopher, we are created and meant to work together, and he is convinced he should do his part to facilitate this, no matter what others might be doing in an opposite direction. In these morning reflections on what he can expect to encounter throughout the day, Marcus is using his reason to prepare himself for having the best relations with others that they will allow, and perhaps beyond what they might ever expect. He will not live reactively and do to others whatever they do to him but will treat others out of the bountiful positive resources of his own strong character. He understands the importance of both good reason and healthy relationality, and that moral character is at the root of any sound and vibrant community.

Plato and Aristotle Behind It All

The Stoics rightly pointed out that all community begins with the original small unit of the family. Every normal baby comes into the world needing love and ready to receive it, reaching out for connection and support, and benefiting from all of it that's offered. The natural affiliations, affections, and duties that can develop in a family setting are to prepare us for our lives in yet broader communities. If we struggle on that small scale of the family unit, we'll likely struggle in larger community contexts as well. And we all naturally look beyond our birth families or other earliest circumstances of nurture for different communities of affiliation and mutuality in which we can feel a sense of contribution and belonging, where we're valued and in turn value others. We're not born into the world to be solitary loners.

Our need to belong

ANECDOTE

The *Los Angeles Times* did a story years ago on why people join often violent street gangs. Their reporters learned that it wasn't fundamentally for access to drugs or money, or primarily for physical protection in dangerous settings, but rather out of a need for a sense of belonging, a deep innate need that was not being met anywhere else in their lives.

WARNING

We all need to feel needed. We all want to make a difference and be appreciated by others for the effort. When this need is taken care of in a positive way, great groups, teams, organizations, and communities arise. When it's not, people can drift off to join any gang, club, cell, or political faction that will have them, however unhealthy and even dangerously toxic it might be. Such is the power and need we have for relationality.

So, just as our need for relationality, or community, has great power for good, it can also have opposite results, as shown by the example of violent gangs. There seems to be a cosmic principle at work in the world around us, something we can call The Double Power Principle: Nearly anything with positive power for good has an equal and opposite power for ill; it's up to us how we use it. For example, technology has great power for good, as used in modern business and medicine, and great power for ill, as seen in modern weaponry, and as it's misused for other forms of harm on social media. Nuclear science does great good in nuclear medicine and clean energy and threatens disaster in war. Likewise, human reason can be used well or badly, to create or destroy. Our relationality is the same. Put to good use, it's the drive behind all the great things we do together. Misdirected, it results in mob violence, political hatred, and harmful sectarianism in many forms. A street gang can destroy a neighborhood. A political cult can take down a nation.

Aristotle on the power of partnership

Before Zeno launched what soon came to be known as Stoicism, Aristotle had proclaimed, "Man is a social animal." In fact, Stoicism got its start not just because one man alone in a room began to develop a philosophy by himself, but because Zeno visited other philosophers and their schools, and then began to have his own independent conversations with other people to discuss ideas with them on the famous "Painted Porch," or the public colonnade known as the Stoa, in the busy central marketplace of Athens. It took all Zeno's friends and associates as a community to launch Stoicism into the world. And this is something modern business is still trying to learn. Community is essential. Partnership is power.

TIP

It's a bedrock truth. Community is crucial for nearly anything you hope to do. When you have a great new idea, you should begin forming a community around it if you want it to make a difference in the world. We can do much more together than we ever could accomplish alone.

REMEMBER

In his great book known as the *Politics*, Aristotle explores the relevance of relationships to human achievement, and he articulates many hints for the outlines of a powerful idea that can be summarized and stated quite simply. The heights of human achievement, the pinnacles of creativity, innovation, and excellence in the world, seem to arise out of a basic formula:

People in Partnership for a shared Purpose.

The key here is people (plural) in a certain sort of relationship (a partnership) guided by something they have in common (a particular sense of purpose). This is the cauldron of human greatness. Aristotle at one point in his book asks what a city is. The Greek word is, again, *polis*, a name for the most fundamental unit of community in ancient Greece, and of course the source of our word "politics." He concludes that a city is not just a construction of roads and buildings or a collection of people living in proximity to each other, but that it is, ideally and in essence, "a partnership for living well."

On further reflection, it seems as if that description might serve as a more extended analysis for any healthy form of human community, whether a family, village, business, volunteer organization, or nation. These should all be viewed as partnerships for living well. If any group or community forgets this idea or departs from its path, things will begin to go badly. We are at our best and do our best together when we work helpfully with other people in partnerships for a shared purpose that will be, at one general level, always the aim of living well, whatever our more specific intentions might be.

The Stoics seem to be proper inheritors of Aristotle's views on community, among the great thinker's many other perspectives that can help us all to return to healthier forms of action and participation in the political sphere. The early Stoics didn't always agree with Aristotle on other things, or even very often overtly consider his views, but they seem to have benefited from many of his ideas that may have been in the air at the time. And so can we.

ARISTOTLE IN NEW YORK ON POLITICS

A few years ago, one of the authors (Tom) was sitting in a beautiful conference room at a great hotel in lower Manhattan, having breakfast with a board of advisors serving a major global technology firm. He'd spoken the previous day to this group of top chief information officers, and chief technology officers from the firm's biggest client companies on the best philosophical wisdom we have for corporate greatness. The floor-to-ceiling glass walls of the room overlooked the Statue of Liberty, gleaming in the early morning sun. The talk around the big table soon reflected the view and turned to politics.

At a certain point, Tom quoted Aristotle on his view that politics is supposed to be a noble enterprise about how best we can live well together. There was a huge, sudden, spontaneous laugh all around the table, with some almost choking on their food, in utter surprise at this unexpected statement. Then, after a moment of silence and a few isolated exclamations, one of the accomplished executives looked around the table, turned his gaze to the philosopher, and slowly said, "How did we fall so far?" Indeed. An amazing discussion was launched, in sight of Lady Liberty's flaming torch.

Platonic perspectives

The Stoics in fact don't often quote or refer to Aristotle as having provided supporting insights for their own views. They were generally more impressed with his teacher Plato, and especially with Plato's fascinating written dialogues featuring his own teacher, Socrates. If Stoicism could be said to have a patron saint, it would be the equally urban Socrates, barefoot and walking the streets of Athens, starting up conversations with friends and strangers about what really matters in life, examining common beliefs, and shredding the illusions that keep people away from what's truly important.

At one point in his writings, Plato represents Socrates as going around and basically calling out to others something like "Man of Athens! You're a citizen of the greatest city in the history of the world. Why is it that all you seem to care about is money and fame? You never give any attention to the state of your own soul." As it turns out, Socrates had no real problem with either money or fame, but his concern was with people chasing external things without first building a proper internal foundation within their own souls. His view seemed to be that if you don't get the inner stuff right, you'll never get the outer stuff right either. Anything out in the world that you chase and succeed in attaining without inner wisdom can then become no more than a new problem or burden, and not the delight you had hoped.

It turns out that the sort of community viewed as important by Plato, Aristotle, and the Stoics is often endangered by people who tend to behave like the proverbial "bull in a china shop." These bull-headed individuals act out of false beliefs and unhealthy emotions, throwing their weight around and disrupting otherwise promising partnerships with versions of negativity and damage they're often not aware that they carry with them wherever they go.

Understanding how important it is for us all to shed such destructive inner baggage, Socrates urged that his fellow Athenians make it a habit to engage in the wisdom work of relentless self-examination, famously saying, "The unexamined life is not worth living." He insisted that his peers examine their beliefs, values, and attitudes and, further, that they engage in such reflection honestly and often. Of course, in response, they insisted that he drink poison and die. So his frequently repeated recommendation wasn't wildly popular at the time. And neither was he. But he was right. Although he was apparently viewed by many as a nuisance to the city and was ultimately executed by public demand, it turns out that the course of human history proves he was deeply wise about the vital importance of the self-reflective task he urged on his fellow citizens. Good souls make for good societies. And creating good souls takes work.

In Plato's *Republic*, Socrates paints the portrait of a political community where everyone has a proper role and does their part in harmony with others, considering all fellow citizens as if they were members of an extended family. He then adds that the leaders of any ideal community or government ought to be philosophers, people who in later Stoic thought might be well described as those best trained to understand and use well both reason and relationality.

Plato depicts Socrates as saying to his friend and conversation partner Glaucon, "Unless communities have philosophers as kings, or the people who are currently called kings and rulers practice philosophy with enough integrity . . . there can be no end to political troubles, my dear Glaucon, or to human troubles in general." Glaucon immediately predicts a poor reception for this idea of philosopher-kings, and jokes that anyone who hears of this might begin to throw things at Socrates in outrage. And he was sadly right, despite the wisdom Socrates had in discerning what it would take for anyone truly to lead others well.

Community and political virtues

The many virtues or forms of human excellence prominently discussed by Plato and Aristotle, and later affirmed by many other philosophers in the Western tradition they launched, such ideal qualities as practical wisdom, justice, courage, and self-control, seem to be crucial for the establishment and maintenance of healthy communities — for the enterprise of living well together. Following their philosophical predecessors, the Stoics went on to name and discuss the importance of many other qualities of emotion, attitude, and character that are also needed for harmonious living together in any form of society. They speak about such things as benevolence, gratitude, forgiveness, acceptance, patience, honesty, discreetness, modesty, affection, courtesy, forbearance, dignity, industriousness, considerateness, kindness, compassion, helpfulness, friendliness, mercy, and many other positive characteristics that we need for flourishing relationships among family, friends, and colleagues, as well as for a positive overall community spirit. It's a list that would serve us all well to use as a template and test for selecting community leaders and political representatives at every level. An absence of such virtues is always a problem, and not just for the individuals who lack them, but for their communities.

REMEMBER

It all goes back to Plato and his teacher Socrates: If we don't do the wisdom work of using our capacity of reason for regular self-examination and proper self-development in the virtues within our own souls, in our hearts and minds, we can never experience the best relationships with others, or the sort of community life in which alone we can feel our best, do our best, and be our best. The inner is the only proper foundation for the outer. The beliefs we hold, the attitudes we maintain, and the emotions we feel will determine how we act in the world and whether we're building or eroding community as we make our own way through our days and years.

Circles of Community and Care

One of the most innovative and vividly helpful ideas about positive community and our larger political life comes to us from a relatively unknown second-century Roman Stoic philosopher named Hierocles. We don't know much about his life, but a few of his thoughts have been passed down to us through the citations and quotations others made of his work in their own documents that have survived the centuries. His most useful idea on community can be spelled out quite simply. It's a picture for our lives as we live them on different levels, and as a map of our various surrounding communities it can be spelled out, or articulated, in several ways. While sticking to the main concepts from Hierocles himself, we'll feel free here to lay out his main idea in a way that's most fitting for our time.

The rings of our lives

Imagine your life as taking place amid a set of invisible concentric circles pictured like the bands of contrasting color in a traditional archery target, with circles or broad circular bands that can be mapped out around you as the starting point, located precisely at the center of the bullseye. The innermost circle of your life is just your own soul, or your heart and mind.

The first job you have in life is, as Socrates suggested, to properly grow and govern your own thoughts and feelings in healthy ways — your beliefs and attitudes and various dispositions — and to perform all that inner activity well. A healthy mind helps make for a healthy body, and then the body returns the favor and supports the clarity and activities of the mind. This inner circle is where it all begins. As you do the inner work well, you can then contribute in positive, healthy ways to the next circle out — one involving your own home and the family members who are closest to you there. As some of the ancients put it, if you manage yourself well, you can then better manage your household well, or at least contribute your proper part at any stage of your life to that context. Good people make for good families.

Perhaps the next circle out can then be imagined as your friends and neighbors, and maybe your fellow students if you're in school, or your business associates or coworkers, in case you're at a stage later in life. Hierocles never makes it completely clear whether these circles are to be distinguished and drawn based on physical proximity, or intimacy of acquaintance, or shared activity, or else by some other measure closely related to these, such as time spent together, or mutual knowledge.

But extrapolating naturally from here in various ways beyond the good friends you see often, perhaps even daily, and maybe also your close neighbors and work colleagues, the next circle out will likely be your city or county, then next your state, then your broader geographical region, and then your nation, and ultimately the world.

Of course, you can draw the circles in a specifically civic way, and then craft another parallel set in a work-related way, where your personal office is one close circle, and then the circles fan out to your industry either regionally, or nationally, and across the globe. Ultimately, Hierocles would want you to see the big picture for your community context at every level and in every way. We're all positioned in circles within circles, and they all should matter to how we think about our lives and actions in the world. Context counts.

The idea behind the concentric circles begins with what we might call "contributory localism." Our first task is to contribute whatever we can to make our closest local circles as good, healthy, and harmonious as they can be. Then it's our job to seek to contribute as we can to make each larger circle better as well, as far as our own efforts may reach.

A good heart and mind contribute to a good family, which contributes to making for a better neighborhood, when then becomes a part of a better city, and so on. Our most immediate duty is to pay attention to what's needed to make our closest circles better, healthier, and stronger, in such a way that they can contribute positively to each of our outer circles. And when we find ourselves operating in any of those more remote circles, our job is to help make sure those outer circles reach back and support healthier inner circles for ourselves and others.

The duties and jobs of other people who live and work in what count as our outer circles are then the same as our general obligations, to work well within their own concentric areas of responsibility, beginning with their own hearts and minds, and to contribute to their outer circles in such a way as to support the inner circles of others as well as themselves. It's quite a picture. Hierocles doesn't go this far in his elaborations of the basic view, but its inner logic allows that we can and should think through all such implications for our vastly interconnected and interdependent time. We need to care for every circle in a positive way, in so far as that is possible for us to do so.

Making the most of our circles

Hierocles gives us a portrait of working well where we are and caring for the larger contexts that surround and support us. It's a depiction of the many communities in which we live and that can affect how we flourish together.

WARNING

A common problem arises in life that can also be diagnosed vividly by this picture of circles. Too many people, in a misguided effort to support and strengthen one or more of their own inner circles, whether it's at the level of family, neighborhood, or village, or even a political community of the like-minded though dispersed, become divisive and tribalistic in a very adversarial way. They start thinking that everything is about "us against them." When you get pulled into this mindset, it's you and yours fighting the world. And it's always a recipe for trouble.

Some of the Stoics have a vivid picture for this divisive tribalism. Marcus Aurelius was an emperor who didn't govern just from the palace but camped out in the worst war zones to lead from the front and lend a hand. He had often seen the horrors of combat and its aftermath up close, including the disturbing sights of severed body parts left on the field of battle. In his writings, he compares any person or group that separates off from the rest of humanity in a selfish, defensive, or adversarial way to such severed limbs, which of course quickly languish and die cut off from the body to which they rightly belong, as the body itself is damaged grievously and often mortally from their removal.

This is a metaphor for antagonistic individualism, and for the aggressive partisan spirit by which people remove themselves from their fellow human beings whom they have come to consider outsiders and enemies. This attitude and related behavior that we see around us so much at the present time tears asunder any broader unity and makes healthy community increasingly hard or impossible. In seeking to preserve, protect, and strengthen their own close circles, people with this divisive spirit ironically weaken the groups they aim to help, as well as the broader context they need so as to flourish.

To the Stoics, our relationality matters deeply, as does our reason. We're here to cooperate and partner in positive ways with each other. When we cut ourselves off from the larger human community, everyone suffers.

Hierocles offers another interesting image connected with these invisible concentric circles that surround us and map our lives. He suggested that the moral or ethical perspective is to reach out to embrace the widest circles and pull them in, imaginatively, to something at least approximating the level of care and affection we owe and normally show to others in our closest circles. Near or far, we're all members of the human family, with a soul spark of reason akin to the divine, a little piece of divinity within ourselves. We're all cousins of the spirit. And we should seek to respect and honor all members of this broader family, however we can, wherever they might be, and however different they may seem from us. Otherwise, our vital and larger unity is broken and we can't flourish as we'd like, or as we should.

The Four Foundations

There's a perspective that runs through much ancient philosophy and is shared in many ways, at least implicitly, by the Stoics. We can put it like this: From the moment you wake up in the morning, until the time you fall asleep at night, you encounter the world along four different dimensions, each of which has an ideal goal or target. We can call them "The Four Dimensions of Experience" and their targets "The Four Foundations of Greatness." They are the bases for excellence in our lives and relationships. Healthy communities require that we respect and nurture:

The Intellectual Dimension that aims at Truth

The Aesthetic Dimension that aims at Beauty

The Moral Dimension that aims at Goodness

The Spiritual Dimension that aims at Unity

We need Truth, Beauty, Goodness, and Unity in our lives just like we need air, food, and water. Without these things we can't flourish as individuals or in community with others. When Hierocles talks about pulling the outer circles of our lives inward, he can be seen as implying that we should think of others, feel toward others, and act so as to treat others — whether in our families or neighborhoods, or across the country, or even in remote parts of the world — in accordance with these four ideals, known as transcendentals, since their importance transcends any particular circumstances and, in principle, should apply to all.

In fact, the way we employ and apply each of these four ideals should be determined by a respect for the other three. Some people tell the truth in ugly ways, and in violation of what's required for goodness, thereby making any form of healthy unity nearly impossible. The early Christian writer known as the Apostle Paul had a powerful phrase: "speaking the truth in love." To an enlightened mind, everything should be somehow answerable to love. Love is just being committed to others intellectually, aesthetically, morally, and spiritually, seeking to honor them with Truth, Beauty, Goodness, and Unity in whatever ways are possible. Harmonious community can result.

The demands of love

The 20th-century philosopher Bertrand Russell once reflected Stoic ideas on all this in a modern way, in a 1959 interview with the BBC:

> Love is wise, hatred is foolish. In this closely interconnected world, we have to learn to tolerate each other. We have to learn to put up with the fact that some people say things that we don't like. We can only live together if we learn the charity and tolerance which is absolutely vital to the continuation of human life on this planet.

REMEMBER

It surprises some people when they first hear that the Stoics talked about love and valued it. The common misunderstanding of Stoicism is that it's a thoroughly anti-emotional view that seeks to free us from any entanglements that could result in an inner vulnerability. People who have only a cursory knowledge of the Stoics seem to think that they valued the good and right, but rarely associate their thought with love. And yet, as we show later (in Chapter 15), the Stoics valued positive emotion, but considered love as more than an emotion, and as a firm commitment of the will to the good of others and their well-being. Marcus Aurelius writes such things as this:

> Happy is the man who does the work of a man. And what is a man's work? To love his neighbor . . . to distinguish false ideas from true, and to contemplate the works of nature. (8.26)

He also contemplates the related importance of unity, the vital level of human connection made possible by love:

> Just as you are part of the whole community, each of your actions should contribute to the whole life of the community. Any action of yours that fails, directly or remotely, to make this contribution, fragments the life of the community, and

jeopardizes its unity. It's a rebellious act, like the man in a town meeting who holds himself aloof and refuses to come to any agreement with his neighbors. (9.23)

In a letter, the Stoic political advisor Seneca explains something about the importance of the unity that only love can attain and uphold. He writes:

I can lay down for mankind a rule, in brief, for our duties in human relationships: Everything you can see comprehending the divine and human is one — we are the parts of one great body. Nature made us related to each other since she created us from the same source and to the same end. She planted in us mutual affection and made us prone to friendships. She established fairness and justice. . . . Our relations with each other are like a stone arch, one that would collapse if the stones did not mutually support one another, and which is upheld in this very way. (*Letters* 95.53-54)

Affection, friendship, fairness, justice, and support are mentioned in just this one passage as important for the health and strength of human community.

THE EMPEROR ON COMMUNITY

While reflecting on the fact that we live in an interrelated and interconnected universe, Marcus Aurelius wrote these things in his *Meditations*:

And because I am related to the other parts that are like me, I will not seek my own advantage at their expense, but I will study to know what is our common good and make every effort to advance that good and convince others not to act against it. If I am successful in this, my life is bound to flow smoothly, as one would expect for the dutiful citizen who always looks out for others and enjoys whatever work his community asks of him. (10.6)

All rational creatures, by nature's deep design and purpose, are made for one another. They are mean to help those who need help, and in no way harm each other. (9.1)

But in whatever I do, whether alone or with someone else, my one objective will be this and only this: to benefit and to live in harmony with the community. (7.5)

The first law of man's being, then, is his sense of kinship. (7.55)

Have I acted unselfishly? Then I've benefited. Hold on to this thought and keep up the good work. (11.4)

> Arm yourself for action with these two thoughts: First, do only what your lawgiving and ruling reason tells you is for the good of others; and second, don't hesitate to change course if someone is able to show you where you're wrong or point out a better way. But be persuaded only by arguments based on justice and the common good, never by what appeals to your taste for pleasure or popularity. (4.12)

> A branch cut from another branch is also, of necessity, cut from the whole tree. Just so, a man estranged from another man is separated from the rest of humanity. But whereas a branch is cut away by someone else, a man cuts himself off from others through his own hatred or neglect, not realizing that at the same time he is cutting himself off from the whole of civilized society. (11.8)

Citizens of the world

In another short passage in his journal, Marcus writes to himself this reminder: "Whether in a city or in the wilderness, you are a citizen of the world." (*Meditations* 10.15) This was an important concept in Stoic thought. As Hierocles showed us, the circles of our lives reach far beyond our neighborhoods and nations and extend to the full reaches of the globe. And if other rational beings ever are found to live on other planets, our circles will extend to them and those distant locations as well. We are citizens of the world, and of the universe, in community with all rational creatures that may exist beyond our precise species and, ideally, in any part of a vast multiverse that either contains or sits apart from our own cosmic neighborhood.

This concept of a broad belonging, or of a cosmic citizenship, a view that's often known as cosmopolitanism, is commonly attributed to Diogenes of Sinope, another role model beloved by the Stoics, an individual also called "Diogenes the Cynic," because he was said to have looked and lived like a stray dog (in Greek, *kunikos* or "doglike"). He is famously reported to have said of himself, "I am a citizen of the world." But the idea of citizenship in a broadest possible community seems to have predated Diogenes and is traced by the Stoics themselves to Socrates. In the *Discourses*, Epictetus comments:

> If what's said by the philosophers on the kinship of God and men is true, then what other course is left for us but the one that Socrates took when, being asked to what country he belonged, said that it never should be answered "I'm an Athenian" or "I'm a Corinthian," but that, "I am a citizen of the universe?" (I.9)

Despite this citation of Socrates by Epictetus, most Stoics seem to have looked to Diogenes for their cosmopolitan inspiration. And Diogenes was in many ways an odd role model to have, as he was an extreme Cynic, often appearing to go out of his way to flaunt behavior that was not socially accepted in his day, or in any day. He was affiliated with a philosophical school or tradition distinct from Stoicism that prized simplicity and poverty above all, urging the elimination of unneeded things and the rejection of all artificial social conventions.

ANECDOTE

Diogenes is said to have lived in a barrel, often strolled around naked, and is reported to have given away all his possessions, except for a clay bowl for drinking water. We're told that he one day saw a slave boy drinking out of cupped hands and then gave away the bowl. He said, "He has the most who is most content with the least." But he was not at all one who embraced and sought to build community. In an excellent scholarly text, *The Stoic Idea of the City*, philosopher Malcolm Schofield says that when Diogenes characterized himself as a citizen of the world, or more literally of the cosmos, "he implied that he was at home nowhere else — except in the universe itself." And Schofield is likely right in that interpretation. When Diogenes said he was a citizen of the broadest context he knew, it was likely because he didn't feel like he fit in with any smaller circle of community. But most of the Stoics would have embraced the view of cosmopolitism for a quite different reason: They felt the broadest possible sense of citizenship precisely because, by contrast with Diogenes, they felt at home in every circle of humanity, at every level, and wanted to endorse a worldview that extended their status as citizens as broadly as possible.

Diogenes may have lacked a sense of local citizenship because he didn't fit in, but more importantly because he spurned local customs and didn't want to fit in. He didn't see his neighborhood or city as contributing to what he valued, or as particularly benefiting him. But the standard Stoic view seems to be very different. We feel the affiliation of community with a place or with a group of people not primarily because we think of it or them as benefiting us, or as contributing to our growth as people, although they certainly do. We feel an affinity because we see that place and those people as an arena where we can ourselves contribute through our attention, care, and action. We see it and them as constituting a stage on which we can create, or join, proper partnerships for living well, in Aristotle's conception, or in which we can have a vital individual role, as perhaps reflected in Plato's *Republic*.

The Stoics saw all people as proper parts of the community, despite their unfortunate and anomalous acceptance of slavery, a form of service and servitude not at the time reflecting race or ethnicity but the vicissitudes of war and conquest. Yet, no philosopher or group of thinkers has ever been right about everything. We appreciate any of their advances when they have discovered new truth or pointed out something that should have been obvious to us, despite their errors on other things. And we can learn from their insights, while avoiding their flaws.

One thing we learn from Marcus Aurelius, if we really pay attention, is that what mainly rips apart communities and disrupts politics in our own time is that we have forgotten those qualities the emperor lauded at the beginning of his *Meditations*, the characteristics of "courtesy and serenity of temper." With those healing attributes, we can do much in our circles of community and life.

THE FIVE RULES OF COSMOPOLITANISM

A contemporary take on the Stoic concentric circles in service to a broader cosmopolitanism could be said to urge you to:

1. Start where you are,

2. Use what you have,

3. Do what you can,

4. Serve all you might,

5. Love with no limit.

It should also be noted that most of the Stoics seemed to see women as either roughly or absolutely equal contributors with men in the formation and composition of community. But this is often clearest in the recorded reflections of Musonius Rufus, the teacher of Epictetus. He believed that women obviously have the same capacity for reason, and so for wisdom and virtue, as men, and that therefore education should be provided equally across the genders. And as properly widespread as that realization is in our own day, despite its still sad lack of universal acceptance, it was quite revolutionary as an idea in ancient Greece and Rome. In this as in other things, the Stoics often led the way.

4

Passions and Emotions

Explore the much-misunderstood Stoic idea of apathy — in case you care.

Dive into Stoic views on friendship and love.

Understand why the Stoics did not fear death.

Chapter **14**

Stoic Apathy: Why You Should Care

For a long time, the word "stoic" with a lowercase "s" has been used to label someone who either shows no emotion or seems to feel none in situations where emotion might be natural, and even healthy. The stoic in our midst appears to be untouched by things that get other people worked up in a visible manner. As everyone else seems emotionally engaged in positive or negative ways by whatever is going on, the individual we think of as a stoic stands aloof and carries on as usual, unperturbed. Onlookers may differ as to whether this is admirable or just odd.

In this chapter, we explore an important idea in Stoic thought that might have given people the idea that such an attitude of aloofness is properly named stoic. We dig deeper to understand what's often called "Stoic apathy," which ends up being a very distinctive mindset, and quite different from what most people now seem to think when they hear the word "apathy." We then work to see what exactly Stoic apathy is meant to be and accomplish. And we end up wondering whether the classic Stoics and their modern followers have been able to get right what they've aimed to achieve with this concept.

Two Ideas of Apathy

ANECDOTE

There's an old joke. But for one of your co-authors, it came bundled in a real-life story. Your current guide typing these words was leading a Summer Seminar for School Teachers sponsored by the National Endowment for the Humanities that brought together some of the best K–12 teachers in America for a month of intellection exploration, freewheeling talk, and philosophical stimulation. Many of the participants had been "State Teacher of the Year" in their various locations, and all were eager to talk philosophy and life in their month together. A seventh-grade instructor told the group about another middle school colleague who had a class full of unruly underachievers. She did her best with the students in the first weeks of the year, but nothing seemed to work. One day she walked into the classroom, went straight to the blackboard, picked up chalk, and wrote out two words in huge letters:

Ignorance

Indifference

She then turned around to the ringleader of the unengaged, apparently lazy, and yet boisterous kids and said, "Bob, what's the difference between ignorance and indifference?" And you know the answer already, right? In a sarcastic tone Bob *actually* said "I don't know, and I don't care." The teacher replied, "Yes! That's right, Bob; perfectly put. See what you can do when you set your mind to it?" Any teacher can deal with the "I-don't-know." We provide information. It's the "I-don't-care" that's so much harder to reach."

Two big problems

WARNING

Perhaps the two biggest problems in modern life are that, in reference to the many dire issues looming over us globally and locally that badly need to be solved, too many people either don't know or don't care about what exactly the issues are and how best they might be tackled. And so the difficulties get worse due to inattention or insufficient intervention. Ignorance and indifference can be big problems in life, but the apathetic disconnect of indifference may indeed be more difficult of the two to solve. When real apathy is present, and especially if it runs deep, it can seem to be nearly untouchable and stubbornly resistant to change. Unfortunately, we see it all around us in the world now. When things seem overwhelming, many people just give up, tune out, and turn off. But that lets things get worse.

An ancient idea and a modern translation

Here's our issue: Google the phrase "Stoic apathy" and you'll likely get 720,000 results or more. It's a common concept, often thought to be a core characterization of how anyone following a Stoic way of life will present themselves to the world and deal with things that come their way. But Stoicism is really supposed to be about growing wise and using our inner power for virtuous choices and actions in this world. And so any application of the common concept of apathy or indifference to Stoicism can be a bit confusing to those first getting to know the Stoic philosophy of life.

Stoicism is known for promoting an attitude or mindset conveyed through an ancient concept that in Greek is expressed by the word *apatheia*. It's a term most often translated into English as apathy, and not just because they sound alike. The English derives from the Greek. But with that translation, modern readers can get a false idea of what the Stoics valued and recommended. It's our job to examine afresh the Stoic notion of apathy. And by the time you finish this chapter, we hope that if you're ever asked what you personally think about the concept, you'll never say that you don't know and don't care.

Definitions and Images in Film

Look up the word "apathy" on the *Merriam-Webster.com Dictionary* and you get these results: (1) lack of feeling or emotion (impassiveness), (2) lack of interest or concern (indifference). A further quick Google search yields "lack of interest, *enthusiasm*, or concern." The Cleveland Clinic even weighs in with a medical definition as "a lack of goal-directed activity," adding the symptomology that it "presents as a lack of emotional expression."

There was a period in American film history when a popular image arose in several forms and then was emulated around the world in other cultures. It was the Wild West Cowboy Problem Solver, or in another form, a laconic private detective, or else a heroic soldier, a guy who saves the day decisively, while acting without apparent emotion. He just did his job, achieved what was needed, and rode off into the sunset with no fanfare at all. The word "stoic" came to be used to describe such a protagonist, whose demeanor was often viewed with admiration by moviegoers, who knew themselves well enough to realize that they couldn't likely marshal such calm determination and effectively targeted action under the duress of intense imminent danger.

The American actor John Wayne, for example, was known for his portrayal of such characters — strong and decisive in the face of evil, but also taciturn, and almost entirely unexpressive. The character of super spy James Bond, played by several top actors, reinforced roughly the same image over decades of film success, adding a touch of urbanity and wit to the mix. Many other leading men, from

Sylvester Stallone and Arnold Schwarzenegger to Matt Damon, Liam Neeson and beyond, have portrayed versions of such a savior of the innocent, the weak and the needy, freeing them from the clutches of evil predators in what seem to be impossible circumstances. This is the guy you want on your side, the stoic hero. Maybe it's even the person you want to be, embodying what has come to be known as "the strong, silent type."

WARNING

This seemed to be a great and noble image until modern psychologists got to work on it and helped us realize that these overt personality traits could be a manifestation of deep emotional damage rather than inner strength. The hero might have long-term psychological problems that caused his natural feelings to be bottled up, or tightly suppressed in a way that was unhealthy for him, and perhaps also for the people closest to him. Sure, he could ride into town and solve a problem, or paraglide into an exotic resort and take out the bad guy, but you wouldn't necessarily want to have him around the house on a regular basis, or report to him at work.

And there's a different problematic form for a lack of emotion. So much bad news in our day comes from all directions that it feels overwhelming to some people, who grow emotionally and motivationally numb, and eventually just shut down. That can lead to the medical diagnosis of apathy. The extreme of this is known as "avolition," a complete lack of motive or energy to carry out ordinary tasks. It can also result from PTSD or a stroke, or several diseases and can be an early sign of dementia or Alzheimer's. It's not at all what the Stoic philosophers recommended that we seek to attain in our lives.

Digging Deeper into Stoic Apathy

Zeno, the founder of Stoicism, apparently praised and urged the wisdom of a certain sort of attitude, often referred to as "apathy," that should be at the core of a proper Stoic mindset. And this can be confusing to a modern student of Stoicism. But a touch more linguistic history can be helpful.

The etymology of the English word "apathy" derives from the Greek privative particle *a,* which was used in compound words to mean "not" or "without," and the term *pathe,* which meant, roughly "passion." So "apathy," in terms of its historic roots, simply means "without passion." But this can be more than a little perplexing to a modern sensibility that normally uses the term "passion" to convey a valued enthusiasm, or a positive measure of emotional energy that seems to be a facilitating condition for success in most difficult endeavors. Business leaders want to hire passionate people for their high energy and commitment. And of course, romantics celebrate passion as a zest for living. Passion seems to characterize the creators and champions in the world. So why would anyone urge on us a life without it?

The Stoics used the term *pathe* that we translate as "passion" quite differently from its modern associations. With the exceptions of what they called "the good passions" of joy, caution, and wish, they thought of a passion as an agitating and disturbing impulse of the soul, an unreasonable movement toward action based on a false judgment that something is good or bad which isn't at all, and whose sheer strength could interfere with our ability to reason well and do the right thing. We preserve hints of this meaning through the present day in the common phrase "crime of passion." A crime of passion isn't the result of admirable zest or positive energy. The phrase is meant to distinguish the act so described from a crime that's the result of premeditation and deliberation, or of reasoning. A crime of passion by contrast is committed in a cascade of ascending emotions, in the pressure of a moment when intense impulses overcome prudence, common sense, and basic moral values to spark, as a result and almost without thought, a heinous act that would never be chosen by a rational consideration. Passion in this sense destroys prudence.

With this as the Stoic idea of passion — that of an extreme and unreasonable impulse connected with a strong false feeling or, attitude, whether of fear, anger, hatred, revulsion, greed, lust, craving, intense pain, or immense pleasure — the contrastive idea of apathy is a form of liberation from all such compulsiveness. It's a form of freedom to think and act rationally and well. That's very different from Bob and the lazy middle school class, or the damaged individual incapable of setting goals or acting on them who gets diagnosed at the Cleveland Clinic. In this precise Stoic sense, apathy does not weaken a person, but in quite the opposite way it provides for a strength not available under the enslavement of troubled impulse and emotion.

In the common modern meaning of apathy as not caring about anything, Stoics aren't apathetic. They care deeply about virtue and vice, and about our reason and our relationships, as well as about the many social and moral roles we naturally play in those relationships. They also care about living in agreement with nature and God, and freeing themselves from anything that would enslave their commanding faculty or guiding inner source, the rational self within that can be the seat of intelligent volition or will.

The Discipline We Need

Plato thought our souls have different parts that could oppose each other. The Stoics had a different view, believing the soul is unified. In their view, no rival compartments of the self can be in tension. But our one soul still has different functions that need to be trained. There is a function of judgment, one of desire, and one of action. Correspondingly, Stoics like Epictetus and Marcus Aurelius thought that an inner discipline should be applied to each: to the judgments we make of the impressions that form in our minds, to the desires that are based on those judgments, and to the impulses toward action that come from both. In one passage in the *Discourses* Epictetus explains that we need to be trained in all these areas and says this:

> The most important and urgent of these areas is the one having to do with the passions. A passion is always a result of frustrated desire or ineffective avoidance. This is the area that involves mental turmoil, confusion, wretchedness, misery, sadness, grief, and fear, and that leaves us envious and jealous, which are passions that make it impossible to listen to reason. The second area has to do with proper conduct, because I should not be as unfeeling as a statue but should maintain my natural and acquired relationships towards gods, father, brothers, children, and fellow citizens. The third area is relevant to those already making progress. It has to do with attaining unquestionable reliability in the other two domains, so that even when asleep, drunk, or depressed, no untested impression slips past one's guard. (*Discourses* 3.2.1–5)

Notice how Epictetus warns against passions in the proper ancient sense and about their dangers, while also distinguishing the desired mindset of *apatheia* from the totally unfeeling nature of a statue. As a Stoic he was not urging on us an elimination of all desires or feelings, but a discipline of them. He speaks of self-mastery and seems to understand its importance not only for our actions, but for our thoughts and emotions as well. Too many people seem to be controlled by their emotions and impulses. It's the essential Stoic perspective that we always need to stay in control of them. And this requires that we are careful about what judgments we make, what beliefs we allow ourselves to form, or what interpretations we give to our impressions.

WARNING

To Epictetus, the trouble of disturbing passions always starts with our judgments. In a very famous passage that's often favorably quoted, he says:

> It's not things themselves that disturb men, but their judgments about these things. (*Handbook* 5)

But this is a classic example of a false dichotomy, since the truth seems to be that some things themselves do disturb us, even with a proper control over our judgments, and yet we are well reminded that many other things bother us only through errant judgment. So, the claim here still shows us how the real battle against disturbing emotions and impulses begins with solid rational control over the judgments we make from our first impressions. Stoicism never tells us not to feel or express emotions, it only wants us not to suffer from experiencing unnecessary and overwhelmingly difficult passions.

REMEMBER

For the Stoics, everything begins with the inner mental impressions that result from our sensations and perceptions, and how we use those impressions. Properly trained, we give our assent only to trustworthy impressions, and not to misleading ones, and never to any distorted interpretations or false extensions of what are basically true and faithful impressions. Likewise, we learn to discipline the desires and impulses that arise out of the interpretations of the impressions we have. We pursue things that seem beneficial, and we avoid those that seem detrimental. We tend to go wrong when we value the wrong things, confusing what isn't in our real interest with what is. Properly trained, we come to desire only what the Logos, or God, would have for us, which is whatever is foreordained and whatever we can attain in virtue. That's the Stoic view. Proper thinking and feeling will most often lead to proper impulses to act, and to rational conduct in our lives.

The Nature of Emotions

So where exactly do such things as emotions, desires, and passions fit into the Stoic view of how we function in the world? It seems that classic Stoics see emotions as arising out of our thoughts, in particular our judgments, and perhaps, led by our desires, when those feelings grow strong enough to result in movements of the soul, they can become unruly passions that are then viewed as dangerously disturbing impulses toward action. But there is twist on this picture that may accommodate more recent modern research into our evolutionary past and its impact on feeling and thinking.

Hot emotions can spark desires, impulses, and actions in a visceral and immediate way. The most primitive parts of our brains seem to encode a variety of tendencies toward emotional reaction that have been connected in a positive way with physical survival value since our prehistoric past. When confronted with something that may injure our bodies or kill us, we naturally and instinctively react with fear, fright, worry, repulsion, or disgust, among other emotions of caution and recoil. And this seems to happen apart from or prior to any detailed information we consciously ponder about the potential threat and its danger. Our ancestors who reacted to objects of this threatening type with emotions and acts of caution or avoidance tended to survive and pass on to their descendants that tendency, and those who did not do so often had their lives cut short, without passing on such contrary and careless habits.

Our emotions can encode information in various ways, a certain knowing before thinking that, expressed as a form of feeling, makes us act quickly. These feelings respond to information when it is manifestly available. That's part of what makes an emotion appropriate to its situation or not. These facts, among others, have led many philosophers to refer to "the cognitive nature of emotion," or "emotional cognitivity." Emotions themselves seem to contain or assume cognitive judgments as to what is true and real, what's valuable or problematic, as well as what's safe or dangerous. And with our neurological wiring, those codifications can spark action more rapidly than any conscious thought process might. It can even happen that the body, confronted with a known danger, reacts even before any overt emotion with an increased heart rate, a jolt of adrenalin, and other manifestations like perspiration and a general tensing or trembling of the muscles. That is then interpreted by the unconscious mind as sensing the presence of imminent danger, and this is encoded by an emotional response to the physiology already in progress. Such a process seems to come as a preloaded tendency or natural endowment that has had long-term survival value. And it could then naturally be seen by Stoics as another function of embodied reason, as well as one over which we could have control once we understood the mechanism.

The Stoics viewed emotion, as well as impulse, as resulting entirely from a proper or improper use of reason. So, on Stoic assumptions, all emotions and impulses can in principle be governed by reason. And that means by us, in our freedom of response.

Most things with power for good seem to have equal and opposite power for ill. Emotions and the impulses they give rise to that the Stoics called passions can obviously distort insight in many situations of exploration, discovery, and assessment. As we have seen repeatedly in early 21st-century political debates and in public and private discussions of issues that have become politicized, heated passions can blind people to clear facts and even cause many to see things that aren't there. Passions, in the strict ancient sense, can be dangerous. But our emotions can also assist us in the search for truth.

People who care about finding the solution to a problem, who are deeply moved with a compassion felt for those suffering with it, will often persist in a determined investigation of the issue longer than those who have no emotional stake in it. And very often, as we've just seen, our emotions can warn us of potential danger or dire need before the rational function of the mind has had a chance to assess the situation we're in. A Stoic can caution us against disturbing passions while recognizing the positive roles of emotion.

In the introduction to this book, we began our adventure with the Stoics by suggesting that much of wisdom consists in knowing what to embrace and what to release. And we also surmised there that it's common to get this wrong, as we seem to frequently embrace what ought to be released, and release what should be embraced. The Stoics want us to get this right. They hope to help us release the false emotions, attitudes, and impulses that get in the way of our best thinking, feeling, being, and doing in the world, in accord with nature, which they think of as suffused with the wisdom and virtue of the Logos, or the benevolent divine rationality that structures everything.

Apathy and Ataraxia

The whole point of *apatheia*, the particular and targeted mindset known properly as Stoic apathy, a mental and emotional state of being without agitating improper passions, is to provide for a certain inner freedom that the Stoics view as otherwise unavailable. That freedom then allows for a condition of the soul known by the Greeks as *ataraxia*, which is usually translated as tranquility, or inner peace. From the Stoic perspective, the foolish are driven by unruly emotions, desires, and passions, while only the wise have inner equanimity, or an unperturbedness of soul. Imagine the surface of a pond on a windless day. This mirrors the soul of the wise. And it's something we can and should work to attain.

In a letter, Seneca characterizes the opposite of wisdom in this matter in strong words:

> Foolishness is low, abject, ungenerous, slavish, and vulnerable to many of the cruelest passions. These passions, which are bullying bosses, sometimes oppressing you one at a time, and sometimes all together, can be cast away by wisdom, which is the only real freedom. (*Letters* 27.4)

How though does wisdom accomplish this exiling of the cruel passions? By showing us that in every case, the disturbance is the result of false judgments, or an improper use of impressions. We leap beyond what we see to what we fear or crave because we think that something is bad when it's not, or good when it's not. When we realize our mistake, we naturally adjust inwardly, and the bullying passions vanish along with the false wind that blew them in.

You've probably known people who are almost always worked up about something, and sometimes seemed to be worked up about everything all at once. In listening to them pour out their tales of woe or exuberance, you've likely come to realize that they were overestimating something, and probably underestimating something else, jumping beyond the available evidence, or putting an extreme value on a mere possibility that it did not seem to merit, pro or con. You may have wanted to tell them to calm down, but if you've accumulated any real wisdom over the years, you know that this almost never works. We can tell ourselves to calm down, and sometimes successfully. But when we suggest that to anyone else, and especially an adolescent or adult, it can have the opposite effect. Telling someone to calm down just makes an agitated person more worked up. It tends to rub an angry person the wrong way, exacerbating the entire situation, as if in seeking to put out a fire, we made the big mistake of pouring more fuel on it.

Stoicism has recommendations for us ahead of time to help us handle the situations of life so well that they rarely or never cause distorting passions to arise in us in the first place. The Stoics remind us that, on their philosophy, only the will and its uses are good or bad. Outer things can never rise to that high level. No external events can strictly be called evil or wonderful, truly terrible, or terrific. Seneca has a great essay on this called "On Tranquility," where he enumerates all the ways we give ourselves completely unnecessary worries. It's not just that we need to be free of all extreme emotions like abject fear and delirious enthusiasm, but that as a path to this freedom, we need to liberate ourselves from the many concerns that weigh us down and prevent us from having the inner peace that should be our natural gift.

Stoic serenity

Imagine *ataraxia*, or stoic calm, not as a void of emotion, desire, or impulse, a state of heart and mind utterly without these things, but rather as one in which gentle breezes of natural and appropriate emotions, desires, and impulses can touch the surface of the mind without disturbing its peace or equanimity. You can get a small and lightweight kite up in these breezes, but don't plan on paragliding. There are absolutely no storms on your horizon, no big booming gusts or blasts aroused within that might dislodge reason or bend it out of shape. The Stoic soul does not allow such strong winds to form and rush through its inner chambers. Its default setting is never the disruptive fluctuation of agitation, delirium, or outrage, but rather the smooth and reliable flow of an ongoing inner peace.

WARNING

Now of course, some Stoics take this need for inner peace to an extreme. Epictetus appears to be an example of that. He seems to want to use the simple distinction between the things we can control and the things we can't control to get us to live with our attention wholly on the former while we overlook or are apathetic about the latter. But as we see in our Chapter 9 on control, the idea of what's completely up to us or wholly within our power is itself an extreme and narrow idea, encompassing few things, and all of them are inner matters of the mind. To then exclude all else as literally "worthless" or "without value" and unworthy of our concern, which is what Epictetus often does, is even more extreme. The former slave clearly wants to render us invulnerable to any disturbance whatsoever, to any emotion of fear or worry, disappointment, or loss, as well as any disturbing passion. But, on reflection, such a result seems impossible. In even the attempt to attain the ideal heights to which this Stoic calls us, we're likely to stumble a lot, and feel a new disappointment and a worry that we'll never manage it. He then inadvertently creates extra worry for us, instead of eliminating those we already have.

The essay Seneca wrote called "On Tranquility" was sparked by a letter from his friend Serenus, a law enforcement official on the night watch in the emperor Nero's palace, who was trying under great pressures to live a Stoic life. But he was endlessly frustrated and troubled that he was not managing to do it well. He was falling short in his own eyes and was disappointed in himself. Seneca writes the essay to help his friend get his bearings and calm down a bit, assuring him that he's experiencing the path of Stoic growth in a natural way. We don't go from being full of inner troubles to being altogether free of them. But if Seneca is right, and he does seem to be, then the extreme project Epictetus has in mind is unnecessary and will be self-defeating in its actual application. As we work to get into a mindset of total freedom from negative emotions, we'll be experiencing new negative emotions due to our inevitable failures and shortcomings along the way to that difficult and perhaps dubious goal. The philosopher will have given us additional burdens of emotion, added to those we already have.

The extremes of Epictetus

Epictetus insists that we focus our attention on only those things over which we have complete control, because this is the only realm where we can totally avoid obstacles and disappointments. The things outside that level of control we should just leave as they are. That's his advice. In one place, he says:

> Do not seek to have everything that happens go as you wish but wish for everything to go as it does in fact happen, and your life will be serene. (*Handbook* 8)

So, regarding all the dire poverty, crime, hatred, misunderstanding, violence, and injustice in the world, this philosopher says: Accept it. Embrace it. No, really. Wish for it to be just as it is and you'll not be troubled by any disparity between your desires and the realities you see around you. But that seems to be an exceedingly high price to pay for inner serenity, if it's even possible at all for a person of normal moral sensitivity to do.

WARNING

What Epictetus urges on us seems to be a formula for a passivity of utter acquiescence and of somehow accepting the unacceptable. Isn't there a better way to establish a bit of inner peace? And after all, do we need complete tranquility within, perfect peace, to operate well and wisely as reasonable beings? Or wouldn't it be enough, after all, just to avoid the worst storms of emotion, desire, and impulse that knock us down and hold us back? Indeed, it can be suggested that emotional invulnerability is a selfish and shortsighted goal. It could be that to experience the depths and full richness of life and contribute to it well, we need to be open and vulnerable, feeling it all, yet not being completely overcome by those feelings. We can just put things into perspective and accept that there are difficulties in the world that, if we have a measure of calm within, we can be more effective in handling and reducing, as we grow in the process of becoming, being, and doing what's best.

Maybe what we need is not to call a bumpy road smooth, or pretend that it is, but to build something like the emotional equivalent of inner shock absorbers, so that as we encounter the real and deep potholes in the road of life we won't be emotionally wrecked and incapacitated by them. In fact, perhaps a gap between desire and reality is needed for our own growth into a deeper and higher spiritual sensibility. It might be that only when we experience the depths can we come fully to appreciate the heights. And perhaps an experience of both is necessary for real personal growth and strength.

A measure of serenity is a very good thing, and Stoic philosophers have many helpful techniques for helping us to attain it, but maybe it's not so important to have perfect serenity as to justify us in isolating ourselves within an impenetrable bubble of concern only for our own inner life, letting the world be what it is without any pushback or resistance from us. It could be better that we instead learn to manage our emotions, desires, and passions, rather than seeking to eliminate all of them that could disturb us in the least.

Epictetus is every bit as good a rhetorician as he is a philosopher. His words can be so rousing as to keep us from wholly registering their implications. For example, consider this series of scattered statements within a talk recorded in the *Discourses* where he's urging on us an invulnerable mindset:

> Just remember your general principles: "What is mine? What is not mine? What has been given me?" (*Discourses* 4.4.29)

Yes, it is important to remember what's up to me and what isn't, and in that sense what's truly mine or not. But does that mean that we should cease to care about most of the facts in the world around us, or that we should fully accept them as they are? Are we supposed to think of them as being literally worthless or unimportant, as Epictetus sometimes says, and best left alone, or do they have some sort of sacred value as from the Logos? Epictetus says:

> Now the time has come for you to discover whether you're one of the athletes who deserve to win, or you belong instead to the multitude of those who travel the world and are everywhere defeated. (*Discourses* 4.4.30–31)

The idea is that if we care about things outside our control and want them to be different from what they are, we are often defeated in our desires. But if we accept everything, we win. But how is "winning" desirable if requires not just being undefeated, but also having no desires whatsoever that could be disappointed or unachieved? The real athletes he evokes here are always concerned about a more common form of winning, not under circumstances where losing has been made impossible, but where they strain to attain their desire of finishing in first place despite the possibility that they'll fall short, coming in behind others. This potential alternative is precisely what makes a win so sweet. And the "multitude" of people mentioned here "who travel the world and are everywhere defeated" aren't perennial losers due to weakness and so to be pitied, but are simply those who like most of us have wishes, desires, hopes, and dreams that can't be guaranteed fulfillment, and are often disappointed in small or large ways. Epictetus wants us to want only whatever happens to happen so that we can't "lose" or "fail" to get what we want. But this is more like giving up, and calling it a victory instead.

Our wily wise guy then enumerates several negative emotions that people can have who operate normally in the world, with dreams and desires for what could be — setting goals, seeking to achieve, and sometimes worrying about falling short, or experiencing the sting of failure with emotions like grief, sorrow, and envy. He says, in an attractive but typically extreme way:

> Do you not wish to free yourself from all this? "And how will I free myself?" Have you not heard over and over that you should eradicate desire completely, direct your aversion to those things that lie within your own moral sphere and to those only, that you ought to give up everything — your body, your property, your reputation, books, turmoil, office, and freedom from office? For if you once turn aside from this course, you're a slave, a subject, you've become vulnerable to hindrance and compulsion, you're entirely under the control of others. (*Discourses* 4.4.33–34)

WARNING

This passage ends with a really strange and in fact self-contradictory conclusion, that if we want anything that's literally outside our control (to get that job, gain a promotion, make peace with a family member, or write posts on social media that help others), we put ourselves "entirely under the control of others," whose cooperation is needed for our desires to be attained. But, on one level, that would be true only if we could not possibly tolerate or ever allow for our desires to be disappointed, and so were "slavishly" willing to do whatever others demanded or required to satisfy our wishes. If we're willing instead to fall short and fail, and to be moderately disappointed, then we're under nobody else's control. And yet, on a deeper level — and please note this carefully — if we agree with Epictetus that things outside our own minds are outside our complete control, then how could having desires regarding those external things ever put us "entirely under the control of others," since *on his own view*, we are external to the minds of those other people and so are literally and necessarily *outside their control* as well? There is a stark inconsistency here, a logical contradiction, and so not all these beliefs of his could possibly be true together, which is what often happens when even good ideas are taken too far. Some defenders of Epictetus may say he's simply exaggerating here to get the attention of his students, and it's just a bit of his characteristic pedagogical hyperbole. But he isn't a marketer or politician who plays fast and loose with the truth. He's supposed to be a lover of wisdom, a philosopher who seeks to use and obey reason to bring us the truth that will liberate us. His words are therefore fair game for logical critique and rejection as inconsistent.

Finding Sensible Peace

Seneca seems to have a more sensible and logical approach to attaining the inner peace or tranquility we need to function well as reasonable and virtuous beings who want to experience happiness. First, he doesn't appear to think we need perfect serenity in our souls. He may even realize this is impossible, despite what others in the Stoic tradition might assume. And he seems to understand that we're fully capable of operating rationally even while experiencing the ups and downs of life, those bumps in the road that are real. We just need to mitigate or manage their emotional effects on us.

TIP

Seneca's practical advice to his stressed-out and downhearted friend is plentiful: Don't let yourself get too busy or bored. Don't take on projects that are too much or too little for you. Either course will bring discouragement and disappointment. Don't overcommit or under-commit but involve yourself in a level of activity that's right for your personality. Cultivate friendships with good people whose own inner resilience will help you with yours. Don't get caught up in craving or mindlessly accumulating money, property, office, status, or fame. All such things bring more worries than you imagine. Practice not getting overly worked up by things that happen. And don't fear calamity or poverty. We can endure both.

This sensible philosopher goes on to point out to his friend that people who are plunged into what are initially very difficult circumstances can and most often do become accustomed to them through the power of habit, and those conditions then begin to feel less burdensome with the passage of time, and so become less of a problem. In noting this, Seneca invents the concept of "The Reverse Hedonic Treadmill," anticipating a twist on the concept of the "hedonic treadmill" popularized by recent psychologists and happiness researchers. We are told from extensive modern findings that human beings are so constituted that every benefit or bliss we crave has the unexpected characteristic that, when we get it, we quickly become adapted to it, and it begins to lose the allure we thought it would always have, eventually allowing us to fall back to the old baseline of felt happiness or its opposite we would have reported before the great boon. Like on a treadmill in the gym, we never make real forward progress. By this process of hedonic adaptation, we get used to nearly any good thing, or nearly any bad thing, so we should all just calm down about the fickle and unpredictable nature of this world.

Seneca goes on: Rather than chasing the biggest and wildest dreams all the time, we should become accustomed to nurturing desires and setting goals that are closer to our level of power, skill, talent, and current circumstances. We can make real progress in such reasonable things, which can then set us up for bolder matters and even greater things, but by moderating our efforts at each level, we render ourselves less vulnerable to the sorts of repeated big failures that can lead to negative passions. We should also regularly remind ourselves of what sort of world we're in, which is a place full of difficulties, diseases, and the inevitability of death at some point. The more we ponder such eventualities, the less shaken we can be by them.

We should seek to become flexible and adaptable with our attitudes and actions, knowing that things are always in flux and shrouded by uncertainty, and so not allowing ourselves emotionally to require a stability or clarity that's not available in the world. We should learn how to frame or interpret situations to empower us, to give us positive possibilities for what's next and the energy to get us there. We need to learn to laugh when we can. We should live authentically, not with the thick disguises of a false superiority that we fear will be seen through, with such an unmasking threatening humiliation.

REMEMBER

Seneca says that to balance society with solitude, we need to withdraw on occasion into ourselves and our own inner resources, refresh ourselves for the demands of the world, and be able to reenter society restored. A little wine now and then won't hurt either, for most of us at least. These are the sorts of pragmatic recommendations we get from the worldly and wise Seneca, not the severe and unintuitive requirements that a more extreme Epictetus would urge on us. Marcus Aurelius is just as practical. In his *Meditations*, he says, "If you seek tranquility, do less." (4.24) And all three of these Romans are Stoics. Who will you choose to follow on this matter? You do have a choice, as all the Stoics frequently remind us. And that's clearly a good thing. *Apatheia*? Sure. *Ataraxia*? Very nice. But there is more than one way to view each of them, to seek them, and to decide when you have enough of either for a good and happy life. Maybe moderation is the nearly universal key.

Too many of us seem to expect either too much of ourselves or too little. Like Epictetus, we go to extremes. And that's why some readers enjoy his brash hyperbole and seek to follow his lead without thinking through all the implications, consequences, and hidden assumptions they're buying into. He's an enthralling teacher and a bit of a Pied Piper. But often we learn best from a charismatic guide not by following him the whole way, but by being goaded by him to think things through more carefully ourselves, picking up some of his recommendations, but leaving others aside, and taking in moderation some of the more exaggerated suggestions he makes.

There's a way to seek more serenity in our lives that doesn't demand desperate measures, or any extremes. It just requires a shift of attention, of emphasis, and of the emotions, desires, and impulses that will naturally accompany that change. We can avoid extremes without being extreme.

Concluding Thoughts on Apathy

Maybe we have just one big job in this world. It has to do with our effort. It's all about trying our best to be and do good, with whatever that means at any given time. It's the effort that counts, far more than the results of the effort. Just try your best and release the rest. It's an idea that could work.

TIP

There is a Yoda-style achiever meme that's very popular in the self-help and personal growth world. It advises us: "Don't try, do." But where the doing begins is in the try and nowhere else. The try is within reach. Those who grab and embrace it have taken the noble path. It's not something that's utterly immune to failure and disappointment — we can come to see that we're not actually trying our best, though we thought we were and are disappointed to realize we really aren't. But getting back on course requires nothing more than a renewed effort, rather than extensive external resources, or the help of lots of other people, who might or might not be interested in giving such help. It's entirely up to us, and that fact would make even Epictetus smile.

The deepest philosophers have redirected us over and over to the effort, the process, to the faithful attempt as where the game of this life is really played. We don't have to love and embrace all the rough edges of the world, but just to accept that they exist to challenge and deepen us. With this attitude or perspective on life, we can grow in the peace that we need within to be our best and do our best in the world. This will free us from the more destructive passions that Stoic apathy is meant to attain.

Chapter **15**

Love and Friendship

In ancient Greece and Rome, love was often in the air. And this very human orientation was also thought about deeply and broadly. So was friendship. Both were seen as central to the human experience. Each could be a support for, and even a crucial ingredient in, a happy life. The Stoics grappled with both concepts, to understand them better and apply them well in their lives.

What is friendship? What's the proper role it can have in a life well lived? How can we experience love better and more deeply in our ongoing adventures? Stoic philosophers had some interesting perspectives on these questions and wanted to help us all become better friends and lovers of our fellow beings. In this chapter, we join their effort. We first explore their ideas on friendship, and then move on into the deeper waters of love.

Two Big Ideas for Friendship and Love

Feelings of affiliation, fun, and trust often lead us into friendships, and of course also into relationships of love. Our feelings can be an important source of information and guidance in life. But of course, they can also get things very wrong. How do we tell the difference? Experience helps. The discernment of wisdom is the real answer. But discernment isn't an algorithm, or the result of any rule that's simple to state and easy to apply. And yet, a sound philosophy of life can help to provide the perspective needed for such discernment. Many people in our time are finding that sort of a philosophy in Stoicism. Perhaps the Stoics can give us needed guidance about friendship and loves. To get clear on the deepest foundations for their views, we'll look first at two other crucial ideas in their philosophy.

The Stoic idea of agreement

Zeno, the founder of Stoicism, is reported by ancient sources to have declared the goal of life to be, simply, "agreement." His successor in leadership over the Stoic school of thought, Cleanthes, felt that this was an incomplete phrasing of the intended answer, and expanded the specification of the goal as "agreement with nature," to spell out what he was sure Zeno had meant. The next head of the school suitably agreed with this, and the idea of "living in agreement with nature" has ever since been one of the central Stoic slogans for how we should conduct our lives. Our job is to live in agreement with nature. That will produce virtue and happiness as its natural result.

Zeno seems to have had a natural intuition that was, appropriately, in agreement with other great wisdom traditions that also put something like harmony, concord, unity, sympathy, concurrence, or agreement at the center of their various worldviews as a core ideal for human life. We're to embody inner and outer harmony. We're to enjoy agreement or unity within our own hearts and minds, among our words and actions, and then in deep ways with other people, as well as nature. The harmony is to pervade all we are, feel, and do. When we're out of harmony, we're not happy or at our peak.

The ultimate condition for human life is not to be disconnected or alienated, fragmented, or at odds, but to connect and flow with the deepest and best in the world, within our own natures, and with each other. Zeno thought that a wise and virtuous person lives in agreement at all levels, with nature, with the Logos or rational intelligence pervading the world, also called God, as well as with himself or herself, and others as we seek the best life.

The Stoic ideal of living in agreement is interestingly not meant to deny the legitimacy of intellectual disagreement among searchers, discoverers, and explorers of reality. As ancient historians tell us, early Stoics often held differing views on a topic. Stoicism, like any other major philosophical school or viewpoint, is not uniform in all its views. Science is the same way. Not all quantum theorists agree on everything. Not all biologists are in full concurrence at the edges of their field, nor are virologists, or anthropologists. Religious traditions and economic schools accommodate disagreements and theoretic differences at both the foundations and the outer reaches of their thought. In a similar manner, Stoics may differ among themselves about how best to live in agreement with nature.

But beneath the intellectual or theoretical disagreements will always be the ideal and reality of a certain fundamental agreement on the basic insights, orientations, and elements that matter most. To live in agreement with nature does not require that we have identical thoughts on all things, but rather involves our coming together around certain fundamentals, while other matters can be debated. The yin always needs its yang.

The point and goal of disagreement in philosophy and life is always the ideal result of ultimate agreement with the truth of the reality in which we live.

So, then, the fundamental background idea of agreement, as embedded as it is in the Stoic worldview and at the origin of Stoic thought, should be crucial for understanding Stoic views on friendship and love. Each of these concepts will either be or manifest a deep form of agreement, or of unity.

And there's a second idea that we should ponder here if we want to grasp more fully what is to come. It's a less familiar idea, but just as important.

The idea of appropriation

The Stoics had a fascinating idea conveyed by the word *oikeiosis* (Oy-keye — as in "eye" — OH-sis), that's often translated as "appropriation." The idea is basically this: When you're born, you come into the world with at least the seed of something like a natural sense of yourself as a distinct being or self, a center of perception and thought with a need for self-concern and protection. And this seems universal. But as you grow, you begin to understand at an unconscious level and then slowly in a more conscious way that your own safety, health, and flourishing are dependent on and involved with the safety, health, and flourishing of the other people closest around you. And so you then tend to emotionally and morally "appropriate" those other people into your circle of concern that's centered on yourself. You bring them in. They come to be recognized as important. You begin to care for them.

In the process of *oikeiosis* or appropriation, your own innate, natural orientation toward self-care grows to involve caring about close others as well, as you come to intuit and then grasp more fully your many and various dependencies, which in your early childhood are simple and strongly one-directional, but then begin to grow in complexity and mutuality.

Next, if you develop in a psychologically healthy way, you gradually begin to reach out beyond this first inner circle of family and start appropriating yet others into your natural commitments of care. Your healthy ongoing interest in the growth or strength of your inner self, as well as the safety and flourishing of your physical body and most immediate context, is seen as not opposed to but entwined with a concomitant care for other people more broadly. You begin to embrace friends and neighbors in community.

This concept of appropriation is important for understanding the full range of Stoic political thought, and it's vital for getting a deeper take on the Stoic idea of what friendship is. Friends come together because of and around various forms of agreement, and bond together out of their mutual appropriation of each other into their individual circles of care. As mentioned in our chapter on community (Chapter 13), the Roman Stoic Hierocles described an imaginary set of concentric circles surrounding each of us, mapping the people in our lives near and far, and giving us a sense of the properly ultimate reach of our care. His belief was that we should reach out to those in our outermost circles and pull them in, appropriating them into our own personal projects of flourishing, while also seeing their proper interests as ideally harmonious with our own.

TIP

In order to understand Stoic views on friendship and love, we'll have to keep in mind this idea of appropriation, and we'll end up asking a deep and fascinating question as to whether at the deepest level we need to engage in a very different but parallel process to appropriation as well, in order for the deepest friendship and love to have a real chance to be what it's capable of being. But first, let's dive right into the basic concepts of friendship and love, as well as the messy and magnificent realities that correspond to them.

True Friendship

We've long celebrated the importance of friendship in life. Popular culture has joined in this acknowledgment with hit television shows presenting us with the images of ideal friendships, with chart-topping songs about being a friend, and in portrayals of great, unforgettable friendships in books and film. And so, as a result, it's a bit ironic that with all this widespread popular appreciation for the role of friendship in life, we're often said to live now with an epidemic of loneliness. The irony is compounded by the fact that we have more tools than ever before meant to bring people together, and yet somehow these very instruments have pushed us apart.

We need a sense of togetherness and community more than ever, a positive, healthy politics, and more harmonious social interactions. Two thousand years ago, philosophers saw this as crucially requiring friendship and love.

Aristotle on friendship

The ancient historian Diogenes Laertius tells us that Aristotle was once asked "What is a friend?" and he reports that the philosopher answered, quite succinctly and provocatively, "One soul dwelling in two bodies." Throughout his work, Aristotle used the phrase "another self" nearly half a dozen times to characterize the status of a friend. Cicero echoed this concept centuries later, but with a tiny hedge, by writing in his essay "On Friendship" that a human being by nature "both loves himself and seeks for another whose mind he may so mingle with his own as *almost* to make one mind out of two." Both philosophers issued a striking claim about friendship. A friend is clearly something special. And though the Stoics are not typically thought to be heavily influenced by Aristotle, even the austere Epictetus alludes to this view of one mind shared by two friends, though likely in a metaphorical way and not to propound it, in the *Discourses* (2.22.24; Oldfather translation).

Aristotle opened a famous discussion of friendship in Book Eight of his *Nicomachean Ethics* by saying, "Without friends, no one would choose to live, though he had all other goods." And oddly, the modern world seems to have inverted that assessment, promoting the quest for external riches and all the luxury markers of wealth so much that it can seem natural and fine if, to get all the other goods, it's necessary to end up without any friends.

Aristotle also gave an analysis of friendship that has echoed through the ages. He distinguished among three kinds of relationships between people that we often call friends, deeming the parties variously: (1) utility friends, or (2) pleasure friends, or (3) complete friends. We can also call them help friends, fun friends, and true friends. It's easy to draw the relevant distinctions as differences we all see in our own lives and relationships.

>> **A utility or helping friendship** is a relationship between two people who provide useful benefits for each other. You often see this in a professional context, or in the circumstances of formal education. Co-workers or professional peers can help each other, offering expertise or connections that benefit the other, and receiving such useful favors in return. Schoolmates study together, helping each other to prepare for a test. Neighbors may offer each other friendly assistance. Utility friends come together over the benefits that create their relationship and, if those benefits ebb, the friendship can too.

>> **A pleasure friend or fun friend** is a person you just enjoy being around, and the feeling is roughly mutual. Aristotle says that this sort of friendship is common among the young, who get a kick out of each other and like to hang out and laugh. Fun friends usually come together around shared interests, and when those interests change or the fun diminishes for any reason, the friendships can also fade.

>> **Complete friends,** by contrast, aren't just attracted to each other out of usefulness or delight but come to appreciate one another as the virtuous people they are, for their character as well as personality, for their goodness, trustworthiness, and reliability. True friends care about each other's flourishing and seek to help provide for and participate in that flourishing, and not just for the benefits or enjoyments they may gain in return. But ironically, complete friendships can be the most reliably productive of benefits of help and fun in both directions over time.

Aristotle seems to see complete friendship as the only true or literal form, and the other relationships based on utility or pleasure as only partially analogous, and so as "friendships" only loosely. The later Stoic philosophers did not seem to approve this looseness of referring to relationships built on mutual help or fun as friendships, and so their own exploration and use of the concept is stricter and is more like what Aristotle thought of as a complete friendship.

REMEMBER

Aristotle believed that a true friendship requires and is rooted in virtue. People who don't seek to live virtuously — meaning those whose thoughts, feelings, attitudes, and actions tend instead to be corrupt or selfish, and either amoral or unethical — can't be true friends. A complete friendship depends on virtuous character on each side. True friends deeply care about each other and are willing to sacrifice convenience or comfort for the good of the other.

Those who do not embody virtue can come together in relationships of convenience around either usefulness or fun, but to the Stoics, these connections don't seem to merit even an extended or analogous use of the concept of friendship. They are viewed as more tenuous and fragile linkages between people that not only can't be relied on to endure but rather can be predicted with confidence not to last.

Stoic friends

There's a passage where Seneca is talking about the importance of how careful we should be in choosing the people we're going to be around on a regular basis, and how cautious we need to be about not getting too close with the wrong people, those who can make a life of virtue and flourishing more difficult. Stressing how hard and yet vital it can be to make such decisions well, and as a result find some real friends to share life with, he writes:

> But nothing can equal the pleasures of faithful and congenial friendship. How good it is to have open hearts as safe repositories for your every secret, whose safekeeping of confidences you fear less than your own, whose conversation soothes your anxiety, whose advice aids with your plans, whose cheerfulness dissipates your gloom, whose very appearance lifts you up! But we should pick friends who are free as far as possible from disturbing desires. Vices are contagious; they spread to those nearest by and infect others by contact. During a plague we need to be careful not to sit near people sick and hot with fever, since we'd be courting danger and drawing in poison with our breath. Just so, in choosing friends we must pay attention to character and take those least tainted. ("On Tranquility" 7.3)

Notice that Seneca does not require that we choose only the perfectly wise and virtuous as companions and friends. He's always more realistic than that. He urges only that we do the best we can with what's available and "take those least tainted" with foolishness and vice. As a result, whenever a Stoic like Seneca befriends you, you can justifiably feel proud to be viewed as, apparently, among the "least tainted" of the available options. Now imagine a marriage proposal from a Stoic: "You're the least tainted of them all!"

THE PEOPLE CLOSE TO YOU

One of your co-authors was on a cross-country flight years ago and struck up a conversation with his seatmate, who turned out to be the founder of a tech startup company, a very smart man who had done well in life up to the time of their chat at thirty-five thousand feet. When the man learned that his traveling companion that day was a public philosopher interested in the practical impact of wisdom, he became quite animated and vocal about how a new therapist a few years back had introduced him to some research in social psychology about how important your friends are to your own trajectory through life. He rummaged through a computer bag and got out a piece of paper and a pen and began to draw vertical columns down the page. He explained. "You're going to like this. It's super cool and sort of mind blowing."

He went on: "Here's what the therapist told me. 'First on the left side of the paper, write down in a column the names of the five closest people in your life, the people you spend the most time around, as a vertical list. They can't all be work people. Then you draw next to them some columns with labels at the top like Financial, Physical, Psychological, Social, and Spiritual. Quickly assess how each person is doing in each category and rate them 0 to 10 on each thing.'"

My seatmate continued: "Then the guy left the room for me to do the assignment, and in a few minutes, he came back in. He smiled at me and pointed to the paper and said something like, 'You're now looking at your future.' And I said, 'What do you mean?' And he explained that we become like the people we're around, so it's important to spend time just with people we really admire and would like to emulate in our own lives."

Then man telling this tale then smiled. Your philosopher said, "Wow. That's interesting. What happened from this exercise?" And the next words the stranger spoke could not have been more unexpected. The man said, "Well, the divorce was easy. But unraveling the business with my partners was much more complicated." True story. And of course, it's okay if you want to take a break from reading right now and go find a piece of paper and a pen. But proceed with caution.

The noble versus the base

In speaking of the wise and foolish, a classic distinction was made between the good and noble on the one hand, and "the base," or imprudent others, where baseness was thought of as a coarse foolishness in thought and conduct, arising from an ignorance of the good and an insensitivity toward its call. Using this concept, Diogenes Laertius draws from the work of Zeno, Chrysippus, and the later influential Stoic Posidonius (135–51 BCE) to sum up some early and middle period Stoic views on friendship, reporting:

> And they say that friendship exists only among virtuous men, because of their similarity. They say that it's a sharing, or community, of things needed for one's life, since we treat our friends as ourselves. They declare that one's friend is worth choosing for his own sake and that having many friends is a good thing and add that there is no friendship among base men, and that no base man has a friend. (*Lives* 7.101.124)

Around two centuries later, Joannes Stobaeus, often referred to as "John," a fifth-century compiler of extracts from more ancient Greek authors, and a valuable source of information about early Stoic views, writes succinctly about the Stoic concept of friendship, saying that:

> Friendship is a community of life. (*Anthology* 102.5l)

He also confirms the report of Diogenes that the founding Stoics believe only the virtuous can be and have true friends, and he roots this in an even deeper relationship between the imprudent and the force guiding the universe:

> Again, they also hold that every imprudent man is an enemy to the gods. For hostility is a lack of consonance and concord about the concerns of life, just as friendship is consonance and concord. (*Anthology* 102.11k)

The idea is that those who in their present state are incapable of fundamental harmony with the gods are equally incapable of it with other human beings, and since friendship requires such a fundamental "agreement" or harmony, those who are described as base are incapable of real friendship.

Stobaeus goes on to draw out the contrast a bit more. He writes:

> Since the virtuous man is affable in conversation and charming and encouraging and prone to pursue goodwill and friendship through his words, he fits in as well as possible with most people; and that's why he's lovable and graceful and persuasive, and again flattering and shrewd and opportune and quick-witted and easygoing and unfussy and straightforward and authentic. And the base man is subject to all the opposite traits. (*Anthology* 102.11m)

He then sums up Stoic views this way:

> They say that friendship exists only among the wise since it is only among them that there is concord about the matters of life, and concord is a knowledge of common goods. For it's impossible to have a genuine friendship, as distinct from a falsely named friendship, without trust and reliability. But since the base are untrustworthy and unreliable and have hostile opinions, there is no friendship among them, although there are certain other kinds of associations and pairings that are held together from the outside by necessity and opinions. And the Stoics say that cherishing and welcoming and love belong to the virtuous alone. (ibid.)

Unless we give up the extreme view held by many classic Stoics that almost none of us is wise, because to be truly wise, you'd have to be perfectly wise, or a Sage, and that such a person exists only once in every few hundred years, it would follow that none of us has friends. And we don't know about you, but the odds are against that. And it seems far too extreme. The poor Sage. Who's *he* supposed to have as a friend? You see the absurdity of this extreme view. In appropriating classic Stoic beliefs, we're either going to have to back off the wild perfection standard for being wise and virtuous, or we'll have to allow friendship for the "almost wise and virtuous." In other words, it seems like we'll have to depart from the classic Stoic tendency to treat concepts like wisdom and virtue in an absolutist way and apply them in a more reasonable and aspirational way, if we hope to have them as more than unrealized ideals.

While describing the Stoic view that real friendship can be experienced only by the virtuous, Stobaeus also summarizes a more general Stoic belief that gives a broader context to the special nature of friendship. He writes of the Stoic philosophers:

> Again, they think it important to understand that nature has brought it about that children are loved by their parents. From this starting point we can follow the development of the shared society that unites humanity. (*Anthology* 103.62)

And he then goes on to say:

> From this, it develops naturally that there is among human beings a common and natural affinity of people to each other, with the result that it is right for them to feel that other humans, just because they are humans, are not alien to them. . . . So, we are naturally suited to gatherings, groups, and states. (ibid.)

People characterized by the classic philosophers as base or imprudent, then, are those who, despite any shred of natural fellow feeling they may still have in their souls, allow selfishness to rule their lives and develop a constant suspiciousness of others, as well as a harshly competitive or combative spirit in suspecting that other people will do them harm from their own selfishness.

Nonetheless, Stobaeus represents the major Stoic thinkers as having enough confidence in natural human affinities, presumably based in the innate process of appropriation summarized at the outset of this chapter, that they are at least moderately optimistic about our general social and political prospects, despite any challenges we might face along the way. And they seem to think that friendships among the virtuous will play a crucial role in dealing with our social and political challenges. Friends are then in this way a source of great and needed social and political power, as well as being an important part of any healthy and flourishing private life.

The positive and the negative

According to Diogenes Laertius, the Stoics identified three major positive emotions that can play an important role in the life of a wise and virtuous person: joy, caution, and a state of wishing well. He also then identifies the "primary forms" of the latter, wishing well, as "goodwill, kindliness, acceptance, and contentment" (*Lives* 7.101.116). And these are obviously all qualities needed for true friendship.

For perspective, Stobaeus summarizes the Stoics as having characterized unhealthy desire as involving "such passions as these: anger and its forms (aggression and irascibility and wrath and rancor and bitterness and such things), vehement sexual desire, and longing and yearning and love of pleasure and love of wealth and love of reputation and similar things" (*Anthology* 102.10.b). Just as obviously, these things will make any true friendship impossible. And they are qualities that characterize those whom the philosophers call base, imprudent, unwise, or simply foolish.

It's no surprise to see the Stoic agree that positive and healthy personal emotions can unite us, while negative and unhealthy ones only divide.

The founding Stoics give us a sense of what friendship is, in the tradition of Aristotle's strictest sense of the term, and what it requires, though as we have noted, they treated it as a nearly unreachable ideal, a step we need not take. When we understand friendship properly, we see that it's a much deeper and richer thing than most people in our day seem to realize. It's not a superficial or static relationship, but it either grows and deepens or else it withers.

In one sense, Aristotle saw the engagement of friendship on the part of any friend, the *philia*, or form of love that makes it possible, as involving an emotion, or cluster of emotions, but in a deeper sense he saw it as like a virtue, or dispositional state. And such a disposition is a basic character tendency toward certain thoughts, emotions, attitudes, and actions.

Ultimately, friendship is a bit like an endeavor, an enterprise of thought, emotion, attitude, and action, with the latter as a culmination of all the former. Being friends in that sense isn't like being Greeks, or fellow human beings, or even distant cousins. It's not an essentially passive relation, but is an active dynamic relationship played out over time, with both friends actively caring about the other and working toward their good for their own sake, and not seeking any benefits, though learning that the benefits may be plentiful as the other party to the friendship does all the same things.

The Interpenetrating Unity of Souls

Have you ever had a friend so good and close, so well attuned to your way of thinking that they could finish a sentence for you, and not in a trivial way, but with a thought that might surprise an onlooker, the same thought you were about to express? Your thoughts often sparked theirs, and the same process flowed in reverse. In fact, maybe you came to a place and form of flow where you weren't just both thinking about something, in the sense that each of you was separately thinking about it and sharing enough of those individual thoughts as to influence what the other might think next, but in a deeper and more entangled sense a single process of thought seemed to be happening in both of you, a single thinking, in a way that could not have been duplicated by the sum total of the two of you apart separately reflecting on the issue and then later reporting your independent results.

You may have heard of siblings, or married people, who at a great distance knew suddenly that the other was in danger of some sort or had just died. You may even have read stories of identical twins, separated at birth and raised by families in different parts of the country with no knowledge of each other, who first meet in adulthood just to discover to their great surprise that they studied the same things in college, entered the same profession, and married people with the same name, who were even born on the same day. It's eerie. And we have no good scientific explanations for it. Yet something strange bringing together minds around identical thoughts, attitudes, emotions, or choices has been reported under very different conditions through history. Could Aristotle have come near this in his image of one soul in two bodies?

Is the self a walled fortress?

We tend to think of the human self, or the conscious mind of the self, as a walled fortress, open to the world through only a few portals that we know of as the senses. But then there are strange phenomena such as "independent discovery" in science, where researchers in different parts of the world who have not been in contact come to the same new idea at the same time. And there's a process of artistic inspiration where the ancients talked of the Muse, and modern artists often speak as if they were passive recipients of songs, or poems, or stories that came from somehow beyond themselves and yet not through the portals that we call our physical senses.

Elizabeth Gilbert wrote a fascinating book on this called *Big Magic*. One of your co-authors had such an experience extended over five years, where a major fictional story came to him in all its details about a place and time in history he did not know much about, producing eight novels of over a million words with uncanny cultural accuracy. Or, in a very different way, many people will report thinking about an old friend for the first time in years and then the phone rings, with that person calling. Coincidence is a lazy and overused concept, stretched far too thin to cover the truth of some things we've experienced and admit we don't understand. But throughout the human journey, we've lived with many things we did not fully grasp.

The walled fortress model of the self then perhaps needs to be rethought as enjoying more access to the broader realities beyond it than our typical image of it would allow. Perhaps there's a basement of the unconscious mind under the floor of the castle, accessed by a trap door that can be opened to let things into consciousness that don't arrive through the known senses. Imagine the basement as under water or having a stream flow through it, and as not being sealed off but surrounded by something more like porous walls, or a sort of latticed mesh, or even like a chain link fence that will allow things to come in that then can percolate up into the conscious mind that we think of as the castle itself. Maybe this is a vivid representation for what the great 20th-century psychologist Carl Jung spoke of as the collective unconscious. There is more accessible to your mind than just what comes through your senses. And perhaps what can happen between great friends is a version of this, and we begin to have what Cicero thought of as *almost* one mind in two bodies, or that Aristotle simply described as one soul dwelling in two bodies.

Distributed cognition

Maybe the mind's thinking can take place in part beyond its own separate identity, and beyond the neurophysiology of the brain that embodies it. In a fascinating book called *Distributed Cognition in Classical Antiquity* (Edinburgh University Press, 2019), a group of distinguished scholars explore various forms of this phenomenon in the ancient world. In a particularly fascinating scholarly paper, "One Soul in Two Bodies: Distributed Cognition and Ancient Greek Friendship,"

New York University professor of Classics, David Konstan examines how a model of thinking that represents it as taking place beyond the confines of a single brain and body may shed light on the views of Aristotle and others in antiquity on this phenomenon of friendship.

The idea of distributed cognition is in its essence very simple. We have a common modern view that thought takes place only in the brain. But consider a girl counting on her fingers, the physicist calculating on a blackboard with chalk, or the immunologist using a computer program to help solve a problem. They're all thinking with the use of something in addition to the neurons in their brains, whether other parts of the body like fingers, or independent objects like chalk and blackboards and computers.

The next step is to consider the possibility that two or more people can do thinking together that's distributed among them in a way that's not just purely individual and additive, but that's a distinctive phenomenon all its own. That's what some of the ancients may have recognized as possible, and as an ingredient in the most intimate of friendships.

A unique virtue

David Konstan, like contemporary philosophers Martha Nussbaum and Zena Hitz, sees Aristotle as viewing friendship not as just an emotion or a feeling state within each of two individuals, but as something that transcends the individual as a "form of life" or "collaboration." There's even a suggestion that, rather than being an emotion, friendship was for Aristotle to be viewed as itself a virtue, or a morally good dispositional state naturally expressed in action, like courage or generosity. And like other standard virtues, it could be seen as a midpoint between extremes of excess and deficiency.

Courage, for example, in the presence of danger is the midpoint between the extreme deficiency of cowardice and the extreme excess of foolhardiness. Generosity in the face of need is the midpoint between the deficiency of miserliness and the excess of profligacy. Friendship then, like courage or generosity, would be a dispositional response to something, in this case another person, a virtuous soul, that's a response somewhere midway between such extremes as flattery and surliness, or sycophancy and enmity. But unlike courage and generosity, it would be a unique sort of virtue, a transpersonal one, essentially dyadic, a pair-bound dispositional state encompassing two people and not just located within each of two utterly separated souls.

Virtue or vulnerability?

This possibility is a challenge for how classical Stoics view the virtues, as belonging wholly to each self, individually, as the stuff of personal power and control within an impregnable fortress of the self. On the Stoic account, whether a virtue is had by a person is entirely up to that individual alone. No one can give you a virtue or prevent you from having it. Nobody can make you courageous or generous or keep you from either of those states of heart and mind. In Stoicism, the virtues are totally up to you, within your complete control. They belong to you as possessions, wholly yours. But if friendship is a virtue, it is one that's not entirely up to you, not completely within your power, involving as it does another person making choices alongside yours to join in a unique collaboration. And that's a problem for the classic Stoic.

The reason ancient Stoics want every ingredient in moral good, and everything necessary and sufficient for happiness or peak well-being, to be within our individual control is that this is what, in principle, makes the soul invulnerable to external threat, disappointment, and discouragement. It makes the self a fortress. The Stoics aren't fans of vulnerability, but friendship seems to bring us fully into the realm of the vulnerable. Two people can't become true friends without being mutually vulnerable. Yet to classic Stoics, this is a precarity not to be countenanced. It's always to be avoided.

And yet, as we've seen, Stoicism views friendship to be at least a preferred indifferent, if not implicitly an actual secondary virtue, arising out of the primary virtues when two or more good people meet and get to know each other intimately well. It's a community of souls, at least, according to the Stoics themselves. And what is the limit of this communing? Is each soul a separate, inviolable, walled castle after all? Or don't the Stoics explicitly acknowledge that we all have within ourselves reason, which is itself a spark or part of the divine? And if we share the same spark, or various sparks of and from the same Logos, then isn't that a foundation for a commonality or unity that goes beyond separated souls at a distance merely acknowledging each other appreciatively, and caring for one another? But if so, it seems to be a possibility that the classic Stoics themselves never identified as such.

There is to our knowledge no existent classic Stoic text embracing Aristotle's conception of complete friendship as involving even metaphorically, or in the Ciceronian sense of "almost," one soul in two bodies. And this may be a lack that derives from an extreme version of Stoic principles that the founders themselves need not have adopted and that we as their students can avoid as we borrow the best of their thought. It's also a view of friendship that brings us a step nearer a view of love that may itself come closer to Stoic practice in antiquity than their own theoretical understanding of love might allow.

Stoics in Love and on It

On the cover of this book, one of your co-authors is identified as a "Stoic guitarist." It's a designation he cherishes, due to the Stoic view of all external things outside our own minds as being "indifferent," and so literally neither good nor bad. Because of that, any true Stoic would of course on principle have to assess this philosopher's guitar playing as "Not bad!" Of course, we should all ignore what else might have to be said.

Stoics have a shaky reputation for love, perhaps largely undeserved, but we can understand. The doctrine of indifferents alone is problematic for any robust account of love, since to each of us every other thing in the world external to our own minds will fall into that category, including other people. Your parents or kids? Indifferents. Your spouse? Indifferent, though perhaps a favorite preferred in the category. So how worked up can you get? Epictetus then doesn't make it any easier with passages like this, using the example of what's perhaps a precious and even loved household item:

> When faced with anything attractive, useful, or that you love, remember to tell yourself what kind of thing it is. Start with the least important stuff. If it's a jug you like, say, "I like a jug," because then you won't be upset when it gets broken. If you kiss a child of yours or your wife, tell yourself that you're kissing a human being because then you won't get upset if they die. (*Handbook* 3)

So it's not just household items. We're supposed to redescribe to ourselves the most precious people in our lives in the most generic way we can, so that "we won't get upset if they die." And just wait; it gets worse. Epictetus says to his students, and this has to be The Greeting Card Sentiment of All Time:

> As you kiss your child, can there be any harm in muttering in an undertone, "Tomorrow, you will die"? (*Discourses* 3.24.88)

Yes. Yes, there can be harm. It sure sounds harmful, at least from the point of view of your child or anyone else who overhears you and calls 9-1-1. And in both these passages, we seem to be confronted with a harshness, or a remoteness from what we naturally think to be the emotional bonds of love and the inevitable implications of grief when a loved person or even a treasured item is lost. But in a passage before the last one cited, Epictetus gives us a sense of what he's really doing in these controversial statements:

> If you kiss your child or brother or friend, never give the impression free reign. Don't allow it to expand as it wants but pull it back. Restrain it in the same way that those who stand behind generals as they're celebrating a victory remind them of their humanity. In much the same way, you too should remind yourself that what

you love is mortal. It isn't something that belongs to you — it's been given to you for the time being, not as a thing irremovable or permanent. It's like a fig or grapes that arrive at a particular time of year, and it would be silly to want them in winter. So, if you long for your son or friend at a time when they aren't given to you, you're longing for a fig in winter. (*Discourses* 3.24.85–87)

The philosopher isn't trying to pull his students back from a full experience of love. He just doesn't want authentic love to shade into a delusion about permanency in this world or into a craving for control where it's not to be found. He hopes to help prevent something healthy from turning into anything that's unhealthy and unrealistic. He isn't meaning to be a killjoy; in fact, to the contrary, he's trying to discourage a mindset that interferes with joy by setting us up for shock and dismay. He would encourage only realistic love.

Epictetus is not blind to the importance of love. He loves virtue. But we should point out that there is a problem looming nearby. In Book Two, Chapter 22 of the *Discourses*, in the first three sections, he reasons that nobody loves anything they consider evil or are indifferent to, but only what they consider good. So he concludes that whoever is unable to distinguish what is truly good from what is bad or indifferent is not able to love properly; only the wise man can make those distinctions correctly, and so only a wise man has the power to love. But a difficulty quickly arises.

Here's the tension, or even a lurking problem of contradiction: Epictetus believes that the only things that can truly be loved are those that are truly good. He also seems to think that (1) nothing is truly good but virtue, and (2) nothing is truly good but what is within the total control or power of each of us. But if our Stoic teacher also wants to believe or acknowledge that we can ever love another person, or humanity at large, or the universe itself, it's clear that no human being is a virtue or is within our total control or power. And of course, humanity, like the universe, is far from being within the scope of our total control. So, then, how can any other person, or humankind, or our home the universe be good in the sense required to be a proper object of love?

It's hard to see how Epictetus could have a reasonable answer to these questions. In his view, every other person is an external object relative to you, exists outside of your own mind and will, and so is to be classified as an "indifferent" rather than a good or bad thing. So is humanity, and our cosmic home. And there are passages where he says that indifferent things are "worthless" or "nothing to me." But if we can love only good things and all good things are within our control, how then are we supposed to be able to love another human being, or humanity, which are not in our control? How do we avoid applying his view of externals as "nothing" and as worthless to the case of other people, and even to our broadest physical home?

It could be that the only answer here is that we can love whatever is intrinsically good or is in some way intimately related to happiness, and that things can count as such in these ways: (1) if they are virtues or things fully within the power of the will, or (2) they are themselves intrinsically good persons with virtues and will, or (3) like the collective "humanity," anything can be a good and can be loved if it is an aggregate entity composed of persons with virtues and wills, or is the Ultimate Source of such persons, such as the universe, or the Logos. On this suggestion, one that's not made in any existing original Stoic document, a friend can be loved as the only sort of external object that we should deem intrinsically good, and friend-ship itself can be loved, either as a virtue of a distinctive sort, or as an aggregate entity composed of persons (the friends) with virtues and wills.

And yet, with these additions, it's hard to see how we're not supposed to grieve the loss of a person, if recognized as a true good. We may have to allow for the propriety of grief after all. And that's always been forbidden by extreme versions of Stoicism. Yet it was allowed by a moderate like Seneca. Without our help in these little additions, though, it looks like Epictetus could be stuck with views that on his own principles are inconsistent with each other. Valuing reason as he did, we hope he'd welcome our suggestion and take it to help attain coherence in being able to value love.

Marcus Aurelius certainly seems to value love, and writes to himself:

> Live in harmony with everything around you, and love without reservations or conditions those with whom you live and work. (*Meditations* 6.39)

You won't find the classic Stoics writing entire treatises about love in all its forms, or even long passages on this crucial human experience, but the concept does crop up frequently and positively enough to convey an appreciation of its role at the core of a life worth living.

REMEMBER

When we think of love not as just an emotion or feeling but more like an engaged commitment of concern and care, of agreement, concord, harmony, and ongoing action in support of what is loved, we can come to understand how, to the Stoics, a love of self, of family and friends, of humanity, and of the universe, or God, as distinct yet related forms of commitment, all play an important role behind the scenes of their philosophy. Love matters.

Sex and Love with the Stoics

In the introduction to her book, *Marcus Aurelius in Love*, Amy Richlin, a professor of Classics, reviews some well-known aspects of the ancient world around gender, friendship, and sexuality prior to the rise of Stoicism and continuing through its various periods. A few remarks should be quoted in full, shocking as they may be to lovers of Stoic thought. The Greek word *prokopton* here simply means student, or one making progress toward truth:

> Much less familiar to modern readers is the position of the early Stoic philosophers on sexuality. Zeno (335–263 BCE) and his successor Chrysippus (280–207 BCE) argued that sex between human beings who have learned the proper principles of respect and true friendship is a good thing, and that the ideal society would be one in which sex was enjoyed freely, without propertarian bonds of marriage. In particular, a young person just turning toward philosophy, the *prokopton*, should be trained by his mentor first through a sexual relationship, which should grow into an understanding of philosophy. (16)

So we have here the report that in early Stoicism: (1) sex was viewed as a good thing between any people who have respect and friendship for each other, regardless of anything else in their lives, or their particular relationship (which Chrysippus took to include forms of incest), and (2) when a young person gets interested in philosophy, he or she should first be trained *through a sexual relationship* with a mentor, which can be philosophically beneficial.

This will shock and rightly disturb most people to hear. When medieval philosopher Peter Abelard got in trouble for an intimate relationship with his student Heloise, he admitted the activity by saying that "Under cloak of study, we practiced love." If he'd been a Stoic, he could have explained that it was just a standard Intro to Philosophy course, properly conducted.

In his anthology of ancient texts, Stobaeus reports about the classic Stoics:

> They say that sexual love is an effort to produce friendship resulting from the appearance of physical beauty in young men at their prime and that is why the wise man makes sexual advances and will have sexual intercourse with those who are worthy of true sexual love, that is, those who are wellborn and endowed with natural ability. (*Anthology* 102.11s)

Diametrically opposed to our sensibilities and expectations today, a common form of mentorship, a teaching relationship, was often expected in ancient Greece and Rome to involve physical affection. The older mentor was attracted to a young student whose potential for virtue was believed to show through a form of beauty and grace that then sparked their wisdom journey together. In recounting the views of Zeno and Chrysippus, among other Stoics, Diogenes Laertius also drew on multiple sources to report:

> They say that the wise man will fall in love with young men who reveal through their appearance a natural aptitude for virtue, as Zeno says in the *Republic,* and Chrysippus in book one of *On Ways of Life*, and Apollodorus in his *Ethics*. (*Lives* 2.7.129)

This historian of thought then goes on in the next sentence to say:

> And sexual love is an effort to gain friendship resulting from the appearance of beauty, and it is not directed at intercourse but at friendship. (*Lives* 2.7.130)

If the aim of the sexual love with students is not the intercourse, but friendship, then it's accepted as fine. Diogenes adds of the Stoics:

> They think that wise men should have their wives in common, so that anyone might make love to any woman, as Zeno says in his *Republic* and Chrysippus says in his *On the Republic* and, again, so do Diogenes the Cynic and Plato. (*Lives* 2.7.131)

While you wrap your mind around all this, we'll throw a little more fuel on the fire with some quotations from *Marcus Aurelius in Love*, which is a compilation of letters between a cultural celebrity of the time, the 39-year-old rhetorician Marcus Fronto, and his young student, the 18-year-old Marcus Aurelius, recently chosen to be the future emperor. The two men got together for lessons and then were often apart for long periods, since Fronto served as a consul in a government office away from Rome. The letters begin at the end of the year 139 CE and continue until late in 148 when the student was 27.

The 46 letters we have are a surprise to read. Young Marcus Aurelius writes in a saucy, funny, playful way that can help us grasp the sensibilities and interpret the tones of voice and mind behind much of what he writes later in life in his journal that was originally untitled, or perhaps headed just with the words "To Himself," and only later was named by others "Meditations." And this title, now standard, is unfortunate, since these private writings breathe a spirit very different from what's known in most traditions as "meditation." In fact, in a recent informal international competition to come up with a more appropriate name for Marcus's journal, one of the co-authors of the present book won with his suggested title: "*How I Try Not to Be an Asshole*, by Marcus Aurelius." It's hard to read the *Meditations* and not think this would be a much better title, but that's perhaps a story for another day.

Let's look at a few samples from these newly translated letters between Marcus the student and Marcus the teacher. First, from the future emperor:

> Good-bye, breath of my life. Should I not burn with love of you when you've written this to me? What should I do? I can't stop. (*Letter* 1)

> Good-bye, ever my sweetest soul. (*Letter* 12)

> I love you as you deserve to be loved. (*Letter* 13)

> I give up, you win: You've clearly surpassed in loving all the lovers who have ever existed. (*Letter* 17)

And so good-bye, kindest teacher, most magnificent consul, and as much as you love me, that's how much you should long for me. (*Letter* 25)

And now from the famous rhetorician, as mentor to his young student:

I engulf myself in your love. (*Letter* 11)

Good-bye my delight, in you I trust, good-bye my happiness, my pride and joy, Good-bye and love me, please in every style, joking or serious. (*Letter* 20)

I'll even swear that I've long since wanted to quit the consulship so that I could put my arms around Marcus Aurelius. (*Letter* 26)

And nobody could ever have pounded such a flame into a lover by potion or charm as you, by what you did, have made me dazed and thunderstruck by your burning love. (*Letter* 33)

What is more delicious to me than your kiss? That delicious scent, that enjoyment, lies for me in your neck and your kiss. (*Letter* 45)

I burn with love for you. (*Letter* 45)

This is not a standard example of the mentor–mentee relationship throughout history, or of that between a teacher and student. In fact, it's hard to read these sentences without thinking: Legal Trouble. Professor Richlin makes the point repeatedly in her endnotes that the two men were throughout the letters using a coded language among the literary, alluding to erotic imagery and passages in writers they would have read. At one point she says:

So whatever the relation of the letters to reality, Marcus and Fronto were playing a game, dangerous but familiar, and the letters themselves are a form of sex on paper. (13)

The letters we have end at about the time that young Aurelius was discovering Stoic philosophy. Fronto was not himself a Stoic, and seemed to be jealous of the popularity the Stoics were enjoying at the time. So their playful and passionate words to each other in their letters don't necessarily display Stoic attitudes, but rather aspects of the culture in which many of the Stoic texts were produced that we read and absorb today.

Fronto was married. His wife, Cratia, gave birth to six children, five of whom died in infancy. She often visited Marcus and his mother, Domitia Lucilla, with her surviving daughter, also called Cratia. Marcus was of course later married as well, to a woman he seemed truly to love named Faustina, but whom he rarely mentioned in writing. Some historians say they had at least 13 children, most lost in early childhood. The Stoic author Seneca was married. The teacher of Epictetus, Musonius Rufus, heartily recommended marriage in his lectures, but Epictetus apparently lived alone until near the end of his life, when he adopted a child and a woman friend moved in to help care for the young one.

Love, gender, sex, and romance all crisscrossed in complicated ways during these times. But the documents that have survived assure us that the major Stoic thinkers of the era were no strangers to the full range of human emotions and commitments encompassing both friendship and other forms of love. We are left in the end, though, wondering whether the standard Stoic concepts and claims allow enough room for capturing the full range and depth of either friendship or love. Their ideas about agreement, appropriation, and virtue are extremely helpful, as far as they go. But do they go far enough? Is there a vulnerability in the deepest forms of love that might be hinted at in a correspondence but that could not be captured in standard Stoic concepts? Stoics are often known for their quest of invulnerability. But perhaps the neglected quality of vulnerability will alone help us understand something deeply needed for the things they felt, beyond the dogmas or principles they articulated.

Consider again their idea of *oikeiosis,* or appropriation, described at the outset of this chapter and meant to identify a natural process in which the self, caring for its own interests, begins to expand its conception of the full range of those interests and starts to care for other people and their concerns as necessary for and essentially connected to its own self-care, as it appropriates others into its circle of interest. But the self is still always at the center in this process, itself an entity often portrayed as a citadel or impregnable fortress. And yet, we've seen that deep friendship and love might require a more permeable or porous metaphor to capture what happens to and with the self in a case of total *philia,* or friendship love. The same surely might be required for a deeper romantic love, and finally the sort of self-giving love for any other humans, for humanity, and ultimately for God and all of creation that is perhaps the greatest form of all, a love that transcends normal friendship and romantic engagement.

Perhaps there has to be a counterpart of *oikeiosis,* an almost opposite-seeming next phase of growth, once appropriation has done its work, a process unrecognized and unacknowledged by the founding and classic Stoics, where the self or soul, instead of continuing to grow in its metaphorical size and strength through the appropriation and inclusion of others, begins in a deep spiritual sense to thin out its walls, to make them more porous, to break down its rigid boundaries, and perhaps to shrink in its own autonomy and sense of separateness, to attain a larger unity no longer to be centered on it, but a unity around and centered on what goes far beyond it. And it is that which the great mystics have whispered and struggled to speak about, or to put into words, as the ultimate stage in our journey where a total vulnerability passes through the deepest alchemy into the greatest form of strength. Perhaps the dynamic of embrace and release that is such a large part of wisdom applies not just to externals but also to the self itself, where these apparent opposites may come together and into play in their own intimate dance.

Chapter **16**

The Fear of Death

To some people, this is the ultimate topic of philosophy. Death inevitably takes away from us the people we love and value. Or first, it comes for us. What is it? How should we think of it? How can we accept this difficult truth?

In this chapter, we explore what the Stoics had to say about this final earthly limit and challenge. We look at their views on death and the fear of death, which for many of us is the most intense and troubling of anxieties. The Stoics sought to liberate themselves and us from this fear and worry. They were sure that the joy they sought required success in this task.

Matters of Life and Death

We're often stunned when a close friend or family member dies, even if we've been prepared for it by a long period of struggle and decline. When death comes as the result of an extended process, it can still shock with its finality and absoluteness. A last breath is taken. A lively soul vanishes out of our lives and leaves a gaping void. They were there a moment ago and now are not. When it happens, it's irreversible and forever. It reminds us of our own fragile hold on life. We'll each get that visit some day and be whisked away from everything and everyone we've cared about in this world.

Death is the great unknown. Will it be like walking through a doorway into a new reality, or flying free of the body, or else transitioning somehow to emerge into a gloriously unimaginable place, or will it be more like the extinguishing of a candle flame in the darkness, or rather perhaps like nothing at all? Is an on/off switch flipped from consciousness to none, or is it a dimmer switch slowly turned down in seconds of fading, gradually to a blank of absolute nothingness, the utter silence of personal extinction? What is it?

Many people believe there is a survival of the soul or core self after death. Many deny it. Almost everyone knows someone who has stories about a near-death experience or contact from beyond, but nobody seems to have proof. All the troubling uncertainty surrounding this one sharp cosmic reality of death creates anxiety, worry, and fear for most people in some way. And these deep reactions impinge on what it may take to live a good life. Can happiness, true well-being in the world co-exist with an undercurrent of fear about the one inevitability of death? This had to be of interest to the Stoic philosophers.

Countless generations of logic students have begun to learn about valid and sound arguments from the simple three-step reasoning involving two premises and a conclusion: (1) Socrates is a man, (2) All men are mortal, and therefore (3) Socrates is mortal. Poor Socrates. Poor us. It's inescapable.

Everyone dies — well, except maybe for the prophet Ezekiel, who reportedly was sent the ancient equivalent of chauffeured air-limo to whisk him into the next life, or perhaps one of the characters in our oldest known story, the *Epic of Gilgamesh*, set in 2,700 BCE, where we learn that a minor character may have received from the gods the gift of immortality. The already ancient man, at the time we meet him, called Utnapishtin, or "The Faraway," would now of course be far and away over four thousand, seven hundred years old, and likely very wise. He would still be among us, though likely under another name, like perhaps Joe Jones, Fred Smith, or Ryan Holiday. But despite a few such ancient stories, it's clear we all need to anticipate a worldly end.

Philosophy as Preparation for Death

If Stoicism had a patron saint, it would be Socrates. And there would be shrines. He was the Ultimate Role Model, the most admired example of proper thinking and living, the superhero in a toga to all the ancient Stoics. He did not fear death, and so we shouldn't either. As you'll soon see, Epictetus gave an argument just like that. And we'll examine it.

The Socratic acceptance of mortality

ANECDOTE

Socrates thought that you'd have to believe things you can't know to be true to think of death as a harm or evil, and so to be feared and avoided as long as possible. He was brought to trial on fabricated charges by people who hated his influence in Athens, and his fame. He was convicted by a large jury and sentenced to death. But he was also given a way out. If he'd just stop doing philosophy in public and act like a normal person, he'd be allowed to live. He replied, "As long as I live and breathe, I shall never cease to philosophize," and thereby both shocked his adversaries and impressed countless generations of people ever since who read the scene in Plato's *Apology*.

But Plato also captured the days that followed, preceding the execution of his teacher, a death that was delayed by certain coincidental events that gave us elaborate conversations that have stood the test of time. In the classic Socratic dialogues, the *Crito* and the *Phaedo*, we hear Socrates talking with friends about his upcoming death. Some are seeking to convince him to escape prison and the unjust sentence. But he refuses. And in the *Phaedo* especially, he explains why. In that dialogue, he tells his friends that philosophy is a preparation for death. And then he goes on to argue for the immortality of the soul. But Posidonius of Rhodes (c. 135–c. 51 BCE), known to history as an influential "middle Stoic," was so shocked by this argument for personal immortality that he rejected the authenticity of the dialogue. He believed it could not represent the real words of Socrates. Surely, he assumed, the real Socratic acceptance of mortality, as well as his courage in the face of death, did not depend on a belief that he would live on in a better realm. It must have come from a deeper and more "Stoic" place than that.

The Stoics' concerns

WARNING

As a matter of fact, there does not seem to have been any strong consensus about the exact fate of the soul, self, or conscious person after death held by all or most Stoics during ancient times. They did agree that the self was, or essentially had, a spark of the divine in it. But what became of this spark at earthly death was a matter of some dispute. Did the spirit (*pneuma* — silent "p") arise out of the body to float off into the heavens to commune with the gods, or was it somehow absorbed back into the essence of the deity from which it had come? Did a merging, as of a drop of water into the ocean, end its journey as a separate consciousness, or would this individual awareness continue, either forever or a very long time, until at least the next conflagration of the universe? But why should the death and rebirth of the material universe affect the existence or continuity of a spark of the Logos, which was believed to survive intact through any conflagration as the basic, fundamental, ultimate structuring force of all — in a modern metaphor, as a bit like a governing software, itself existing as a program in a kind of physical state that could transfer across and reinstall in any relevant cosmic hardware?

The Stoics could not agree on this. And that's no surprise, because where would the evidence be? But given the many cosmic details on which they did seem to be sure, just as far removed from decisive evidence, this is a bit odd. You'd think they'd want to be clear on the soul and its future. But it's often true that what's closest to home can be the most perplexing of all.

In one passage, Marcus Aurelius expresses some basic concerns about the issue in a vivid way. He's clearly worried over the issues and articulates his concerns in words you might hear during an all-night dorm room bull session. He comes up with an argument from analogy comparing our bodies and souls and writes this about death, using a picture of our souls rising through the air from this event, and leaving our bodies that remain:

> If our souls survive, how does the air find room for them, all of them, since the beginning of time? How does the earth make room for all the bodies buried in it since the onset of time? They linger for whatever period, then through change and decomposition make room for others. So too with souls that inhabit the air. They linger a bit and then are changed — diffused and kindled into fire, absorbed into the Logos from which all things spring, and so make room for new arrivals. (*Meditations* 4.21)

In this passage he seems to land on the "reabsorption into the Logos" view. But that would still leave questions unanswered about the ongoing status and consciousness of these souls or divine parts reunited into their home. We can certainly be reunited with old friends or reabsorbed into a community without ceasing to be who we individually are. And yet, can such a metaphor hold? Marcus does not spell out final conclusions with any specificity.

In the *Phaedo*, Plato represents Socrates as being confident about his future after execution, but even then, he hints at the intellectual humility that characterized his entire philosophical career, holding as he did that his own wisdom must consist in knowing that he did not know so many vital and central things that others purported to know. He could believe that the soul in this life is imprisoned in the body and that its release would be better for it without also holding precise theories about the afterlife.

TIP

Commentators have differed over what exactly Socrates could have meant in characterizing philosophy as a preparation for death. Perhaps philosophy strips away the illusions that make us cling too tightly to this world. It could be that philosophy helps us discover the values and ideals needed for living a good life, which is both a preliminary and needed preparation for what comes next, for dying a good death. Philosophy can break the hypnotic trance of the material world and open us up to deeper and greater realities. Even by helping us think more clearly and reason more carefully, it can in principle help to inhibit irrational fears of anything, including death. But whatever exactly it meant to Socrates, the Stoic philosophers certainly adopted this view in their own ways. They believed that philosophy has resources of insight sufficient to reconcile us to the ups and downs of this world and even to our ultimate worldly end. But they approached this final issue in several different ways. We'd like to profile and examine a few of them by looking at what the three main Roman Stoics had to say. But first, a word about the competition.

Two Epicurean Efforts to Calm Us Down

Those other very popular philosophers in ancient times, the Epicureans, produced two famous arguments with which they tried to show us that we should not fear death. We can call them "The Symmetry Argument" and "The Impossibility of Harm Argument." Epicurus himself is best known for the latter, and his follower Lucretius for the former. We'll begin with symmetry. And we should recall that the Epicureans believed death to be the annihilation of the conscious aware self, so if they can help us to accept even that, which was their aim, they'll be accomplishing something impressive.

The Symmetry Argument

The Symmetry Argument goes like this: Before your birth, you did not exist for a very long time, perhaps an infinite duration. After your death you will not exist for a very long time, perhaps an infinite duration. It makes no sense to view the long span of time that existed before your birth without you in it and feel terror, fear, or worry about that nonexistence. So, since the future after your death is the symmetrical mirror image of that, it makes equally no sense to view the span of time without you in it after your death and feel terror, fear, or worry about that nonexistence. Next issue.

Wait. Can things be that simple? The Epicureans want us to be reasonable. A potentially infinite span of nonexistence is what it is, however we might be related to it in time. What's appropriate as an attitude toward it then should not vary from one time to another, any more than from one place to another. If humans should fear death, then it doesn't matter whether they live in Paris or Dallas. And it should not matter whether they're living in the first century or the twenty-first. Likewise, it should not matter to you that you won't exist after your death, since it doesn't matter to you that you didn't exist prior to your birth. You're fine with the latter, the pre-life nonexistence. You should be equally fine with the post-life nonexistence. The situation is equal in all relevant respects, and so our attitudes toward each time should be the same.

Does this convince you? Isn't there a crucial difference the Epicureans are over-looking? Did they indulge in too much wine with dinner and forget something relevant to the issue? After all, you weren't around to contemplate a coming extinction before the first long gap of you-lessness. And you are in fact around now to contemplate your coming extinction — if death is what the Epicureans think it is, a total "lights out." The previous nonexistence did not loom ahead as a big reversal of fortune. This one does. You couldn't have anticipated your prior nonexistence, since you were not around to do so. You can and must anticipate the coming attraction. So the situations aren't symmetrical after all. Described generally enough, they can of course seem to be. But any two things can seem alike if we leave out enough relevant detail. It's what's called a specious argument, seemingly but not actually good.

This argument can be paralleled with another equally bad one that clearly goes wrong. It doesn't bother you when a stranger across town is injured in the gym. So it shouldn't bother you when you are injured in the gym. Symmetrical situations call for equal responses. But there's also a crucial asymmetry here, right? You're personally involved in one situation.

This is of course the form of a common Stoic argument: Suppose your favorite vase is broken and you're upset. The Stoics will point out that if this happened to a stranger across town, you would not be upset, and then they say you should not be upset here either. A broken vase is a broken vase, wherever it happens. But this is silly. In one case it's your special vase, and in the other case it isn't. And that's a crucial difference that makes a difference.

Some people do seem to find the Symmetry Argument about death convincing. There's no accounting for taste. But most feel it's more of a trick, like a magic illusion, not persuasive at all. Clever, but no. Those who give it as a persuasive argument tend to do so with great confidence, but confidence doesn't necessarily track rationality or truth. And we're confident of that.

The Impossibility of Harm Argument

The Impossibility of Harm Argument has been even more widely discussed and has fascinated people ever since it first appeared. It wouldn't be an exaggeration to say that it's one of the most interesting and clever short arguments ever invented. Here's one way of presenting it:

1. At any time when you exist, your death does not exist.

2. What does not exist cannot harm you.

3. At any time when your death exists, you do not exist.

4. What does not exist cannot be harmed. So:

5. It's impossible for death to harm you.

6. It makes sense to fear only things that can harm you. So:

7. It makes no sense to fear death.

We hope you feel better now. But once more, you may worry that a rabbit has been pulled out of a hat. The magician did not vanish. The girl didn't really get sawed in half. It was an illusion. So is this. But wait, what's wrong with the argument? It merely points out that all times that exist can be divided into two categories: (A) those times in which death can't harm you, because of something about it, and (B) those times when you can't be harmed by death, because of something about you. But those two categories then collapse into one: All those times that ever exist, which you now can see are times in which no harm comes to you from death. So don't worry, be happy.

WARNING

Sometimes, we come across an argument that seems too good to be true: It appears to prove what it sets out to prove, yet we can't help but suspect we've been tricked. And we can often begin to test our suspicion by creating a parallel argument that's obviously absurd to perhaps see why our intuitions rejected the first argument. Then we can go looking more carefully for the cause, where things went wrong in the first argument, where the trick was.

Imagine someone arguing against speed limits and seat belt laws and saying that they are passed to prevent certain fatal harms, but it makes no sense for you to fear harm from a fatal automobile crash in which you're killed, because any time at which you exist is a time that such a crash fatality for you does not exist, and any time such a fatality exists is a time you do not, so there is no time occupied by both you and a crash fatality of you. And if you cannot occupy the same time, there is no time when such a thing can be harmful to you. So, speed limits and seat belt laws don't prevent the real harm they were passed to help prevent.

Or suppose someone is opposed to sensible nuclear weapons agreements between countries and argues that it makes no sense to fear the nuclear annihilation of all life, because — and you can fill in the blanks here. Something is clearly going wrong in such arguments. And many rational people will conclude that this is enough to reject the version of such an argument that Epicurus offered. Sorry, we're not convinced. Next.

TIP

But perhaps we can say more. This could well be like the Symmetry Argument, where the reasoning can seem to work largely because relevant details are left out. Consider, for example, line two of the argument: "What does not exist cannot harm you." The argument just talks about you and your death, as a state of your nonexistence. But perhaps there are other things to consider, such as any things in the world that do exist when you do and can lead to or cause your death, like bullets, cars, diseases, nuclear weapons, and on and on. And maybe these things that do share existence with you can be rationally feared in their capacity of potentially killing you because they lead to something that would be of great harm to the present you: a forthcoming stretch of time never ending when, because of just one of them, your plans, projects, prospects, conscious experience, loves, and interests can no longer exist and play out as positive features of reality, with ongoing conscious benefits to you that you enjoy. And if these things can rationally be feared because of what they lead to, then what they lead to can itself be rationally feared, since the harm of these other things derives entirely from bringing that about. And nothing is harmful because of what it leads to if it leads to something good or neutral, but only because it leads to something harmful.

This is just an example of how two very famous Epicurean arguments can fall short. But that other band across town known as the Stoics had their own hit parade arguments. So, let's look at them in the next section.

Epictetus Against Fearing Death

The ancient Stoics viewed death as a natural and necessary part of life. We mention in our chapter on desires (Chapter 10) an idea circulating at the time that among our many desires, some are natural and necessary, some are natural but unnecessary, and others are neither natural nor necessary. The latter were to be shunned, or else treated with great caution, those in the middle category were acceptable, but the first category encompassed the desires most to be approved. So the combination of natural and necessary was already in a positive column of human thinking, and the Stoics aimed to file death there, too, however different it might otherwise be. They believed death is a natural process and that all things in the universe are subject to the cycles of birth, growth, and death. And of course, since the founding Stoics emphasized the importance of living in accordance with nature and accepting the natural order of things, they were keen to point out that this includes our accepting and even embracing the fact that all living beings eventually die.

TIP

Rather than fearing death, the Stoics encouraged using it well. They saw a contemplation of our own mortality as a way of gaining perspective to appreciate the present moment more. They believed that by recognizing the transitory nature of life, we can develop a greater sense of gratitude for what we have now, the fullness of life that we currently enjoy. And this thought might also help us with two of the biggest problems we face: (1) the ongoing, frequent temptation of putting things off, or procrastination, and (2) a sort of oblivious, mindless, nonattentive plod through the present. A keen sense of the inevitable approach of death and so of the limited time we have available can help erode the strength of each temptation. Death makes any needless delay seem less desirable. Its reality can encourage us to act while we can. And it encourages us to savor the moments we have. There are even slogans for this. Remembering our mortality, "*Memento Mori!*" can encourage us to make the most of today: "*Carpe Diem!*"

REMEMBER

To the Stoics, the end points of birth and death, if pondered properly and incorporated well into our thinking, can give us a vivid sense of our finitude, or the limitations of our time here, which used well can then help focus us on the importance of living fully, wisely and virtuously, with excellence, and feel the urgency of making the most of our limited time on earth.

Many of the early Stoics believed in the soul's survival of bodily death, but fewer details have survived from their thought on this than we would like. Yet the scholar A. A. Long concluded in his book *Hellenistic Philosophy*, "no Stoic postulated unlimited survival or immortality" (213n). And in his careful study *The Stoics*, the late F. H. Sandbach wrote of their views about the soul after death, "The psyche, which was a mixture of air and fire 'in tension,' would hold itself together for a time, contracted into a spherical shape and risen to the upper air: the weaker souls would break up first and only those of the ideal wise men would persist until finally caught up in the conflagration that would end the world-cycle" (83). Diogenes Laertius told us, "Cleanthes indeed holds that all souls continue to exist until the great conflagration," but Chrysippus says that only the souls of the wise do (*Lives* 7.156–157). The fiery death of the universe that ancient Stoics postulated as the end of this current cosmic cycle and the birth of the next one would be definitively bad news for our poor souls, wise or otherwise.

Of course, there is no simple list of essential views for being a Stoic, though some of the fundamentals are clear enough. And there may be room for a sufficient revision of their physics to allow for a bit of Platonizing or Christianizing on this issue about survival of death. A modern philosophical Stoic with such sympathies could indeed argue that since the Logos was postulated to survive the conflagration, this loving and rational God could support the continued survival of souls in some form or other if that would be best for the total good. But this is a bit of speculation divergent from the scant evidence we have concerning classic Stoic views.

One thing the early Stoic teachers all did have in common on the topic of death was to agree among themselves that the inevitable cessation of this earthly life should not worry us or spark fear. We should anticipate it with perfect serenity. The reasoning they then offered us about death was meant to help with that. They gave several sorts of arguments to make their case. We can usefully begin with some reasoning from Epictetus.

The Judgment Argument

In the *Handbook*, Epictetus gives this reasoning:

> People are troubled not by things, but by their judgments about things. Death, for example, isn't frightening, or else Socrates would have thought it so. No, what frightens people is their judgment about death, that it's something to fear. So, whenever we're obstructed or troubled or distressed, we should blame only ourselves. (*Handbook* 5a)

What's the argument, exactly? Let's consider carefully the first sentence in this passage from the *Handbook*: "People are troubled not by things but by their judgments about things." Many modern readers of the Stoics love this statement and like to quote it. And we can understand why, since it removes all threats from the realm of things we can't control and relocates them to the safer, more manageable realm of things we can control. We have no power over hurricanes, tornadoes, wildfires, unemployment, and the fact of death, but we can control how we think of such things. We can control our own judgments. So if the dangers or real threats aren't in the things but only in how we think about them, that's just great, because it gives us a sense of power. It's too bad that this is not true, because it's certainly a power we'd love to possess. But we can't so easily defang the world with magic words.

Now, if Epictetus had just said, "People are *often* troubled not by things but just by their judgments of things," we'd have here a better statement. And that's because we do frequently fear things that aren't real dangers, we project onto things scary properties or frightening implications they don't have, we jump at shadows, and we should just generally calm down. But it doesn't follow from this that we're always wrong, that external events never have in themselves a power of harm or cause our fear. To conclude that would require a convincing argument, and of course elsewhere Epictetus tries such an argument, seeking to persuade us that the only harm is moral harm, or damage with respect to the personal inner arena of virtue and vice, detracting from the one and encouraging the other. And surely, it does make sense to fear becoming a worse person or being derailed from progress in becoming a better person. And yet, how good is the argument that these things are the only things that objectively carry a threat or danger of harm?

Animal bites can inflict bodily damage and severe pain, and so can bullets and bombs, car accidents, and falls, storms and fires. The same things can inflict death. But Epictetus wants us to believe that these things never themselves trouble us, but that only our judgments that they are harmful do so. But what if our judgments are true? What if we judge something to be dangerous and harmful precisely because it is?

WARNING

A classic Stoic will call everything regarding the physical body an "indifferent," and literally neither good nor bad, since bodily health isn't necessarily and always an aid to virtue or a guarantee of happiness, and bodily problems don't necessarily and always detract from our virtue. But from that, it doesn't follow that things that can damage the body can't be viewed as objectively harmful. If health and bodily integrity, and an absence of severe pain, can be generally or even just situationally be judged rightly as "preferred indifferents," isn't something that objectively threatens to take them away a real threat, regardless of our judgments? It's hard to see what answer Epictetus could have to this question, or how it could be convincing.

It looks like Epictetus has given us a false dichotomy here and not a true start on what will be a good argument. But in the same passage he tries another tack when saying, "Death, for example, is not frightening, or else Socrates would have thought it so." Here, instead of leading us to a broader argument about indifferents and where real harm is found, he gives us the example of a revered wise teacher.

The argument now takes this form: Surely, if death were dangerous and to be feared, Socrates would have feared it, but he didn't, so it must not be. But of course, this assumes that Socrates would have had all knowledge regarding death sufficient to ground the right attitude toward it, and Socrates had made a career of admitting how much he didn't know about the things that matter most, things that most people unjustifiably assume they know. And he saw his own wisdom as centrally consisting in his acknowledged ignorance. As a matter of fact, his own reason for not fearing death seemed more aligned with a very different argument, that to be justified in fearing something, we must know or reasonably believe that it's harmful, and he didn't think he was in the right position to know enough about death to satisfy that condition.

To assume, as Epictetus apparently does when he gives this argument, that if death were properly frightening, Socrates would have known enough about that fact to be frightened by it is simply to believe something that seems false. Why would Socrates have had special access to such knowledge, despite often claiming he didn't have any such special access at all, and that neither do we?

If there's a good argument to be had from the example of Socrates, it's not one that begins with a claim that if death were harmful or properly frightful, then Socrates would have known that and feared it. It would be the very different reasoning that Socrates himself used when he pointed out that it makes no sense to fear something unless you know it to be harmful, and we don't know enough about death to know that. And maybe even that argument wouldn't be altogether convincing either, because perhaps it's not just knowledge of harm that properly justifies fear, but an uncertainty about the matter can be all that's needed when the stakes are high enough.

Most of us accept that in some circumstances, uncertainty can be enough to justify fear. And neither Socrates not Epictetus refutes that suggestion. So, the Judgment Argument does not work. But wait, there's more.

The Avoidance Argument

In another place, Epictetus tries a different argument, as if realizing he needs a more convincing case. He says:

> When death seems bad, the idea we need to have at hand is that it's proper for us to avoid things that are bad, but death is unavoidable. (*Discourses* 1.27.7)

And then later in the same passage:

> I can't avoid death, but might I not avoid being frightened by it? Am I bound to die grieving and trembling with fear? (ibid.)

Epictetus here offers us a general principle he thinks we can all agree to, and then an application of it to death. The principle is this: "It's proper for us to avoid things that are bad." He then points out that we can't altogether avoid death. He concludes that since it can't be properly avoided, death must not be bad, and so it's wrong to fear it. I can avoid this fear, but I can't avoid death. It's proper to fear what I can avoid, but not what I can't. So let's focus on fearing fear itself and then as a result acting to avoid it, as we often do with a lesser fear, like of public speaking. That's a very clever move of reasoning, but we now need to examine the argument carefully to see if it can properly convince us. Otherwise, we should avoid the Avoidance Argument itself.

Let's lay out the core reasoning in the first quote in a more transparent logical form and even tuck in some of the concerns of the second quote. We get:

1. If something is bad, then it's proper for us to avoid it.

2. If something is proper to avoid, it must be avoidable.

3. Death is not avoidable. Therefore:

4. It's not proper to avoid death. Therefore, surprise:

5. Death isn't bad.

6. If something isn't bad, it's not proper to fear it. Therefore,

7. It's not proper to fear death.

So, cheer up, says Epictetus. Aren't you glad we got that out of the way?

On the surface, this looks pretty good. We have here an argument in two parts. The first part is composed of lines 1–5 and seeks to establish that death isn't a bad thing, and the second argument, composed of lines 5–7, tries to then show that it's not proper to fear death.

TECHNICAL STUFF

For all you readers who are logic geeks: The first part of the argument proceeds by the universally accepted logic principle of *Modus Tollens* (*if p then q; not q; therefore, not p*), and the second by a version of the equally dandy *Modus Ponens* (*if p then q; p; therefore, q*). But you don't have to know these names, however helpful they might be to impress your friends.

When you think hard about lines 1–5, you will find the reasoning persuasive in the sense that *if* the premises are all true, the conclusions will be true. Epictetus hopes you'll be impressed enough to walk away without any further worry about the argument . . . or death. And yet there's more to examine.

>> **Here's an initial flaw:** Consider the first premise, or line 1. "If something is bad, then it's proper for us to avoid it." Why should we accept this central claim as true? Imagine you're a rock climber and just slipped off a sheer rock face high above the canyon floor. You're plummeting and will in moments crash to the ground. You surely think of that as a bad thing, but then remember that if something is bad, it's proper to avoid it. Would you then rightly realize that since you can't avoid the now inevitable crash to come, it must not be a bad thing after all? Absolutely not. Maybe the premise, to be true, needs to be reformulated to state more carefully: "If something is bad, then it's proper for us *to try to avoid* it." And as soon as you begin to lose your grip and slip, you'll surely *try to avoid* crashing to the ground, and you can indeed try; and it will be right to view such a crash as a bad thing.

>> **A second matter:** So let's make that change to premise one, and then for the sake of consistency in the argument, it's a change we'll need to make to the second line too, which then becomes: "If something is proper *to try to avoid*, it must be avoidable." And that can look just fine, even applied to death, because whenever you see a truck bearing down on you and jump back, trying to avoid death, you can find that it is indeed avoidable at that time, as on many occasions. But then, the next step, line 3 ("Death is not avoidable"), will be false, since, as we've just seen, it often is possible to avoid death, as we avoid it daily by careful living.

Obviously, what Epictetus needs for the argument to work is another change in the second premise and then here in the conclusion as well. He needs line 2 to be "If something is appropriate *to try to avoid*, it must be *ultimately avoidable*." Then, to be true, line 3 will become: "Death is not ultimately avoidable." And the argument can go through. But wait. Why should we accept the new version of the second line? Why should we buy the claim that "If something is appropriate *to try to avoid*, it must be ultimately avoidable"? So changed, this now seems to be false. We just saw that it's proper to try to avoid death in rock climbing, while crossing the street, and in many other situations. If Epictetus wants us to change our minds about this only because death is not ultimately and forever avoidable, and then redescribe what we do in rock climbing and jumping from the path of a truck as not "avoiding death" but as merely postponing it, he'd better have a good reason, because on each of those occasions, when we're successful, it looks like we have precisely avoided death, which would itself otherwise have happened right then.

Let's get the suitably altered argument in front of us for one last assessment:

a. If something is bad, then it's proper to try to avoid it.

b. If something is proper to try to avoid, it must be ultimately avoidable.

c. Death is not ultimately avoidable. Therefore:

d. It's not proper to try to avoid death. Therefore:

e. Death isn't bad.

f. If something isn't bad, it's not proper to fear it. Therefore,

g. It's not proper to fear death.

Let's grant line a. We can accept it in this new version. And in its new version, line c looks fine too. But line b now looks false, from what we've just seen. It's appropriate for us to try to avoid death today and tomorrow and every day we can, even though it's not ultimately avoidable.

And there's a second problem with line b that's almost too small to mention, but we'll do so anyway. It seems proper for us to try to avoid things that we rationally believe to be avoidable, whether they ultimately are or not. When you see the truck coming at you, you can properly try to avoid it, even if it's literally too late. You just have to think you have a chance, or hope you do, whether you really do or not. To accommodate this, Epictetus would need to change the end of lines b and c from the words "ultimately avoidable" to the alternative phrase "such that it is rational to believe or hope that it is ultimately avoidable." But even that won't help Epictetus. A reformulated line c would be false, as certain billionaires in Silicon Valley now show us in their widely publicized tech-based rational hope and belief that they'll find a way to avoid death, uploading themselves into the cloud, whether they actually can or not. In this argument itself, failure is not "such that it is rational to believe or hope that it is ultimately avoidable." Sorry.

REMEMBER

So, this argument from Epictetus fails. When we fix parts of it to make them look true, those fixes show another part to be false. We remain free to fear death if we're so inclined. But most likely, we don't enjoy having such a fear at all. So let's continue to look for a good argument. Surely, there is one.

The Ignorance Argument

Elsewhere in the *Discourses*, Epictetus says this:

> We treat death as something to flee from, while we're careless, negligent, and unconcerned in forming a judgment about it. Socrates was right to call death and so on bogeys. Masks appear scary to young children and frighten them with their weirdness, and we too are affected in much the same way by events, for precisely the reason children are scared by bogey masks . . . What is death? A bogey-mask. Turn it around and you'll see it for what it is. Look! Now it can't bite! Now or later, your body is bound to be separated from your spirit, just as it was separated before. If it's now, what is there to complain about, seeing that, if not now, it will be later? (*Discourses* 2.1.14–17)

Of course, the last sentences are an allusion to previous arguments, with all their problems. If death is just a scary mask, then what's it covering that isn't scary at all? The truth must be that here Epictetus is assuming something like the normal Stoic view that death is a natural transition from this world to something else, and that since it's natural and decreed by a benevolent God, it must not be bad or properly scary *if* we were just to see it as it is. And yet, to describe death as a "natural transition" is again leaving out crucial aspects of it, and amounts to a form of fallacy that cannot and should not remove whatever worries or fears we might have about death.

But then, Epictetus may have something much simpler in mind here. We see only the scary appearance of death. We are ignorant as to what's really behind the mask. It makes no sense to fear what we don't know. So, stop it already.

REMEMBER

And yet, as we mentioned before, a fear of the unknown amid uncertainty and where a lot is at stake is perhaps one of the most common forms of fear. And part of the worry is that problems we see are bad enough, but those we don't even know about can be worse. The worry or fear is that the unknown may be hiding much worse than we imagine. But again, Epictetus will not convince most people here that they should abandon fear in the face of their own mortality. This is not the argument we were seeking. But there's more.

The Acceptance Argument

Epictetus has a big bag of tricks in hand and seems always to be ready with another line of reasoning to help dislodge us from our fears. He keeps impressing us with new lines of thought waiting in the wings. But lots of arguments won't alone solve the problem. If you're trying to carry water, and each bucket you own has a big hole in it, then having ten leaky buckets won't necessarily get the job done. We need good arguments, not just lots of them.

In one passage Epictetus gives an example of a man who suddenly learns he's been sentenced to the harsh penalty of exile, but he won't have to leave immediately. He takes the news with acceptance and so calmly as to suggest to the messenger that they go grab something to eat first, since it's mealtime. He can go into exile when the time comes. Our Stoic guide says these words of approval, and then ratchets the example up a notch:

> That's what it is to have trained yourself properly, to have made desire immune to impediment and aversion, immune to encountering what it wants to avoid. I am condemned to death. If it happens straightaway, I die. If after a short delay, I eat first, since the time has come for lunch, and then I'll die later. How? As is proper for someone who's giving back what was not their own. (*Discourses* 1.1.31-32)

The key principle here is acceptance of what is not within our control, which Epictetus likes to characterize as "not our own." He says later:

> There's no point in laying claim to what isn't yours. Always bear in mind what is and what isn't yours, and then you'll be impervious to anxiety. (*Discourses* 2.6.8)

Apply this to an idea of immortality on earth, a life without death, which isn't ours, since it isn't within our power, and you have the Acceptance Argument. What's yours, you can do something about, you can act on; what's not yours is simply to be accepted for what it is. It's pointless to be worked up about anything that isn't properly ours. In the *Handbook*, Epictetus says:

> Instead of wishing that things would happen as you'd like, wish that they would happen as they do, and then you'll be content. (*Handbook* 8)

Death, though exceptional in many ways, should not be an exception here, to a Stoic. Wish that your death will happen whenever and wherever it will indeed happen, and you can be content, since if such a wish can't be thwarted, what's there to worry about? In another place, he says:

> So, what must we do? Make the best of what's up to us and take everything else as it comes. And how does it come? As God wishes. (*Discourses* 1.1.17)

But then an objection is raised, and he gives a response:

> "But being hanged is unbearable, isn't it?" — Except that when a person thinks it's a reasonable thing to do, then he'll go and hang himself. (*Discourses* 1.2.3)

The argument here seems to be that if death were inherently terrible and essentially fearful, and especially if, as people represent it to be, it is the worst thing imaginable, then nobody would ever select it as a rational option, what's needed, or the thing to choose as a situational exit. But people sometimes do, as in terrible and incurable illness. So it's no exception to the rule after all. It's neither good nor bad, but indifferent, most often rationally dispreferred, but on rare occasions, situationally chosen. In either case, when it comes, like any intrinsically indifferent thing, it's to be accepted.

Here, Epictetus alludes to a controversial Stoic stance on suicide, the idea of "The Open Door." The principle is simple: Sure, it's a tough world, but we've been given the equipment needed to manage it, the reason and the virtue, the insights and techniques we need. And then if it ever becomes so difficult as to be literally unbearable, there is another resource we've also been provided by the benevolent designer of nature: The door to leave is always open. In another place Epictetus metaphorically and vividly says:

> Has someone made the house smokey? If it's not too bad, I'll stay. If it's too much, I'll leave. What you need to remember and keep in mind is this: The door is open. (*Discourses* 1.25.18)

This is of course the door of rational suicide. But the Stoics are adamant to say that this should not be an option that's chosen quickly or easily. They like to use the analogy of a soldier at a difficult post who is to stay and fight under almost any circumstances. But there are rare extreme situations where the general will signal a retreat, and then it's proper to leave the post. Epictetus in another passage says this about giving up his body and leaving this world:

> As long as I don't give it up irrationally, or out of weakness, or for a trivial reason. Again, that's not what God wants, because he needs the universe to be as it is and the earth to be populated by creatures such as us. But if he sounds the retreat as he did for Socrates, I must obey him as a soldier obeys his commanding officer. (*Discourses* 1.29.29)

Seneca adds a cautionary note about the idea of the open door in a letter:

> For we need to be warned and strengthened in both directions — not to love or to hate life too much. Even when reason advises us to make an end of it, the impulse isn't to be adopted without reflection or quickly. The brave wise man should not beat a hasty retreat from life; he should make a becoming exit. And above all he should avoid the weakness that's taken possession of so many, a lust for death. (*Letters* 24–25)

The point Epictetus wants to make regarding the fear of death is that if this open door can ever be rational to choose, if it can ever be preferable to select death over another option, then death is not essentially bad, or the worst possible thing, but rather, in rare circumstances, can be a preferred choice.

Our guide then reassures his students, with an ending of typical hyperbole:

> The time of your stay here is short, and easy to endure for people with your convictions. What tyrant or thief or law can strike fear into those who regard the body and its possessions as of no importance? (*Discourses* 1.9.17)

When something is damaged, destroyed, or taken away, and is of no real importance, we accept what's happened. And we don't fear it in advance. The philosopher thinks we should apply that same principle to life and death:

> If a man endeavors to incline his mind to these things and to persuade himself to accept of his own accord what necessarily must happen to him, he will have a very reasonable and harmonious life. (*Fragments* 8)

ANECDOTE

One more quote, and a long one because it's so good. Epictetus begins by asking his students to imagine getting on a boat for a trip, then he instantly switches into the first person, putting himself in the place of those students and saying what he would want them to say or think:

> Suppose you're going on a voyage. What is it within my power to do? To choose the captain and the crew, and the day and time of departure. Then a storm falls on us. Why should that be any concern of mine? I've done all I can. Coping with the storm is someone else's business, the captain's. But now the ship is starting to sink. What can I do? All I can do is do what I can. So, I drown without fear, without screaming, without cursing God, knowing that everything that's born is bound to die. I'm not a form of everlasting life but a human being, a part of the universe as an hour is part of a day. Like an hour, I'm present and then I pass. So, what difference does it make to me how I pass, whether by drowning or fever? Some such thing is going to see to my passing anyway. (*Discourses* 2.5.10–14)

TIP

The idea is simple. There is only one rational response to something that's both natural and necessary, and so inevitable, and that's emotional acceptance. And this, without argument, might be his most convincing line.

Marcus Aurelius Weighs in on Death

Epictetus may have the most considerations and even arguments against fearing death. But Marcus Aurelius may have spent more of his time and mental energy wrestling with the issue. It often comes up in his journals. He can't quite manage to shake it. And because of this, he's a good guide for most of us, who can find ourselves in the same position. We can't quite put the issue to rest, as hard as we might try. It nags at us. It won't go away.

The Sameness Argument

Marcus apparently ruminated a lot about how short life can be. He'd lost many children at very young ages. He was around soldiers dying all the time at or before the prime of life, as they sought to defend Rome. He had chronic illnesses and can't have been confident about his own longevity. And we find him writing notes to himself like this during a military campaign:

> Even if you're going to live three thousand more years, or ten times that, remember: you cannot lose another life than the one you're living now, or live another one than the one you're losing. Whether a man lives for a long time or a short duration, it amounts to the same. The present is the same for everyone, and it should be clear that a brief instant is all that's lost. For you can't lose either the past or the future. How could you lose what you don't have? (*Meditations* 2.14)

This is in different ways both an attractive passage and puzzling. The emperor is trying to reassure himself that no matter whether he lives a long or short life, it doesn't matter, it amounts to the same thing in the end. Suppose he's cut down long before he eventually could have died of a ripe old age. He shouldn't worry in any case about what otherwise could have been because nobody can live lives other than the actual one given to them.

WARNING

And as to the length of this one life, whether he dies at one age or another, at one time or another, Marcus tells himself that he loses only one brief instant. But which instant is that? Is it the last one he lives as a conscious or even then unconscious soul connected to a body on this earth? But how is that instant lost if it's indeed had and lived? Does he then lose only the next instant to come, the first moment of his death that otherwise could have been a moment of his life? And if so, why is it just this one moment that's lost, rather than every moment beyond this one that also would have been or could have been lived? If a man can lose only what he has and if nobody has the past or future, then how can he lose even that one instant, the first and next *in the future* he would have had, but as things are, won't have? The passage is puzzling. And yet, on some level, we can get what Marcus is trying to say. If you're going to die at some point, you shouldn't worry so much about when. A moment is a moment. It's all the same. But is it? Is it all the same? It might not be the same to the guy who survives the battle that kills the man standing next to him, and having lived through it, goes on to enjoy 40 more years of a happy meaningful life. Ask him: "Would it have been all the same if you'd died that day in battle?" He'd say no. And who is the philosopher to disagree?

In another passage Marcus writes:

> Suppose a god announced that you were going to die tomorrow "or the next day." Unless you were a complete coward you wouldn't kick up a fuss about which day it was. What difference could it make? Now realize that the difference between years from now and tomorrow is very small. (*Meditations* 4.47)

It's as if he's telling himself again that it's all the same whether he dies sooner or later; it really doesn't matter, or shouldn't, and there should be no worry or fear that death might be imminent rather than more distant from the present moment. And measured by a cosmic scale of billions of years, perhaps there wouldn't seem to be a big difference between tomorrow and 40 years from now. But to the man or woman who gets those extra days and years and uses them well, it's not all the same. The argument seems to depend on a fallacy we've noted before: If you leave out enough relevant detail, almost any two things can look the same. Squint your eyes, move a distance away, and two very different things may seem alike, but they're not the same at all.

This is clearly not the sort of detailed, multi-step logical argument that Epictetus was ready at the drop of a toga to create for the conclusion that death ought not be feared. First, these musings are more about the timing of death and life's relative shortness. They're about an abrupt end that, when it comes, arrives completely for all, affecting each person in that one moment in what is, in one big sense, the same way. It's an absolute ending, no matter how far in years or days it may be from the beginning of that soul's time in the world. Maybe Marcus thinks it's the "what," not the "when" that matters.

So, what about the "what"? How would he advise us? As Marcus approaches his own end, and comes near the end of his journal, he writes later:

> Death holds no terrors for the man who calls good whatever happens in due season, who cares more that his actions are rational than that they are numerous, and to whom it matters not whether his view of this world is long or short-lived. (*Meditations* 12:35)

TIP

Appropriateness and rationality are important in ways that mere duration alone is not. When we allow anxieties, worries, or fears to arise about duration, he seems to be implying, we're thinking about and focusing on the wrong things. Or to reverse the point, when we're thinking about the right things, when we're well focused and properly oriented in life, we'll have no worries or fears about our duration here, the length of our stay. Do you agree?

The Natural and Liberating Argument

In a beautiful passage pondering his own future death, whenever it might come, Marcus tells himself:

> You boarded, you set sail, you've made the passage. Time to disembark. If it's for another life, well, there's nowhere without gods on that side either. If to nothingness, then you will be liberated from the tyranny of pain and pleasure, and from

bondage to your earthly shell, your body, which is of so much less value than what serves it. (*Meditations* 3.3b)

It's as natural to get off the boat of this life as it was to get on it for such a voyage as this. And regardless of what's next, no terrible harm will befall you. Either the rational benevolent gods that exist here are to be found there too, in which case you'll have a new existence in a fundamentally rational and good realm, likely with its own challenges which you can handle as you did those you've faced here; or else there is simply no nothing to come that could contain difficulties or pain. In either case, there's nothing to fear.

This reasoning seems to reflect in an interesting way some aspects of the most famous Epicurean argument about harm, but with good and rational gods thrown in for support. In any case, no terrible harm awaits us on the other side. And this should be enough to dispel our worries. But is it?

Marcus keeps reminding himself that death is as natural as anything else. In another passage, he writes this to remind himself of the overall context of death and his own best role in the story:

> In short, know this: Human lives are brief and trivial. Yesterday bodily fluid, tomorrow embalming fluid or a pile of ash. To pass through this life as nature demands. To give it up without complaint. Like an olive that ripens and falls, praising its mother, thanking the tree it grew on. (*Meditations* 4.48)

REMEMBER Recall the vision of the founding Stoics. What is our goal? To live in agreement with nature. To live consistently with who we are and where we are. An olive has the same job. It grows, ripens, and falls, in agreement with the larger overarching nature and its own small nature. So should we.

Again, death is altogether natural, another part of our life in nature, the nature that has supported those who came before us, as well as our own journey so far. Marcus keeps returning to this point and writes:

> I walk through what's natural, until the time comes to sink down and rest, to entrust my last breath to the source of my father's seed, of my mother's blood, of my nurse's milk, of my daily food and drink through all these years, to what sustains my footsteps and the use I make of it, the many uses. (*Meditations* 5.4)

In the middle of this overarching and undergirding home of nature, within our sustaining cosmic environment, formed and guided by a rational and good Logos, death seems a universal, ineluctable part. Will we treat it differently from all else? Will it alone strike terror and deep anxiety into us? What would justify our singling out this one part of the natural cycle in such a way and taking it as if it's inimical to who and what we are, different from all else?

The emperor often reflects on the great people who have gone before him and whose names live on after they've died. At one point he says to himself:

> Don't fear death but welcome it. It too is one of the things required by nature. Nature sends it, along with everything else. Like growth and maturity. Like a new set of teeth, a beard, and the first gray hair. Like sex and pregnancy and childbirth. Like all the other physical changes at each stage of life, our dissolution is no different. So, this is how a thoughtful person should await death, not with careless-ness, or hastily, or with disdain, but simply viewing it as one more natural process. Now you anticipate the child's emergence from its mother's womb; that's how you should await the hour when your soul will emerge from its container.
> (*Meditations* 9.3)

TIP

Life is full of beginnings and endings. Death is certainly one of the latter. Perhaps it's also one of the former. Regardless, it's natural and is to be accepted as such. Some of the Stoics would say it's to be embraced, even loved. Is that possible? Can we go that far? Can you?

To Marcus, death is not only natural and to be accepted as such, but it's also lib-erating. He writes later in the passage just quoted this reminder:

> Or maybe you need some tidy aphorism to tuck away in the back of your mind. Well, consider two things that should reconcile you to death: the nature of the things you'll leave behind you, and the kind of people you'll no longer be mixed up with. (*Meditations* 9.3)

It's hard not to smile at this. He goes on in the same entry to say:

> But now? Look how exhausting it all is! This chaos we all live in. It's enough to make you say to death, "Come quickly, before I start to forget myself, like them." (ibid.)

You can tell that, like most of us today, this leader's work involved things that were unpleasant, and people who were the same. He writes:

> Stop whatever you're doing for a moment and ask yourself: Am I afraid of death because I won't be able to do *this* anymore? (*Meditations* 10.29)

Again, whether he's thinking of war, some leadership challenge, or a personal problem, his honesty is engaging. He's trying to put death into a perspective that will take away its sting. It's natural, it happens to everyone, it's necessary, and it's in fact liberating. But there's more.

The Normal Change Argument

We live in a universe of constant change. Heraclitus knew it. So did the early Stoics. They even celebrated it. But other philosophers in the West then seemed to forget this for a long time, seeing solid substance as the building block of the world and change as secondary. Modern physics appears to loop back to the older vision of flux at the foundations. Marcus certainly saw everything as always in a state of transition. And this was his big-picture perspective for our own deaths. He advises himself in these words:

> Think about them all, the waves of change and alteration, endlessly breaking. And see our brief mortality for what it is. (*Meditations* 9.28)

In this, he was sharing a vision with Epictetus, whose talks had come to him in written form and had made an impression. The older philosopher imagined someone bemoaning their own impending death and then his own response:

> "But now it is time to die." Why say "die"? Make no tragic parade of the matter but speak of it as it is: It is now time for the material of which you are constituted to be restored to those elements from which it came. And what's terrible about that? (*Discourses* 4.7.15–16)

In another passage, Epictetus says:

> Why is there such a thing as death? For the cyclical perpetuation of the universe. The universe needs not only the things that currently exist in it but also those that are to come and those that have already been and gone. (*Discourses* 2.1.18)

Marcus takes this up and writes:

> You've functioned as a part of something, you'll vanish into what made you. Or to be restored to the Logos from which all things spring. By being changed. (*Meditations* 4.14)

He had earlier given himself an example:

> Alexander the Great and his mule driver both died, and the same thing happened to both. They were absorbed alike into the life force of the world or dissolved alike into atoms. (*Meditations* 6.24)

The great man and his servant both came from the life force, and they both returned there in a natural transition. And all those things we think about the most, like who's the emperor and who's the mule driver, all the categories of rank and status, of work and wealth, vanish as everyone returns to the source.

REMEMBER

The world is full of change and transformation. Everything is in transition, and the flow unites things in one big dance of existence. We have each faced many transitions before, endings and beginnings, and can face the one called death, because each has been a preparation for it. The emperor writes:

> When we cease from activity, or follow a thought to its conclusion, it's a kind of death. And it doesn't harm us. Think about your life: childhood, boyhood, youth, old age. Every transformation was a kind of dying. Was that so terrible? Think about life with your grandfather, your mother, your adopted father. Realize how many deaths and transformations and endings there have been and ask yourself: Was that so terrible? Then neither will the close of your life be, its ending and transformation. (*Meditations* 9.21)

Marcus would likely have loved what his fellow Stoic Seneca one day wrote to his friend Lucilius about death, when he said:

> That day you fear as the end of all things is the birthday of your eternity. (*Letters* 102, 26)

TIP

Death is simply another transition, another natural change, in a world of transitions and changes. Why should we fixate on it in terror or anxiety? It's either something or nothing. And Marcus is convinced: If it's something, it's something good, since the same Logos is in charge. If it's nothing, then it's nothing bad, for likely the same reason. So we can ease up and relax a bit and accept it with a measure of peace. Half of wisdom, after all, is perspective. Marcus seems to have an intuitive feel for that, and so instead of giving us multi-step logical arguments, he offers us reminders and perspectives, a fresh framing for what troubles us, so that we can see it anew with our sensibilities perhaps transformed, which then display in their own way the importance of transformations and transitions in the realm of the real.

In his last journal entry, preceding his last breath, Marcus writes to himself:

> You've lived as a citizen in a great city. Five years or a hundred, what's the difference? . . . And to be sent away from it not by a tyrant or a dishonest judge, but by Nature who first invited you in, why is that so terrible? Like the impresario ringing down the curtain on an actor: "But I've only gotten through three acts!" Yes. This will be a drama in three acts, the length fixed by the power that directed your creation, and now your dissolution. Neither was yours to determine. So, make your exit with grace, the same grace that's been shown to you. (*Meditations* 12.36)

The Stoics were right in thinking that at times there's no greater inspiration for us than the example of one good person, seeking to live the wisdom and virtue we each need. The powerful words of this man to himself can have an effect for some that's unrivalled by any systematic argument or treatise.

Seneca's Quantity or Quality Argument

Seneca wrote an amazing essay called "On the Shortness of Life." His main message was that life is long enough if you know how to invest it well. And that's a powerful reminder we all need in our day. He also wrote to his friend Lucilius about these matters, regarding life and death and our proper attitudes toward each. And we see in those letters various principles and arguments to reconcile us to the inevitable. We'll look at a few.

Again, Stoic wisdom is often about perspective. Seneca writes to his friend:

> We should strive not to live long but to live rightly, for to achieve a long life you need only fate, but for right living you need the soul. A life is long enough if it's a full life. But fulness is not reached until the soul has given itself its proper good, until it has assumed control over itself. What benefit does this older man derive from the eighty years he's spent in idleness? A person like him hasn't lived, he's merely lingered a while through the years. He's just been a long time dying. (*Letters* 93, 3–4)

We'll also see in Seneca the standard Stoic view that we should not fear death, but he also stresses that we should strive not to leave life until we've exercised such control over ourselves as to attain the wisdom and virtue needed for experiencing why we're here: to attain a fulness of life. Here's a visual. Imagine yourself looking at a timeline of the last century and this one, perhaps placed within the context of former and future times. How wide or long across the page will your own personal lifeline be? Seneca writes:

> I urge you, my dear Lucilius, let's see to it that our lives, like jewels of great price, are worthy of note not because of their width but because of their weight. Let's measure them by their performance, not by their duration. (*Letters* 93, 3–4)

In one of his essays on inner peace, he writes this remarkable passage:

> The sage does not need to walk timidly and grope his way. He's so sure of himself that he doesn't hesitate to face Fortune and will never give ground to her. He has nothing to make him afraid of her, for he considers not only his stuff, property, and position but even his body and eyes and hands, all that a man cherishes in life, even his own personality, to be temporary holdings, and he lives as if he were on loan to himself and is ready to return the whole sum cheerfully on demand. But the knowledge that he does not belong to himself does not cheapen him in his own sight. He performs all his duties as diligently and well as a devout and holy man guards any property trusted to him. When the order to return these things comes, he won't argue with Fortune but say, "I'm thankful for what I've held and enjoyed. My management of your property has paid you dividends, but as you order me to give it back, I do so, and I withdraw cheerfully and gratefully." (*On Tranquility* 11)

Later in the same passage he says:

> What hardship is there in returning from where you came? A man will live ill if he doesn't know how to die well. (ibid.)

In fact, Seneca in one place elides the stark difference between living and dying, giving his friend the example of an ancient time-keeping instrument:

> I remember one day you were working with the well-known thought that we don't suddenly fall on death but gradually approach it by slight degrees. We die every day. For every day, a little of our life is taken from us. Even when we're growing, our life is on the wane. We lose our childhood, then our boyhood, and then our youth. Counting even yesterday, all past time is lost time. The very day that we're now spending is shared between us and death. It's not the last drop that empties the water-clock, but all that previously has flowed out. Likewise, the final hour when we cease to live does not of itself bring death, it just completes the death process. We reach death at that moment, but we've been a long time on the way. (*Letters* 24, 19–20)

And Seneca doesn't have a clear or certain view of what comes next. He says:

> Death either annihilates us or strips us bare. If we are then released, there remains the better part, after the burden has been withdrawn. If we're annihilated, nothing remains. Good and bad alike are removed. (*Letters* 24.18)

We have here bodily life characterized as a "burden" or as involving a burden, and death as a release. But a quick word on this translation, which is a standard one. Compare this passage with another one that's a bit of a shock on first reading, where Seneca represents himself as in a dialogue, with his own surprising statement given first, which is then questioned:

> A whole life seems scarcely sufficient to learn the single principle of despising life. "What? Did you not mean 'control' instead of 'despise'"? "No. Controlling is the second task. For no one has controlled his life aright unless he's first learned to despise it." (*Letters* 111, 5)

He's advising his friend not to take these things too seriously, not to grab onto them with either worry or delight, fear or joy. Our delight and joy are in wisdom and virtue, in choosing and doing well within the sphere of our freedom. Externals are never really ours. And we're never fully free with respect to them. So we should not deal with them graspingly or with a fierce clinging attitude or emotion. We should let go, loosen our grip, or release them in a deep and existential sense.

But Seneca's best advice about life and death comes in a lengthy passage within one letter where he is talking with Lucilius about an older friend of theirs named Bassus, who is close to death. He writes of the man:

> A great pilot can sail even when his canvas is torn. If his ship is coming apart, he can still put in trim what remains of her hull and hold her to her course. This is what our friend Bassus is doing, and he ponders his own end with the courage and countenance that you'd regard as undue indifference in a man who so contemplated another's. (*Letters* 30, 3)

He goes on:

> This is a great accomplishment, Lucilius, and one that needs long practice to learn: To depart calmly when the inevitable hour arrives. (*Letters* 30.4)

He then says of the man:

> For he talks freely about death, trying hard to persuade us that if this process contains any element of discomfort or of fear, it is the fault of the dying person and not of death itself. Also, that there is no more inconvenience at the actual moment than there is after it's over. "And it is just as crazy," he adds, "for a man to fear what will not happen to him, as to fear what he will not feel if it does happen." Or does anyone imagine it will be possible that the cause by which feeling is removed can itself be felt? "Therefore," says Bassus, "death stands so far beyond all evil that it is beyond all fear of evils." (*Letters* 30, 5–6)

And Seneca then interjects:

> For I must tell you what I think. I hold that one is braver at the very moment of death than when one is approaching death. For death, when it stands near, gives to even inexperienced men the courage not to seek to avoid the inevitable. (*Letters* 30, 8)

And he finally concludes about the admirable Bassus:

> He says that it's as foolish to fear death as to fear old age, for death follows old age just as old age follows youth. He who does not wish to die can't have wished to live, for life is granted to us with the condition that we'll die. To this end our path leads. Therefore, how foolish it is to fear it, since men simply await what's sure, but fear what's uncertain. Death has its fixed rule, fair and unavoidable. Who can complain when he's governed by terms that include everyone else? (*Letters* 30, 10–11)

Bassus does have a lot of wisdom, but in this last report from Seneca, he clearly equivocates on the concept of uncertainty, which is to say he uses it in two different ways. He says that we naturally fear what's uncertain, but that death is unavoidable and therefore certain, so we should not fear it but merely await it. The fallacy of equivocation here is that while the occurrence of death is certain, its actual nature is not. And that amply allows for us to have a reasonable fear that it will involve harm of the most serious kind.

TIP

And yet, old Bassus and his exemplary attitudes lead us to a deep thought. What if the Logos is extremely clever, as would be expected? And so, God gave us opposites together, granting life on the condition of death, as an unavoidable certainty, in the sense that it definitely will happen. Even if the tech guys in Silicon Valley figure out a way to upload themselves into the cloud and improbably share that with the rest of us, the sun will burn out, and either an eventual cosmic conflagration will eliminate all suns and clouds, or the alternative of a heat death entropy flattened universe will have the same result of cessation for all. So, in this phase of life, or the existence we have in this universe, death is unavoidable. Well, then, what good is worry? What use is it? What job will fear do? It's not as if those negative attitudes will give us the alertness, focus, and creativity to figure out an avoidance strategy. And nothing else of positive value would seem to result. Perhaps death is a built-in unavoidable precisely to habituate us to an ultimate form of acceptance. And if we can learn to accept that great approaching mystery, then we can learn to accept and be courageous before all of life's other and lesser challenges. That's the thing with Stoic perspectives, as well as with adversities or challenges and, for that matter, opportunities: It's up to us how we use them. And when we learn to use them well, perhaps then indeed, all is well.

In a *Fragment*, Epictetus said:

> If a man endeavors to incline his mind to these things and to convince himself to accept of his own accord what necessarily must happen to him, he will have a very reasonable and harmonious life. (*Fragment* 8)

REMEMBER

Contemporary public philosopher and author Brian Johnson likes to talk about going from theory to practice to mastery. Perhaps a properly Stoic attitude toward death is a matter ultimately of more than theory and argument, but of habituation, of what Seneca calls a practice, a way of thinking, feeling, and acting cultivated over time, perhaps with difficulty for a while, but then with more ease as the habits settle in and become a part of us. The ultimate result will then be one of mastery, and that involves our beliefs, attitudes, and emotions in a highly elevated and settled state, poised to help us to live our best earthly lives in every moment. The Stoics hope to start us on the way but can't promise that they'll lead us the entire distance we need to go. That will largely be up to us, as it should be, from a Stoic point of view.

5

Stoic Virtues

Contemplate the four master virtues, which are so important in ancient thought and in today's world.

Learn to be more emotionally resilient and at peace in a turbulent world.

Chapter **17**

The Master Virtues

The Stoics believed, along with many other ancient philosophers, that there are master virtues, and that if you can master those masters, you're well on your way to the best possible life. As we saw in Chapter 8, they were convinced that virtue overall is the goal or "final end" of human life, a view that had been put forward by their predecessors the Cynics and that found clear echoes in the moral teaching of Socrates.

For the Stoics, virtue is not merely a good or even the highest good, but the only true good. It's the be-all and end-all of human existence. Those who have virtue have perfect wisdom and perfect happiness and live a blessed life akin to the gods. Those who lack virtue are miserable and vicious and even "mad" according to some of the older Stoics. In this chapter, we explore the Stoic view of virtue more fully. What is it, exactly? How did the Stoics think of it? Which virtues did they see as most important, and why? Let's begin by delving into the somewhat old-fashioned-sounding notion of virtue.

The Nature of Virtue

One of the big obstacles to explaining Stoicism today stems from the vitally important and central idea of virtue. As noted in Chapter 8, to modern ears, talk of virtue smacks of Victorian prudery and a kind of rigid moral uptightness. Such connotations are quite foreign to Stoicism. As we saw earlier, Zeno and

Chrysippus defended incest, "a community of wives," sex with any willing teen, and argued quite impractically in an ideal state no one would wear clothing that fully conceals any part of the body (Long and Sedley, *The Hellenistic Philosophers*, section 67). In general, the early ancient Stoics were far from being prudes and tended toward a more Cynic and opposite extreme.

Arete, or excellence

As explained earlier, the English word "virtue" is derived from the Latin word *virtus* that was used to translate the Greek *arete*, which means "excellence." So, when the ancient Stoics spoke of virtue, they weren't thinking of modern notions of chastity, clean living, and the like, but what it means to be an excellent human being living an excellent life. To understand Stoic teaching on virtue, we then need to understand what the Greeks more generally meant by *arete*.

WARNING

As classical scholar Tad Brennan explains, the Greeks spoke of *arete* (excellence) in three different but related senses. One applies to anything that can have any kind of distinctive excellence or good quality at all. So, Socrates notes (Plato, *Republic* 353b) that pruning knives have *arete* if they cut well, as they are designed to do. In a slightly broader sense, living things have *arete* if they have qualities that perfect their natures and lead them to their natural ends, as swiftness is an excellence in cheetahs and keen eyesight is an excellence in eagles. Finally, humans have *arete* if we have character traits such as courage, self-control, and honesty that are essential to being good moral persons and living excellent and fulfilling lives. Cicero is thinking of these latter two senses of virtue when he says that "virtue is nothing other than nature, brought to perfection and developed to the highest extent." Since virtue, for the Stoics, consists in following nature, and since humans are by nature rational animals, virtue is perfected rationality.

Good habits

Aristotle famously describes the virtues as good *habits*, that is, as stable acquired dispositions that make a person good. This is true of most human virtues. We don't speak of a person as being generous, for example, unless they consistently display generosity, and not just on rare occasions. But not all human excellences are habits. Having healthy teeth and attractive hair are excellences but not habits in the sense of acquired settled dispositions. Still, most of the qualities that we usually think of as distinctive virtues, such as kindness, humility, trustworthiness, and courage, meet Aristotle's definition of habits, or settled dispositions, that make one good.

Usually, when we think of virtues, we think of *moral* virtues, like justice, honesty, and generosity. But as Aristotle points out, there are intellectual virtues — good habits of the mind or intellect — as well as moral ones. Important intellectual virtues include open-mindedness, curiosity, love of truth, intellectual humility, attentiveness, "logicalness" (a propensity to reason logically), and intellectual persistence. Intellectual virtues are habits that help us think and learn well, whereas moral virtues are habits that help us to be good and live well.

The Stoic View of Virtue

In developing their own view of virtue, the Stoics drew heavily from prior thinkers such as Diogenes, Socrates, Plato, and Aristotle, but they also added many distinctive twists of their own.

From the Cynics

Drawing from the Cynic philosophers, the Stoics took these ideas:

>> **Virtue is the only true good.** Though Stoics believed that nonmoral goods such as life, health, knowledge, and good friends have value, they are not strictly good. As they saw it, nothing is truly and strictly good unless it always and unconditionally benefits its possessor and can never be possessed by a bad person. Only moral virtue, they argued, meets these two conditions. Moral virtue is thus the only true good.

>> **Virtue is sufficient for happiness.** Contrary to most Greek thinkers (as we report in some detail in Chapter 10), the Stoics held that nothing is needed for complete happiness or peak well-being except virtue. Virtue, in fact, is the sole component of and contributor to human happiness.

>> **Virtue consists in "following nature."** As we've seen, the Cynics were back-to-nature types who taught that civilization is corrupting and that we should "live naturally," in the sense of rejecting all human conventions and enjoying simple lives of virtue, independence, and self-sufficiency. The Stoics agreed that we should "follow nature," but in a very different way. They believed that humans are essentially rational animals. Our good, therefore, consists in living rationally, not in sleeping on the ground or having sex just anywhere outdoors like wild animals. Since the Stoics were also deeply religious, they held that "following nature" was equivalent to "following God," the one absolutely perfect being, who the Stoics saw as the source of moral law. This is why Epictetus says that "in all that he says and does, [one] must act in imitation of God" (*Discourses* 2.13).

From Socrates

Then drawing from Socrates, the Stoics borrowed these ideas:

» **Virtue is a form of knowledge.** Socrates taught that anyone who truly and deeply knows what is good will always do what is good. Everyone naturally and unavoidably desires what will benefit them as a good thing or increase their well-being. Nothing but virtue contributes (greatly) to well-being. So, anyone who truly understands what is virtuous will automatically do what is virtuous. Any wrongdoing that may appear to be due to "weakness of will" is thus really because of ignorance. Though people are still responsible for their actions, all wrongdoing is strictly involuntary, since, according to both Socrates and the Stoics, nobody acts contrary to what they truly believe to be in their own interest.

» **No harm can come to a good person.** At his trial, Socrates famously said that "no harm can come to a good person, either in this life or the next one." As we noted in Chapter 2, he believed this because he held that nothing can truly harm a person except moral or spiritual damage to the soul, which a good person would never permit. The Stoics fully agreed with Socrates on this point. The only evil, they held, was moral wickedness, and a completely good person would never sacrifice their virtue for any reason. We may naturally ask: What of *involuntary* loss of virtue, due to senility, a stroke, brainwashing, or some other cause that impairs moral reasoning and deliberation? Curiously, the Stoics seem not to have given much thought to this possibility, though Chrysippus did concede that virtue could be lost due to intoxication or "an excess of black bile," that is, a deep depression due to biological causes. It may be that they believed that only actual wrongdoing, and not loss of virtue as such, was strictly bad, though this is hard to reconcile with their claim that virtue is the sole good and trumps all other forms of value. If virtue can be lost by means of a stroke or other involuntary causes, it is not fully within one's control, contrary to what Epictetus and other Stoic thinkers claim.

Stoic paradoxes relating to virtue

Aside from these borrowings, the Stoics added a number of their own distinctive teachings on virtue. These included some bold and hard-to-swallow claims known as "Stoic paradoxes." Three of the most striking Stoic paradoxes regarding virtue are:

» **Virtue and vice do not come in degrees.** Just as a line is either straight or not straight, the Stoics believed that an act is either virtuous (i.e., fully virtuous) or it is not. All sins or misdeeds are equal in moral gravity because they all involve an intention to deviate from the law of right reason and share the crucial attribute "not completely virtuous." And the same absolutism applies to people. You can't be more or less virtuous. You can't be a little virtuous and in the process of growing in virtue, since it does not have degrees. You either are completely virtuous or you aren't virtuous at all, and in fact are completely wicked. According to the Stoics, those who lack perfect virtue are wholly vicious, lack all virtues, and possess all vices (plus the nonmoral defect of being mad). In their view, there is no middle ground. But then, oddly and also paradoxically, the Stoics do seem to allow that there can be moral progress, so that one person can be closer to achieving virtue than another, while still sadly being wholly vicious. The progress they make is thus not progress *in* virtue, since virtue does not come in degrees, but progress *toward* virtue. Being virtuous is thus a bit like switching on a light. One person may be closer to the light switch than another, but until the light is switched on, the room is still dark. Unlike with horseshoes and hand grenades, close is not good enough when it comes to virtue.

» **He who has one virtue has them all.** This is what ethicists call "the unity of virtue thesis." Socrates, Plato, and Aristotle all defended it in one form or another. On its face, the thesis seems implausible. We've all known people who seem to possess one virtue (e.g., honesty) but appear to lack another (e.g., sensitivity). The Stoics, however, believed that perfect virtue requires a deep, firm, and fully accurate knowledge of what is good and bad, beneficial or harmful. All individual virtues presuppose such knowledge, and anyone who possesses this kind of understanding will have all the virtues. Virtue is knowledge; the wise possess all relevant knowledge of what relates to virtue; and so, the wise possess all virtues. Thus, when an individual seems to have one virtue and lack another, appearances are deceptive in one way or another. Perhaps the apparent virtue is merely a counterfeit and not the real thing. Or the seeming lack of virtue is based on a misunderstanding on our part. On the unity thesis, it's always a full package deal. Since, for Stoics, only Sages possess all the virtues and Sages are extremely rare, the unity thesis implies that there is very little actual virtue in the world, only the appearance of such.

REMEMBER

Modern Stoics generally reject or ignore most of the classic Stoic paradoxes. Many of the paradoxes depend on parts of Stoic teaching that were not universally accepted even in ancient times, and today such claims are often seen as exaggerated or extreme.

The Four Cardinal Virtues

Following Plato, the Stoics identified four primary virtues that they believed lie at the root of all morality. In medieval times, these virtues came to be called "cardinal virtues" (from the Latin *cardo*, or "hinge") because they were seen as fundamental, and all the other virtues were thought to depend on them. The four cardinal virtues are courage ("fortitude"), self-control ("temperance" or "moderation"), justice, and practical wisdom ("prudence"). Let's consider them in that order.

Courage

As the French philosopher André Comte-Sponville has remarked, courage is the most universally admired virtue. Historically, all cultures have praised the brave and condemned the cowardly. From Homer's *Iliad* and Virgil's *Aeneid* to J.R.R. Tolkien's *Lord of the Rings* and J. K. Rowling's *Harry Potter* novels, courage has been a persistent theme of great literature. Of course, this virtue has different facets or modes of presentation. Courage can take many forms. We speak, for example, of physical courage, moral courage, intellectual courage, emotional courage, and so forth. But what do these various forms of courage have in common? What is courage, exactly?

Modern Stoic Ryan Holiday has suggested memorably that courage is "laying your ass on the line," but this seems overly broad, which is understandable, since in the passage quoted, he doesn't seem to be trying to define it as much as to recommend it. As Aristotle notes in more of a spirit of definition, courage is a kind of mean or midpoint between two opposite vices: cowardice and rashness. Both rashness and courage seem to involve "laying your ass on the line." But this is a virtue only when it involves the *proper* management, control, and overcoming of fear and risk, which is to say, when it doesn't shade into rashness, foolhardiness, or impetuosity. Since fear is one of the strongest human emotions and self-preservation is one of our most powerful instincts, we greatly admire those who, at real personal risk, act courageously for the good of others.

A woodcarver has a skill that can be seen as a form of practical knowledge. So does a potter. She knows how to make beautiful pots. The doing cannot be separated from a knowing. A wisdom is involved. Following Socrates, the Stoics saw all virtues as forms of knowledge or practical wisdom. They defined justice, for example, as the knowledge (or "science") concerned with properly distributing individual deserts (Long and Sedley, *The Hellenistic Philosophers*, section 61). In a similar way, they defined courage as the knowledge or science of "things that are fearful and not fearful and neither of these (ibid.). Unlike Aristotle, who saw courage as exemplified primarily in warfare, the Stoics defined it more broadly. According to Cicero, courage is displayed in both "indifference to outward circumstances" and in the performance of "deeds not only great and in the highest degree useful, but extremely arduous and laborious and fraught with danger" (*On Duties* 1.66). It then includes a knowledge of what must be uncomplainingly endured as well as an understanding of how to manage and overcome fears for the sake of important ends. So courage in this broader conception may shade into elements of persistence, determination, and grit.

It's important to remember that virtues are typically dispositions to think and act in a certain way, and not simply emotions or feelings that you have. Many courageous people will report after their heroic deed that they didn't feel particularly brave or heroic, but that they just saw what needed to be done and got busy doing it, regardless of the threat or danger they faced. To onlookers, the main feature of the situation might have been its danger and the fear that could produce, but to the courageous person who took action, the most significant fact is often that something had to be done. A value was at stake and, accordingly, someone or something had to be respected, preserved, or saved in order to honor that value.

One reason for seeing courage as a basic or cardinal virtue is that it seems to enter into the exercise of all the other virtues. Doing what is just, for example, often requires great courage. It's also frequently needed to control one's emotions and appetites, and thus act "temperately," in situations where there might be powerful social pressure to do the opposite. Most difficult and worthwhile things in life involve risk, and consequently the courage to face and surmount those risks.

WARNING

Courage has one feature that seems to make it an awkward fit in the Stoic catalogue of virtues: It's a trait that seemingly can be possessed by bad people as well as good people. Corrupt people can boldly do bad things. This creates a problem for Stoic ethics because of the strict Stoic definition of "good." As we have seen, classic Stoics refuse to count anything as good unless (1) it unconditionally benefits its possessor and (2) it can never be possessed by a bad person. Courage can seem to fail both these two conditions. In reply to the second point, Stoics would likely appeal to their doctrine of the unity of virtue. If having one virtue implies having them all, then a bad person, despite appearances, cannot be truly courageous but at most can display a convincing counterfeit of the virtue that's never the real thing. And in reply to the first point, Stoics would say that the virtue of courage does benefit a person in all possible circumstances, despite any superficial appearances to the contrary, because the possession of courage entails a possession of complete virtue, which for Stoicism is the sole good and the goal of life. Likewise, a bad person can never be truly courageous because if they were, they would have all the virtues, and so would not, in fact, be bad.

REMEMBER

Stoicism overall demands great emotional control, a commitment to the common good over personal gain, and a strong devotion to virtue above all other ends. As such, the practice of Stoicism requires real ethical and psychological fortitude.

CATO THE YOUNGER: STOIC MODEL OF COURAGE

One of the most admired Roman Stoics was Cato the Younger (95–43 BCE), also known as Cato of Utica. Born into a distinguished family, Cato became a Stoic at a young age and had a distinguished political career, along with a reputation for total honesty and integrity. In an age of declining morals and growing threats to Roman freedom, Cato stood like a rock for traditional Roman values and the preservation of the Roman Republic. When Caesar was on the verge of overthrowing the Republic and becoming a dictator, Cato opposed him to the bitter end.

On the final night of his life, when he and his troops were hopelessly besieged by Caesar's legionnaires in the North African city of Utica, Cato threw a dinner party for his friends where they discussed the Stoic maxim that only the wise are free. After the party, Cato twice read Plato's *Phaedo*, a dialogue in which Socrates discusses his hopes for an afterlife just hours before he was forced to commit suicide. After taking his sword from a reluctant servant, Cato declared, "Now I am my own master." Toward dawn, he stabbed himself in the abdomen. When Cato awoke to find that a doctor had sewn up his wounds, he ripped out the stiches (grossness warning), pulled out his guts, and died. As the great French essayist Michel de Montaigne said of him, Cato "had to die rather than look on the face of a tyrant."

Self-control

One of the things the early Stoics most admired about Socrates was his amazing ability to control his emotions and physical appetites. Socrates was never known to become angry, display fear, get drunk, or indulge base desires at the expense of reason and moral goodness. He led an extremely self-disciplined life, focused entirely on what he termed "care of the soul" and gave no personal consideration to wealth, fame, power, or most other worldly values.

Today, many therapists and life coaches report that the two biggest challenges their clients face are (1) self-awareness and (2) self-management, the latter of which is just another term for the ancient virtue of self-control. If you think about it, a huge portion of the world's problems — and perhaps many of the difficulties in your own life — stem from a lack of self-knowledge or self-control. How much better off we'd all be if we just had a little more self-discipline and impulse control! And yet, it's a bit of a paradox for the Stoics to have named self-control as a needed virtue, since we typically think of it as a good thing only in contrast with weakness of will, which Stoics reject as a reality in our lives.

Remember that in the Stoic view of human nature, there aren't any unruly, irrational parts of us (desire, emotion, the Freudian unconscious, etc.) vying with reason for influence over our behavior. Vice, or bad thought and action, is supposed to result only from ignorance and not from any form of weakness of will (*akrasia*) that tempts us away from what we know to be right and that needs to be shut down by reason exercising firm temperance and self-control.

So, on Stoic theory, where exactly is self-control needed? What is its use? Perhaps a classic Stoic would say that we need a measure of self-control to resist deceptive impressions about what is good and desirable, and that we then need self-discipline in order to pay attention to what reason shows us to be true and right, and then to remember it so that we'll always act in accordance with what we properly know to be in our own best interest. On this view, the virtue of self-discipline isn't needed to wrestle us away from our own irrational inclinations, but rather to resist the world's many illusory appearances about what is truly good, and then to persist in a commitment to what we've come to realize.

The strangeness here is that in most views of self-control, this virtue has to do with things like emotions and strong desires but not primarily with our interpretations of how the world appears to us. Perhaps, though, this is where all self-control really begins. But however well or poorly this virtue is explained by classic Stoic theory, and however similar or different it might be on their various views, it is embraced by all as a vital good for us all. And the Stoics are certainly right about that. As the great German philosopher Immanuel Kant (1724–1804) said, "Without disciplining his inclinations man can attain to nothing. Therefore, in self-mastery there resides an immediate worth, for to be lord of oneself is to be independent of all things."

In fact, Stoicism demands an unusual degree of self-mastery because it rejects many human feelings and values that are widely considered normal or natural. Stoics totally reject such common emotions as anger, hatred, fear, envy, jealousy, pity, mercy, lust, sadness, disappointment, frustration, grief, and sorrow. They deny that we should care deeply about "externals" such as health, physical appearance, possessions, reputation, or career success. They even tend to deny that we should feel upset at the loss of a loved one (Epictetus, *Handbook* 3; Seneca, *Letters* 74) or at the reception of any sort of bad news (Epictetus, *Discourses* 3.18). Their ideal was one of perfected rationality and godlike imperturbability that regards nothing but moral goodness and wisdom as actually having high value or being of great concern. They favor what the philosopher Nietzsche would in his own way call a radical "transvaluation of values." It's easy to see, then, why Stoics would view self-control as central to virtue and the good life. For without it, we become prey to all sorts of irrational and upsetting impulses and become incapable of imitating the rock-like virtue of Socrates and the unruffled serenity of the gods. It's a tall task, but as Cicero says: "The greater the difficulty, the greater the glory."

Justice

Together, the virtues of courage and self-control might be said to be the master virtues of our own soul's "domestic affairs," that is, the proper management and direction of our interior selves. For the Stoics, justice is the master virtue of "foreign affairs," that is, our conduct toward others. They defined justice as giving each person their "due," that is, treating them as they deserve (Cicero, *On Duties* 1.5; Stobaeus, *Anthology* 5b5), a definition that was later enshrined in Roman law. Justice requires keeping our promises, paying our debts, treating others with respect and dignity, recognizing their merits, distributing benefits and burdens fairly and equitably, and respecting other people's rights. More broadly, it requires treating people as they deserve, which, of course, isn't always easy to discern.

How much punishment does a typical bank embezzler deserve? Which job applicant deserves the job? Which college applicant deserves to be admitted? What grade should a student get on a class presentation? Who deserves to win the talent show? What would a just immigration policy involve? What would a fully just society be like? These are, or can be, hard questions because moral desert is often difficult to ascertain or calibrate, and people disagree about what kinds of distributions and treatments are "due." This may be one reason why the Stoics believed that Sages are so rare. Sages, by definition, have complete virtue, including perfect justice and infallible judgment. They never make mistakes or draw erroneous conclusions. In fact, all their actions are fully virtuous and morally correct. Everything Sages do is a "right action" (*katorthoma*), even the seemingly neutral acts of brushing their teeth or picking up a pebble (Long and Sedley, *The Hellenistic Philosophers*, p. 365). Treating everyone along the way and all one's fellow citizens with perfect justice would seem to require an almost godlike knowledge of the proper bases of desert, which few if any of us can claim. That many of the ancient Stoics, as smart and attuned to moral issues as they might have been, yet believed that slavery, sexism, the killing of unwanted babies, a father's near-absolute authority over his wife and children, and imperial conquest and colonization were just and fair should teach us a good measure of humility in our own judgments of what people are "due." Justice is one of many ideals that is as difficult at some times to apply as it is important at all times to seek.

TIP

Justice is in a sense about deep agreement or harmony in our actions and lives, a harmony with the most fundamental structures of rationality and benevolence. It's not a mere fairness fantasy cooked up by powerless people to impose on the powerful, as some critics of morality maintain. Justice is meant to connect in small and large ways with the deep structure of things. And it's crucially related to human well-being and happiness.

Wisdom

The last cardinal virtue is practical wisdom (or "prudence"). Aristotle helpfully distinguishes between theoretical wisdom, which focuses on the pursuit of truth for truth's sake, and practical wisdom, which focuses on how we can live and act well. Some thinkers, such as Aristotle and the great medieval philosopher Thomas Aquinas (c. 1225–1274) define practical wisdom relatively narrowly as a kind of means-end rationality. On this view, practical wisdom is not concerned with what our goals are or should be (which we derive from other sources, such as virtue or divine revelation) but only with intelligent, efficient, and proper ways to achieve our goals. The Stoics, however, seem to have conceived practical wisdom more broadly, defining it as "knowledge of which things are good and bad and neither" (Diogenes Laertius, *Lives* 7.92), which can be thought to imply a knowledge of correct goals as well as sound and effective means to achieve those ends.

For Stoics, then, practical wisdom involves a firm and deep grasp of what things are truly good (namely, virtues and virtuous acts), what things are bad (namely, vices and vicious acts), and what things are neither good nor bad (everything else). Since the Stoics believed that some indifferent things also have "selective" value or disvalue, practical wisdom must also relate to them, since as Cicero points out (*On Moral Ends* 3.12), so much of life is rightly concerned with matters of health, work, leisure, family, friends, avoidance of pain, and other things that the Stoics considered neither strictly good nor strictly bad. A person of practical wisdom (the *phronimos*) will be skilled at not only pursuing what is truly good and avoiding what is truly bad, but at wisely and ethically dealing with other things in life that have any legitimate form of positive and negative value.

Can we be more specific about what a practically wise person would know and be able to do? The late and influential Harvard philosopher Robert Nozick offered a helpful general summary:

> What a wise person needs to know and understand constitutes a varied list: the most important goals and values of life — the ultimate goal, if there is one; what means will reach these goals without too great a cost; what kinds of dangers threaten the achieving of these goals; how to recognize and avoid or minimize these dangers; what different types of human beings are like in their actions and motives (as this presents dangers or opportunities); what is not possible or feasible to achieve (or avoid); how to tell what is appropriate when; knowing when certain goals are sufficiently achieved; what limitations are unavoidable and how to accept them; how to improve oneself and one's relationships with others or society; knowing what the true and unapparent value of various things is; when to take a long-term view; knowing the variety and obduracy of facts, institutions, and human nature; understanding what one's real motives are; how to cope and deal with the major tragedies and dilemmas of life, and with the major good things too. (Nozick, *The Examined Life*, p. 269)

In short, practical wisdom or prudence requires perspective, deep insights into the human condition, a clear sense of what is important in life, and a deep grasp of what is needed to live a good and fulfilling life.

The noted literary scholar and popular Christian writer C. S. Lewis defines practical wisdom as "practical common sense, taking the trouble to think out what you are doing and what is likely to come of it." As such, the acquisition of practical wisdom seems to require a good deal of mature thought and wide experience; predicting what is "likely to come of" one's actions is no simple business, as stock market pros and quite a few disgraced politicians can attest! This is likely one reason why the Stoics denied that young children can possess any virtues, or moral responsibility (Seneca, *Letters* 124) until they reach "the age of reason" at about age fourteen. Here the Stoics seem to have underrated the ability of children to grasp basic concepts of right and wrong and possess at least a rudimentary form of practical wisdom. A great many children, at quite a young age, seem to display an innate sense of fairness and unfairness, both in their complaints about the behavior of peers, and in their occasional heartwarming acts of affection to others.

Evaluating the four cardinal virtues

Of the four cardinal virtues, which is the most important? Cicero argued that justice is "the most glorious and splendid of all the virtues," since it is the cement that holds society together and permits us to enjoy the fruits of civilized life. A strong case can be made, however, for seeing practical wisdom as the fundamental virtue, because in a way it includes all the other virtues. As the knowledge of living and acting well, and of knowing what is good, bad, and different, the virtue of practical wisdom presumably includes an understanding of how to act justly, temperately, and courageously, as the early Stoics reportedly maintained. As noted earlier, Zeno, in the spirit of Socrates' dictum that virtue is knowledge, taught that all virtues are ultimately forms of prudence or practical wisdom. Justice, for example, is wisdom about deserved distributions, courage is wisdom about which things should be feared or endured, and self-control is wisdom about matters requiring choice about which desires, pleasures, and so forth are truly worth pursuing. As the most general and inclusive virtue, practical wisdom would seem to have a kind of primacy among the cardinal virtues. Without wisdom to know what is just, temperate, and courageous, ethical life would be largely blind.

The Stoics considered the four cardinal virtues the most basic virtues and the beating heart of morality. Are they? Can a persuasive case be made that, say, love, or kindness, or caring, or benevolence, or reciprocity might be equally or more fundamental? Inquiring minds want to know! What do you think?

Chapter **18**

Finding Resilience and Inner Peace

I n addition to the four cardinal virtues of prudence, courage, justice, and self-control that the Stoics thought should form and structure a good life, they recognized and sought to cultivate many other virtues, including resilience, inner calm, acceptance, kindness, dutifulness, considerateness, public spiritedness, and piety, to mention a few. The virtues are those strengths of mind and heart that enhance your life, raise your game, and support your happiness or well-being amid all the challenges, opportunities, and even struggles of life.

In this chapter, we focus on resilience and inner peace. We look at a wealth of Stoic techniques for bouncing back from hard knocks and maintaining inner calm. Such techniques lie at the core of Stoicism as a practical philosophy of life. As we have seen in earlier chapters, ancient Stoics saw philosophy as a way of life, not merely a body of theoretical teachings. Stoic schools were regarded as doctor's clinics for ailments of the soul, with therapies for the treatment of negative and unhealthy passions. They were places for training self-discipline, not merely for transmitting information. All Stoic teaching was ultimately aimed at the achievement of virtue, wisdom, and enduring serenity.

To that end, the ancient Stoics worked out a host of spiritual or psychological practices that Stoics still use today. Arrayed together and deployed as needed, they function as something almost like mixed martial arts for the mind. In this chapter, we lay out some of the most powerful of those practices.

Resilience: The Art of Bouncing Back

Resilience is the ability to withstand or recover quickly from hardships or difficulties. A rubber ball is resilient because it rapidly springs back into its original shape after being pressed or squeezed. A highly resilient person is able to bounce back rapidly from disappointment, fright, anxiety, trauma, grief, or any form of emotional upset and regain both composure and psychological equilibrium. As Seneca and Marcus Aurelius both noted, resilient individuals are even able to gain inner strength through adversity, becoming better, stronger, and more confident by treating their challenges as opportunities for growth. Let's look at a few key Stoic resilience-building practices.

Live in the present moment

As Marcus Aurelius reminds us, "each of us lives in the present moment" (*Meditations* 3.10). Often when we feel unhappy or distressed, we can find on examination that it's rooted in painful feelings about the past or worries about the future. In the blur and busyness of everyday life, we too often forget that life is a miracle and that there is joy in the simple acts of breathing, walking, listening to the laughter of children, and feeling the sun and wind on our faces. The past is a memory, and the future is yet to be born. All that we have is now. To find calmness and recenter ourselves often requires nothing more than bracketing off fretful thoughts of the past or future and finding stillness and contentment in the present moment.

TIP

The technique here could not be simpler. Whenever you find yourself upset, worried, or distressed about anything, ask yourself whether your thoughts and feelings are dwelling in the present, past, or future. If it's something from the past, whether distant, or yesterday, or five minutes ago, pull yourself back into the now, into the fresh moment of the present. Release that past event or situation. Choose instead to embrace a new beginning now.

The same is true if you're worried about something five minutes from now, tomorrow, next month, or next year. Take note of the source of that concern, and then remind yourself that the future is sufficiently elusive as not likely to conform to our worries. Each new moment produces new possibilities for coping with any difficulty, and new resources could come your way at any time. Worry assumes it knows more than it can. Pull your heart and mind back from those times yet to come and call yourself back to the present, which is usually calmer and less anxious than the hypothetical futures we fret about. Breathe. Relax your soul.

REMEMBER

You can certainly plan for the future and learn from the past, but you can never do either very well when you're worked up with troubling emotions. Allow them to dissipate first and then you can tackle whatever you do need to think about from other times. But it's more likely that you can engage in this productively when you're emotionally well anchored in the inner peace that the present moment allows. There is a deep sense in which resilience exists only in the present moment.

Adopt the view from above

Stoics stress the importance of keeping things in perspective. When we find ourselves upset, frequently it's because of little things that we'll later realize won't matter at all a year from now, or perhaps even next week. We blow things up, or "catastrophize" them, as modern psychologists say. We make them seem much bigger and more important than they are. This may be an exaggerated distortion of a natural tendency that has evolutionary survival value when it operates properly. We're sensitive to the negative, to threats and dangers, and precisely so we can avoid them. But as descendants of ancestors who often lived on the edge of survival with too few resources, we often have in the back of our minds a "more is better" mentality. When this operates in modern life, that assumption easily leads to a fever of acquisition and hoarding. And it can also function to distort our natural early warning system. If to be vigilant is good, we assume that to be hypervigilant is better. If something looks bad, we assume that it's worse than it seems. That way, we can be better protected, we think. And we're more often wrong than right. As a result, we live with needless and, ironically, self-defeating stress.

To combat this lack of proper and accurate perspective, Stoics often recommend a kind of mental exercise called "the view from above." Suppose you're commuting to work, or just going to the grocery store in your car, and you encounter a rude driver. At the moment, as you seethe with shock, irritation, and then resentment, it feels like a big deal. But is it? No.

TIP

Try looking at the situation from a larger perspective. Imagine yourself floating high above the earth, looking down at yourself in traffic. From that vantage point, you seem like an ant, scuttling along like countless others. Rude drivers are not a major disturbance in the Force, and in a day or two you will forget the whole thing. So, why wait? Let it go now.

We do ourselves no favor by allowing our day to get ruined by such small matters. Tell yourself just to forget it. The other driver may be upset at bad news, or hurrying to the hospital, oblivious to others. They may not have seen you, distracted by a very difficult high-pressure situation at work, or a sudden personal disappointment, or else too little sleep last night. We're offended because we see their behavior as directed at us, and that may not be what's going on at all. We may not even be on their radar. And even if they are being a jerk, what's the importance of that in the sweep of space and time? Jerks will be jerky. Why should you expect anything different? Amid the infinities and immensities, it should make us smile if it affects us at all. And we can just remind ourselves that we are also often insufficiently attuned to the implications of our behaviors for other people, even those who are close to us. Maybe we just need to give the bad driver a break.

Having reframed an initially distressing situation, we can recover emotionally and regain our inner balance, poise, and peace. We should remind ourselves that those who go through the world highly vulnerable to upset have a weakness and not a strength for dealing with the ups and downs of life. We need not be among their number. We can rise above it with inner equilibrium.

Look at the situation objectively

We are quick to make negative value judgments. Our car gets dented in a parking lot and we viscerally shudder with panic or outrage and immediately think, "That's terrible. How can this happen to me? Who did this and didn't leave a note? This was clearly a person with no moral compass, or an idiot who has no care about the damage they're doing. The world is full of hideous people. I can't afford this now. I don't have the time or the money for this." Or we call a customer service line and get put on hold for the longest hour of our lives and think, "This is just stupid. It's awful. So unnecessary. So totally insensitive. Completely unprofessional. These people do not respect my time at all. I'm nothing to them. Me — the one who helps pay their salaries! Who do they think they are to treat me like this? It's a monstrous insult. I'm going to give somebody a piece of my mind." We tense up. We fume within. As the instant critics of others, we're hardly living our own best lives in the moment.

Stoics believe that this constant tendency to project rash value judgments onto the world is a prime source of dissatisfaction. Something happens and we rush to judgment, adding our own assessments that often go far beyond what's immediately before us. We think, "This is horrible!" Or "This is amazing!" We say, "This is the best thing ever!" Or "This is the worst thing possible!"

The Stoics urge us to combat this tendency by adopting a strategy the French classical scholar Pierre Hadot calls "objective representation." In objective representation, we view events simply as value-neutral happenings in the world and separate out any value judgments (pro or con) that we instantly may be inclined to impose on those events. So, the objective representation "my car got dented" is better in the moment because it simply describes what actually happened, and

"That's terrible" is my superimposed value judgment on the event. For Stoics, nothing is terrible except immoral thought or choice, and we risk imposing that harm on ourselves when we run beyond the objective situation that's available to us and begin harshly judging others or our fate. We cause ourselves all kinds of unnecessary mental distress and act irrationally by making rash and false value judgments about the world.

The classic Stoics would tell us to "stick with impressions" or what we actually perceive. We need to pull ourselves back from any value judgments we might be adding to the situation, which Stoics believe are often wrong and unwarranted. We judge countless things to be "bad," without reflecting that only immorality is bad, and that no one does wrong willingly. We also pronounce things to be "good" without realizing that only virtue is good and that virtue (by which the Stoics meant complete virtue) does not often exist in this flawed world.

We should realize how easily we rush to judgment, notice it when we're starting to do it, and call ourselves back to an objective representation of what's before us.

Cut people some slack

Feelings of anger and resentment toward others who we believe have wronged us are a prime source of mental discontent. Harboring such feelings requires a great deal of negative energy. The Stoics believed that everyone, deep down, wants to be good. Everyone does in the moment what they think to be good, whether they're right about that or wrong. But nobody wants to be wrong. So, if they are, they're suffering that condition, and are not likely to be just doing so perversely. Those who offend us are mistaken about where their true good lies. Understanding this can help us overcome any feelings of anger and resentment we may be feeling and get us back on an even emotional keel.

When someone does something that offends us, we should always remember that they just did something, and we freely took offense. We need to release that sense of offense. Nobody can insult us entirely from their own power. For a real insult to happen, we have to give them that power. And why should we? Why not take it back? Remember how important it is in life to embrace and release wisely. It's the Stoic perspective that any insult, or any offense, should be released as soon as possible. Be resilient. Or better yet, be fine quality Teflon, never scratched in the first place.

With the right mindset, you can retain our peace, and so your power, in situations where others are losing theirs. But you need to be mindful of your first reactions. When you feel anger, or offense, cut it off that instant.

TIP

There's an old Stoic metaphor that helps. When you're walking slowly, it's easy to stop and change direction. But if you're running at top speed, it's impossible to just stop or radically change direction. A negative emotion just cropping up in your heart is walking. You can stop it and should. If you don't, it will quickly begin to run, and you will lose your immediate power over it. It will gain control of you and take you where it wants you to go. And that's not wise or desirable. It's not a source of strength.

Take a walk on the wild side

Often, the quickest way to calm a troubled mind is to step outdoors, breathe deeply, and take a walk. But of course, it's not recommended to take a meditative stroll on a busy thoroughfare, or the interstate, or a long walk off a short pier. Any stroll that's in nature is best, in a park, or even down a quiet street surrounded by trees and shrubs, birds, and a random squirrel, if you can find one. Hint: Be known to carry nuts. Numerous studies have found that a walk in beautiful surroundings can reduce stress, lower blood pressure, calm anxiety, elevate mood, and boost other measures of well-being.

Humans evolved as hunter-gatherers on the African plains and are built for walking long distances. As Aaron Sussman and Ruth Goode note in their book, *The Magic of Walking*, when we're in the flow of a good walk our brain waves change and something miraculous happens. "We become unconscious of weight, or of locomotion; we are aware only of rhythm. It is a sensation akin to swimming, in which the water bears our weight. To hit your stride is to discover a new sensation, the experience of moving as effortlessly as the deer bounds, the horse gallops, the fish swims, and the bird flies."

REMEMBER

When we go for a leisurely walk anywhere in nature that even remotely replicates a pastoral setting, we disconnect from the frenetic artificial world of concrete, steel, deadlines, Zoom meetings, and emails and reconnect with something fundamental and elemental. It can recharge and restore.

The main rivals of the Stoics, the Epicureans, may have gotten some things wrong, but they rightly set up camp outside of Athens in a beautiful place they called "The Garden," as if they knew that natural beauty is conducive to contemplation, wisdom, and the inner peace they saw as the peak of worldly pleasure. We each need time in nature every day to reconnect and recenter.

Keep Stoic basics ready to hand

As Seneca says, when tough times hit, it's good to own core Stoic teachings that have "gone deep and sunk in for a long time, and not merely colored but thoroughly permeated the soul" (*Letters* 70:30). We learn from the Stoics best when we're not just being instructed by them, or enlightened, but actually trained in new habits of thought, emotion, attitude, choice, and action. That's why we say to keep Stoic basics ready to hand, like the tools they're meant to be, and not just ready to mind, as if quick, clever slogans are all we need.

At times of great stress or temptation, it's easy for the intellect to be overwhelmed by desires or emotions that are rooted in our physical natures. As Aristotle noted, the only effective defense is to make virtuous action habitual, so that our wills are always strongly pre-aligned with what's good. This comes only from training, practice, and such a deep absorption of sound ethical teaching that it becomes second nature.

Suppose, for example, that someone grossly insults you. In our modern political moment, it happens. For a Stoic, it would not be proper to respond to this with anger, however "natural" such a reaction may seem. Though even a highly trained Stoic might react to such an affront with a momentary spasm of involuntary rage — a purely physical sensation that the Stoics called a "pre-passion" — he or she would quickly bring the emotion under control of the rational will and intellect. But to accomplish this, the person would need to be "permeated," as Seneca says, with Stoic teachings about the true nature of good and evil and the need to control disturbing passions such as anger and fear.

STOICISM AND MODERN PSYCHOLOGY

Two influential forms of modern cognitive psychotherapy — rational emotive behavior therapy (REBT), founded in the 1950s by Albert Ellis, and Cognitive Behavior Therapy (CBT), launched by Aaron Beck in the early 1960s — were influenced by Stoicism and harmonize with it on many points. Though they differ in some important ways, both rational emotive behavior therapy and cognitive therapy are based on the idea that psychological problems are caused by irrational thinking and can be alleviated by helping patients think and behave more rationally. For example, a neurotic patient might suffer from a tendency to "catastrophize" feared events, seeing them as far worse than they are. The goal of a rational emotive behavioral therapist or cognitive therapist is to help such a patient form more realistic attitudes, and thus to reduce anxiety and cope better with life. Another common irrational belief that leads to problems is the idea that we must be perfect in everything we do. Such an idea is unrealistic and causes people unnecessary distress.

Ancient Stoicism is similar to psychotherapies like cognitive behavioral therapy in stressing rationality, personal happiness, and the origins of psychological problems in poor thinking. It differs, however, in prioritizing virtue and in its doctrinal commitments to concepts like the Logos, fate, radical acceptance, and souls as fragments of the divine.

Soldiers drill, firefighters and other first responders train until virtue becomes habit and courage a way of being in the world. When we've been trained by good philosophy, wisdom gets inside us, almost within our DNA, and we don't have to consider at length how to act in a challenging situation, since the right actions will arise from the right thinking and feeling that have resulted from our training. This will then produce the emotional resilience from grasping Stoic teaching thoroughly and absorbing it deeply.

The Stoic Quest for Inner Peace

Modern Stoic William Irvine says that for him, Stoicism is centrally about the quest for the Stoics called *ataraxia*, or inner peace. For the ancient Stoics, however, tranquility was not the primary goal of life but both a facilitating condition and a proper side effect of virtue, which the Stoics held was the only true good. For Stoics, tranquility is not strictly good because it also can be possessed by a bad person (for instance, through a use of mood-altering drugs or meditation). Yet, the Stoics believed that gods and Sages enjoy perfect happiness, contentment, and imperturbability (what the Stoics might call "true tranquility"). They experience no discontent because they possess complete well-being, have no passions to disturb them, and know that we live in a universe in which everything happens for the best.

As Epictetus notes, from a Stoic point of view dissatisfaction is a form of impiety because it amounts to a kind of false accusation that God is mismanaging the universe (*Discourses* 1.39). For Stoics, the only legitimate form of discontent is discontent with our own lack of virtue, which is the only bad thing in the universe we can fully control. In the light of this, the Stoics developed a wide range of practices designed to promote mental tranquility and inner peace. For many modern Stoics, these practices are among the most helpful features of their philosophy. Let's take a look at a few of the most widely used in our time.

Anticipate possible adversities

While negativity of almost any sort is typically avoided by classic Stoics, there is one use of negative visualization they recommend as helpful. A Stoic aid for maintaining inner calm and virtue is to anticipate possible future hardships like poverty, illness, or failure as though they were occurring right now or certainly will in the future. Seneca calls this technique *praemeditatio malorum*, or premeditation of evils, though the Stoics are merely using a common expression here, since they did not regard things like poverty or sickness as literally evils. The thought behind the practice is that, as Seneca writes, "The blow of an evil foreseen comes softly" (*Letters* 76.34).

By anticipating things that can go wrong in the future, we can plan for such contingencies and prepare ourselves emotionally, as well as in other ways in advance of their occurrence, to meet them more effectively. On the contrary, when we blithely and unconsciously imagine that we are magically immune from rejection, sickness, job loss, a romantic breakup, or other adversities, such blows when they do come can fall hard. By reflecting in advance on how things like poverty and sickness and other such difficulties are not true evils but are rather only challenges that we have the internal resources to meet, we can face them with greater fortitude and confidence when they occur.

In this way, negative visualization is a form of mental training like what the military and others in dangerous jobs undertake to strengthen and position themselves well to deal with any adversity they may meet. Visualization engages the imagination. And the imagination seems to have a power over emotion, attitude, and action that the intellect alone lacks. Thus, to engage the imagination as well as the intellect can go a long way in such preparatory training. It's an exercise well worth using on a regular basis.

Practice morning and evening meditations

The Stoics also recommended a regular practice of morning and evening reflection as a form of spiritual discipline. For many, the morning meditation is aimed at fortifying ourselves to meet the challenges of the day. So, Marcus reminds himself of coming challenges when he writes:

> Say to yourself at daybreak: I shall come across the meddling busybody, the ungrateful, the overbearing, the treacherous, the envious, and the antisocial. (*Meditations* 2.1)

Here the emperor clearly is engaging in a *praemeditatio malorum*, anticipating the inevitable problems and annoyances he will face during the day and preparing himself to meet them well. This is an exercise intended only for the morning, before entering the challenges of the day. It doesn't require a detailed imagination of specific adversities but consists more in a mere listing of challenging possibilities the day may bring. It's a reminder for the heart and mind not to be surprised, but to take such things in stride.

The focus of the evening meditation is somewhat different. Seneca writes:

> When the light has been taken away and my wife has fallen silent, aware as she is of my habit, I examine my entire day, going through what I have done and have said. I conceal nothing from myself, I pass nothing by. (*On Anger* 3.36)

As this passage makes clear, the purpose of the evening Stoic meditation is not to anticipate future adversities, but to examine our recent activities and current conscience with moral improvement in mind. Each night, the Stoic would himself ask some questions about the day just lived through, such as:

>> What did I do wrong?

>> What did I do right?

>> What duty did I leave undone?

>> What progress did I make today?

>> What can I do better in the future?

By means of honest self-examination — and it has to be utterly honest — we can improve, day by day, and move closer to consistent virtue and the mental serenity that Stoics believe is a necessary side effect of virtue. We are growing and developing beings, changing every day. With such an exercise, we can take control of that process of change and direct it for the better.

Start journaling

One of the most common Stoic spiritual practices is journaling. What we know today as Marcus Aurelius's *Meditations* was originally his personal journal of philosophical memoranda. Making a habit of daily or regularly jotting down your thoughts about the practice of Stoicism has several benefits. It's a powerful way of clarifying your thoughts, tracking your growth and progress, processing your emotions, recording important insights, reminding yourself of key Stoic teachings, practicing gratitude, and engaging in a continuing process of self-examination and self-discovery.

By journaling, you cross an important threshold between merely reading and thinking about Stoic philosophy to actually practicing it. As the popular author Ryan Holiday notes, quoting the French philosopher Michel Foucault, Stoic journaling can be a "weapon of spiritual combat." Journaling, Holiday writes, is "a way to practice philosophy and purge the mind of agitation and foolishness and to overcome difficulty, to silence the barking dogs in your head. To prepare for the day ahead. To reflect on the day that has passed . . . It's spiritual windshield wipers, as the writer Julia Cameron once put it." (Holiday, *Stillness Is the Key* 55, 57)

Act with a reserve clause

An ideal Sage, Epictetus says, would have his will so perfectly aligned with God's that he never desires anything that fails to occur (*Discourses* 2.14.7). But is this possible? Many of our desires seem to be involuntary. Don't we unavoidably desire drink when we're thirsty, food when we're hungry, rest when we're fatigued, sleep when we're tired, and pain relief when we have a headache? And aren't such desires sometimes unfulfilled?

To address this problem, Stoics in part advocated willing with what later scholars have dubbed a reserve clause. A reserve clause involves desiring with a kind of proviso or if-then qualifier (Seneca, *On Tranquility* 13). So, a Stoic would not think, "I want to go to Rome on Monday," but rather "I want to go to Rome on Monday, if fate permits." Or, as Socrates once said, "I will come to you tomorrow, Lysimachus, as you propose, God willing" (Plato, *Laches* 201c). In this way, it's possible for all our desires to be fulfilled and for us to remain unperturbed no matter what happens. Never do we impiously desire something that turns out to be contrary to God's will and hence opposed to the overall good of the cosmos.

You'll often hear modern religious people in different traditions doing this, saying things like "See you next week, God willing!" Or as Muslims would put it, "We'll meet at the concert tomorrow, inshallah" (if God or Allah wills, and these Taylor Swift tickets aren't fake).

One other Stoic technique for aligning our wills with whatever happens, so as never to be disappointed, is simply to will that whatever happens will happen. And yet it's difficult not to be a little more specific than that in our daily lives, and that's where the reserve clause becomes both operative and important. And it can actually help, if God approves.

REMEMBER

Stoics don't require that we all go around adding this phrase aloud to every future tense wish, promise, or plan. Their intent is that we at least silently assume the reservation and conform our psychological expectations to the reality that God's plan might or might not align with our own and that we ought to incorporate this into our mindset so as to avoid disappointment, or being at odds with the gods.

Practice voluntary discomfort

Stoics believe that if we approach hardships well, they can toughen us and make us more resilient. For example, a person accustomed to cold weather finds cold easier to bear, and a runner who has done many hard workouts finds that such training requires less effort. Building on this insight, some ancient Stoics embraced and advocated occasional bouts of self-deprivation as a way to harden themselves and strengthen their power of will. They believed that this can also relieve us of needless worries. Too many moderately affluent people, for example, fear the ongoing possibility, however remote it might be, of falling into poverty. So, Seneca writes his friend and advises the following about eating and other things in daily life:

> Set aside a certain number of days, during which you'll be content with the scantiest and cheapest fare, and with coarse and rough dress, saying to yourself the while: "Is this the condition I feared?" It's precisely in times of immunity from care that the soul should toughen itself in advance for occasions of greater stress, and it is while Fortune is kind that it should fortify itself against her violence. (*Letters* 18).

This is a bit akin to *praemeditatio malorum* as a preparation for adversity, but it involves more than making lists or imagining things; it requires doing some practical things differently. Eat rough bread and drink only water for a few days. Sleep on the floor. Many modern Stoics regularly practice forms of voluntary discomfort, like taking cold showers, intermittent fasting, getting up really early, sleeping on wooden floors without a pillow, and, worse yet, putting the smartphone away, turning off the television, and staying offline for an entire day or more of living like people once did, as hard as it is for most of us to get our heads around such deprivation. Stoics believe that these practices not only improve our general resilience and willpower but can have many emotional and health benefits as well. This break from doom-scrolling and comparison-making on social media alone will have amazing effects.

Contemplate impermanence

As we saw in Chapter 5, Marcus Aurelius meditated frequently on the impermanence of all things. Reality, Stoics believe, is an ever-changing flux in which nothing is permanent. Time is a kaleidoscope of constantly changing patterns, a never-ending cycle of coming-to-be and ceasing. Marcus writes:

> Existence is like a river in continual flow, its actions a constant succession of change, its causes innumerable in their variety. Hardly anything stands still, even what is most immediate . . . So, in all this, it must be folly for anyone to be puffed with ambition, racked in struggle, or indignant at his lot — as if this was anything lasting or likely to trouble him for long." (*Meditations* 5.23).

Reflecting on the impermanence of all things can contribute to inner peace because we're less bothered by difficulties, knowing they aren't likely to last, and less attached to enjoyable things we know are fleeting and easily lost. Focusing on the flux of all things, we realize that nothing can be grasped, clutched, owned, or permanently possessed. Reminding ourselves of this impermanence can also deepen our sense of life's value. As the Buddhist monk Thich Nhat Hanh remarks, "Impermanence teaches us to respect and value every moment and all the precious things around us and inside us."

But on the surface here, we seem to be in the neighborhood of a paradox. We're urged by the Stoics to ponder change and impermanence precisely to relieve us from undue attachment to either the pleasant things or the negatives in our lives. They're hoping that when we remember the flux of the world, we'll be better able to value things properly, and to let go of things, not fall in love with the passing, or wallow in the miseries of life's struggles.

TIP

So *carpe diem*! Seize the day! Squeeze the moment for every drop of its grace! Embrace the precious things before they vanish! But won't such a mindset make us even more attached to the momentary? The simple answer is no. Enjoyment and appreciation, even at high levels, are not the same thing as attachment. They often go hand in hand only because people don't understand the difference. We can appreciate and relish something without needing it, without clinging to it, without attaching our emotions to it in an unhealthy way. And we should appreciate every moment in precisely that way.

THIS TOO SHALL PASS

The legendary Notre Dame football coach Lou Holtz loved to have his teams run the ball. He was naturally averse to the passing game. He liked to say, "When you throw the ball, three things can happen — two of them bad. I don't like the odds." And that would bring a smile to the face of even the most ardent advocate of the forward pass. You football fans will know right away what he meant. But for all other readers, when a quarterback throws the ball, it can of course be caught by his teammate, the intended receiver, for a positive gain, a first down, or even a touchdown. And that's ideal. But it can also be an incomplete pass, and a waste of effort, which is certainly bad. Or the thrown ball can be intercepted, caught by an opposing player, which is very bad indeed, since it gives them possession or maybe even a touchdown. So, three things can happen, two of them bad. That's why the coach said he didn't like the exciting passing game that most fans love precisely because of the excitement. But when you walked into the coach's office at Notre Dame, you would be met by a sign on his desk providing great Stoic wisdom for life and football. It said, "This too shall pass." And this statement, while reminding us of the constant impermanence of the challenges we may face, just might have also given sports journalists and fans a hint of hope for the coach calling something other than a running play now and then.

If we remind ourselves, "This too shall pass," we protect ourselves against being too puffed up by the nice things that happen, and too pushed down and defeated by the adversities that come into our lives. Most people live emotionally on a roller coaster, getting too excited about some things and too depressed about others, skyrocketing to extreme highs or plummeting to terrible lows. Keeping in mind impermanence can help us moderate our emotions well. While we can still appreciate the delights and take seriously the challenges, we remember their evanescence.

Contemplating impermanence properly can help us to both embrace value and release need and graspingness at the same time. It can be a tricky balance, but it can also be crucial for a life of resilience and inner peace.

Adopt good role models

Stoics believe that it's important to have good role models. For many of us, it's often easier to see what is morally good if we simply ask, "What would role model X do?" rather than to engage in some complex pattern of moral reasoning, which we, being far from perfect, could easily botch. Because of this, Seneca quotes with approval Epicurus's advice that we should "cherish some good man and keep him always before our eyes, so that we will live as if he were watching and do everything as if he could see us" (*Letters* 11.9).

Seneca then adds his own advice with the words:

> Choose someone whose way of life as well as words and whose very face as reflecting the character that lies behind it have won your approval. Be always pointing him out to yourself either as your guardian or as your model. There is a need, in my view, for someone as a standard against which our characters can measure themselves. Without a straight ruler to put it up against, you won't correct what's crooked. (*Letters* 11.10)

REMEMBER

A good role model can provide a concrete pattern and a vivid reminder of what it means to live a virtuous life. In tough situations we should call such a person to mind. What would she do? What would he advise or approve?

For some fans of the Stoics, these philosophers themselves can be in the choir of role models. What would Epictetus say here? What would Marcus do, or at least complain about not having done when he wrote in his journal later in the day? A good role model, even a character in fiction, if vividly enough brought to mind, can help us become more resilient in the face of challenge and disappointment, while also more serene in how we carry on.

Focus on what you can control

As we saw in Chapter 9, Epictetus urges focusing on what we can control. He goes overboard in claiming that externals are "nothing to us" (*Discourses* 1.29.23, 3.4.14) and that we should avoid all desires for things that lie outside our control (*Discourses* 4.1.84, *Handbook* 14). Your health, your daughter's happiness, your dog's welfare, your grades, your job performance, your car's reliability, your marriage, and your retirement plans are all worth serious care and concern, though none of them is completely within your control.

But Epictetus is certainly right that people often worry unnecessarily about things over which they have no real control. If your flight is delayed, for example, stressing over that is simply wasted energy and pointless negativity. Whenever you confront the inevitable, you must choose between responding to it with a positive or negative mindset, and positivity is always better. Positivity radiates good energy to those around us and positions us to think more clearly and creatively, and then to act more properly to solve whatever challenge we face. When we redirect our hearts and minds to what we do have some measure of control over, we allow ourselves a bit of this positivity. This is an insight of permanent value, some Stoic wisdom we should all take to heart and build into our daily lives.

Now, of course, as we suggest in Chapter 9, the things we confront in life don't so easily and simply divide into the two boxes of "things we can control, and things we can't control" or into the two exclusive categories of "things within or outside our power," as Epictetus seems to have thought. It's more like a spectrum that may be a bit different for each situation, and we'll find ourselves somewhere on that spectrum, either toward the end where we have no control, or closer to the side where we have an impressive amount of it, or at least influence. We may lack total control in a situation, as we do in most, but still have some influence or sway. And that influence can alter over time, up or down the spectrum, growing or diminishing as things change, which, as we've just seen, things most often do. But at any time and place, we will become more resilient, and we'll enjoy more peace and positivity, when we focus most on what we can likely do something about, and release for the moment anything farther from our control or influence.

Growing in, or as the classic Stoics would say, toward wisdom, will allow us to develop the discernment to know what to embrace and what to release, and that can be, as Epictetus always wanted, a very liberating thing.

Curb your desires for externals

Like Buddhists, Stoics see desire as a prime source of dissatisfaction and discontent. We desire love, popularity, job promotions, and financial or athletic success, and are disappointed if we don't get them. So, what's the solution? It's not to eradicate all desires, as Epictetus sometimes exaggerates to say (*Discourses* 4.4.33, *Handbook* 48), for this is neither possible nor in fact desirable. Desire is what motivates us, and a person who lacked all desire could quickly be extinguished by death. Our most basic desires keep us alive. Our higher desires grow us into the people we're capable of being.

A more sensible strategy is to curb our desires and direct them to healthier channels. This is what Stoics do when they de-emphasize the value of indifferents such as wealth, power, fame, status, and pleasure and instead stress the importance of wisdom and virtue. There's nothing wrong with desiring things like health, good relationships, and financial success, but we should not place such value on them that we're devastated if we fail to achieve them at the levels we had wanted. There can be no healthy resilience or mental tranquility without some mastery of our desires. They should be neither outsized nor directed at unworthy objects. We need to be in charge of our desires, not the other way around.

TIP

There is a spiritual or philosophical exercise available to us for desire management. If we find ourselves crushed by a disappointment, or perhaps overly elated by a success in such a way that our emotions, attitudes, and actions are departing from our own healthy norm, we should seek right away to identify any desire that might be behind the emotional disturbance. What is it? Why do we have it? What can we do to moderate or more properly control it? We can begin to take charge of our emotional lives in a healthier way if we're more self-aware and self-managed regarding desire.

There is an art of desire that, when cultivated and practiced wisely, can lead to our desiring well and rightly. As the Stoics saw, swollen or misdirected appetites cause endless problems and disappointments. Lao Tzu said, "There is no greater calamity than lavish desires." The Stoics would fully agree.

Practice *Amor Fati*

In Chapter 4, we examine Epictetus's view of radical acceptance. He believed that we should accept everything that happens in life, not merely grudgingly or resignedly, but cheerfully and gratefully. This is the idea of what Nietzsche later called *amor fati*, or a love of fate. For Stoics, it's rooted in their belief in a providential world order. As we've seen, the Stoics thought that God is in complete control of world events and that all things happen for the best. God sees to it that even apparent disasters such as floods, earthquakes, plagues, and famines work out for the long-term good of the universe. And if this is so, the Stoics believed, it would be improper and impious for us to grumble or complain about anything that happens. Even if you suffered all the calamities of Job, you should welcome and embrace them, for as the Bible says, "The judgments of the Lord are true and righteous altogether" (Psalms 19:9). And this is true for Stoics who call the Logos Lord.

As we note earlier, it is not clear that it's psychologically possible to sincerely love and welcome *everything* that befalls us in life. If you're being boiled in oil, you might say and pretend that you love what's happening to you, if you're really trying, maybe too hard, to be a Stoic, but it's doubtful this is what you truly feel and believe. Nor is it clear that it's appropriate to respond to all events with cheerful and grateful acceptance. If your daughter was assaulted and badly beaten, how should you respond? In such cases, talk of "love of fate" and grateful acceptance seems wholly misplaced. Between there and total rage, there is more likely to be a proper range of reaction.

It's clear why the Stoics placed such value on radical acceptance: It could undoubtedly contribute to mental tranquility. A person who sincerely and deeply accepts an event will not be troubled or disturbed by its occurrence. Or at least, not initially. But it's important to keep in mind that Stoic acceptance applies only to past and present events. If my dog falls into a well, Stoics teach that I should not be disturbed by that, since it reflects God's all-wise and all-good will. But the fact that my dog fell into the well does not imply that God wants my dog to stay there and drown and wishes me to make no effort to save him. Nothing in Stoic teaching implies that I should accept my dog's inevitable demise as a result of the situation. Past and present events, on the Stoic view, reveal God's will perfectly, but his *future* will is difficult to know. If I believe that my dog can be saved, I will feel an urgent desire to rescue him, making perfect mental tranquility in the situation impossible.

So, while Stoic acceptance can be an important aid to inner calm, it doesn't guarantee it entirely. Complete imperturbability seems to be an impossible ideal for such vulnerable, feeling, and desiring creatures as we are. And yet to practice acceptance as a habit wherever it's possible and fitting will indeed help us both with resilience and with that inner serenity that's a boon and a boost as we continue to live in a world of opportunity and challenge. Tranquil enough may be a useful concept here, and everywhere in our journeys.

All told, the Stoics created an impressive toolkit of practices and techniques to promote emotional resilience and inner peace. Many people find that these reminders and exercises help them live better, happier, less anxious lives.

6

Stoicism Today

Meet some modern-day Stoics and their exciting work.

Explore what's happening in modern and contemporary Stoicism.

Chapter **19**

The Stoic Next Door: The Popular Revival of Stoicism Today

As we saw in Chapter 5, Stoicism effectively died as an organized movement not long after the death of Marcus Aurelius in 180 C.E. After a very successful 500-year-long run as one of the most popular philosophies of life in ancient times, it finally faded like an aging rock star, keeled over, and breathed its last.

As paganism and the Roman Empire slowly crumbled in the years following Marcus's death, Stoicism was outcompeted by more consoling philosophies and faiths like Christianity and Neoplatonism that had greater mass appeal.

After the triumph of Christianity in the fourth and fifth centuries of the Common Era, Stoic philosophy was nearly universally seen as a pantheistic and materialistic pagan philosophy that held dangerously misguided views about God, the soul, fate, the goal of life, and life after death.

As we've seen, Stoicism continued to have some influence after the Roman era. Key Stoic teachings about natural law, divine Providence, the cardinal virtues, submission to the divine will, and the governance of unruly passions and appetites were absorbed into Christian thought and practice. The writings of ancient Stoic philosophers like Seneca, Epictetus, and Marcus Aurelius, as well as those heavily influenced by the Stoics, like Cicero, continued to be read in medieval and modern times and exerted great influence on major thinkers such as Boethius, Erasmus, Montaigne, Descartes, Spinoza, David Hume, Adam Smith, Jean-Jacques Rousseau, and Immanuel Kant. Yet, as practical matter, Stoicism essentially expired when Marcus Aurelius took his last breath in a Roman fort on the wintry Danubian frontier. It was no longer an intellectual and spiritual "live option" for any but a select few.

Fast forward to today. Stoicism is red hot. Business leaders and celebrities have embraced it. Books on Stoicism have topped national bestseller lists and abound in the philosophy sections of bookstores. Major newspapers, magazines, and other mass media outlets have reported widely on the popular resurgence of Stoicism, and Stoic-themed blogs, podcasts, conferences, and online groups have exploded in popularity. And of course there are T-shirts. Much of this renewed interest in Stoicism has been centered in the United States, a country not usually known for its warm embrace of ancient philosophies or other highbrow "isms" that originated in distant lands. In this chapter, we ask: What explains this remarkable revival? What led to it? What accounts for the huge and surprising appeal of ancient Stoic philosophy in our time? Who are the major figures in the modern Stoicism movement, and what are they saying?

The Rise of Modern Stoicism

If you go back to, say, the mid 1960s, Stoicism was not of great interest to either scholars or general readers. Case in point: Check out the entry on Stoicism in the prestigious eight-volume *Encyclopedia of Philosophy*, published in 1967. The entry is short, quite a bit shorter, in fact, then the entries on such then-hot-button topics as recursive function theory (don't ask) and the linguistic theory of the a priori (again, don't ask). A glance at the bibliography of the Stoicism entry also reveals something interesting. With the exception of one reference to a work on Stoic logic, one to a work on Stoic physics, and one to a book on Roman Stoicism originally published in 1911, all the citations are to works by French or German scholars. There's not a single citation to any recent work in English on Stoic ethics or Stoic philosophy in general. Nada. Zilch. The Void.

What could explain such a puzzling entry? Two things. First, philosophy in general was in the doldrums in the mid-1960s. That was the heyday of linguistic philosophy, when most professional philosophers believed it was their job to clarify issues and dissolve confusions by parsing language, rather than to weigh in on the existence of God, the meaning of life, or other traditional philosophical questions. Stoicism was centrally concerned with two things — the ultimate nature of reality and the nature of the good life — that most philosophers then believed were not in their job descriptions. There was also no demand among students for Stoicism courses in most colleges and universities.

Second, though English-speaking scholars were then doing important work on Plato and Aristotle, they had little interest in Stoicism or other Hellenistic philosophies. Aside from a few scholarly works on Stoic physics and logic, and A. S. L. Farquharson's major two-volume translation of and commentary on the *Meditations* of Marcus Aurelius (1944) that his mother may not even have read, virtually no books of note on Stoicism were published by Anglo-American scholars between the mid-1920s and the mid-1960s.

The therapists

The first stirrings of renewed interest in Stoicism lay, in fact, in psychology, not in philosophy. Beginning in the late-1950s, forms of psychotherapy began to emerge that drew heavily on Stoic thought. The first was rational emotive therapy (now called rational emotive behavior therapy, or REBT), founded by the American psychologist Albert Ellis (1913 – 2007). Drawing in part on the psychological theories of Alfred Adler (1870 – 1937), Ellis argued that "emotional pain or disturbance . . . usually originates in some irrational or illogical ideas." Much like the Stoics, he believed that anxiety, depression, and many other psychological problems are rooted in "unrealistic, illogical, self-defeating thinking." The "cause of upsets," he said, "lies mainly in people, not in what happens to them."

The philosophical origins of REBT, Ellis stated, go back "especially to Epicurus and the Stoic philosophers Epictetus and Marcus Aurelius." In treating his clients, Ellis would frequently quote Epictetus's saying that "people are disturbed not by things, but by the view which they take of them." In 1961, Ellis teamed with fellow psychologist Robert Harper to write *A Guide to Rational Living*, which became one of the top-selling self-help books of all time and put Stoic philosophy on the radar screens of millions of ordinary readers.

Another form of psychotherapy that emerged a little later than REBT and was also influenced by Stoicism is cognitive behavior therapy (CBT), or cognitive therapy, for short. Founded by Aaron Beck in the early-and mid-1960s, CBT is currently the most popular form of psychotherapy. According to Beck, the basic premise of CBT — that "the individual's view of self and the personal world are central to behavior" — "originated in Greek Stoic philosophy." According to CBT, common psychological disorders such as depression, anxiety, paranoia, and panic disorder are caused by "systematic biases in information processing," that is, by faulty, dysfunctional thinking. Depression, for example, is often due to irrationally negative views of self and the future. Anxiety disorder is typically the product of an exaggerated sense of physical and psychological danger. Morbid stage fright is often caused by "catastrophized" thinking that exaggerates the risks of public speaking. And so on.

WARNING

Cognitive therapists help patients "correct faulty information processing" and "modify assumptions that maintain maladaptive behaviors and emotions." Though similar to REBT in many ways, cognitive therapy differs in viewing faulty information processing as maladaptive but not necessarily irrational. In contrast to REBT, CBT also insists that different psychological disorders often spring from radically different forms of faulty thinking and require very different forms of therapy. Though Stoicism, a full-scale worldview and philosophy of life, clearly differs from REBT and CBT, which are simply clinical therapies aimed at curing psychological disorders, they are similar in seeing poor thinking as a major source of human unhappiness and emotional and behavioral problems.

The sixties

In addition to these developments in psychology, there were important new trends in philosophy in the 1960s that helped prepare the way for current revival of Stoicism. As noted in Chapter 1, one was the growing popularity in the West of Buddhism, Hinduism, and other Eastern wisdom traditions. Like Stoicism, Buddhism and Hinduism, at least in some strands, embrace pantheism and impermanence. They also stress the importance of nonattachment and mental tranquility, the role of desire in causing suffering and unhappiness, and the need to control unhealthy emotions such as anger, worry, envy, greed, and fear.

WARNING

Buddhism and Hinduism differ, of course, in major ways from Stoicism. Stoicism, for example, rejects reincarnation, which is central to both Buddhism and Hinduism. There are also no counterparts in most strands of Buddhism and Hinduism to the Stoic doctrines of materialism, virtue as the sole and sufficient good, and "cosmic optimism" (the view that this is the best of all possible worlds). Still, there are striking similarities between Stoicism and both Hinduism and Buddhism that no doubt helped prepare the way for a Stoic revival.

Two other developments in philosophy during the 1960s also likely contributed to renewed interest in Stoicism. One was existentialism, which enjoyed a huge vogue in the 1950s and 1960s. In general terms, existentialism is a philosophy that stresses individual freedom, authenticity, individualism, choice, commitment, and responsibility. Leading existentialists include Søren Kierkegaard, Jean-Paul Sartre, Albert Camus, Karl Jaspers, and Martin Heidegger. The popularity of existentialism in this era brought more public attention to philosophy as relevant to our daily lives and the ways we think about what we do and how we live. We should say more.

Existentialism

Though some fans of Stoicism have claimed that there are close parallels between Stoicism and Existentialism, there are actually major differences. Existentialists, for example, typically reject materialism, pantheism, fate, virtue as the only good, natural law, and the objectivity of values, all of which Stoics (or at least ancient Stoics) embrace. But there are some real similarities between the two viewpoints. One involves Sartre's notion of "despair." (The existentialists were always talking about cheery topics like abandonment, forlornness, suicide, anguish, death, and despair. Most of them presumably were not a lot of fun at parties.) In his famous 1945 lecture, "Existentialism Is a Humanism," Sartre defines despair as the recognition that the world, and especially the actions of other people, are outside of my control and that I must accordingly limit myself to that which lies "within my own will." He writes:

> Beyond the point at which the possibilities under consideration cease to affect my action, I ought to disinterest myself. . . . When Descartes said, "Conquer yourself rather than the world," what he meant was, at bottom, the same . . .

Clearly, Sartre's notion of "despair" (the French word is *désespoir*, which signifies lack of hope and does not connote bleak sadness, as the English *despair* does) is similar to Epictetus's idea that we should focus on what we can control and let the rest go.

Virtue ethics

The other development in more recent philosophy that had a clear impact on the revival of Stoicism was the rediscovery and increasing popularity of virtue ethics in the 1950s and 1960s in the work of ethicists such as Elizabeth Anscombe and Philippa Foot, and later on, the immensely influential Alasdair MacIntyre. According to virtue ethics, the principal focus of moral theory should be on questions of character, virtue, and wisdom, not on maximizing good consequences or identifying correct moral rules, as most mainstream ethical theories then held. Virtue ethics brought renewed attention to the Stoics, because Stoicism was a prime example of an ancient philosophy that embraced virtue ethics. In Stoic ethics, the main focus is on good moral habits and intentions rather than on the consequences of action, because consequences are out of our control and are externals that should be of little concern.

In addition, Stoicism clearly prioritized virtue, wisdom, and good character and made no systematic effort to formulate any detailed code of moral rules, though as a friend of the philosophy, Cicero does a bit of that in his Stoic-influenced book, *On Duties*. As virtue ethics gained traction in moral philosophy in the 1960s and 1970s, as well as in later years, there was naturally new interest in Stoicism.

A renewal of scholarly work

Whatever the precise causes, there was a significant upsurge in scholarly attention to Stoicism that began in the late 1960s and early 1970s. Major works on Stoicism published in this period included Ludwig Edelstein's *The Meaning of Stoicism* (1966), Gerard Watson's *The Stoic Theory of Knowledge* (1966), John Rist's *Stoic Philosophy* (1969), Josiah B. Gould's *The Philosophy of Chrysippus* (1970), A. A. Long's edited volume, *Problems in Stoicism* (1971), and his monograph *Hellenistic Philosophy* (1974). Since that time, scholarly books on Stoicism have continued to pour forth from the presses, and over the past decade or so, have become a flood.

Renewed scholarly interest in Stoicism began to gain a modest amount of professional attention in the 1960s. But what about widespread popular interest in the Stoics? When did Stoicism begin to become the pop phenomenon it is today? How did it leap from seminar rooms and library collections onto the bestseller lists of our time?

Cultural attention

One big catalyst was the writings of Admiral James Stockdale in the 1970s and 1980s. Stockdale was a POW in North Vietnam for over seven years. During his captivity, Stockdale endured brutal conditions and was tortured repeatedly. After his release, he credited Epictetus for helping him survive and cope with the terrible ordeal. In April 1978, five years after his release, Stockdale published an article titled "The World of Epictetus" in the *Atlantic* magazine that sparked a lot of popular interest in the Stoics. Later, Stockdale wrote a number of books, including *A Vietnam Experience* (1984) and *Courage Under Fire: Testing Epictetus's Doctrines in a Laboratory of Human Behavior* (1993) that created similar buzz. For his leadership and heroism, Stockdale received the Congressional Medal of Honor. In 1992, he served as Ross Perot's running mate in Perot's failed bid for the presidency, which drew further attention to his appreciation for Stoicism.

Another major milestone in the popular resurgence of Stoicism was the publication in 1998 of Tom Wolfe's novel *A Man in Full*, which was a *New York Times* #1 bestseller. Wolfe's novel tells the story of two very different men who each have a kind of conversion to an austere brand of Epictetian Stoicism, which totally changes their lives. Inspired in part by Stockdale's experiences in Vietnam and including copious quotations from Epictetus, the novel stirred interest in Stoicism among non-academic readers.

FORAYS INTO POPULAR PHILOSOPHY

One of your co-authors (Tom) got an urgent phone call in 1998 from the publisher of his then-recent book *If Aristotle Ran General Motors*, asking him to stop whatever he was doing and write a book on the Stoics very quickly, in 90 days, long before the current wave of interest in Stoicism. Tom Wolfe's novel *A Man in Full*, had just debuted atop the *New York Times Bestseller List* and featured Stoicism in its plot just enough to pique but not satisfy readers' curiosity about this ancient philosophy. Tom had been speaking to Fortune 500 companies about the wisdom of the ages and had seen first-hand the opportunity of interpreting ancient philosophy for modern living and current business challenges. He had been circulating some private writings on Seneca and Marcus Aurelius to the CEOs who were bringing him into their companies to speak to their executives and even broader audiences. And so he managed to do the job in the time required. But when he turned in the completed manuscript, his editor had the bad news that Wolfe's book had fallen off the list and that there was no longer any interest in a popular book on the Stoics.

It was six more years before anyone wanted to publish *The Stoic Art of Living*. Tom has always wished for a banner across the cover, "Dozens of Copies in Print" to reflect sales prior to the popular concern about Stoicism. And yet among the dozens who have read the book were many corporate leaders who reported that it was the only book they'd ever read two or three times, cover to cover, back-to-back, finishing the last page and starting again on page one. One said, "Everyone in financial services ought to read this book right away." And that was because Tom had highlighted the gems of wisdom in Stoic writings that could be of help to people now in their lives and careers. The goal wasn't a deep dive into Stoic doctrine, but a focus on Stoic thoughts that might help people now. So he was working hard long ago at the task that authors like Ryan Holiday have now built into an empire. And he, along with his co-author of the current book, understand what it takes to translate, interpret, and sometimes remodel ancient ideas into a form that can have a positive powerful impact in the present. Purists will always carp. But in the end, philosophy isn't the prized possession of university departments, to be protected and guarded just for the few, but rather an amazing and vitally important enterprise that needs to be injected into the cultural mix in every era. Some of those who do it well will have serious academic degrees, and others will simply have a keen intellectual interest, a personal enthusiasm, and a talent for communication that can spread ideas broadly through the zeitgeist.

WARNING

Prior to all this, the writings of French classical scholar Pierre Hadot (1922 – 2010) had created considerable popular interest in Stoicism and ancient philosophy more generally in France, as they still do today. Hadot's widely read books *Exercices spirituels et philosophie antique* (1981, translated into English in 1995 as *Philosophy As a Way of Life*), *La citadel intérieure* (1992, translated into English in 1998 as *The Inner Citadel*), and *Qu'est-ce que la philosophie antique?* (1995, translated into English in 2002 as *What Is Ancient Philosophy?*) popularized the idea of philosophy as a way of life, rather than simply a "discipline" one studies, like calculus or organic chemistry; introduced French readers to Stoic psychological practices such as the view from above, premeditation of adversities, and concentration on the present moment; and effectively refuted the then-common idea that the Stoics were grim, impassive, and totally anti-emotion. Unlike so many French philosophers of his day, Hadot wrote clearly and engagingly and aimed his books at scholars and general readers alike. His works had a major impact, not only in France, but in the United States and Great Britain when they were translated into English.

The notion that the ancient Stoics were stern, emotionally constipated guys who advocated an attitude of what David Hume calls "sullen apathy" was also effectively critiqued in Lawrence Becker's important book, *A New Stoicism* (1998; revised edition 2017). Becker (1939 – 2018) was a major American philosopher who specialized in ethics and political philosophy. He became attracted to Stoicism, in part, because of his lifelong struggles with polio. Wheelchair-bound since he was a child, Becker amazingly typed all his books and his many academic articles with his toes. In *A New Stoicism*, he seeks to imagine how Stoicism might look today if it had never died out in antiquity but had continued to evolve and improve in response to modern science and subsequent intellectual currents in general. The result is a form of Stoicism that keeps its traditional stress on virtue and "happiness" (reconceived by Becker as a form of "ideal agency" rather than any kind of pleasurable state of mind or "feeling happy"), but that totally drops talk of Stoic cosmology, God, providence, natural law, an afterlife, and many other traditional Stoic teachings.

Becker persuasively argues that "no Stoics ever held the view that the Sage's life should be empty of affect, emotion, and passion," but he does concede that the ancient Stoics were too negative on many of what we today would call "emotions." He argues that the classic Stoics embraced an exaggerated view of self-sufficiency and so were too quick to think that the Sage's life would be an emotionally tranquil one (*A New Stoicism*, rev. ed., 151). A defensible updated version of Stoicism would recognize that even Sages may experience "passions an Aristotelian would find wildly immoderate" (149).

WARNING

Becker's book is quite scholarly and at times even technical, so it was not widely read by nonacademic readers when it was first published. However, it did have a big impact on later writers like philosophers William Irvine and Massimo Pigliucci, who also sought to offer updated versions of Stoicism and popularized many of Becker's ideas.

Leading Figures in Modern Stoicism

So, by the late 1990s, stirrings of renewed interest in Stoicism were in the air, but it wasn't even remotely close to being the pop phenomenon it is today. That was largely the result of four writers — William Irvine, Donald Robertson, Massimo Pigliucci, and perhaps most of all, Ryan Holiday — who succeeded in repackaging Stoicism in a new and attractive form that resonated with busy and stressed general readers. In this section, we profile these four horsemen of modern Stoicism.

William B. Irvine

The first really big catalyst for the current rise of the modern Stoicism movement was the publication in 2009 of William B. Irvine's *A Guide to the Good Life: The Ancient Stoic Art of Joy*.

Irvine's background

Irvine is a professional philosopher, trained at UCLA, who taught for nearly four decades at Wright State University, and is now retired. Early in his career, he focused on ethics and political philosophy, authoring two provocative academic books on parental rights that argued, among other things, that parents should be licensed and that eugenics is acceptable under certain conditions. Later, Irvine says he lost interest in writing for other professional philosophers and began addressing his thoughts to more general readers. In 2005, he published *On Desire: Why We Want What We Want*, a wide-ranging and multidisciplinary study that explores both the science of desire and also how we should think about desire if our goal is lasting happiness and mental tranquility. In a preview of his later work on Stoicism, Irvine argues that the secret to enduring happiness is to learn to want what we have, not to try to bend the world to our wishes.

In a blog post titled "On Becoming a 21st Century Stoic," Irvine says that when he was writing *On Desire* he was thinking about becoming a Zen Buddhist. That changed, however, as he dug deeper into his research. Zen Buddhism, he decided, was too opposed to reason and analytical rigor, and offered no guarantees for a speedy life-improvement and inner peace. In the Stoics, however, which he now read seriously for the first time, he found just what he was looking for: a practical philosophy of life that values reason, is adaptable to the modern world, and provides proven techniques for reducing stress, coping with adversity, and achieving inner calm and contentment. So Irvine became a practicing Stoic and began writing *A Guide to the Good Life*.

Much to Irvine's surprise, the book made a big splash when it appeared in late 2008 (with a copyright date of 2009). Unlike *On Desire*, which was targeted at both academics and general readers, *A Guide to the Good Life* is obviously aimed at a non-academic audience. It's clear, engaging, filled with interesting stories and personal anecdotes, and almost entirely jargon-free. Why did the book strike such a chord? A brief summary of its key points will make clear why.

Irvine's thought

Stoicism, Irvine argues, offers a simple, practical philosophy of life that helps curb negative emotions, enhance positive emotions like joy and delight, and lead to mental calm and greater life satisfaction. The ancient Stoics discovered a whole toolbox of effective techniques for reducing negative emotions and achieving a happy, tranquil life (*Guide*, 245). These tools include psychological practices like negative visualization (imagining that bad things are happening to you to reduce their possible impact), focusing on what you can control, voluntary discomfort, and a regular practice of mindfulness and meditation (*Guide*, Part 2). They also include powerful bits of advice, such as to care little about externals like fame, wealth, and status; to recognize that humans are inherently social animals and to be conscientious in fulfilling our social duties to others; to learn to master unhealthy emotions such as anger, frustration, and grief; to develop mental toughness and emotional resilience in the face of insults, exile, old age, and other adversities; to practice minimalism and a simple lifestyle; and not to fear death (*Guide*, Part 4).

Irvine went on to convey that, unfortunately, the Stoics mixed in a lot of bad philosophy and outdated science and theology with these powerful psychological techniques and helpful pieces of advice. But that's okay, because Stoicism can easily be "modernized" to keep what is useful and throw out what's false or outdated (*Guide*, 242).

Irvine himself became a practicing modern Stoic of this sort and has found it very effective in reducing negative emotions, improving life satisfaction, and achieving greater peace of mind and regular experiences of Stoic joy and delight (*Guide*, 275). A modernized Stoicism of the sort he has "customized" (*Guide*, 244) and "cobbled together" (*Guide*, 242) from various ancient Stoic writers and modern perspectives admittedly isn't for everybody. People differ in their personalities, values, and circumstances, and so there is no life philosophy that works for everybody (*Guide*, 246, 248). But Irvine does claim that "Stoicism is a wonderfully effective way to gain tranquility" (*Guide*, 246). Anyone who shares his belief that tranquility is the proper goal of life (*Guide*, 274) should consider giving Stoicism a try. There's little to lose by doing so, and potentially much to gain (*Guide*, 279).

TIP

Clearly, this is powerful stuff. A simple, practical, evidence-based way to vanquish bad emotions, nurture good emotions, and find joy, happiness, and inner peace! For many readers, Irvine seemed to have discovered a long-forgotten happy pill, a virtual psychological cure-all. It's hard to imagine why, at the time, there weren't late night TV infomercials with 800 numbers touting this remarkable tonic.

Conclusions on Irvine

But wait, alert readers may be thinking. How "Stoic" is Irvine's "cobbled together," modernized Stoicism? What happened to the Logos, souls as fragments of the divine, virtue as the sole good and goal of life, radical acceptance, providence, fate, natural law, cosmic citizenship, the Stoic paradoxes, an afterlife, eternally recurring cosmic cycles — all that good stuff the ancient Stoics were always talking about? Gone. Most are not even mentioned by Irvine. Stoicism, in Irvine's rendition, has morphed into pop psychology and a medley of life hacks focused almost exclusively on managing negative emotions and achieving tranquility. Irvine has been touting a potent tonic he calls "Stoicism," but gives little clue to unsuspecting readers that this is very different from actual historic Stoicism.

Irvine himself is unfazed by such criticism. He rightly notes that most of his readers "won't be concerned with preserving the purity of Stoicism. For them, the question is, does it work?" (*Guide*, 245). And Irvine is quite right that a modernized Stoicism such as he favors does often "work" (as do Buddhism, Taoism, cognitive therapy, Transcendental Meditation, and possibly ancient Druidism as well, done in the right ways). Stoicism, seriously practiced, can demonstrably reduce stress, improve coping skills, build emotional resilience, curb unhealthy emotions, and boost happiness. But is Irvine's modernized Stoicism *real* Stoicism, or is it simply Stoic-flavored pop psychology, a weaker version of philosophical Miller Lite watered down from the ancient brew?

It's really largely the latter, in our view. The ancient Stoic belief that virtue is (1) the only true good, (2) necessary and sufficient for human flourishing (*eudaimonia*), and (3) the proper goal of life isn't an accessory a shiny new "customized" Stoicism can toss out. It lies at the core of authentic Stoicism and defines how Stoicism differed from other ancient philosophies like Platonism, Aristotelianism, and Cynicism that also stressed virtue and human flourishing. The same is true of the Stoic belief in radical acceptance. For ancient Stoics like Epictetus, acceptance lies at the heart of what virtue means. As modern Stoics Massimo Pigliucci and Gregory Lopez point out, Irvine's brand of Stoicism "veers

Epicurean" in its claim that tranquility, not virtue, is the goal of life (*A Handbook for New Stoics*, 316).

Irvine's *Guide* is subtitled "The Ancient Stoic Art of Joy," and he talks a lot in the book about how Stoicism can lead to more frequent experiences of joy and delight. This surely helped book sales, because as emotions go, joy and delight are two of the most popular. But as we've seen, the ancient Stoics used "joy" (*chara*, in Greek) in a highly specialized way. The founding and classic Stoics recognized only three "good passions" (*eupatheiai*): joy, wish (*boulesis*), and caution (*eulabeia*). Only Sages, or the perfectly wise, can experience any of these good passions, and all are directed solely at either virtue or vice. Only joy is an emotion in the modern sense. Joy, in Stoic doctrine, is a "reasonable elation" about one's present possession of complete virtue. Wish is a "reasonable striving" for the future continued possession of perfect virtue, and caution is a "reasonable avoidance" of future vices or loss of virtue (Diogenes Laertius, *Lives* 7.116).

As we've seen, the ancient Stoics believed that Sages are excedingly rare; consequently, so too are experiences of Stoic "joy." Irvine quotes a number of passages from Seneca and Musonius (*Guide*, 7-8), but without alerting readers that these writers were speaking of joy in a specialized, nonstandard sense. Irvine himself uses "joy" in an unusual way, meaning by it "a kind of objectless enjoyment — an enjoyment not of any particular things but of all this" — the simple, astonishing fact that the world exists and that one is able to live in it (*Guide*, 275). Joy, in Irvine's special sense, is certainly a wonderful feeling, but clearly it has really *nothing* to do with the ancient Stoic concept of joy, which focused entirely on the possession of virtue, apart from a positive feeling.

Equally misleading is Irvine's discussion of what he terms positive and negative emotions. He rightly notes that the ancient Stoics were not totally anti-emotion; as we have seen, they conceded that there are a few "good passions," that there are "pre-passions" that are in no way culpable, and that many affections that we today would call emotions (for example, parental love) are "preferred" and accord with nature, and therefore valuable and licit. But Irvine misleadingly states that the Stoic goal "was not to banish *emotion* from life, but to banish *negative emotions*" (*Guide*, 7), while also nurturing "positive emotions — particularly joy" (*Guide*, 10). This makes Stoicism sound eminently sensible and pleasingly up-to-date. Who doesn't want to get rid of "negative emotions" and experience only "positive" ones? Wouldn't we all be far happier, and wouldn't the world be a far better place, if we could all experience positive emotions and rid ourselves of all negative ones? This isn't philosophy, but the emotive happy-talk of advertisers and politicians. And again, what does it have to do with the ancient Stoic view of emotions, which, as we've seen, in its standard form categorically rejected pity, empathy, grief, fear of pain, fear of the death of loved ones, and all other emotions ("positive" *or* "negative") that stemmed from false beliefs about what was truly good or bad? Irvine's concern has very little at all to do with these authentic Stoic themes.

On the whole, then, Irvine's *Guide to the Good Life* offers an attractive but misleading picture of Stoicism. But it did sell very well, and so attract fans and imitators. On the upside, it accomplished what Irvine hoped: It revivified Stoicism and made it once again a live option for people looking for a practical, effective philosophy of life that makes sense in the modern world. The current, vibrant modern Stoicism movement in several ways largely stems from Irvine's book. On the downside, however, this popular book set an unfortunate precedent and launched a whole series of Irvine-esque books, blogs, and podcasts that offer radically stripped-down and oversimplified versions of "Stoicism" that are really little more than a hodgepodge of philosophically gussified bits of pop psychology. It must immediately be added that not all of Irvine's many imitators and successors fall into this category. Some offer versions of modern Stoicism that, while aimed at non-specialist readers, are sophisticated and harmonize fairly well with authentic Stoicism, but with a few plausible modern add-ons and updates.

Donald Robertson

One of the best-known modern Stoics is the Scottish psychotherapist Donald Robertson. He is the author of numerous books on Stoicism, including his excellent *Stoicism and the Art of Happiness* (2013), and more recently, *How to Think Like a Roman Emperor: The Stoic Philosophy of Marcus Aurelius* (2019), *Verissimus: The Stoic Philosophy of Marcus Aurelius* (a graphic novel, co-authored with Zé Nuno Fraga, 2022), and a biography of Marcus Aurelius from Yale University Press (2024).

Robertson's background

Born in Irvine, Scotland, Robertson was raised in a working-class home in nearby Ayr, dropped out of school at age 16, and was placed in a special program for troubled kids. As he explains in *How to Think Like a Roman Emperor*, his life began to turn around in his late teens when he started reading Plato's *Dialogues* and discovered Socrates.

Robertson got a certificate in computing from Ayr and a master's degree in mental philosophy (i.e., philosophy of mind) at the University of Aberdeen. Later, he switched to psychology and became a practicing clinical psychotherapist and therapist trainer in London for many years, specializing in cognitive behavioral therapy.

In his 30s, Robertson discovered the writings of French classical scholar Pierre Hadot and was struck by the similarities between Stoicism and cognitive behavior therapy. Since then, Robertson has been one of the most active and respected members of the modern Stoicism movement, authoring numerous books, cofounding the nonprofit organization Modern Stoicism in 2012, serving as owner/moderator of the popular Stoic Philosophy Facebook group and one on

LinkedIn, and founding the Plato's Academy Centre in 2021, dedicated to rehabilitating the original site of Plato's Academy in suburban Athens as a place of philosophical and literary discussion. Robertson has a website on the online platform Substack titled "Stoicism: Philosophy as a Way of Life," where he publishes a blog, an email newsletter, a podcast, interviews, and offers occasional courses for paid subscribers. He moved to Canada in 2013 and now divides his time between Canada and Greece.

Robertson's thought

As a trained psychotherapist, Robertson is especially interested in ways in which Stoicism and psychotherapy (especially rational emotive behavior therapy (REBT) and cognitive behavior therapy (CBT)) are related. In books such as *The Philosophy of Cognitive-Behavioural Therapy* (CBT) (2010), *Build Your Resilience* (2012), *Stoicism and the Art of Happiness* (2013), and *How to Think Like a Roman Emperor* (2019), Robertson explores such parallels in detail. He notes that Stoicism was a major philosophical influence on both REBT and CBT, and that many of the therapeutic techniques employed by these psychotherapies are similar to certain Stoic spiritual exercises. For instance, both Stoicism and CBT believe that psychological problems such as anxiety, depression, paranoia, morbid introversion, and panic disorders are often rooted in poor thinking, what CBT calls "cognitive disorders" or "dysfunctional interpretations." Moreover, both employ techniques such as mindfulness meditation; decatastophizing imagery, which involves visualizing why future events are not likely to be as horrible as one fears; cognitive distancing, a way of creating a mental space between yourself and a situation, allowing for a more rational and objective perspective; objective representation, separating your value judgment of a thing from the thing itself; and "the view from above," which recommends looking at a situation from a broader or more "cosmic" perspective.

Robertson's preferred version of modern Stoicism is a mix of classic Stoic themes and psychotherapeutic strategies drawn from CBT. While CBT and Stoicism do share some commonalities, they also have notable differences. Key contrasts include:

» Stoicism is a wide-ranging worldview and philosophy of life; CBT is a form of psychotherapy aimed at curing or alleviating certain kinds of psychological disorders.

» Stoicism is a normative theory that embraces a clear set of values (e.g., that virtue is the only good and the final end of life); CBT is an evidence-based branch of therapeutic science that focuses solely on psychological disorders and is neutral on value questions such as the *summum bonum* (highest good), the value of indifferents, the cardinal virtues, the importance of social duties service for the common good, and whether virtue comes in degrees.

CBT employs many therapeutic techniques that have no parallels in Stoic teaching and in some cases conflict with classic Stoic doctrine. For instance, Robertson notes that one common therapeutic technique used in CBT is values clarification. In values clarification, a therapist uses Socratic questioning to help patients get a clearer picture of the values they currently hold. Unlike in Stoicism, no judgments are made in CBT about the correctness of those values; cognitive therapists are interested in patients' values only insofar as they are deemed dysfunctional, not insofar as they are "irrational" or "incorrect." In addition, unlike Stoicism, CBT does not view all intense and reason-hindering emotions (even "negative" ones such as fear, anger, grief, and lust) as "bad" or "irrational." In fact, as Robertson notes, cognitive behavioral therapists often try to *elicit* intense emotions from their patients as a form of "stress inoculation" to build up more resistance to emotional disturbance in the future. The ancient Stoic and modern CBT views of emotion are thus quite different and, in fact, incompatible in some ways.

Conclusions on Robertson

TIP

Unlike Irvine, who often presents a one-sided view of ancient Stoicism, Robertson is a quite reliable guide to classic Stoic beliefs and practices. His *Stoicism and the Art of Happiness* (2013) is one of the best and clearest introductions to Stoic thought. Readers should be aware, though, that the version of modern Stoicism Robertson presents includes a good bit of modern psychology that does not always harmonize with some ancient Stoic teachings. Like Irvine, he offers a modernized form of Stoicism that omits any concept of a pantheistic God, divine Providence, life after death, souls as fragments of the divine, natural law, *amor fati*, and many other ideas central to ancient Stoic thought. That said, Robertson is an excellent, engaging writer and an insightful guide on both ancient and modern Stoicism.

Massimo Pigliucci

Among the leading modern Stoics, the biggest philosophical heavyweight is arguably Massimo Pigliucci (pronounced *Pilly-oochi*; the "g" is silent, unlike Massimo himself, fortunately), who currently serves as the K. D. Irani Professor of Philosophy at the City College of New York.

Pigliucci's background

Born in Liberia and raised in Rome, Pigliucci holds a doctorate in genetics, a Ph.D. in evolutionary biology, and a Ph.D. in philosophy. The author of more than a dozen books, he is an avowed atheist who has written extensively in defense of science and against creationism, intelligent design, and pseudoscience. In a 2015 op-ed piece in the *New York Times*, Pigliucci announced that he had become a practicing Stoic. Two years later, he published *How to be A Stoic* (Basic Books, 2017), a major work in the modern Stoicism movement.

Pigliucci's thought

In *How to be a Stoic*, Pigliucci explains that he was attracted to Stoicism because it is "a rational, science-friendly philosophy that includes a metaphysics with a spiritual dimension, is explicitly open to revision, and, most importantly, is eminently practical" (*How to Be a Stoic*, 5). Drawing heavily from Epictetus, he explores in the book what it means to embrace a Stoic lifestyle, as well as various psychological exercises Stoics can use to make progress in applying Stoicism to daily life. Like Irvine, Pigliucci says very little about Stoic physics, logic, or theology; he focuses only on what he feels are the practical teachings of Stoicism.

Also like Irvine and Robertson, Pigliucci believes that Stoicism needs to be updated in certain ways to fit with modern science and modern values. For example, he points out that science has shown that our beliefs, feelings, and desires are not as much in our control as Epictetus assumed. You cannot, for example, just decide not to believe that Germany lost the Second World War; your belief that it did automatically tracks your sense of the supporting evidence. Pigliucci also denies that Stoics must believe in any kind of higher power.

WARNING

In a more recent book, *A Field Guide to a Happy Life* (2020), Pigliucci explores more fully what updates to historical Stoicism he believes are needed, especially in the case of his favorite Stoic, Epictetus. Among the changes he recommends are:

» Externals don't need to be despised or avoided, as Epictetus urged.

» There is no need to cultivate indifference to human loss, as Epictetus also claimed.

» No Logos or other higher power need be invoked. In particular, modern Stoics need not believe that the entire universe is a rational animal and that the cosmos is providentially directed (*Field Guide*, 118-124).

» Talk of natural law should be dropped. "There are — so far as we know — no laws of ethics, no law giver, no cosmic essence. Only human experience and wisdom" (*Field Guide*, 137).

» Virtue is not the only good. Externals, such as health and friendship, are also goods, though of a lower rank (*Field Guide*, 113). Though these goods are often outside our control, they also deserve our care and our focus.

» The strong Epictetian doctrine of *amor fati* (love of fate) should be softened. Speaking of difficulties or adversities, he says: "You cannot love something that is not the result of benevolent Providence. But you can accept with equanimity whatever happens, being glad when things go your way, serene when they don't" (*Field Guide*, 135).

Conclusions on Pigliucci

Pigliucci calls an updated Stoicism that includes these and other changes he proposes "Stoicism 2.0." Taken together, they clearly amount to some pretty big changes. Are they too big? If you drop the whole religious side of Stoicism, the idea that virtue is the only true good, the belief in radical acceptance, and the idea that externals should be of little concern, have you modified Stoicism or abandoned it? What teachings *are* central and defining elements of authentic Stoicism, and does Pigliucci's Stoicism 2.0 adequately preserve those features? Could a non–Stoic, such as Socrates or Cicero, substantially embrace Pigliucci's Stoicism 2.0? Which teachings do *you* see as nonnegotiably basic to Stoicism? It's a tricky question we'll take up in the next chapter.

Ryan Holiday

By far the best-known modern Stoic today is former marketer and public-relations guru Ryan Holiday, author or co-author of several bestselling Stoic-centric books, including *The Daily Stoic* (2016), *The Obstacle Is the Way* (2014), *Ego is the Enemy* (2016), and *Stillness is the Key* (2019), as well as being highly active on social media and host of the hugely popular *Daily Stoic* podcast and daily email.

Holiday's background

Unlike Irvine and Pigliucci, Holiday is not an academically trained professional philosopher. His background is interestingly different. Born in Sacramento, Holiday dropped out of college at age 19 to work as a research assistant for Robert Greene, author of the unabashedly Machiavellian books, *The 48 Laws of Power* (1998), *The Art of Seduction* (2001), and other controversial works. While in college, Holiday became friends with Tucker Max, author of such humorist "fratire" classics as *I Hope They Serve Beer in Hell* (2006), *Assholes Finish First* (2010), and *Sloppy Seconds: The Tucker Max Leftovers* (2012). It was through the advice of Max and Dr. Drew Pinsky that Holiday discovered the writings of Marcus Aurelius and Epictetus, whose pearls of wisdom he plastered on the walls of his college dorm room.

ANECDOTE

While still in his early and mid-20s, Holiday served as marketing director and later advisor to American Apparel, the giant LA-based clothing manufacturing and marketing chain that imploded not long after Holiday left the company. It was during his tenure at American Apparel that Holiday published a shocking and widely read exposé of the seamier side of digital media, *Trust Me I'm Lying: Confessions of a Media Manipulator* (2012), in which he admitted to engaging in all sorts of dark arts to manipulate the media and sell products. After moving to a small ranch near Austin, Texas, Holiday published *The Obstacle Is the Way: The Timeless Art of Turning Trials into Triumph* (2014), which became a #1 *Wall Street*

Journal bestseller. That book launched his career as a Stoic pundit and prominent self-help and motivational speaker. Since then, he has authored numerous Stoic-themed books, including *Ego Is the Enemy* (2016), *The Daily Stoic: 366 Meditations on Wisdom, Perseverance, and the Art of Living*, co-written with Stephen Hanselman (2016), *Stillness Is the Key* (2019) (a #1 *New York Times* bestseller), *Courage Is Calling* (2021), and *Discipline Is Destiny* (2022). To date, his books have sold more than six million copies.

Holiday's thought

Holiday is the least "academic" of the four leading modern Stoics we have profiled. His books and blog posts are immensely engaging and read a bit more like the great motivational writers of the recent past, from Norman Vincent Peale to the present, or at times even more like highly effective modern ad copy than conventional philosophical prose. Here's a short sample of his writing from *The Obstacle Is the Way*, speaking of the importance of persistence:

> It's okay to be discouraged. It's not okay to quit. . . . It's *supposed* to be hard. Your first attempts *aren't going to work*. It's going to take a lot out of you — but energy is an asset we can always find more of. It's a renewable resource. Stop looking for an epiphany, and start looking for weak points. Stop looking for angels, and start looking for angles. There are options. Settle in for the long haul and then try each and every possibility, and you'll get there. (*Obstacle*, 80-81)

Note the short, snappy diction, the inspirational and motivational tone, and the overtly practical, success-oriented focus. It reads almost like Zig Ziglar or Tony Robbins channeling Aristotle. It's very effective. Holiday's books feature many engaging inspirational stories, well told, and insightful quotes, but little in the way of close philosophical reasoning or rigorous analysis. Yet it's a style and a message that resonates with millions who otherwise would never have picked up a book on philosophy. By the ample testimonials to be seen all over the Internet, he's helping bring insight to a lot of people who need encouragement, or a little "edge" in what they're seeking to accomplish.

In a dust-jacket blurb, Holiday's popular publisher Portfolio/Penguin describes him as "one of the world's bestselling living philosophers." Whether Holiday is himself a philosopher or else simply a very talented student of philosophy, a sort of wisdom evangelist and needed public-relations guy for the ancients who channels many of the great philosophers on daily podcasts, we'll leave to others to debate. But this raises the broader philosophical question of what it is to be a philosopher, both in the ancient sense and in modern times. Socrates didn't have anything like a Ph.D. but was a master of analysis and new, formative thinking.

REMEMBER

Perhaps Holiday is closer to the "way of life" and "therapy of the soul" sense of philosophy as a calling than the vast majority of current professors of philosophy in colleges and universities. It may not matter whether he's considered a "Stoic thinker" or a "Stoic life coach." But it's important to note that Holiday, like other modern proponents of Stoicism, isn't a 100-percent traditional Stoic. Mirroring his hero Marcus Aurelius, he's a bit eclectic and mixes non-Stoic elements into his philosophical stew.

For instance, like his mentor Robert Greene, he often talks about strategies for achieving career success, peak performance, and victory over one's competitors. So, in his hugely readable book on the Stoic cardinal virtue of self-control, *Discipline is Destiny,* he has chapters titled "Dress for Success," "Clean Up Your Desk," Hustle, Hustle, Hustle," "Just Work," and "Be Best." Here we're in the personal success world of Napoleon Hill's classic *Think and Grow Rich,* or Robert Greene's *The 48 Laws of Power* and, apparently, many miles away from the Socratic-initiated and Cynic-inspired anti-worldly Stoicism of Epictetus, with its frequent talk of caring nothing for externals, "despising" the body, curbing your desires, and being content with what you have.

WARNING

Or consider Holiday's chapter titled, "What's Right Is What Works" in *The Obstacle Is the Way.* There he suggests an approach to life and career success he calls "radical pragmatism" (*Obstacle,* 101). This involves "focusing on results instead of pretty methods," believing that "if you've got an important mission, all that matters is that you accomplish it," not worrying about "how you get your opponents to the ground, . . . only that you take them down," and in, in general, adopting the mindset that what's right is "any way that works" (*Obstacle,* 99, 100). What does pragmatism of this "the-means-justify-the-end" sort have to do with historic Stoicism? Really, nothing. In fact, it's clearly antithetical to classical Stoicism with its stress on virtue, moral objectivity, justice, and the common good. Here again we are in the amoral, success-oriented world of Greene's *The 48 Laws of Power* and far from the Socratic ethics of the Stoics that teaches that "it is never right to do a wrong" (Plato, *Crito* 49a), that virtue is the sole good, and that we should just "do the right thing. The rest doesn't matter" (*Meditations* 6.2).

It's important to keep this in mind when we're reading Holiday and most other modern Stoics: What we're hearing at some points may not be authentic Stoicism but some modern perspective that has seeped in from a thought-world very different from the one inhabited by Epictetus or Marcus Aurelius. And yet, because of that, lots of readers are being reached with bits of ancient wisdom, blended with the can-do ethics of modern personal growth and high achievement literature.

Conclusions on Holiday

Not surprisingly, Holiday has taken flak from academics who object to what they call his "oversimplified presentations" of Stoic teachings, his apparent lack of concern for close analysis and scholarly rigor, his attempt to convert Stoicism into a mantra of peak performance and personal success, and his extraordinary success in gaining both fame and fortune with what at times can feel like a relatively casual approach to the details and demands of the classic Stoic tradition.

As the previous chapters make clear, we have some sympathy with such assessments. And they raise important questions about the nature and role of philosophy in our time. We'll explore such concerns more fully in the next chapter, where we'll consider the pros and cons of modern Stoicism and raise questions as to what it is to adopt or transform an ancient way of thinking and living, so that we might be said to be doing in our time what various ancient thinkers were doing in theirs, and in continuity with the traditions of thought and action they created, rather than just creating our own mix tape of snappy themes woven into the distinctive rhythm of our time.

All things considered, it's hard not to be impressed with Holiday's clear talent, work ethic, and achievement. He clearly is an A-list writer, storyteller, speaker, and strategist who, at a remarkably young age and with incredible effort and determination, has built a business empire centered on — of all things!—ancient Greek and Roman philosophy. Any way you slice it, that's quite a feat. There's a sort of genius evident in his handling of a mosaic of materials from across the centuries, as well as in his ability to translate those teachings in ways that busy, stressed, aspiring people today can understand. He often clearly seeks to get things right historically, and more often than not succeeds well where others might go astray.

Although credentialed professional philosophers may turn up their noses at successful popularizers like Holiday, let's not forget the bottom line: Millions of people who never would have picked up a philosophy book are now eagerly reading and discussing Seneca, Epictetus, and Marcus Aurelius, and thinking about the Big Questions of life. As former philosophy professors ourselves who spent our entire professional careers working to inspire such enthusiasm for the great thinkers and their thoughts, we can only toast that remarkable achievement.

Chapter **20**

Modern Stoicism

I n the previous chapter, we told the story of how Stoicism — an ancient Greek and Roman philosophy long thought to be outdated and defunct — rose again under the guise of a revised modern Stoicism and became the huge and growing pop cultural movement it is today.

In this chapter, we want to look more closely at this modern version. What is it exactly? How does it differ from historic Stoicism? Is it real Stoicism or, as some critics have charged, just a brand of Stoic-flavored pop psychology? What are its major strengths and weaknesses? And what's its future likely to hold? Does modern Stoicism have real staying power or is it destined to be a blip on the ever-changing screen of contemporary culture, a flash in the pan?

What Is Modern Stoicism?

Before we can honestly assess its pros and cons, we need a clear picture of what modern Stoicism is. But that's a little tough, because as we saw in the last chapter, the modern movement is diverse and takes many shapes.

For instance, some forms of modern Stoicism stick fairly closely to the historic teachings of ancient Stoicism, whereas others propose major changes. There are three kinds of major changes: rejections, omissions, and add-ons.

All versions of modern Stoicism *reject* some classical Stoic teachings. For instance, all modern Stoics reject outdated parts of Stoic physics, such as an earth-centered universe, the notion that there are four basic physical elements (earth, air, fire, and water), and the possibility of foretelling the future by reading the entrails of animals or other ancient methods of divination. Also, no modern Stoic would defend culturally dated Stoic teachings on matters such as slavery (see Diogenes Laertius, *Lives* 7.23), infanticide (see Seneca, "On Anger" 1.15),the acceptability of cannibalism and incest (see Long and Sedley, *The Hellenistic Philosophers*, 430–31) and the sexist notions that women are "born to obey (see Seneca, "On Firmness" 2.1) and should generally remain indoors (see Musonius Rufus, *Lectures and Sayings* 4.5).

Other classic Stoic doctrines are rejected by many modern Stoics, but not all. Though most leading modern Stoics are agnostics or atheists and abandon the idea of a pantheistic God, so-called traditional Stoics like Chris Fisher retain belief in the Logos as a living rational animal of which we are all parts (Chris Fisher, "What Is Traditional Stoicism?," online). Likewise, some modern Stoics such as Ryan Holiday and Matthew Van Natta hold on to a robust Stoic belief in *amor fati* (love and cheerful endorsement of all events), though most modern Stoics opt for less demanding forms of acceptance.

Finally, some historic Stoic teachings are rejected by only a few modern Stoics. For example, few, if any, modern Stoics seem to follow Massimo Pigliucci (*Field Guide*, 113) in denying the classic Stoic tenets that virtue is the only good and that externals cannot be of substantial value.

Outright rejection is just one way that modern Stoics sometimes modify ancient Stoic beliefs. Another is by *omission*. Many modern Stoics *say nothing* about many key parts of classical Stoic teaching. Usually, this includes nearly all of Stoic physics, logic, and theology, as well as some of the more difficult or implausible ethical teachings, such as the idea that all vices are equal, that anyone who is not perfectly virtuous is wholly wicked, that one should not feel distress at the death of children or friends (Seneca, *Letters* 74; Epictetus, *Manual* 3), and that we should "despise" the body and physical pleasures (see Marcus Aurelius, *Meditations* 2.2; Seneca, *Letters* 51, 59, 92; Epictetus, *Discourses* 3.21, 4.79). As we saw in the last chapter, the practice of cherry-picking attractive parts of ancient Stoic teaching and passing over the rest in silence is one reason for the surprising popular revival of Stoicism in our time. If the only Italian food you'd ever had was spicy meatballs in red sauce, would you rightly think that you love Italian food, or would it be more accurate just to say you love spicy meatballs in red sauce?

A third way that some modern Stoics have modified historic Stoic teaching is by *adding things* that ancient Stoics didn't believe, and sometimes vigorously would have rejected. We noted two prominent examples of this in the previous chapter when we looked at Ryan Holiday's invocation of the very *non*-Stoic pragmatist notion that "what's right is what works." Massimo Pigliucci's claim (*Field Guide*, 137) that there are no ethical norms grounded in natural law, but that all morality is rooted simply in "human wisdom and experience" is another very non-Stoic add-on, and more akin to the rampant forms of moral skepticism or relativism that the Stoics, following Socrates and Plato, battled in ancient Greece.

It's easy to see from such examples how diverse modern Stoicism is. It's not really a single philosophy, but an unruly and argumentative *family* of philosophical views. This makes it hard to define "modern Stoicism" in a way that covers all bases and leaves nothing important out.

TIP

A very general definition or characterization of "modern Stoicism" is probably the best we can do, and we suggest the following:

Modern Stoicism is a contemporary popular movement and family of philosophical views aimed at reviving Stoicism as a practical philosophy of life and adapting it to modern values and perspectives. Its main focus is on applying Stoic principles to everyday life, with the goal of helping people become happier, wiser, and more virtuous and emotionally healthy.

We think this description captures what modern Stoicism — in all its many shapes and sizes — is basically about. Readers who wish to explore how to define it might wish to check out a helpful article, "Symposium: What Is Modern Stoicism?" online.

Key Differences: Ancient and Modern

By now, it should be clear that there are major differences between ancient and modern versions of Stoicism. Those contrasts are often concealed by defenders of modern Stoicism who may not wish to bring attention to how large those differences are. Based on what we have learned about both ancient and modern forms of the philosophy, we can now sum up what the key contrasts are. They can be grouped into the following topics:

>> Theoretical ambitions

>> Intellectual foundations

>> Attitude toward religion

>> Plausibility

>> Central focus

>> Intended audience

>> Argumentative and rhetorical styles

Let's begin with the first.

Theoretical ambitions

As we've seen, ancient Stoicism was a comprehensive worldview rooted in ideas that derived from many sources, including Heraclitus, Socrates, ancient Cynicism, Plato, and, to a lesser extent, Aristotle. It gave confident answers to a whole range of big questions about the ultimate nature of reality, the structure of the cosmos, the existence and nature of God, the human soul, life after death, causation, free will, human knowing and perception, logical reasoning, the proper role of emotions and how to manage them, the nature of good and evil, what it means to be an ideally good and wise person, and the purpose of human existence and of the cosmos itself. It was, in short, a highly "dogmatic" creed in the ancient sense that it had large intellectual ambitions and was firmly committed to the truth of its claims.

REMEMBER

In most guises, modern Stoicism is much less intellectually ambitious. It's a greatly *streamlined* version of Stoicism. Modern Stoics mostly focus on practical questions: How can I happier? Less stressed? More in control of my emotions? More emotionally resilient? Less anxious in social situations? More adaptive to change? Less angry? A better person? These are a lot easier to answer than the huge intellectual conundrums about God, the nature of reality, the point of human existence, and so on that the ancients confronted.

If we have learned anything from the long history of Western philosophy, it's that it's hard to come up with confident answers about ultimate questions. In this respect, modern Stoicism holds a clear edge over classical Stoicism.

Intellectual foundations

As noted in Part 1 of this book, the intellectual foundations of ancient Stoicism are reasonably clear. Scholars tell us that it was largely a patch job, a crazy quilt stitched together from a picture of the cosmos borrowed largely from Heraclitus and Plato, a logic borrowed from Aristotle and then refined in important ways, and a radical ethics of virtue, wisdom, acceptance, and self-sufficiency taken from mostly from Socrates and the Cynics.

The intellectual foundations of modern Stoicism are a lot murkier and diverse. Ancient Stoic physics, theology, and logic almost totally disappear. The radical

Socratic/Cynic ethic remains, but usually in a watered-down form that Socrates and Diogenes would hardly recognize. In most versions of modern Stoicism, the core values are simply those of "the modern world and modern values," with a great deal drawn from the feel-good Oprah-verse of contemporary self-help, success, and personal growth literature common to the affluent West.

Modern Stoicism promises the moon: calmness, mental clarity, resilience, emotional regulation, positivity, joy, closer relationships, inner strength, mindfulness, mental discipline, becoming present, the ability to "thrive in a world out of your control," and, in some high-octane versions, "ruthless pragmatism," "relentless persistence," and the ability to turn obstacles into opportunities, and even, metaphorically of course, "shit into sugar" (Holiday, *Obstacle*, 5, 69). This feels like we're a long way from the austere and almost monkish world of Epictetus's *Discourses* or the melancholy and resigned world-weariness of Marcus's *Meditations*. And as we'll see, it's unclear whether modern values and beliefs can support an authentically Stoic outlook.

Attitude toward religion

As we saw in Chapter 2, early Stoicism was very much a religious or spiritual philosophy, grounded in a faith in a benevolent pantheistic divine Being, the Logos. Indeed, noted classical scholar and author Edith Hamilton has said that Stoicism "was a religion first, a philosophy only second" (*The Echo of Greece*, 157). This religious bent is plainly evident in Cleanthes's famous "Hymn to Zeus," Seneca's "On Providence," Cicero's Stoic-influenced *On the Nature of the Gods*, and Epictetus's *Discourses*, which brims with piety toward a personal and caring divinity on nearly every page.

Modern Stoicism, by contrast, tends to be secular in spirit. Most leading modern Stoics are not religious, or even openly hostile to religion, and it's often claimed by them that it's possible to be full-fledged practicing Stoic without any religious or spiritual beliefs at all. That would surely be a surprise to the Greek founders of Stoicism, as well as to the late Roman Stoics, who often found themselves persecuted by the Roman Christian authorities precisely because of their unorthodox religious views.

Plausibility

Ancient Stoicism had a plausibility problem in antiquity, and in its full-blown form would have an even greater one today. Key features of the classic Stoic worldview were hard for even most ancient Greeks and Romans to swallow.

As we've seen already, the ancient Stoics delighted in paradoxes such as:

>> No harm can come to a good person.

>> No one does wrong willingly.

>> Nothing is good except virtue.

>> Virtue is sufficient for happiness and complete well-being.

>> Pain, sickness, and death are not evils.

>> All vices are equal.

>> Anyone who lacks one virtue, lacks them all.

>> Anyone who lacks perfect virtue is utterly wicked.

>> A Sage is not upset by the deaths of friends and loved ones.

>> We should welcome and cheerfully accept whatever happens in life.

As we saw, Stoics had deep, complicated explanations for these and other paradoxes, but they were always tough sells with the proverbial man in the Agora and were sharply criticized by Platonists, Epicureans, Skeptics, and other rival schools of thought. Moreover, ancient Stoics were widely charged with holding self-contradictory beliefs. For instance, they affirmed both free will and inexorable fate, despite the obvious difficulties in reconciling the two. They also asserted that this is the best of all possible worlds, while conceding that it contains practically no actual goodness (i.e., perfect virtue) and that probably all then-living persons were totally wicked.

Finally, as both ancient and modern commentators have noted, there is an obvious tension between the Stoic ideals of virtue, which for them require active engagement in public affairs, family affection, and the fulfillment of social roles, and the ideal of complete freedom from passions and mental "perturbations" other than involuntary "pre-passions" (see Seneca, *Letters* 74 and "On Tranquility" 2.4; Epictetus, *Discourses* 1.18.21, 4.4.9). Except perhaps for the gods and any Spock-like Vulcans who may be secretly living among us, politics and family life tend to lead to quite a few "perturbations!" In other words, the twin Stoic ideals of perfect virtue and imperturbability seem to be incompatible as human beings are now constituted. These are some of the reasons why Stoicism petered out as an organized movement not long after the death of Marcus Aurelius (180 CE), and why, until now, there has never been a serious attempt to revive it, except possibly for the brief Christian "Neo-Stoicism" movement in the late Renaissance.

By design, modern Stoicism faces a much less severe plausibility problem. It was specifically tailored to appeal to people with modern values and contemporary problems. Modern Stoicism strips away most of the highly questionable features of ancient Stoicism and keeps the most credible and attractive parts — its broad ethical concerns and its psychological practices for attaining greater happiness and mental strength.

REMEMBER

The central claims of modern Stoicism are quite modest. It doesn't promise perfect happiness, absolute serenity, and complete virtue; it merely asserts that one can achieve *greater* happiness, calmness, resilience, mental fortitude, and so forth by following its teachings. Thousands of practicing Stoics today can attest that such claims are true.

And as Dr. Tim LeBron notes, there is a fair amount of empirical evidence from the use of well-being questionnaires that Stoicism can increase healthy emotions and reduce negative ones (LeBron, "Why Stoicism Is More Relevant Than You Think," *Psychology Today*, January 14, 2023, online). Generally speaking, modern Stoicism is less intellectually ambitious and makes fewer, more modest, and better-substantiated claims than ancient Stoicism does. It also discards or passes over without mention many of ancient Stoicism's most questionable or even provably false claims. So, on the whole, modern Stoicism is a good deal more believable and appealing than ancient Stoicism would be today.

Central focus

Most forms of modern Stoicism have a different focus than ancient versions. The main focal point of the founding and classic Stoics was virtue, which they saw as sufficient for complete well-being and as the only true good. By contrast, in most versions of modern Stoicism, virtue plays second fiddle to happiness and inner calm.

As we noted in the last chapter, modern Stoic William Irvine explicitly says that his preferred version of Stoicism focuses on the attainment of tranquility and freedom from emotional pain, not virtue. Most modern Stoics pay at least lip service to the traditional Stoic claim that virtue is the only good, with happiness being a necessary by-product of it. But they mainly talk about how Stoic teachings can boost happiness, in the modern sense of *feeling* happy and contented, by teaching coping strategies, curbing unhealthy emotions, increasing mindfulness, developing greater impulse control, and so forth.

This is a big difference between ancient and modern Stoicism, and as Irvine notes (*Guide*, p. 42) a selling point for modern Stoicism. There's a reason why there are tons of ads and click-bait Internet articles that promise happiness, but few that promise virtue. There don't seem to be hordes of people out there frantically googling "How can I be more virtuous?"

Intended audience

Another obvious difference between ancient and modern Stoicism is the target audience. Though Epictetus lectured to mixed audiences and Seneca's *Letters from a Stoic* was almost certainly written with a wide readership in mind, most ancient Stoic writings were probably aimed primarily at advanced students and fellow philosophers. It's hard to believe, for example, that Cleanthes's treatise "On Categorems" or Chrysippus's work on "Probable Conjunctive Reasons" were popular page-turners in their day.

In contrast, nearly all works of modern Stoicism are clearly aimed at general, non-specialist readers. Holiday's *The Obstacle Is the Way* (Portfolio/Penguin), Robertson's *How to Think Like a Roman Emperor* (St. Martin's Griffin), and Pigliucci's *How to Be a Stoic* (Basic Books) were all published by popular nonacademic presses and aimed at mass-market audiences, even though these broad audiences now include growing numbers of self-professed practicing Stoics. They presuppose no prior knowledge of Stoicism or philosophy in general, are written clearly and accessibly, often feature engaging inspirational stories, and typically involve few if any complex arguments, specialized terms, or careful analyses. This is true of nearly all other recent books on modern Stoicism.

REMEMBER

Unlike the general thrust of ancient Stoicism, modern Stoicism is very much mass-market "pop philosophy" in the genre of Robert Pirsig's *Zen and the Art of Motorcycle Maintenance*, Benjamin Hoff's *The Tao of Pooh*, or, more recently, Don Miguel Ruiz's *The Four Agreements*, or even Jordan Peterson's *12 Rules for Life* and Mark Manson's *The Subtle Art of Not Giving a F*ck*.

Argumentative and rhetorical styles

The final big difference that should be highlighted between ancient and modern Stoicism deals with how these philosophies are generally presented, and specifically in their argumentative and rhetorical styles. When we read the surviving fragments and second-hard reports of ancient Stoic authors like Chrysippus or Posidonius — though this is less true of the great Roman Stoics, whose writings survived largely because of their popular appeal — we find ourselves in a world of "professional" or high-level philosophy akin to some of the more advanced writings of Plato or Aristotle. Arguments are often dense and complex. Close and detailed analyses are given. Terms are carefully defined. Specialized vocabulary is frequently used. Objections are stated and examined fairly and in detail. Claims are carefully qualified. Theoretical and speculative issues are discussed as well as practical ones. The principal focus is on wisdom and truth, not on winning converts or whipping up enthusiasm for a philosophical school.

Modern Stoicism, broadly speaking, is very different. Like much of pop philosophy, there is a general lack of argument, or where there is in fact some measure of reasoning, it most often lacks in rigor. When arguments are presented, they tend to be short, simple, and easily grasped. Careful critical analyses and close readings of texts are rare. Critical terms and phrases such as "virtue," "happiness," "emotions," "acceptance," "living in the present," and "things we can control" are used loosely and left undefined. Technical or specialized terms are seldom employed in precise ways, though transliterated Greek terms are often to be seen, as a sort of hot spice to the stew.

Obvious objections are often ignored or not closely examined. Engaging, illustrative stories are frequently and effectively told. The focus is almost exclusively on practical matters of success, mental health, or felt happiness, with perhaps a little dose of virtue ethics thrown in. The tone is often inspirational or hortatory. There is a striking difference in diction, particularly in the writings of the uber-popular Holiday, who uses short words, punchy short sentences, easily digestible short paragraphs, and powerful, emotively charged language, not unlike a political ad, a rousing locker room motivational speech, or a compelling commercial for Chevy trucks. The Stoic: Built Like a Rock.

REMEMBER

In sum and generally speaking, ancient Stoicism tends to be:

>> Religious or spiritual

>> Dogmatic

>> Intellectually ambitious in what it claims to know or prove

>> Grounded on relatively clear philosophical and religious foundations

>> Careful in its borrowings from rival philosophical traditions

>> Theoretical as well as practical

>> Focused mainly on virtue as the goal of life

>> Often aimed at advanced audiences and not a large popular movement

>> Rigorous in argumentation

>> Complex and often specialized in diction

>> More focused on truth than motivation or inspiration

>> Implausible in many of its core claims

Modern Stoicism, on the other hand, tends to be:

>> Secular

>> Relatively undogmatic

>> Much less intellectually ambitious

>> Comparatively unclear and disparate in its intellectual foundations

>> Often eclectic in its borrowings from non-Stoic sources

>> Practical

>> Focused mainly on happiness or tranquility rather than virtue

>> Aimed at general audiences and part of a large popular movement

>> Rarely rigorous in argumentation

>> Simple and easily understandable in diction

>> Often motivational or inspirational in tone

>> More plausible in its central claims

MORE GREAT READS ON MODERN STOICISM

In exploring modern Stoicism, we've looked mostly at the work of four major voices in the modern Stoicism movement: William Irvine, Donald Robertson, Massimo Pigliucci, and Ryan Holiday. But there are lots of great books out there on modern Stoicism! For those who like to cut to chase and quickly get up-to-date on what modern Stoics are saying, we especially recommend the following:

Matthew J. Van Natta, *The Beginner's Guide to Stoicism: Tools for Emotional Resilience & Positivity* (Althea Press, 2019): When friends ask for an easy-to-read intro to modern Stoicism, we recommend this. It's compact, lively, very well-written, and packed with practical advice you can use every day.

Jonas Salzgeber, *The Little Book of Stoicism: Timeless Wisdom to Gain Resilience, Confidence, and Calmness* (self-published, 2019): This is another great beginner's intro to modern Stoicism. Clear, fun, and highly practical. The heart of the book is a very helpful discussion of over 50 Stoic psychological practices.

Modern Stoicism: Down and Upsides

Like all forms of popular philosophy, modern Stoicism has its pros and its cons. Let's begin with the downsides. We should warn you that there are no "experts" on what modern Stoicism gets right and what it gets wrong. The distinction is more like a matter of informed opinion and careful judgment. What follows is just our currently best personal take on these matters.

Modern Stoicism: The cons

As we see it, major concerns with modern Stoicism in many of its contemporary guises include a general lack of rigor and precision, unclear intellectual foundations, and worries about whether it is similar enough to historic Stoicism to count as real Stoicism, or instead is just a mishmash of Stoic-inspired life hacks. Let's take a brief look at these possible problem areas.

Lack of rigor and precision

Most books on modern Stoicism are works of commercialized pop philosophy. They are written for broad mass audiences and published to sell and make money for the authors and publishers. Inevitably, that means less rigor, precision, accuracy, depth, balance, and often less conceptual clarity than one would find in a book written by and for scholars, or other mostly smaller and mainly intellectual audiences. Hence, we get the problems of oversimplification, loose argumentation, overgeneralization, one-sidedness, and occasional inaccuracy or confusion that its critics often allege.

REMEMBER

None of the four most prominent modern Stoics — Irvine, Robertson, Pigliucci, and Holiday — are academically trained experts on ancient Greek and Roman philosophy. It's not surprising, then, that they sometimes get things wrong or offer a passage that could mislead. For example, Donald Robertson is a very careful and accurate scholar whose books are some of the very best introductions to both ancient and modern Stoic thought. And yet, in the midst of an engaging passage even he can say that "the teachings of Zeno and Cleanthes were simple, practical, and concise" (*How to Think Like a Roman Emperor*, 34). Yet we have long lists of the writings of Zeno and Cleanthes, many of which were clearly theoretical and complex (Diogenes Laertius, *Lives* 7.174-75, 7.4).

As noted above, one common problem with modern Stoicism is a lack of reliable clarity in their use of key terms. For instance, they often urge us to "focus on things we can control and let the rest go." But what things exactly *can* we control? And "control" in what sense? And what does it mean to "let the rest go"? Ignore completely? Have little concern for? Not worry about? Not freak out over? As we note in Chapter 9, these are precisely the questions we need to ask if we are to make proper sense of this frequent modern Stoic mantra, but they are questions that modern Stoics themselves rarely pose.

Unclear intellectual foundations

Most modern Stoics jettison most of the philosophical, scientific, and religious underpinnings of ancient Stoicism. It's doubtful that adequate foundations remain to support such common modern Stoic claims as:

>> Virtue is the only true good.

>> We should practice Stoic love of fate, cheerfully welcoming and even loving whatever befalls us, our loved ones, or events in the world.

Consider the first claim, that virtue is the only strict or true good, and that all other things of value, if in fact there are any, are "indifferents." That's a bold claim, and on its face hard to believe. Isn't premium chocolate chip ice cream good? A hard-earned A on your final exam? Pleasant, sunny weather on your wedding day? Migraine relief? A diagnosis that you are cancer-free? What basis did the ancient Stoics have for believing that, literally, nothing but human virtue is truly good?

One reason, we saw, was their faith in Socrates as a model Sage. Socrates had said that "no harm can come to a good person." The only way this can be true, Stoics reasoned, is if vice is the only evil and virtue is the only good. A good person, they thought, must be totally "self-sufficient" regarding whatever can contribute to his or her complete happiness or well-being (*eudaimonia*). Only virtue and vice are totally in our control, at least ideally. So, virtue is the only good, or utterly reliable contributor to well-being, and vice is the only evil, or intrinsic detractor from well-being.

WARNING

This, clearly, is an unconvincing argument. Couldn't Socrates have been mistaken when he declared that no harm can befall a good person? Who died and made him omniscient? How could he possibly have known such a thing? Why should we accept vice as the only harm? And why must a good person be totally self-sufficient when it comes to their own well-being? Isn't this a godlike ideal that's totally inappropriate for us? Doesn't "sh*t" that never actually becomes "sugar" happen to all desiring, feeling, hoping, and dreaming beings like us? Aren't there more rough edges to life for even the most spiritually advanced of us than such an idealized portrait could allow?

Fortunately, the Stoics had another argument for their paradoxical claim that virtue is the sole good. Seneca nicely lays it out in Letter 74 to Lucilius:

> Whoever makes up his mind to be happy should conclude that the good consists only in what is honorable [*honestum*, Seneca's Latin translation for the Greek word *arete*, meaning "virtue" or "excellence"]. For if he regards anything else as good, he is, in the first place, passing an unfavorable judgment upon Providence, since upright men often suffer misfortunes, and the time which is allotted to us is short and scanty, if you compare it with the eternity allotted to the universe (*Letters* 74.10)

This is a clear and straightforward argument for the Stoic view that virtue is the only good. Seneca reasons: If anything other than virtue were good, God could be faulted for the way he has distributed goods and evils. In particular, God would be to blame for causing bad and undeserved things to happen to good people, as in the case of small children dying of cancer. God is perfect and would never allow bad things to happen to good people, or otherwise act unjustly. So, virtue is the only good.

Is this a convincing argument? We'll leave that for you to decide. What we want to point out is that such an argument is totally dependent on Stoic beliefs about religion. No God, no fated events, no Providence: no argument. So again, we must ask: Can modern Stoics who want to throw out Stoic physics and theology still give a good reason that virtue is the only true good? Or must they throw in the towel, as Massimo Pigliucci does, and concede that *many* things are good other than simply virtue, as Plato and Aristotle held, but the Stoics strenuously denied?

Much the same goes for a modern Stoic belief in love of fate. Hard-core ancient Stoics like Epictetus had a perfectly clear rationale why we should not merely minimally, grudgingly, or resignedly "accept" whatever happens in the world, but cheerfully, gratefully, and wholeheartedly welcome and actually love it: A perfect and all-wise God wills it, and therefore it must be good and in fact ultimately for the best. Is this a great argument? For reasons we've suggested earlier, probably not. Not all believers in a creator God think that such a being would also meticulously orchestrate worldly events in every detail. For one reason, such a view makes it very difficult to acknowledge any substantive version of freedom in human actions. But it's where the very religious Epictetus is coming from.

WARNING

Modern Stoics, on the other hand, seem to be up a creek without a paddle when it comes to love of fate. It's true that cheerfully accepting whatever happens can lead to greater serenity. But do we *want* to be serene about things like racial injustice, radical climate change, nuclear proliferation, threats to democracy, and ethnic cleansing? *Can* we be serene when we witness child abuse or see a crowded school bus on fire? Serenity, it seems, is greatly overrated. And maybe you agree, as well. More inner peace is great, but perfect and unbroken tranquility may be too much to ask or expect. At some level we must admit that it looks like humans are *supposed* to hurt.

So again, it seems fair to ask: Do modern Stoics, with their picky gleanings from ancient Stoicism, still have the theoretical resources to defend the key Stoic beliefs that they do endorse? We think this remains an open question.

Is modern Stoicism <u>real</u> Stoicism?

Many critics have charged that modern Stoicism isn't genuine Stoicism at all but merely a cheap knockoff that leaves out literally essential parts of authentic Stoic teaching. Georgetown University philosophy professor and longtime Stoicism expert Nancy Sherman makes this charge in a widely read 2021 *New York Times* guest editorial titled, "If You're Reading Stoicism for Life Hacks, You're Missing the Point." Sherman writes:

> Today, Stoicism is not so much a philosophy as a collection of life hacks for overcoming anxiety, meditations for curbing anger, exercises for finding stillness and calm — not through "oms" or silent retreats but through discourse that chastens a mind: "The pain isn't due to the thing itself," says Marcus Aurelius, "but to your estimate of it." In this mind-set, the impact of the outer world can fade away as the inner self becomes a sanctuary. The focus narrows to that self — me, isolated from the social structures that support me or bring me down.

This may be one strand of classic Stoicism, hyperbolized in the much-quoted epigrams of the Greek Stoic Epictetus, but it is by no means the whole of it. The me-focused view misses ancient Stoicism's emphasis on our flourishing as social selves, connected locally and globally.

Here Sherman offers two basic criticisms: (1) Unlike ancient Stoicism, modern Stoicism is not a comprehensive philosophy of life but more like a collection of life hacks for reducing anxiety, curbing anger, and so forth. (2) Modern Stoicism leaves out, or gives short shrift to, vital parts of authentic Stoicism, such as the idea that humans are essentially social beings. Modern Stoicism is too much about self-protection, self-help, and a retreat to an unconquerable inner citadel that can protect you from risk but also isolate you from vital social connections.

Is this a fair criticism? Perhaps not entirely. It's true that modern Stoicism, in most of its current popular iterations, is not a comprehensive philosophy of life but mostly a set of psychological coping tools combined with a loose framework of broadly ethical beliefs. But it's a bit misleading for Sherman to suggest that modern Stoicism is nothing but an assortment of life hacks. Even William Irvine and Ryan Holiday, who *do* offer a lot of life hacks, retain healthy chunks of ancient Stoic doctrine. And the life-hacks charge applies even less to Donald Robertson and Massimo Pigliucci, both of whom serve up meaty dishes of ancient Stoic belief. As for Sherman's charge that modern Stoics are too self-focused, that's at best a half-truth. Modern Stoicism does focus more on self-protection, self-help, and distress-avoidance than most ancient Stoics did. See Cicero's Stoic-channeling book *On Duties* for a good example of how socially oriented Stoic ethical and political thought was. On the other hand, *all* major modern Stoic thinkers emphasize the social nature of humans and the importance of other-focused virtues such as justice.

That said, it's still a legitimate question whether modern Stoicism is similar enough to its ancient ancestor to count as *real* Stoicism. To answer that, we need to know, of course, what "real" Stoicism is. And that's tough, because even the ancient classic forms were diverse and there's no agreement, even among scholars, about what's really essential to it, or required for it.

WARNING

The label "Stoicism," like many big abstract terms such as "freedom," "democracy," and "justice," seems to be what philosophers call an "essentially contested concept," one that can't be defined in any simple uncontroversial way. Like "Christianity," we're never going to agree on exactly what the term means. Fair enough. But consider this: Can we at least agree on a few things that Christianity is definitely *not*? If somebody says, "Oh, Christianity? That's all about Buddha and karma and reincarnation," no informed person is going to fall for that. And might we then also go further and pick out a few things that Christianity definitely *is*, like a religious or spiritual tradition based on the teachings and person of Jesus? In such a way, we might be able to get a good enough grip on what Stoicism definitely is and isn't to rule out certain forms of modern offshoots from being the real deal.

We're not going to try to do that now, because it would take us into deep waters. But as we suggested in the previous chapter, one current form of modern "Stoicism" — Massimo Pigliucci's so-called Stoicism 2.0 — seems a likely candidate for possible expulsion from the true Stoicism team. Pigliucci, as you'll recall, rejects many classic Stoic beliefs, including commitments about God, the soul, living in agreement with nature, love of fate, moral objectivity, seeing externals as irrelevant to well-being, and, most importantly, the key Stoic idea that virtue is the only good and sufficient for happiness (*Field Guide*, 134–37). Has Pigliucci left the friendly folds of Stoicism and become a Stoicizing eclectic, like Cicero or Plutarch were in ancient times? And does that matter? What do *you* see as the essential and nonnegotiable set of beliefs for true Stoicism?

Modern Stoicism: The pros

So much for modern Stoicism's downsides — or what some might see as its downsides. What about its upsides or advantages? We see mainly four.

Broad impact

Modern Stoicism has clearly had a positive impact on many thousands of lives. Go online and you'll find countless testimonies of people who say that Stoicism has helped them become calmer, less anxious, less stressed, less materialistic, more self-disciplined, more self-aware, and more resilient. Many vow that it's changed their lives for the better. Some even claim that Stoicism has literally saved their lives. It's a contention you're not likely to hear about Hegelianism or Neoplatonism. "Kant Saved My Life" isn't primed to become the next big Internet meme or T-shirt proclamation. But Stoicism seems to be making a big and healthy difference for lots of people who would not ordinarily be reading or talking about a philosophy at all.

Positive results

Though some purists might object to certain facets of modern Stoicism, it can't be denied that its central messages and recommended "life hacks" are overwhelmingly positive. Put wisdom and virtue first. Control your emotions. Be self-disciplined. Be brave. Be just. Act for the common good. Roll with the punches. Make light of your troubles. Don't sweat the small stuff. Focus most on what you can control. Treat setbacks as opportunities. Be reasonable. Be mindful. Seek perspective. Take the long view. Live an examined life. Be philosophical. Let go of unhealthy attachments. Be unconquerable. Live always aware, as Gandalf reminds us, that you are "only quite a little fellow in a wide world" and part of something much bigger than yourself.

These are the central and enduring messages of both ancient and modern Stoicism. And they are just what our sick, stressed-out souls need in an increasingly crazy world. Imagine for a moment that everyone over the age of ten or twelve suddenly and completely became either a classic or modern Stoic for the rest of their lives in emotions, attitudes, actions, and beliefs. Surely the world would radically improve in an instant and for the good of all. It would be a profound and wonderful sort of alchemy, a transformation that otherwise people could only dream of. And just as surely, to the extent that anyone individually adopts these bits of advice, improvement happens.

Renewed scholarship

Modern Stoicism has sparked a surge of both popular *and scholarly* interest in Stoicism. Partly as a response to all the public buzz about Stoicism, some first-rate scholarly works have appeared on Stoicism, including A. A. Long's *Epictetus: A Stoic and Socratic Guide* (2004), Emily Wilson's *The Greatest Empire: A Life of Seneca* (2015), Margaret Graver's *Stoicism and Emotion* (2007), and William O. Stephens's superb *Marcus Aurelius: A Guide for the Perplexed* (2012), to name just a few. And most of these academic works are informative to a general reader, and even helpful to the serious student of Stoicism outside any classroom.

Attention to philosophy

REMEMBER

Modern Stoicism has *a lot* of people thinking and talking about four of the wisest thinkers who ever walked the planet: Socrates, Seneca, Epictetus, and Marcus Aurelius. That's all for the good. So, too, is the fact that people are talking and thinking not only about Stoicism but about philosophy in general.

Philosophy is hot now, probably hotter than it's ever been in the United States and in other parts of the world. And mostly that's due to Ryan Holiday, Donald Robertson, and other leading modern Stoics who are showing how an ancient wisdom tradition can continue to change lives for the better today.

Though history suggests that philosophical fashions have a relatively brief shelflife — think of transcendentalism, pragmatism, beat generation existentialism, and peak Zen Buddhism, along with the alternative spirituality movements of the 1960s and 1970s in American history — it's possible that modern Stoicism has greater staying power and more enduring mass appeal. At its heart, Stoicism is a form of "Socraticism" rooted in the perennial wisdom of Socrates. His stress on wisdom and virtue; indifference to fame, wealth, and most other conventional values; rock-like strength in the face of changing fortune; constant self-examination; and fearless questioning of social falsehoods lie also at the heart of authentic Stoicism. For these reasons, modern Stoicism is likely to remain an attractive working philosophy of life for many thoughtful, questioning souls for many more years to come.

7

The Part of Tens

Peruse our suggestions for ten books every Stoic should read (after this one).

Discover ten great Stoic blogs and podcasts.

Chapter **21**

Ten Books Every (Budding) Stoic Should Read

The already large literature on Stoicism has recently become a flood. If you're new to the topic, where should you begin? Well, first, thank you for starting here with us. Probably the best place to go now is to begin with the great Roman Stoic thinkers themselves, and especially the Big Three: Seneca, Epictetus, and Marcus Aurelius. All three are quite readable.

For translations, we strongly recommend that you avoid older ones with their archaic "thee's" and "thou's." Find good recent versions instead. We especially like Seneca's *Letters from a Stoic* (Penguin Classics, translated by Robin Campbell) and *Seneca: Dialogues and Essays* (Oxford University Press, translated by John Davie); Then for Epictetus, go to: *Epictetus: Discourses, Fragments, Handbook* (translated by Robin Hard for Oxford World Classics), and an even more recent translation, *Epictetus: The Complete Works*, by Robin Waterfield for The University of Chicago Press; and for the Emperor's journals try the Modern Library edition of Marcus's *Meditations* (translated by University of Virginia classist Gregory Hays). Also, *The Emperor's Handbook*, translated by the brothers C. Scott Hicks and David V. Hicks is very good and easy to read. For those of you who might be looking for more precisely literal translations of the *Meditations*, G.M.A. Grube's (Hackett) and Martin Hammond's (Penguin) are quite good. Hammond's edition also has extensive explanatory notes and an excellent Index. But there are many other fine recent translations as well. It's a growth industry these days.

After you've read the Big Three Stoics and digested their thoughts, then you may want to go dip into some of the recent great books on Stoicism listed below and briefly described. Any of them can be very helpful in your adventures into Stoic philosophy.

The Inner Citadel: The Meditations of Marcus Aurelius

Pierre Hadot, (1998). Hadot (1922 – 2010) was a distinguished French scholar on ancient philosophy who taught for many years at the Collège de France in Paris. His *The Inner Citadel* (first published in French in 1992) had a major impact on the modern Stoicism movement. It's a commentary on the *Meditations*, with fascinating background on how it came to be written, what currents of thought influenced it, and what Marcus chiefly tries to do in his jottings. Hadot's book is scholarly in tone and a bit demanding, but still mostly easy to read. He was the first to point out the importance of the threefold Stoic disciplines of action, assent, and desire for understanding Marcus and other leading Stoics. His book is especially helpful about the influence of Epictetus on Marcus's thought and on the importance of the common good in Stoic ethics.

A Guide to the Good Life: The Ancient Art of Stoic Joy

William B. Irvine, (2009). Irvine's *Guide to the Good Life* was a breakthrough book in the modern Stoicism movement. Written in clear, jargon-free English by a contemporary philosopher who considers himself a Stoic, it was the first book to galvanize popular interest in Stoicism as a credible philosophy of life in the English-speaking world of today. Much of it is practical, offering specific suggestions on how to apply Stoic wisdom to everyday life. By highlighting ancient Stoic teachings on joy and other good passions, Irvine punctures old stereotypes about

Stoics as dour, stiff-upper-lip killjoys. His interest is primarily in Stoicism as a way to tranquility rather than to virtue. It could be viewed as one-sided in places, but it's still a pretty virtuous read. Add to this his more recent book *The Stoic Challenge: A Philosopher's Guide to Becoming Tougher, Calmer, and More Resilient*, and you'll have even more great examples of how a philosophical guide finds great usefulness in these ancient ideas.

The Stoic Art of Living: Inner Resilience and Outer Results

Tom Morris, (2004). Stoicism helps us manage our emotions, deal with anxiety, and find inner calm, but can it also help us achieve high-level success in business, sports, academics, and other important life pursuits? Drawing on the timeless wisdom of Seneca, Epictetus, and Marcus Aurelius, Morris makes a case in this earlier book on Stoic ideas that it can. Quoting extensively from the great Roman Stoics, he presents Stoicism as a treasury of powerful insights into the good life and — perhaps surprisingly — as also offering a guide to outstanding and proper success in "preferred indifferents," such as business and athletics. (A concluding note: This entry was suggested and written by Greg, not the Stoically humble Tom.)

How To Be a Stoic

Massimo Pigliucci, (2017). In this widely read book, Pigliucci, a distinguished philosophy professor at the City College of New York, recounts how he came to abandon secular humanism and instead adopt Stoicism as a personal credo of meaning and purpose. While struggling through a midlife crisis of sorts, Pigliucci came to embrace Stoicism as "a rational, science-friendly philosophy that includes a metaphysics with a spiritual dimension, is explicitly open to revision, and, most importantly, is eminently practical." To underscore the practicality of Stoicism, Pigliucci concludes the book by discussing twelve helpful Stoic spiritual practices culled from Epictetus's writings. His later book, *A Field Guide to a Happy Life* (2020), is shorter and aimed at busy non-specialists. Based mainly on the *Manual* of Epictetus, the *Field Guide* offers a boldly updated version of Stoicism for modern readers.

How to Think Like a Roman Emperor: The Stoic Philosophy of Marcus Aurelius

Donald Robertson, (2019). Robertson, a Scottish psychotherapist and popular author and podcaster, has long been a major figure in the modern Stoicism movement. His earlier book *Stoicism and the Art of Happiness* (2013) offers a clear and engaging overview of Stoic thought that will be helpful to any beginner wanting to apply Stoic practices to his or her own life. In the more recent *How to Think Like a Roman Emperor*, he delves more deeply into the life and teachings of Marcus Aurelius, frequently drawing on the insights of modern cognitive behavioral therapy to reveal how Stoicism can relieve anxiety, build emotional resilience, and help us cope with life's rough patches. Perhaps because Robertson was not originally trained as a historian of ancient Greece or Rome, his own work on the backgrounds of the Stoics comes alive with a vividness needed for us to understand the importance of their thought in their own time, as well as how it can so powerfully translate to ours. His ability to engage in creative imaginative reconstructions might surprise some stodgy academics, but he's good at what he does. This book nicely shows how ancient Stoicism dovetails at many points with modern psychotherapy. We won't even mention his helpful foray into the graphic novel format with *Verissimus* (oops, there we did), but all his recent work has been important in bringing Stoic thought vividly into the challenges of modern life.

The Stoics (2nd edition)

F. H. Sandbach, 1994. For readers wishing to dig a little deeper into the thought of the ancient Stoics, including their complex views of God, nature, and humanity, Sandbach is an excellent guide. A long-time Professor of Classics at Cambridge University, he offers a clear and comprehensive account of all aspects of Stoic teachings, including their psychology, logic, philosophy of nature, ethics, and theology. As a bonus, the book is available in an inexpensive paperback edition from Hackett Publishing. An excellent companion to Sandbach, also published by Hackett, is Brad Inwood and Lloyd P. Gerson's *The Stoics Reader: Selected Writings and Testimonia* (2008). Inwood and Gerson offer lucid translations of key passages from Diogenes Laertius, Stobaeus, Cicero, and other ancient sources that reveal the complex and systematic accounts ancient Stoics developed in their three major disciplines of physics, logic, and ethics. But Sandbach is the place to start.

The Obstacle Is the Way

Ryan Holiday, (2014). Though some of Holiday's books are highly eclectic and touch only lightly on historical Stoicism, *The Obstacle Is the Way* is organized explicitly around what he terms the three Stoic disciplines of perception, action, and will, and draws extensively from ancient Stoic thought. With his trademark clarity and high-energy brio, Holiday artfully uses examples of famous people such as Steve Jobs, Thomas Edison, and Ulysses S. Grant, among many others, to illustrate the Stoic ju-jitsu art of turning setbacks into springboards to greater success and strength of character. If the contemporary wave of interest in Stoicism had a rock star, this would be the guy. Holiday is currently the most popular figure in the modern Stoicism movement and has played a huge role in bringing ancient wisdom to the attention of a wide reading and listening public through bestselling books, blogs, podcasts, newsletters, and major media appearances. Like Tom Morris's *The Stoic Art of Living*, Holiday's *The Obstacle Is the Way* is aimed at busy philosophical newbies who want to improve their lives and propel themselves to greater success.

The Daily Stoic

Ryan Holiday and Stephen Hanselman, (2016). This bestselling book is a collection of 366 short daily readings on practical Stoic themes such as acceptance, virtue, resilience, courage, and overcoming the fear of death. Each entry includes a brief reading from an ancient Stoic thinker, followed by a short commentary. Hanselman, a Harvard-trained editor and literary agent, did the translations, and Holiday wrote the commentaries. A helpful glossary of key terms and passages is tacked on at the end. Many people have used this book to integrate Stoic perspectives and practices into their daily lives. Lots of readers have reported going completely through it more than once, and with some, many times, in order to fully absorb its lessons. Reading and pondering a page of this daily devotional is a great way to begin or end your day on a note of Stoic calmness and inspiration. Use it to jump-start your own jottings, and get started on your own Stoic journal of philosophical insight.

Epictetus: A Stoic and Socratic Guide

A. A. Long, (2002). This is, and has long been, the best general introduction to Epictetus. Long, a former University of California, Berkeley classics professor, might fairly be described as the Dean of Stoic Studies. This relatively short book, published by Oxford University Press, is written with both academics and non-academics in mind and is quite readable. It includes fresh translations of many key passages in Epictetus's works and is particularly helpful in bringing out the Socratic and Cynic origins of so much of Epictetus's thought. An epilogue explores the influence of Epictetus on later thinkers from his time to ours. Long is one of the top recognized academic experts in the field, and his work is always both insightful and deep. If you feel in the mood to be a star student, take on this book as you would a great lecture class.

Breakfast with Seneca: A Stoic Guide to the Art of Living

David Fideler, (2022). Of the three great Roman Stoics, Seneca, Epictetus, and Marcus Aurelius, Seneca seems to be the least read and the least generally favored today. And that's a shame. One reason for this may be that his golden philosophical nuggets are often buried in prosy passages in his essays, letters, or tragedies and are not always easy to dig out. But when you come across one, you light up. He provides some of the most vivid metaphors and amazing slogans for Stoic success in the world. Fideler's insightful, easy-to-read book on his thought offers an expert travel guide to Seneca's Stoic philosophy for general readers. Topics include how to overcome worry and adversity, how to curb anger, the vital importance of friendship, dealing with death and grief, and finding love, gratitude, and inner peace. Thomas Jefferson was reading Seneca's *Letters to Lucilius* (in Latin) on his deathbed. Fideler's engaging book helps us understand why.

BUT WAIT! THERE'S MORE!

The books listed in this chapter are some great places to start, but don't stop here! There are too many other interesting, entertaining, enlightening, and useful recent books on the Stoics and on Stoicism for us to name. Go look up John Sellars' great little *Lessons in Stoicism,* for example, or Nancy Sherman's *Stoic Wisdom,* or her earlier *Stoic Warriors.* A friend of ours has been reading William Ferraiolo's *Slave and Sage* to good effect. And we could go on. Trust us, as we've read most of the recent offerings. You should see our bookstore bills. And it's a safe guess that more will soon be forthcoming. So stay tuned if your interest in the Stoics continues. Your local public library may have lots of recommendations about other books to peruse as well. Go talk to your librarian. They can be amazing resources for this or any topic.

Chapter **22**

Ten Great Stoic Blogs and Podcasts

Modern Stoicism has a vibrant online community. Fans of Stoicism regularly connect on social media sites such as Facebook and Reddit, in virtual Meetup groups, and on a variety of online conferences, courses, and other forums. Stoic-themed blogs and podcasts are also very popular, and new ones pop up constantly online. Listening to Stoic podcasts while working out or taking a long walk "in agreement with nature" is a great way to multitask! This chapter lists some of the best blogs and podcasts we've found. But there are other great ones, too.

Daily Stoic Blog

Daily Stoic blog posts are, as the name suggests, posted daily. Written by #1 *New York Times* bestselling author Ryan Holiday and his Austin-based team, Daily Stoic posts are usually short and often centered around a quotation or two by a major Stoic thinker such as Seneca or Marcus Aurelius. Holiday is a poised and charismatic guy with a background in marketing, and the posts tend to be upbeat, breezy, and focused on self-help and personal growth. Common topics include coping with grief, strategies for achieving happiness, reducing stress, managing negative emotions, achieving peak performance, and dealing with daily annoyances. Visitors can sign up for a free daily email meditation delivered each morning to their inbox.

Stoicism Today Blog

Stoicism Today, founded in 2012, is the official blog of the British-based Modern Stoicism organization (the group that sponsors Stoic Week and the annual Stoicon conference). Free articles and essays are put out each Saturday, with interviews and event announcements posted at other times during the week. Blog posts are authored by guest writers as well as by members of the Modern Stoicism organization. Normally, the posts are longer and more academic in flavor than those in Holiday's Daily Stoic. Typical posts are between 1,500 and 4,000 words in length.

Figs in Winter Blog

Massimo Pigliucci, the well-known author of *How to Be a Stoic*, *A Field Guide to Happiness*, and other widely read books on Stoicism, writes this informative blog (a successor to his earlier Philosophy As a Way of Life blog on Medium). But get that credit card ready, because, unfortunately, full access requires a paid subscription to Substack. Pigliucci, who holds doctorates in both evolutionary biology and philosophy, is one of the best informed and most insightful writers on Stoicism today and one of the best commentators on ways to update ancient Stoic ideas for today's world. Posts from his first Stoic-themed blog *How to Be a Stoic* (2015 – 2018) are still available for free online. Postings tend to be somewhat scholarly in tone but are written quite accessibly. The *How to be a Stoic* blog posts include very helpful and detailed critical commentaries on Lawrence Becker's important but very scholarly book *A New Stoicism* (rev. ed. 2017) and Margaret Graver's *Stoicism and Emotion* (2007).

Stoicism: Philosophy as a Way of Life

Prominent Stoic author and psychotherapist Donald Robertson writes this reader-supported blog/email newsletter together with a number of guest contributors. Articles usually appear once or twice a week and are typically relatively short. Many posts explore connections between Stoicism and psychotherapy, but the topics are wide-ranging and informed by Robertson's deep knowledge of ancient and modern Stoicism. Full access to the posts requires a subscription to Medium.

Traditional Stoicism Blog

A small but energetic band of self-proclaimed Stoics today denies that ancient Stoicism requires any significant updating in light of modern science and philosophy. They support classic Stoicism, including its materialistic physics, pantheistic theology, and providential world order. The Traditional Stoicism Blog is aimed at such unabashedly old-style Stoics. Hosted by Chris Fisher, second Scholarch of the College of Stoic Philosophers, the Traditional Stoicism Blog is committed to a version of Stoicism with clear spiritual underpinnings. The same traditional Stoics group hosts the Stoicism on Fire podcast.

Daily Stoic Podcast

Hosted by Ryan Holiday, the Daily Stoic Podcast features short (2-3-minute) audio versions of its email meditations on weekdays and longer episodes on Saturdays and usually once or twice during the workweek. The longer episodes frequently include interviews, sometimes with Stoic scholars but often with public figures who are interested in Stoicism or Stoic-related themes such as self-discipline, reducing anger, or overcoming adversity. Recent interview guests have included actor Matthew McConaughey, voting rights activist Stacey Abrams, pop singer Camila Cabello, and authors Malcolm Gladwell, Steven Pinker, and Sebastian Junger.

The Walled Garden Podcast

The Walled Garden Philosophical Society is an international community of philosophers, artists, and seekers dedicated to bringing ancient wisdom into the modern world. Simon Drew, CEO of the Walled Garden, is a frequent host of the weekly, approximately hour-long Walled Garden podcast (formerly known as The Practical Stoic). Other regular hosts include Kai Whiting, Juan Perez, Sharon Lebell, and other well-known figures in the modern Stoicism movement. Though Stoic-related themes are common on the Walled Garden podcasts, they range broadly over topics in psychology, music, poetry, and spirituality.

Stoic Meditations Podcast

Massimo Pigliucci does these short (two-minute) five-times-a-week reflections on Stoic themes. Or rather did do them, because the podcasts ended in August 2022. They are still worth noting here, however, both for their quality and their range. In all, Pigliucci produced almost 1,100 *Stoic Meditations* podcasts from 2017 to 2022, which continue to be available on Spotify and other websites. They remain a gold mine for serious fans of Stoicism.

Stoicism: Philosophy As a Way of Life Podcast

Prominent Stoicism author Donald Robertson does these podcasts roughly weekly or biweekly. They range widely in length, from about ten minutes to over an hour. Many feature interviews, often with well-known figures in modern Stoicism and other guests. Robertson, a clinical therapist by training, is an expert guide on all things Stoical and always has interesting and informed things to say. The Scottish-born Robertson also seems to be a really nice guy, which is always a good thing in a Stoic. Donald's spouse, Kasey Robertson, may be even nicer, if that's in fact possible, and is also making contributions to our current discussions of Stoicism, both behind the scenes and up front, online and off.

Stoic Coffee Break Podcast

Erick Cloward hosts this weekly podcast on how to use Stoicism to improve your life. Podcasts are typically about 10 minutes long, though some episodes feature longer interviews. Cloward's talks are soothing and laid back, and some are quite frank about issues in his own life. A fine way to add some Stoic calmness to your coffee break!

Index

A

acceptance, 38–39, 50–52, 188

Acceptance Argument, 271–274

action, desire and, 145–147

Addison, Joseph, 157

Adler, Alfred, 321

adversity, 45, 306–307

Aeneid (Virgil), 292

Aeschylus
  Agamemnon, 80–81

afterlife, 35–36, 74–75

Against the Professors (Empiricus), 75

Agamemnon (Aeschylus), 80–81

age of reason, 298

agreement, Stoic idea of, 236–237

Agrippina (empress), 43

Alexander the Great, 39

Allen, Woody, 60, 73

American Apparel, 335

amor fati, 314–315, 340

ancient Stoicism
  demise of, 63–64
  modern Stoicism compared with, 341–348

Anecdote icon, 3

anger, controlling, 45–46

animal pain, 86–87

Anrold, Matthew, 63

Anscombe, Elizabeth, 323

antagonistic individualism, 209–210

Anthology (Stobaeus), 242–244, 252, 296

anthropocentric view, of humanity, 73–74

anti-body themes, 61

Antigone (play), 184

Antipater, 42

Antisthenes, 28

Antonine Plague, 56, 57

apatheia, 38

apathy
  about, 61–62, 219, 222–223, 234
  ataraxia and, 227–232

discipline and, 224–225

film and, 221–222

finding sensible peace, 232–234

ideas of, 220–221

nature of emotions, 225–227

sullen, 325

Apollo, 69

Apollonius of Chalcedon, 55

Apology (Plato), 75, 259

"Appointment in Samarra," 80

appropriation, Stoic idea of, 237–238

Aquinas, Thomas, 189, 297

arete, 97–98, 288

argumentative styles, in ancient compared with modern Stoicism, 346–348

Aristotle
  about, 9, 31–32, 336
  on anger, 46
  anthropocentric view of, 73–74
  on citizens of the world, 214
  on courage, 292
  on Earth's place in the universe, 70
  on free will and responsibility, 81
  on friendship, 238–240, 244, 247
  influences on, 24
  logic of, 342
  on matter, 68
  on natural law, 202–207
  on nature, 87
  Nicomachean Ethics, 239
  on politics, 204, 205
  Politics, 204
  on power of partnership, 203–204
  on resilience, 305
  on universal law, 184, 186, 187
  on virtues, 288

Arnold, E. V.
  Roman Stoicism, 74–75

Arrian, 47

The Art of Seduction (Greene), 335

Assholes Finish First (Max), 335

ataraxia, apathy and, 227–232

Atropos, 78

Atticus, Herodes, 54

attitude toward religion, in ancient compared with modern Stoicism, 343

Augustine, St., 86, 154, 158, 189

Aurelius, Annius, 56

Aurelius, Commodus, 56–57

Aurelius, Lucius, 56

Aurelius, Marcus
  about, 12, 14–15, 19, 20, 23, 40, 42, 53–54, 75
  on challenges, 307
  on community, 212–213
  conversion to Stoicism, 55
  on death, 260, 274–280
  death of, 319, 320, 344
  on demands of love, 211–212
  demise of ancient Stoicism, 63–64
  on discipline, 224
  early influences on, 54–55
  Ellis on, 321
  on eternal recurrence, 72
  on gratitude, 201
  Holiday on, 337
  on human race, 185
  on impermanence, 310–312
  on inner citadel, 83
  on journaling, 308
  Meditations, 58–59, 60, 86, 87, 102–103, 111–112, 170–174, 181, 185, 186, 188–189, 202, 212–213, 233, 251, 253, 260, 275–280, 300, 307, 308, 310, 321, 340, 343, 359, 360
  on money, fame and happiness, 102–103
  on natural law, 194
  personal tragedies and death, 56–58
  philosophical themes of, 59–62
  on pleasure and pain, 170–175
  reign as emperor, 55–56
  on resilience, 300
  writings of, 320

autonomous act, 83

Avoidance Argument, 268–270

avolition, 222

B

"back-to-nature" approach, 28, 29

Bacon, Francis, 43

Barry, Dave
  Live Right and Find Happiness (Though Beer Is Much Faster), 62

base, noble versus, 242–244

Bassus, 283–284

Beck, Aaron, 305, 321–322

Becker, Lawrence E.
  A New Stoicism, 190–191, 325–326

The Beginner's Guide to Stoicism: Tools for Emotional Resilience & Positivity (Van Natta), 348

belief
  in a temporary afterlife, 74–75
  universality of, 71

belong, need to, 203

Benevolent Nature, 147

The Bhagavad Gita, 140

Big Magic (Gilbert), 246

Birley, Anthony
  Marcus Aurelius: A Life, 57

Blackstone, William, 190

blogs, recommended, 365–368

Bobzien, Suzanne
  Determinism and Freedom in Stoic Philosophy, 83, 87

Boethius, 64, 320
  The Consolation of Philosophy, 88, 90

Bond, James, 221

books, recommended, 359–364

Breakfast with Seneca: A Stoic Guide to the Art of Living (Fideler), 364

Brennan, Tad, 288

Buddhism, 140, 322

Build Your Resilience (Robertson), 332

Burrus, 43

C

Campbell, Robin, 359

Campbell, Tanner, 16

Camus, Albert, 322

cardinal virtues, 38, 291–298, 319–320

care, circles of, 207–215

Carneades, 42

Cassius, Avidius, 56

Cassius, Dio, 57

Cato the Younger, 294

central focus, in ancient compared with modern
    Stoicism, 345

Chadwick, Henry, 60

Channing, W. E.
  Note-book: Joy, 167

Cheat Sheet (website), 3–4

Christianity, 60, 63, 64, 319, 353

Chrysippus, 33, 40, 42, 47, 75, 77, 82–83, 87, 89, 184–185,
    194, 195, 242, 252, 287–288, 290, 346
  "Probable Conjunctive Reasons," 346

Cicero
  about, 42, 190
  on compatibilism, 82
  on courage, 292
  De Legibus, 167
  on divine Providence, 90
  On Duties, 187–188, 292, 296, 323, 353
  On Fate, 82, 83
  on God, 70
  On Moral Ends, 297
  on natural law, 185–186
  On the Nature of the Gods, 71, 74, 77, 87, 185–186, 343
  "On Firmness," 340
  "On Friendship," 239
  on Principle of Excluded Middle, 80–81
  on self as a walled fortress, 246
  on virtue, 288

circles of community and care, 207–215

citizens of the world, 29–30, 213–215

citizenship, as a basic component of natural law,
    188–189

Claudius (emperor), 43

Cleanthes, 34, 40, 63, 75, 236, 349
  "Hymn to Zeus," 343
  "On Categorems," 346

Clotho, 78

Cloward, Erick, 368

Coelho, Paolo, 158

cognition, distributed, 246–247

cognitive behavior therapy (CBT), 305, 321–322, 332–333

cognitive restructuring, 46

commitments, desire and, 144–145

Common Era, 319

common good, relationships, reason, and, 131–132

common law, as a basic component of natural law,
    188–189

community
  about, 197
  Aristotle and, 202–207
  Aurelius on, 212–213
  circles of care and, 207–215
  citizens of the world, 213–215
  cosmopolitanism, 215
  demands of love, 211–212
  foundations, 210–211
  need to belong, 203
  philosophers as social advisors, 197–199
  Plato and, 202–207
  political virtues and, 206–207
  power of partnership, 203–205
  reason and relationality, 199–200
  rings of our lives, 207–209
  roots of, 199–202
  self and society, 200–202

The Compact Oxford Dictionary, 108

compatibilism, 82–84

complete friend, 239

Comte-Sponville, André, 292

The Consolation of Philosophy (Boethius), 88, 90

contentment, as a component of happiness, 103, 104

contributory localism, 208

control
  about, 119–120
  alternate strategy, 138–142
  another spectrum, 130
  common good, 131–132
  concept of, 124–130
  desires, 125–126
  dichotomy of, 49–50, 120–123
  emotional relationship to goals, 139
  goals, 125–126
  inner citadel or fortress, 128–129
  modern Stoic's strategy, 133–137
  needless worry, 129
  options about, 126–128
  path of action, 140–142

control (continued)

  power and, 121–123

  problem of external goals, 131–137

  reason, 131–132

  relationships, 131–132

  trying our best, 137–138

  value judgments, 125–126

  wants and, 121–123

  wisdom, 140

cosmic holists, 69–70

cosmic optimism, 51–52

cosmopolitanism, rules of, 214

cosmos, place of humanity in the, 73–76

courage, 247, 292–294

Courage Is Calling (Holiday), 336

Courage Under Fire: Testing Epictetus's Doctrines in a Laboratory of Human Behavior (Stockdale), 324

Crates, 31

Crito (Socrates), 259

Critolaus, 42

cultural attention, 324–327

Cynicism, 31

Cynics, 28, 29–30, 36, 44, 61, 108, 184, 195, 289

D

Daily Stoic blog, 365–366

Daily Stoic podcast, 367

The Daily Stoic: 366 Meditations on Wisdom, Perseverance (Holiday and Hanselman), 335, 336, 363

Damon, Matt, 221–222

Darwin, Charles, 192

Davie, John, 359

De Legibus (Cicero), 167

death. *see also* fear of death

  of Aurelius, 56–57

  fatalism and, 80

Declaration of Independence, natural law in, 190

Descartes, René, 320

design argument, 71–72

desire

  about, 125–126, 143–144

  action and, 145–147

  commitments, 144–145

  "The Desire Satisfaction View of Happiness," 151–153

  facets of happiness, 160

  finding flaws, 154–156

  gap between satisfaction and, 157–158

  happiness and, 150–156, 162

  managing, 147

  of only what is true, 148–149

  opportunity for hope, 156–162

  problem of evil, 149–150

  ridding yourself of, 158–159

  for that which is, 160–161

  thought and, 145–147

  whatever should be will be, 147–148

"The Desire Satisfaction View of Happiness," 151–153

detachment, 61–62

Determinism and Freedom in Stoic Philosophy (Bobzien), 83, 87

determinists, 35

Dewey, John, 9

Dhammapada, 140

Dialogues (Plato), 331

Dialogues Concerning Natural Religion (Hume), 91

dichotomy of control, 49–50, 120–123

Diogenes of Babylon, 42

Diogenes of Sinope, 27–30, 213–214

Diogenes the Cynic, 47

discipline, apathy and, 224–225

Discipline Is Destiny (Holiday), 336, 337

Discourses (Epictetus), 47, 50, 51–52, 55, 74, 75, 83, 168, 178, 180, 188, 213–214, 224, 230–232, 239, 249–250, 268, 271, 272–274, 279, 289, 295, 306, 308–309, 312–314, 340, 343, 344

Discourses, Fragments, Handbook (Epictetus), 115–117, 120, 168–169, 224, 229, 249, 266, 272, 274, 284, 295, 312–314, 359

dispreferred, 110–112

distributed cognition, 246–247

Distributed Cognition in Classical Antiquity, 246–247

Divine Fire, 35

divine Providence, 72, 76, 77, 89–92, 319–320

Divine Reason, 38

divine will, 319–320

Doctor Faustus (Marlowe), 167

Domitian (emperor), 47

The Double Power Principle, 203

Drew, Simon, 367

Durant, Will, 55

E

Earth, place in the universe of, 70

Ecclesiastes (Book of the Bible), 72–73

The Echo of Greece (Hamilton), 343

Edelstein, Ludwig
  The Meaning of Stoicism, 324

Ego Is the Enemy (Holiday), 335, 336

ekpyrosis, 72

Ellis, Albert, 305, 321
  A Guide to Rational Living, 321

Ellison, Harlan, 119

Emerson, Ralph Waldo, 9

emotional control, 38

emotional relationship, to goals, 139

emotions
  nature of, 225–227
  philosophy as a therapy for, 43–44

The Emperor's Handbook, 359

Empiricus, Sextus, 70
  Against the Professors, 75

Encyclopedia of Philosophy, 320

enjoyment, as a component of happiness, 103, 104–105

Epaphroditus, 47

Epic of Gilgamesh, 123

Epictetus
  about, 12, 15, 17, 19, 40, 42, 44, 47–52, 70, 75, 82, 214, 254–255
  on *amor fati,* 314–315
  on death, 258, 264–274, 279
  on desires, 125
  on discipline, 224
  Discourses, 47, 50, 51–52, 55, 74, 75, 83, 168, 178, 180, 188, 213–214, 224, 230–232, 239, 249–250, 268, 271, 272–274, 279, 289, 295, 306, 308–309, 312–314, 340, 343, 344
  Discourses, Fragments, Handbook, 115–117, 120, 168–169, 224, 229, 249, 266, 272, 274, 284, 295, 312–314, 359
  Ellis on, 321
  Epictetus: The Complete Works, 181, 359
  extremes of, 229–232
  on fate, 351
  on focusing on what you can control, 312–313
  on happiness and desire, 160–161
  on inner peace, 147
  on love, 249–251
  The Manual, 187, 340
  on natural law, 194
  Pigliucci on, 334
  on pleasure and pain, 168–170
  on reserve clause, 308–309
  on serenity, 228–229
  Stockdale on, 324
  Wolfe on, 324
  writings of, 320

Epictetus
  Discourses, Fragments, Handbook, 115–117, 120, 168–169, 224, 229, 249, 266, 272, 274, 284, 295, 312–314, 359

Epictetus: A Stoic and Socratic Guide (Long), 354, 363–364

Epictetus: The Complete Works (Epictetus), 181, 359

Epicureanism
  pull of pleasure and, 163–167
  Stoic objections to, 166–167

Epicurus, 164–166, 321

epidemic of loneliness, 198–199

Erasmus, 320

ethics
  about, 32
  facts and, 191–193
  virtue and, 291, 323

eudaimonia, 101, 105, 109, 110, 329, 350

evening meditations, 307–308

evil
  about, 36–37
  God and, 85–88
  natural, 86–87
  problem of, 149–150

The Examined Life (Nozick), 297

existentialism, 9, 323

"Existentialism Is a Humanism" (Sartre), 323

externals, curbing desires for, 313–314

Ezekiel, 258

F

facts, ethics and, 191–193

fame, 102–103

Farquharson, A. S. L., 321

fate
  about, 77–79
  free will and, 81–82
  gone rogue, 79–81
  Stoic, 88–92

Faustina, 57
fear of death
  about, 257
  Acceptance Argument, 271–274
  acceptance of mortality, 259
  arguments against, 261–264
  Aurelius on, 274–280
  Avoidance Argument, 268–270
  Epictetus on, 264–274
  Ignorance Argument, 271
  Impossibility of Harm Argument, 262–264
  Judgment Argument, 266–268
  matters of life and death, 257–258
  Natural and Liberating Argument, 276–278
  Normal Change Argument, 279–280
  philosophy as preparation for death, 258–261
  Quantity or Quality Argument, 281–284
  Sameness Argument, 275–276
  Seneca on, 281–284
  Stoic concerns of, 259–261
  Symmetry Argument, 261–262
Ferraiolo, William
  Slave and Sage, 364
Fideler, David
  Breakfast with Seneca: A Stoic Guide to the Art of
    Living, 364
A Field Guide to a Happy Life (Pigliucci), 191, 334, 340, 341,
    353, 361
A Field Guide to Happiness (Pigliucci), 366
film, apathy and, 221–222
fire, 69
Fisher, Chris
  Traditional Stoicism blog, 367
  "What Is Traditional Stoicism," 340
flaws, finding, 154–156
Foot, Philippa, 323
forces
  of nature, 86
  virtue and, 98–99
The 48 Laws of Power (Greene), 335, 337
Foucault, Michel, 308
The Four Agreements (Ruiz), 346
"The Four Dimensions of Experience," 210–211
"The Four Foundations of Greatness," 210–211
Fraga, Zé Nuno
  Verissimus: The Stoic Philosophy of Marcus Aurelius, 331

free will
  about, 77–78
  fate and, 81–82
  responsibility and, 81–84
freedom
  from external matters, 117–118
  philosophy as happiness and, 18–19
  Stoic, 83–84
  true, 48
Friedman, Milton, 87
friends, Stoic, 240–245
friendship. see love and friendship
Fronto, Marcus Cornelius, 54, 254
fulfillment, as a component of happiness, 103, 104
fun friend, 239
The Functionality Principle, 179

G

Gaius, 189
Gates, Bill, 45
generosity, 247
Gerson, Lloyd P., 34
  The Stoics Reader: Selected Writings and Testimonia, 362
Gilbert, Elizabeth
  Big Magic, 246
glass empty view, 151–152
glass full view, 153
glass half empty view, 152
glass quarter full view, 152
glass three-quarters full view, 152–153
goals
  about, 125–126
  emotional relationship to, 139
  external, 131–137
God
  evil and, 85–88
  nature and, 69–73
good, 28, 36–37
good habits, virtue and, 288–289
Goode, Ruth
  The Magic of Walking, 304
Gould, Josiah B.
  The Philosophy of Chrysippus, 324
Gracián, Baltasar, 157
gratitude, Aurelius on, 201

Graver, Margaret
  Stoicism and Emotion, 354
The Greatest Empire: A Life of Seneca (Wilson), 354
Greece, 39–40
Greeks
  on fatalism, 80–81
  Greek law (nomos), 184
  lifestyle of, 54
Greene, Robert, 337
  The Art of Seduction, 335
  The 48 Laws of Power, 335, 337
Grube, G. M. A., 59, 360
A Guide to Rational Living (Harper and Ellis), 321
A Guide to the Good Life: The Ancient Art of Stoic Joy (Irvine),
  133–137, 191, 327, 328–329, 330–331, 345, 360–361

H

Hadot, Pierre
  about, 43, 112–113, 302
  The Inner Citadel, 111–112, 146, 326, 360
  Philosophy As a Way of Life, 326
  Robertson on, 331
  What Is Ancient Philosophy?, 325
Hadrian, 57
Hamilton, Edith
  The Echo of Greece, 343
Hammond, Martin, 360
A Handbook for New Stoics, 329–330
Hanh, Thich Nhat, 310
Hanselman, Stephen, 16
  The Daily Stoic, 363
  *Lives of the Stoics: The Art of Living from Zeno to Marcus
    Aurelius*, 336
happiness
  from within, 162
  about, 150
  desire and, 150–156
  "The Desire Satisfaction View of Happiness,"
    151–153
  facets of, 160
  money, fame, and, 102–103
  philosophy as freedom and, 18–19
  relationship with virtue, 37–39
  surface complexity of, 103–105
  virtue and, 101–107
  virtue as being sufficient for, 28–29

Hard, Robin, 359
hard knocks, coping with life's, 44–45
hardships, 45
harm
  to good people, 26, 290
  good people and, 114–115
Harper, Robert
  A Guide to Rational Living, 321
Harry Potter (Rowling), 292
Hays, Gregory, 58, 61, 359
Hegelianism, 354
hegemonikon, 73
Heidegger, Martin, 322
The Hellenistic Philosophers (Long and Sedley), 78, 194,
  265, 288, 292, 296, 324, 340
helping friendship, 239
Hera, 69
Heraclitus the Obscure, 22–23, 55, 58, 69, 184, 342
Herman, Pee-Wee, 61
Heroic Public Benefit Corporation, 97
Hick, John, 88
Hicks, C. Scott, 359
Hicks, David V., 359
Hierocles, 208, 209, 210, 238
higher law, 184
Hill, Napoleon
  Think and Grow Rich, 337
Hinduism, 140, 322
Historia Augusta, 57
Hitz, Zena, 247
Hobbes, Thomas, 198
Hoff, Benjamin
  The Tao of Pooh, 346
Holiday, Ryan
  about, 188, 292, 335, 340, 341
  background of, 335–336
  conclusions on, 338
  Courage Is Calling, 336
  Daily Stoic blog, 365–366
  Daily Stoic podcast, 367
  *The Daily Stoic: 366 Meditations on Wisdom,
    Perseverance*, 335, 336, 363
  Discipline Is Destiny, 336, 337
  Ego Is the Enemy, 335, 336
  on life hacks, 352
  *Lives of the Stoics: The Art of Living from Zeno to Marcus
    Aurelius*, 336

Holiday, Ryan *(continued)*
  as a major voice in modern Stoicism, 348
  The Obstacle Is the Way: The Timeless Art of Turning Trials into Triumph, 335–336, 337, 343, 346, 363
  Stillness Is the Key, 308, 335, 336
  thoughts of, 336–337
  Trust Me I'm Lying: Confessions of a Media Manipulator, 335
Holtz, Lou, 311
Homer
  Iliad, 292
hope, opportunity for, 156–162
How to be A Stoic (Pigliucci), 333–334, 361, 366
How to Think Like a Roman Emperor: The Stoic Philosophy of Marcus Aurelius (Robertson), 331, 332, 346, 349, 362
hubris, 123
humanity, place of in the cosmos, 73–76
Hume, David
  about, 9, 85, 320
  Dialogues Concerning Natural Religion, 91
  on sullen apathy, 325
"Hymn to Zeus" (Cleanthes), 63, 343

I

I Hope They Serve Beer in Hell (Max), 335
icons, explained, 3
If Aristotle Ran General Motors (Morris), 325
"If You're Reading Stoicism for Life Hacks, You're Missing the Point" (Sherman), 352
Ignorance Argument, 271
Iliad (Homer), 292
impact, modern Stoicism and, 354
impermanence, 58–59, 310–312
Impossibility of Harm Argument, 262–264
impressions, 115, 180
incorporeals, 68
indifference, 36–37, 109–113
inner citadel/fortress, 128–129
inner peace. *see also* resilience
  about, 299–300, 306
  anticipating possible adversities, 306–307
  curbing desires for externals, 313–314
  impermanence, 310–312
  journaling, 308

  morning and evening meditations, 307–308
  practicing *amor fati,* 314–315
  reserve clause, 308–309
  role models, 312
  voluntary discomfort, 309–310
  what you can control, 312–313
inner things, 113–114
The Inner Citadel (Hadot), 111–112, 146, 326, 360
intellectual foundations
  ancient compared with modern Stoicism, 342–343
  modern Stoicism and, 350–352
intelligence, 71
intended audience, in ancient compared with modern Stoicism, 346
interpenetrating unity of souls, 245–248
Inwood, Brad, 16, 34
  The Stoics Reader: Selected Writings and Testimonia, 362
Irvine, William B.
  about, 16, 49, 194
  background of, 327–328
  conclusions on, 329–331
  On Desire: Why We Want What We Want, 327–328
  A Field Guide to a Happy Life, 191
  A Guide to the Good Life: The Ancient Art of Stoic Joy, 133–137, 191, 327, 328–329, 330–331, 345, 360–361
  on inner peace, 306
  on life hacks, 352
  as a major voice in modern Stoicism, 348
  on Stoicism, 345
  The Stoic Challenge: A Philosopher's Guide to Becoming Tougher, Calmer, and More Resilient, 361
  thoughts of, 328–329

J

James, William, 9
Jaspers, Karl, 322
Jefferson, Thomas, 190
Johnson, Brian, 97, 284
journaling, 308
Judgment Argument, 266–268
judgments, wariness of, 116–117
Jung, Carl, 246
jus gentium, 189
justice, as a cardinal virtue, 296

K

Kant, Immanuel, 295, 320
Kierkegaard, Søren, 322
King, Martin Luther, Jr., 189
knowledge, virtue as a form of, 290
Konstan, David, 246–247

L

Laches (Plato), 309
Lachesis, 78
Laertius, Diogenes
    about, 31, 32, 35, 37, 238
    Lives, 75, 77, 164, 242, 244, 252–253, 297, 330, 340, 349
    on positive emotions, 244
    Principle Doctrines, 164
"The Lazy Argument," 89
LeBron, Tim
    "Why Stoicism Is More Relevant Than You Think," 345
Lectures and Sayings (Rufus), 340
lekta, 68
Lessons in Stoicism (Seller), 364
Letters from a Stoic (Seneca), 359
Letters to Lucilius (Seneca), 43, 74, 75, 154, 175–177, 212, 227, 253–254, 273, 280, 281–283, 295, 298, 304–305, 306, 310, 312, 340, 344, 346, 350–351, 364
Lewis, C. S., 298
life
    philosophy and, 14–16
    as a sewer, 61
life and death matters, 257–258
Life of Cato the Censor (Plutarch), 167
The Little Book of Stoicism: Timeless Wisdom to Gain Resilience, Confidence, and Calmness (Salzgeber), 348
Live Right and Find Happiness (Though Beer Is Much Faster) (Barry), 62
Lives (Laertius), 75, 77, 164, 242, 244, 252–253, 297, 330, 340, 349
Lives of the Stoics: The Art of Living from Zeno to Marcus Aurelius (Holiday and Hanselman), 336
Locke, John, 9, 190
logic, 32
Logos, 22, 33–34, 35–36, 69, 70, 73, 77, 82, 90, 98, 111, 147, 149–150, 184
Long, A. A.
    Epictetus: A Stoic and Socratic Guide, 354, 363–364
    Hellenistic Philosophy, 265

The Hellenistic Philosophers (Long and Sedley), 78, 194, 265, 288, 292, 296, 324, 340
    Problems in Stoicism, 324
Lopez, Gregory, 329–330
Lord of the Rings (Tolkein), 292
love and friendship
    about, 235
    Aristotle on friendship, 238–240
    demands of, 211–212
    distributed cognition, 246–247
    Epictetus on, 249–251
    idea of agreement, 236–237
    idea of appropriation, 237–238
    ideas for, 235–238
    interpenetrating unity of souls, 245–248
    people close to you, 241
    self as a walled fortress, 245–246
    sex and love, 251–254
    Stoic friends, 240–245
    Stoics in and on love, 249–251
    true friendship, 238–245
    unique virtue, 247
    virtue compared with vulnerability, 248
Lucretius, 164

M

MacIntyre, Alasdair, 323
The Magic of Walking (Goode), 304
A Man in Full (Wolfe), 324, 325
Manson, Mark
    *The Subtle Art of Hot Giving a F*ck*, 346
Manual (Epictetus), 187, 340
Marcomannic Wars, 56
Marcus Aurelius: A Guide for the Perplexed (Stephens), 354
Marcus Aurelius: A Life (Birley), 57
Marcus Aurelius in Love, 253
Marlowe, Christopher
    Doctor Faustus, 167
Martyr, Justin, 55
masses, failure to appeal to the, 63
master virtues
    about, 287
    cardinal virtues, 291–298
    nature of virtue, 287–289
    Stoic view of virtue, 289–291

materialists, 32–33

matter, 68

Maugham, Somerset, 80

Max, Tucker

  Assholes Finish First, 335

  I Hope They Serve Beer in Hell, 335

  Sloppy Seconds: The Tucker Max Leftovers, 335

The Meaning of Stoicism (Edelstein), 324

meditations, 307–308

Meditations (Aurelius), 55, 57, 58–59, 60, 61, 73, 86, 87, 102–103, 111–112, 170–174, 181, 185, 186, 188–189, 202, 212–213, 233, 251, 253, 260, 275–280, 300, 307, 308, 310, 321, 340, 343, 359, 360

Merriam-Webster Dictionary, 108, 221

middle Stoic, 259

Middle Stoicism, 42

Mies van der Rohe, Ludwig, 186

Mill, John Stuart, 192–193

modern Cynics, 30

modern psychology, Stoicism and, 305

modern Stoicism

  about, 339–341

  ancient Stoicism compared with, 341–348

  leading figures in, 327–338

  natural law and, 190–194

  pros and cons of, 349–355

  rise of, 320–327

  strategy of, 133–137

Modus Ponens, 269

Modus Tollens, 269

money, 102–103

monists, 33

Montaigne, Michel de, 43, 320

Montesquieu, Charles de, 9

Moral Essays (Seneca), 154

Moral Essays II (Seneca), 178

moral evil, 87

moral philosophy, 13

moral showboating, 100

moral value, 109

moral virtue, 98

morning meditations, 307–308

Morris, Tom

  If Aristotle Ran General Motors, 325

  The Stoic Art of Living: Inner Resilience and Outer Results, 325, 361, 363

mortality, Socratic acceptance of, 259

motion, proof from, 71

Musonius, Irvine on, 330

N

National Endowment for the Humanities, 220

Natural and Liberating Argument, 276–278

natural evils, 86–87

natural law

  about, 183–185, 319–320

  basic elements of, 186–189

  Cicero on, 185–186

  in Declaration of Independence, 190

  modern Stoicism and, 190–194

  pros and cons of, 191–194

  in Roman law, 189–190

  Zeno on, 194–195

natural philosophy, 13

naturallistic fallacy, 191–192

nature

  God and, 69–73

  of virtue, 287–289

needless worry, 129

Neeson, Liam, 221–222

negativity, 244–245, 306–307

Neoplatonism, 64, 319, 354

Nero, 43, 47

A New Stoicism (Becker), 190–191, 325–326

Nicomachean Ethics (Aristotle), 239

Nietzsche, Friedrich, 314

noble, base *versus,* 242–244

Normal Change Argument, 279–280

Note-book: Joy (Channing), 167

Nozick, Robert

  The Examined Life, 297

Nussbaum, Martha, 247

O

objectivity, looking at situations with, 302–303

The Obstacle Is the Way: The Timeless Art of Turning Trials into Triumph (Holiday), 335–336, 337, 343, 346, 363

oikeiosis, 237–238, 255

On Anger (Seneca), 45, 307, 340

"On Becoming a 21st Century Stoic" blog post, 327

On Benefits (Seneca), 181, 201
"On Categorems" (Cleanthes), 346
On Desire: Why We Want What We Want (Irvine), 327–328
On Duties (Cicero), 187–188, 292, 296, 323, 353
On Fate (Cicero), 82, 83
"On Firmness" (Cicero), 340
"On Friendship" (Cicero), 239
On Moral Ends (Cicero), 297
"On Providence" (Seneca), 85, 88, 343
On Stoic Self-Contradictions (Plutarch), 77
On the Nature of the Gods (Cicero), 71, 74, 77, 87, 185–186, 343
On Tranquility (Seneca), 228, 229, 240–241, 281–282, 309, 344
on virtues, 292
"One Soul in Two Bodies: Distributed Cognition and Ancient Greek Friendship," 246–247
optimism, cosmic, 51–52
ought-from-its fallacy, 191–192
outer things, 113–114

P

paganism, 63
pain
  about, 163
  Epictetus on, 168–170
  Marcus Aurelius on, 170–175
  Seneca on, 175–177
  with the Stoics, 167–177
  using sensations and situations, 178–181
"Painted Porch," 203–204
Panaetius, 42, 47, 72
pantheism, Stoic, 69–70
partnership, power of, 203–204
passions, 45, 223, 305, 319–320
passivity, 88–92
path of action, 140–142
Paul (Apostle), 211
peace, finding sensible, 232–234
Peale, Norman Vincent, 336
The Perfect Satisfaction Axiom, 156
periodic conflagrations, Stoic belief in, 72–73
Perot, Ross, 324
pessimism, as a philosophical theme of Aurelius, 59–62
Peterson, Jordan
  12 Rules for Life, 346

Phaedo (Plato), 260
Phaedo (Socrates), 259
Philip of Macedon, 39
philosophers, 16, 197–199
philosopher's cloak, 54
philosophical assessments, of pleasure, 167
philosophy
  life and, 14–16
  meaning of, 10–11
  modern Stoicism and, 355
  pop, 346
  popular, 325
  as preparation for death, 258–261
  rise of competing, 63
  sides of, 12–14
  Stoic, 8–10
  as a therapy for emotions, 43–44
Philosophy As a Way of Life (Hadot), 326
The Philosophy of Chrysippus (Gould), 324
The Philosophy of Cognitive-Behavioural Therapy (Robertson), 332
physics, 32
Pigliucci, Massimo
  about, 16, 191, 194, 333
  background of, 333
  conclusions on, 335
  A Field Guide to a Happy Life, 334, 340, 341, 353, 361
  A Field Guide to Happiness, 366
  How to be A Stoic, 333–334, 361, 366
  on Irvine, 329–330
  on life hacks, 352–353
  as a major voice in modern Stoicism, 348
  Stoic Meditations podcast, 368
  thoughts of, 334
Pindar, 184
Pinsky, Drew, 335
Pirsig, Robert
  Zen and the Art of Motorcycle Maintenance, 346
Pius, Antonius, 55
Plato
  about, 24, 31–32, 38, 46, 53, 55, 58, 61, 70, 73–74, 167, 194, 342
  Apology, 75, 259
  Dialogues, 331
  Laches, 309
  on natural law, 202–207

Plato *(continued)*

   Phaedo, 260

   Republic, 78, 129, 206, 214, 288

   Robertson on, 331–332

   Sophist, 68

   on souls, 224

plausibility, in ancient compared with modern Stoicism, 343–345

pleasure

   about, 163

   Epictetus on, 168–170

   Epicurean pull of, 163–167

   Epicurus on, 164–166

   Marcus Aurelius on, 170–175

   philosophical assessments of, 167

   Seneca on, 175–177

   Stoic objections to Epicureanism, 166–167

   with the Stoics, 167–177

   using sensations and situations, 178–181

pleasure friend, 239

Pligliucci

   A Field Guide to a Happy Life (Pigliucci), 191, 334, 340, 341, 353, 361

   A Field Guide to Happiness (Pigliucci), 366

Plutarch, 33, 55, 64, 82

   Life of Cato the Censor, 167

   On Stoic Self-Contradictions, 77

pneuma, 69, 70

podcasts, recommended, 365–368

politics

   Aristotle on, 204, 205

   community and political virtues, 206–207

Politics (Aristotle), 204

pop philosophy, 346

Pope, Alexander, 60

popular philosophy, 325

Posidonius, 42, 242, 259, 346

positive, 244–245

positive results, modern Stoicism and, 354

power, wants and, 121–123

practical philosophy, 13

praeneditatio malorum, 307

precision, modern Stoicism and, 349–350

preferred, 110–112

pre-passion, 305

present moment, living in the, 300–301

Primal Reality, 69

Principle Doctrines (Laertius), 164

Principle of Excluded Middle, 80–81

"Probable Conjunctive Reasons" (Chrysippus), 346

problem of evil, 149–150

Problems in Stoicism (Long), 324

providence, 77–78, 147

psychological depreciation, 62

psychotherapy, 321

Pythagoreanism, 31

Q

Quantity or Quality Argument, 281–284

R

radical acceptance, 50–52

rational emotive behavior therapy (REBT), 305, 321, 322, 332–333

rational living, 36

rationality, 71

reality

   about, 67

   anthropocentric view, 73–74

   belief in temporary afterlife, 74–75

   Earth's place in universe, 70

   finding truth in outdated notions, 76

   God and nature, 69–73

   matter, 68

   place of humanity, 73–76

   Stoic arguments for God, 70–72

   Stoic belief in periodic conflagrations, 72–73

   Stoic pantheism, 69–70

reason

   relationships, common good, and, 131–132

   as a root of community, 199–200

relationality, as a root of community, 199–200

relationships

   emotional, 139

   reason, common good, and, 131–132

Remember icon, 3

Republic (Diogenes the Cynic), 194

Republic (Plato), 78, 129, 206, 214, 288

reserve clause, 308–309

resilience. *see also* inner peace
  about, 299–300
  adopting view from above, 301–302
  cutting people slack, 303–304
  keeping basics at hand, 304–306
  living in the present moment, 300–301
  looking objectively, 302–303
  walking on the wild side, 304

responsibility, free will and, 81–84

"The Reverse Hedonic Treadmill," 232–233

rhetorical styles, in ancient compared with modern
    Stoicism, 346–348

Richlin, Amy, 251–252, 254

rigor, modern Stoicism and, 349–350

Rist, John
  Stoic Philosophy, 324

Robbins, Tony, 336

Robertson, Donald
  about, 16, 62, 89, 331
  background of, 331–332
  Build Your Resilience, 332
  conclusions on, 333
  *How to Think Like a Roman Emperor: The Stoic Philosophy
    of Marcus Aurelius,* 331, 332, 346, 349, 362
  on life hacks, 352–353
  as a major voice in modern Stoicism, 348
  The Philosophy of Cognitive-Behavioural Therapy, 332
  Stoicism and the Art of Happiness, 331, 332–333
  Stoicism: Philosophy as a Way of Life blog, 366–367
  Stoicism: Philosophy as a Way of Life podcast, 368
  thoughts of, 332–333
  Verissimus: The Stoic Philosophy of Marcus Aurelius, 331

Rodin, August, 197–198

Rogers, Fred, 201

role models, 312

Roman law, natural law in, 189–190

Roman Stoicism (Arnold), 74–75

Rome
  about, 39–40, 41
  Epictetus, 42, 47–52
  Seneca, 42–46

Rousseau, Jean-Jacques, 320

Rowling, J. K.
  Harry Potter, 292

Rufus, Musonius, 47, 171–172, 214, 254–255
  Lectures and Sayings, 340

Ruiz, Don Miguel
  The Four Agreements, 346

Russell, Bertrand, 157, 211

Rusticus, Junius, 55

S

Sages, 44, 47, 48, 330

Salzgeber, Jonas, 16
  *The Little Book of Stoicism: Timeless Wisdom to Gain
    Resilience, Confidence, and Calmness,* 348

Sameness Argument, 275–276

Sandbach, F. H.
  The Stoics, 67, 265, 362

Sartre, Jean Paul, 198, 322
  "Existentialism Is a Humanism," 323

satisfaction, gap between desire and, 155–156, 157–158

Schofield, Malcolm
  The Stoic Idea of the City, 214

scholarly work, renewal of, 324

scholarship, modern Stoicism and, 354–355

Schopenhauer, Arthur, 60

Schwarzenegger, Arnold, 221–222

Scipio the Younger, 42

Sedley, D. N.
  The Hellenistic Philosophers (Long and Sedley), 78, 194,
    265, 288, 292, 296, 324, 340

self
  society and, 200–202
  as a walled fortress, 245–246

self-control, as a cardinal virtue, 294–295

self-evidence, 185

self-preservation, as a basic component of natural
    law, 187

Seller, John, 16
  Lessons in Stoicism, 364

Seneca, Lucius Annaeus
  about, 10–11, 14, 17–19, 20, 40, 42–46, 82, 111
  On Anger, 45, 307, 340
  On Benefits, 181, 201
  on death, 273, 280
  on demands of love, 212
  on desire, 154
  Irvine on, 330

Seneca, Lucius Annaeus (continued)
  Letters from a Stoic, 359
  Letters to Lucilius, 43, 74, 75, 154, 175–177, 212, 227, 253–254, 273, 280, 281–283, 295, 298, 304–305, 306, 310, 312, 340, 344, 346, 350–351, 364
  Moral Essays, 154
  Moral Essays II, 178
  on natural law, 194
  "On Providence," 85, 88, 343
  on peace, 232–234
  on pleasure and pain, 175–177
  on the problem of evil, 85–86
  Quantity or Quality Argument, 281–284
  on role models, 312
  Seneca: Dialogues and Essays, 359
  on Stoic teachings, 304–305
  On Tranquility, 228, 229, 240–241, 281–282, 309, 344
  on voluntary discomfort, 309–310
  writings of, 320
Seneca: Dialogues and Essays (Seneca), 359
sensations, using, 178–181
serenity, 228–229
Severus, Claudius, 55
sex and love, 251–255
Sextus of Chaeronea, 55, 70
Shaw, George Bernard, 157
Sherman, Nancy
  "If You're Reading Stoicism for Life Hacks, You're Missing the Point," 352
  Stoic Warriors, 364
  Stoic Wisdom, 364
situations, using, 178–181
sixties, 322
slack, cutting people, 303–304
Slave and Sage (Ferraiolo), 364
Sloppy Seconds: The Tucker Max Leftovers (Max), 335
Smith, Adam, 320
Snow, Nancy, 16
sociability, as a basic component of natural law, 187–188
social advisors, philosophers as, 197–199
society, self and, 200–202
Socrates
  about, 21, 24–25, 36–37, 44, 47, 61, 83–84, 184, 206, 207, 208, 288, 292, 336, 342–343, 350
  on acceptance of mortality, 259
  on care for the soul, 25

Crito, 259
  on death, 267–268
  on doing wrong willingly, 27
  on harm to good people, 26
  Phaedo, 259
  on self-control, 294
  on virtue, 26, 27, 290
Socratism, 355
soft determinism, 83
Sophist (Plato), 68
Sophocles, 184
souls
  interpenetrating unity of, 245–248
  Socrates on care for the, 25
space, Stoics on, 68
Spinoza, Baruch, 320
spiritual disciplines, 146
Stallone, Sylvester, 221–222
Stephens, William O.
  Marcus Aurelius: A Guide for the Perplexed, 354
Stillness Is the Key (Holiday), 308, 335, 336
Stobaeus, Joannes
  Anthology, 242–244, 252, 296
Stockdale, James, 324
  Courage Under Fire: Testing Epictetus's Doctrines in a Laboratory of Human Behavior, 324
  A Vietnam Experience, 324
  "The World of Epictetus," 324
Stoic Coffee Break podcast, 368
Stoic Meditations podcast, 368
Stoic Philosophy (Rist), 324
Stoic Sagehood, 88
Stoic Warriors (Sherman), 364
Stoic Wisdom (Sherman), 364
Stoicism
  about, 7, 31–32
  conversion of Aurelius to, 55
  meaning of philosophy, 10–11
  modern psychology and, 305
  revival of, 319–338
  rise of, 39–40
  using wisdom with the, 17–20
  as a way of thought, 8–10
  wisdom and, 11–20
Zeno of Citium, 31, 32–39

Stoicism and Emotion (Graver), 354

Stoicism and the Art of Happiness (Robertson), 331, 332–333

Stoicism: Philosophy as a Way of Life blog, 366–367

Stoicism: Philosophy as a Way of Life podcast, 368

Stoicism Today blog, 366

The Stoics (Sandbach), 67, 265, 362

The Stoics Reader: Selected Writings and Testimonia (Inwood and Gerson), 362

The Stoic Art of Living: Inner Resilience and Outer Results (Morris), 325, 361, 363

The Stoic Challenge: A Philosopher's Guide to Becoming Tougher, Calmer, and More Resilient (Irvine), 361

The Stoic Idea of the City (Schofield), 214

The Stoic Theory of Knowledge (Watson), 324

"The Stoic Trichotomy," 126

strategies, alternate, 138–142

*The Subtle Art of Not Giving a F*ck* (Manson), 346

Symmetry Argument, 261–262

T

The Tao of Pooh (Hoff), 346

Taylor, Richard, 80

Technical Stuff icon, 3

Thales, 23

"That There is No Need of Giving Many Proofs for One Problem" lecture, 172

theoretical ambitions, in ancient compared with modern Stoicism, 342

theoretical philosophy, 13

therapists, 321–322

Think and Grow Rich (Hill), 337

The Thinker (sculpture), 197–198

Thoreau, Henry David, 9

thought, desire and, 145–147

time, Stoics on, 68

Tip icon, 3

Tolkein, J. R. R.
  Lord of the Rings, 292

Traditional Stoicism blog, 367

true freedom, 48

true friendship, 238–245

true tranquility, 306

Trust Me I'm Lying: Confessions of a Media Manipulator (Holiday), 335

truth, finding in outdated notions, 76

12 Rules for Life (Peterson), 346

Tzu, Lao, 314

U

Ulpian, 189, 190

unity of the virtues, 99

universality of belief, 71

universe, Earth's place in, 70

use, value and, 115–118

utility friendship, 239

V

value judgments, 125–126

Van Natta, Matthew J., 16, 340
  The Beginner's Guide to Stoicism: Tools for Emotional Resilience & Positivity, 348

Verissimus: The Stoic Philosophy of Marcus Aurelius (Robertson and Fraga), 331

Verus, Lucius, 57

Verus, Marcus Aurelius. *see* Aurelius, Marcus

vice signaling, 101

vices
  about, 99
  virtue and, 112–113, 290–291
  virtue compared with, 106–107

A Vietnam Experience (Stockdale), 324

view from above, adopting, 301–302

Virgil
  Aeneid, 292

virtue ethics, 323

virtue signaling, 100–101

virtues. *see also* master virtues
  about, 95–96
  arete, 97–98
  cardinal, 291–298
  at the center, 98–100
  compared with vice, 106–107
  Diogenes of Sinope on, 28–29
  elements of, 38
  force and, 98–99
  good, bad, and indifferent, 107–118
  happiness and, 101–107

virtues *(continued)*
   happiness coinciding with, 105–106
   harm of good people, 114–115
   inner and outer things, 113–114
   money, fame, and happiness, 102–103
   nature of, 287–289
   progressing toward, 99–100
   relationship with happiness, 37–39
   Socrates on, 26, 27
   Stoic indifference, 109–113
   Stoic simplification of, 105
   Stoic view of, 289–291
   surface complexity of happiness, 103–105
   unique, 247
   use and, 115–118
   vice and, 99, 112–113, 290–291
   vice compared with, 106–107
   virtue signaling, 100–101
   virtus, 96–97
   vulnerabilities and, 248
virtus, 96–97
visualization, 307
Voltaire, 91
voluntary discomfort, 309–310
vulnerabilities, virtue and, 248

W

The Walled Garden podcast, 367
wants, power and, 121–123
Warning icon, 3
Waterfield, Robin, 359
Watson, Gerard
   The Stoic Theory of Knowledge, 324
Wayne, John, 221

Western philosophy
   about, 21–22
   Diogenes of Sinope, 27–30
   Heraclitus the Obscure, 22–23
   Socrates, 24–27
What Is Ancient Philosophy? (Hadot), 325
"What Is Traditional Stoicism" (Fisher), 340
"Why Stoicism Is More Relevant Than You Think"
      (LeBron), 345
wild side, walking on the, 304
Wilde, Oscar, 167
Wilson, Emily
   The Greatest Empire: A Life of Seneca, 354
wisdom
   about, 140
   as a cardinal virtue, 297–298
   meaning of, 11–16
   using with the Stoics, 17–20
Wolfe, Tom
   A Man in Full, 324, 325
"The World of Epictetus" (Stockdale), 324
world-weariness, 60

Z

Zen and the Art of Motorcycle Maintenance (Pirsig), 346
Zen Buddhism, 9, 327–328, 355
Zeno of Citium
   about, 31, 32–39, 42, 71, 105–106, 163, 184–185, 222,
      242, 252, 287–288, 298, 349
   on natural law, 194–195
   on Stoic idea of agreement, 236
Zeus, 69, 83, 111, 147
Ziglar, Zig, 336

About the Authors

Tom Morris has long been one of the most active public philosophers and top business speakers in the world. After an undergraduate degree at UNC-Chapel Hill, where he was a Morehead-Cain Scholar, and a PhD in the two departments of Philosophy and Religious Studies at Yale, Tom was a Professor of Philosophy for fifteen years at the University of Notre Dame before launching into a new adventure as an independent thinker, advisor, and guide to the wisdom of the ages.

He is the author of more than thirty books, from pioneering academic works to national bestsellers and other popular titles, including *True Success, If Aristotle Ran General Motors, Philosophy For Dummies, The Stoic Art of Living, If Harry Potter Ran General Electric, Socrates in Silicon Valley, The Oasis Within, Plato's Lemonade Stand*, and *The Everyday Patriot*. His work has been featured on NBC, ABC, CNN, and NPR, in top newspapers and magazines globally, as well as on many great contemporary podcasts. Visit Tom at www.TomVMorris.com where you can discover more resources for your personal quest to understand the world and make it a little better.

Gregory Bassham is a former Professor of Philosophy at King's College (Pennsylvania). A native of Oklahoma, Bassham received his BA and MA from the University of Oklahoma, and his PhD from the University of Notre Dame. Among his many books are: *The Bedside Book of Philosophy* (2021), *Environmental Ethics: The Central Issues* (2020), *The Philosophy Book: 250 Milestones in the History of Philosophy* (2016), *Critical Thinking: A Student's Introduction* (7th ed., 2023, written with three co-authors), *The Ultimate Harry Potter and Philosophy* (2010), and *The Lord of the Rings and Philosophy* (2003, co-edited with Eric Bronson). A long-distance runner and avid hiker, Bassham has twice run the Boston Marathon. Before retiring to become a full-time writer, he taught Stoicism in his college courses for nearly three decades.

Dedication

Tom would like to dedicate this book to his wife and partner of 50 years, Mary, who has managed to extend her Stoic sphere of control to include him, at least on most days.

Greg dedicates this book to his wife, Mia, for her love, encouragement, and Epictetian patience and forbearance.

Authors' Acknowledgments

We'd first like to thank Jennifer Yee, Best Possible Acquisitions Editor of the *For Dummies* series, for having the idea that this book should exist, and then trusting the two of us to write it in record time. Thanks also to our wonderful Development Editor, Tim Gallan, most stoic and benevolent of development editors in the known world and, we suspect, beyond. We are also immensely grateful for Amy Handy, our graceful and astute copy editor, Kristie Pyles, our magnificent managing editor, and the world-class professor, mountain biker, and camper Aaron Simmons, our technical reviewer, who all, while working on this manuscript, got exactly what they needed from the Stoics for dealing with the likes of us.

Publisher's Acknowledgments

Acquisitions Editor: Jennifer Yee

Development Editor: Tim Gallan

Copy Editor: Amy Handy

Technical Reviewer: Aaron Simmons, PhD

Managing Editor: Kristie Pyles

Production Editor: Saikarthick Kumarasamy

Cover Image: © AlexSava/Getty Images

Take dummies with you everywhere you go!

Whether you are excited about e-books, want more from the web, must have your mobile apps, or are swept up in social media, dummies makes everything easier.

Find us online!

dummies.com

dummies
A Wiley Brand

PERSONAL ENRICHMENT

9781119187790	9781119179030	9781119293354	9781119293347	9781119310068	9781119235606
USA $26.00	USA $21.99	USA $24.99	USA $22.99	USA $22.99	USA $24.99
CAN $31.99	CAN $25.99	CAN $29.99	CAN $27.99	CAN $27.99	CAN $29.99
UK £19.99	UK £16.99	UK £17.99	UK £16.99	UK £16.99	UK £17.99

9781119251163	9781119235491	9781119279952	9781119283133	9781119287117	9781119130246
USA $24.99	USA $26.99	USA $24.99	USA $24.99	USA $24.99	USA $22.99
CAN $29.99	CAN $31.99	CAN $29.99	CAN $29.99	CAN $29.99	CAN $27.99
UK £17.99	UK £19.99	UK £17.99	UK £17.99	UK £16.99	UK £16.99

PROFESSIONAL DEVELOPMENT

9781119311041	9781119255796	9781119293439	9781119281467	9781119280651	9781119251132	9781119310563
USA $24.99	USA $39.99	USA $26.99	USA $26.99	USA $29.99	USA $24.99	USA $34.00
CAN $29.99	CAN $47.99	CAN $31.99	CAN $31.99	CAN $35.99	CAN $29.99	CAN $41.99
UK £17.99	UK £27.99	UK £19.99	UK £19.99	UK £21.99	UK £17.99	UK £24.99

9781119181705	9781119263593	9781119257769	9781119293477	9781119265313	9781119239314	9781119293323
USA $29.99	USA $26.99	USA $29.99	USA $26.99	USA $24.99	USA $29.99	USA $29.99
CAN $35.99	CAN $31.99	CAN $35.99	CAN $31.99	CAN $29.99	CAN $35.99	CAN $35.99
UK £21.99	UK £19.99	UK £21.99	UK £19.99	UK £17.99	UK £21.99	UK £21.99

dummies.com

dummies®
A Wiley Brand